organizational values. It has also been stated that transformational leadership occurs when leaders and followers interact in such a way that they are elevated and committed to some great cause external to the relationship (Swanson et al., 1993). An example is the transformational role played by Martin Luther King, Jr., in leading millions of Americans of all races to support the civil rights movement of the 1960s.

Transformational leadership is dynamic because leaders enter into a purposeful and mutually supportive relationship with followers who are activated, motivated, and sustained by it. In the police field, the challenge for the police chief executive is to help police officers redefine their role and accept responsibility for following in a constantly changing, transformational environment. The key ingredients in developing an effective leadership/followership strategy are genuine participation, communication, shared decision making, equity, self-control, and interdependence.

The transformational approach emphasizes the importance of people, commitment, leadership, and empowerment. Here leadership is not the exercise of power, but the empowerment of others to help set and achieve mutually acceptable goals or objectives. Good police supervisors and administrators cultivate effective followership by creating and nurturing collective ownership of the enterprise based on a common culture, shared values, mutual respect, trust, problem solving, and collaborative risk taking (Rippy, 1990).

Situational Leadership®*

Situational leadership theories recognize that the workplace is a complex setting subject to rapid changes. Therefore, it is unlikely that one best way of leadership would be adequate for these varying situations. Simply, the best way to lead is dependent on the situation.

Paul Hersey[†] and Kenneth A. Blanchard (1977) presented a model of situational leadership that has been used in training by many major corporations and the military services. Their model emphasizes the leader's behavior in relationship to followers' readiness (see Figure 3–8). The **situational leadership** requires the leader to evaluate follower readiness in two ways: willingness (motivation) and ability (competence).

Situational leadership® takes into account worker readiness; readiness is defined as the capacity to set high but attainable goals, the willingness to take responsibility, and the education and/or experience of the individual or the group. Figure 3–8 depicts the situation leadership model; the various levels of follower maturity are defined as:

R1: The followers are neither willing nor able to take responsibility for task accomplishment.

R2: The followers are willing but are not able to take responsibility for task accomplishment.

R3: The followers are not willing but are able to take responsibility for task accomplishment.

* Situational Leadership is a registered Trademark of the Center for Leadership Studies, Inc. Used with permission. All Rights reserved.

[†]Hersey, P. (1985). *Situational Selling* (Escondido, Calif.: Center for Leadership Studies).

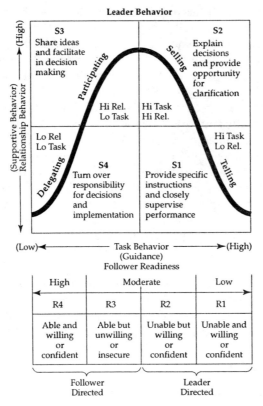

FIGURE 3-8. Situational Leadership
Source: Copyrighted material. Center for Leadership Studies, Escondido, CA. All rights
reserved. Used with permission.

> R4: The followers are willing and able to take responsibility for task ac-
> complishment (Hersey, 1985:27).

Task behavior, shown in Figure 3–8, is essentially the extent to which a leader
engages in one-way communication with subordinates; relationship behavior is
the extent to which the leader engages in two-way communication (by providing positive reinforcement, emotional support, and so on).

There are four basic styles of leadership that are associated with task
accomplishment; the definition of these four styles of leadership are characterized as follows:

> S1: *Telling.* High task–low relationship style characterized by one-way
> communication in which the leader defines the roles of followers and
> tells them what, how, when, and where to do various tasks.
> S2: *Selling.* High task–high relationship behavior is provided by two-way
> communication and socioemotional support to get followers to volun-
> tarily buy into decisions that have been made.
> S3: *Participating.* High relationship–low task behavior indicates both leader
> and follower have the ability and knowledge to complete the task.
> S4: *Delegating.* Low relationship–low task behavior gives followers the oppor-
> tunity to "run their own show" with little supervision (Hersey, 1985:20).

The bell-shaped curve in the style-of-leader portion of Figure 3–8 means that, as the readiness level of followers develops, the appropriate style of leadership moves correspondingly. For example, a police supervisor who has a subordinate whose readiness is in the R3 range (able but unwilling) would be most effective in employing an S3 (participating) style of leadership.

They asserted that leaders could reduce their close supervision and direction of individuals and increase delegation as followers' readiness to complete tasks increased.

The difficulty of this style of leadership is its dependence on leaders to diagnose follower ability and then adjust their leadership style to the given situation. This is often easier said than done.

Contingency Theories

During the late 1950s and early 1960s, several researchers (Burns and Stalker, 1961; Woodward, 1965) attempted to show that no single leadership style was appropriate for all job situations. Then, the publication of Harvey Sherman's *It All Depends* in 1966 made a major statement. Sherman believed that "There can be no ideal design that will fit all times, all situations, all objectives, and all values. These forces are in constant flux" (Sherman, 1966:57). Therefore, situational

---

Case Study 3–2
Where to Begin When a Veteran Comes In

Officer Maria Sanchez has 17 years of experience, mostly in undercover narcotics and vice in detectives. She is a capable officer with numerous departmental commendations and awards for her work. As a result, Sanchez was selected to be a member of an elite multiagency vice and narcotics task force.

On the first day of her new assignment, Sanchez met with her new supervisor, Sgt. Webster. He is from another agency and did not know Sanchez outside the selection interview process and review of her personnel file.

Sgt. Webster was also assigned recently to the unit from patrol division where he gained a reputation as a perfectionist and detail-oriented person. Webster assumed responsibility for breaking in all new team members to ensure they knew exactly what, when, where, and how they should perform their tasks. Webster had developed a four-week orientation for all new members.

After two weeks of basic orientation, including an elementary review of drug law, raid procedures, vice laws, and so on, Sanchez has become extremely frustrated with Sgt. Webster and asks why she is not allowed to participate in drug and vice raids with the rest of her team. She argues that she has worked with the task force on many occasions, is very familiar with operational procedures, and could demonstrate her abilities if Webster would only allow her to work with the rest of the team. Webster denies her request.

The next day, Sanchez submits a memo to the lieutenant in charge of the task force, requesting reassignment back to her previous agency. In the memo, Sanchez states that she believes Sgt. Webster is treating her differently from other people in the unit and does not have any respect for her past experience and work. She does not believe she can work under these conditions where she is "treated like a child."

1. Could this problem have been avoided? How?
2. What situational style of leadership was Sgt. Webster employing?
3. How would you assess the maturity level of Officer Sanchez?
4. Discuss what style of situational leadership would be more appropriate for this situation.

McGraw-Hill College

*A Division of The **McGraw·Hill** Companies*

POLICE SUPERVISION

Copyright © 1999 by The McGraw-Hill Companies, Inc. All rights reserved. Printed in the United States of America. Except as permitted under the United States Copyright Act of 1976, no part of this publication may be reproduced or distributed in any form or by any means, or stored in a database or retrieval system, without the prior written permission of the publisher.

This book is printed on acid-free paper.

1 2 3 4 5 6 7 8 9 0 DOC/DOC 9 3 2 1 0 9 8

ISBN 0-07-303342-1

Editorial director: *Phillip A. Butcher*
Sponsoring editor: *Nancy Blaine*
Marketing manager: *Leslie Kraham*
Project manager: *Christina Thornton-Villagomez*
Production associate: *Debra R. Benson*
Senior designer: *Crispin Prebys*
Supplement coordinator: *Becky Szura*
Compositor: *Carlisle Communications, Ltd.*
Typeface: *10/12 Palatino*
Printer: *R. R. Donnelley & Sons Company*

Library Congress Cataloging-in-Publication Data
Glensor, Ronald W.
    Police Supervision / Ronald W. Glensor, Kenneth J. Peak, Larry K.
Gaines
      p.   cm.
    ISBN   0-07-303342-2
    Includes bibliographical references and index.
    1. Police—Supervision of.   I. Peak, Kenneth J., 1947–
II. Gaines, Larry K.   III. Title.
HV7936.S8G54   1999
363.2'068'3 dc—21   98-08620

http://www.mhhe.com

Police Supervision

Ronald W. Glensor
Reno, Nevada Police Department

Kenneth J. Peak
University of Nevada, Reno

Larry K. Gaines
California State University—San Bernardino

McGraw-Hill College

Boston   Burr Ridge, IL   Dubuque, IA   Madison, WI   New York   San Francisco   St. Louis
Bangkok   Bogotá   Caracas   Lisbon   London   Madrid
Mexico City   Milan   New Delhi   Seoul   Singapore   Sydney   Taipei   Toronto

Police Supervision

To my wife, Kristy, and children, Breanne and Ronnie, for their continuous support and patience. And to my parents, Charles and Helga, and brother, Tom, who endures the daily challenges of being a first-line supervisor.

—*R. W. G.*

To my brother, Dan: supervisor (sergeant) and manager (captain) in the past, administrator (undersheriff) at present, and perhaps chief executive officer (sheriff) in the future.

—*K. J. P.*

To my father, Keith, and mother, Tyree, who provided me with a good education and a firm grasp of life.

—*L. K. G.*

About the Authors

RONALD W. GLENSOR, Ph.D., is a Deputy Chief of the Reno, Nevada, Police Department (RPD). He has more than 23 years of police experience and has commanded the department's patrol, administration, and detective divisions. Glensor has provided training on a variety of police topics for more than 250 police agencies throughout the United States and in Canada, Australia, and the United Kingdom. In 1997 he received the prestigious Gary P. Hayes Award conferred by the Police Executive Research Forum in recognition of his contributions and leadership in the policing field. He served a six-month fellowship as problem-oriented policing coordinator with the Police Executive Research Forum in Washington, D.C., and received an Atlantic Fellowship in public policy, studying repeat victimization at the Home Office in London. His publications include *Community Policing and Problem Solving: Strategies and Practices* (2d ed, 1999) (co-authored with Kenneth J. Peak). Glensor is an adjunct professor at the University of Nevada, Reno, and instructs at area police academies and criminal justice programs. Glensor has a Ph.D. in political science and a master's of public administration from the University of Nevada, Reno.

KENNETH J. PEAK, Ph.D., is professor and former chairman of the Criminal Justice Department at the University of Nevada, Reno (UNR), where he was named "Teacher of the Year" by the UNR Honor Society for 1984–85 and concurrently served as acting director of public safety in 1989. Recent publications include *Policing America: Methods, Issues, and Challenges* (2d ed., 1997) and *Justice Administration: Police, Courts, and Corrections Management* (2d ed., 1998). He has published nearly 50 journal articles and additional book chapters on justice-related subjects. He currently serves as chairman of the Police Section, Academy of Criminal Justice Sciences, and is past president of the Western and Pacific Association of Criminal Justice Educators. He entered municipal policing in Kansas in 1970, and subsequently held positions as criminal justice planner for southeast Kansas; director of the Technical Assistance Institute, Washburn University of Topeka; director of university police, Pittsburg State University; and assistant professor at Wichita State University. He received two gubernatorial appointments to statewide criminal justice committees in Kansas. Professor Peak holds a Ph.D. from the University of Kansas.

LARRY GAINES is professor and chair of the Criminal Justice Department at California State University—San Bernardino. He began his police career as a communications officer with the Kentucky State Police, and later became a police officer with the Lexington, Kentucky, police department. He is a past president of the Academy of Criminal Justice Sciences and past executive director of the Kentucky Association of Chiefs of Police. He received his doctorate in criminal justice from Sam Houston State University. He has published a number of books and papers in police operations, police administration, drug policies and enforcement, and white-collar crime. His academic emphasis has been the study of organizations and management, with particular interest in personnel administration and planning. He currently is pursuing research on police personnel issues.

Preface

To say the job of a supervisor is important to the success or failure of an organization is an understatement. Indeed, to say that supervisors are *vital* to an organization does not exaggerate their importance. This is especially true in policing, where the supervisory role will increase to an even higher level as we enter the next millennium. Changing demographics, increased diversity within neighborhoods and the workplace, shifting crime trends, and emerging technologies will challenge police organizations to their limits in the coming decades. For supervisors to perform their duties competently, there must be a considerable expansion of the knowledge, skills, and abilities required to organize and oversee employees. This fact becomes more certain as an increasing number of police agencies adopt models of community policing and problem solving and officers engage in collaborative approaches to crime control and prevention.

Supervisors must continue to serve at the forefront of leadership in police command structures during these challenging times. These functionaries must assume responsibility for directing, controlling, motivating, coaching, and leading sworn and nonsworn employees not only during routine patrol operations, but also during dangerous tactical and critical incidents.

This textbook describes how these challenges can and must be met. It brings theory to practice by emphasizing the applied aspects of supervision. The book will also help the reader to confront the major supervisory issues of the day. Part I examines the supervisory process, specifically, the place of the supervisor in a police organization, the supervisor's roles and responsibilities, theories of leadership and motivation, and communication, negotiation, and conflict management. Part II explores the major component of a supervisor's overall responsibility: human resources. The five chapters in this section consider the supervisor's role in training and professional development; evaluation and performance appraisal;

stress, wellness, and employee assistance programs; ethical issues, values, and liability; and officers' rights, discipline, and appeals. Part III looks at the daily work of the police and details the supervisor's functions in the deployment and scheduling of personnel, patrol operations and special situations, tactical operations and critical incidents, and community policing and problem solving. Part IV looks at future trends and challenges for the policing profession and its supervisors.

We wrote this text for several audiences: academics and trainers who are in a position of imparting knowledge about police supervision to others; students who want to learn about the role and functions of police supervisors; contemporary police supervisors; and those persons interested in being promoted to a supervisory position. Both student and instructor will find the text readable and comprehensible. Figures, tables, and photographs accompany each chapter and enhance the themes discussed. Key terms and review questions facilitate the reader's learning of the concepts. Case studies will challenge the student and encourage further class discussion.

ACKNOWLEDGMENTS

The collaborative effort to bring this book to fruition was made possible with the input, counsel, guidance, and moral support of several people. The authors wish to acknowledge several colleagues who contributed to its development, especially Acting Dean Gary Cordner, College of Law Enforcement, Eastern Kentucky University, who authored Chapter 2, "Supervisory Roles and Responsibilities."

We are also grateful to the book's reviewers, Dennis C. Brown, University of Nebraska at Kearney; Thomas H. Carr, University of Maryland; C. Wayne Johnston, Akansas State University; Peter K. Manning, Michigan State University; and James D. Stinchcomb, Miami Dade Community College, who provided us with their insights and guidance, and contributed much toward making *Police Supervision* a better effort.

We further thank Captain James Albrecht, New York City Police Department; Sheriff Richard Kirkland, Washoe County, Nevada; and Lieutenant Phil Galeoto, Reno, Nevada, Police Department, for their generous photo support. Of course, we bear sole responsibility for any shortcomings in the final product.

Finally, we greatly appreciate the various kinds of assistance provided by the technical support staff at McGraw-Hill: Nancy Blaine, sponsoring editor; Christina Thornton-Villagomez, project manager; and Charles Olson, copyeditor.

Ronald W. Glensor

Kenneth J. Peak

Larry K. Gaines

Contents in Brief

Contents

PART THREE
Supervising Police Work: Deployment
and Daily Operations   235

10.   Deploying and Scheduling Personnel   237

List of Figures and Tables

The Supervisory Process

1

Introduction to the Book and Police Supervision

No organization, regardless of its character, can rise higher than the quality and competency of its supervisory officials.

—AUGUST VOLLMER

We are born in organizations, educated by organizations, and most of us spend much of our lives working for organizations. We spend much of our leisure time paying, playing, and praying in organizations. Most of us will die in an organization, and when the time comes for burial, the largest organization of all—the state—must grant official permission.

—AMITAI ETZIONI

INTRODUCTION

Purpose of the Book

Those of us who have ever held a position, unless we were self-employed or began immediately as the boss, had a supervisor to whom we reported. That supervisor probably had a hand in showing us how to do our work and certainly was responsible for making sure that we did it properly. Even persons who have not yet entered the working world probably experienced supervision in school, in sports, in the Boy Scouts or Girl Scouts, or in other nonwork settings. Supervision is a crucial element of any organized activity.

This book is about police supervision. However, to cover the topic thoroughly and to provide as much useful information as possible, we must maintain a dual approach by (1) examining supervision in general while (2) focusing narrowly on supervision in police organizations. All supervisors, whether police sergeants, construction bosses, or office managers, share similar concerns and duties.

It is also true that every organization is unique. Police departments in particular are different from most other kinds of organizations for the simple reason that policing is significantly different from most other kinds of work. In addition, the police supervisor's job has recently been made even more unique by virtue of the Peace Officer's Bill of Rights, discussed thoroughly in Chapter 9.

Police supervisors are unique in that during the course of a day they will not only directly oversee several employees but also will possibly supervise a life-threatening situation or a critical incident or disaster. While supervisors may not have ultimate command and control over critical incidents or disasters, they are often the first responder at the scene; their actions and directions over subordinates will be vital in determining the eventual success of the police in dealing with the problem at hand.

A number of textbooks have been written on police management and administration (these terms are discussed more fully below), addressing the roles and responsibilities of chiefs of police or sheriffs and middle managers such as captains and lieutenants. However, in focusing on the first-line supervisor, this text is grounded on the assumption that the reader is an undergraduate or possibly even a graduate student, or a neophyte practitioner, possessing only a fundamental knowledge of police organizations and operations. This text is intended to assist people who are interested in learning more about the police supervision, practitioners preparing for their first promotional rank, and new and experienced supervisors seeking to improve their skills. It will help to lay the foundation for the reader's future study and experience. This text also assumes that a *practical* police supervision perspective is often lost in many other texts; therefore, while necessarily delving into supervisory theory, our intent is to focus on the practical aspects of a supervisor's job.

Key Terms

Although the terms *administration, management,* and *supervision* are often used interchangeably, each is a unique concept that occasionally overlaps with the others. **Administration** encompasses both management and supervision. It is a process whereby a group of people are organized and directed toward achieving the group's objective. The exact nature of the organization will vary among the various types and sizes of agencies, but the general principles used and the form of administration are often similar. Administration focuses on the overall organization, its mission, and its relationship with other organizations and groups external to it. **Management,** which also is a part of administration, is most closely associated with the day-to-day operations of the various elements within the organization. Finally, as we indicated above, **supervision** involves the direction, on a one-to-one basis, of staff members in their day-to-day activities.

Confusion may arise because a chief administrator, manager, or supervisor may at various times need to act in all three capacities. Perhaps it is most useful to define top-level personnel as administrators, midlevel personnel as managers, and those who oversee the work as it is being done as supervisors (Tansik and Elliott, 1981).

Finally, the terms **police officer, law enforcement officer,** and **peace officer** are generally interchangeable. They may refer to municipal or rural police officers, deputy sheriffs, highway patrol, troopers, state police, and others holding local, state, or federal peace officer status. For the purpose of this text, the term *police officer* will generally be used to refer to all the positions noted.

Organization of the Book

The 14 chapters of this book are organized to provide the reader with an understanding of the key elements of police supervision from both theoretical and applied perspectives. To understand the challenges of police supervision, we must first place it within the "big picture" of a police organization. Thus, in Part I, "The Supervisor in a Police Organization," we introduce the theory of supervision, the roles and responsibilities of supervisors, personnel leadership and motivation, and effective communication and negotiation in an organization.

Part II, "Supervising Human Resources," covers personnel training, evaluation, stress and wellness, ethical issues and liability, and the rights and discipline of subordinates. Part III, "Supervising Police Work," contains related matters that are more applied to police work in nature and reviews supervisors at work, both on and off the streets; it considers what supervisors need to know concerning officer deployment and scheduling, patrol and special operations, tactical and critical incidents, and under the community policing and problem solving philosophy. Part IV, "Epilogue," provides a look at future trends and challenges.

Also note that the following chapters each contain two case studies that allow the reader to contemplate the kinds of problems police supervisors routinely confront. Discussion questions follow each case study. With a fundamental knowledge of the criminal justice system and a reading of the chapters, the reader should be in a position to engage in some critical analysis—and, we hope, some spirited discussions—of the issues involved and arrive at several feasible solutions to the problems presented.

The remainder of this chapter sets the stage for subsequent chapter discussions of police supervision. First we define organizations and then look at police agencies as organizations and bureaucracies. We conclude the chapter by providing some practical concepts for supervisors, borrowing from the historical writings of Confucius and Machiavelli as well as some modern-day observers.

DEFINING ORGANIZATIONS

Organizations are entities of two or more people who cooperate to accomplish one or several objectives. In that sense, certainly the *concept* of organization is not new. Undoubtedly, the first organizations were primitive hunting parties. Organization and a high degree of coordination were required to bring down huge animals, as fossils from as early as 40,000 B.C. reveal (Tansik and Elliott, 1981:1).

An **organization** may be formally defined as "a consciously coordinated social entity, with a relative identifiable boundary, that functions on a relatively continuous basis to achieve a common goal or set of goals." (Robbins, 1987); "consciously coordinated" implies supervision. "Social entity" refers to the fact that organizations are composed of people who interact with one another and with other people. "Relatively identifiable boundary" alludes to the organization's goals and the public served (Gaines et al., 1991:43). Following is an analogy to assist in understanding organizations:

> Organization corresponds to the bones which structure or give form to the body. Imagine that the fingers were a single mass of bone rather than four separate fingers and a thumb made up of bones joined by cartilage so that they are flexible. The mass of bones could not, because of its structure, play musical instruments, hold a pencil, or grip a baseball bat. A police department's organization is analogous. It must be structured properly if it is to be effective in fulfilling its many diverse goals (Gaines et al., 1991:9).

It is important to note that no two organizations are exactly alike and, as we will note throughout the text, there is no one best way to supervise within an organization.

POLICE AGENCIES AS ORGANIZATIONS AND BUREAUCRACIES

Certainly police agencies fit the description of an organization. First, these agencies are managed by being organized into a number of specialized units (e.g., patrol, traffic, investigation, records). Administrators, managers, and supervisors exist to ensure that these units work together toward a common goal. If each unit were to work independently, that would lead to fragmentation, conflict, and competition and subvert the goals and purposes of the entire organization. Second, police agencies consist of people who interact within the organization and with external groups, and they exist to serve the public. The development of an organization should be done with careful evaluation, or the agency may become unable to respond efficiently to community needs. For example, the implementation of too many specialized units in a small police department (e.g., street crimes, bicycle patrol, media relations, and administration) may commit too many personnel to these functions and result in too few patrol officers. As a rule of thumb, at least 55 percent of all sworn personnel should be assigned to patrol (Guyot, 1979:253–84).

Police administrators, through a mission statement, policies and procedures, a proper management style, and a number of other means, attempt to ensure that the organization maintains its overall goals of crime suppression and investigation, and that it works amicably with similar organizations. As the organization becomes larger, the need becomes greater for people to cooperate to achieve the organizational goals. Formal organizational structures, which assist in this endeavor by spelling out areas of responsibility, lines of communication, and the chain of command, are discussed in Chapter 2.

Police organizations everywhere are also bureaucracies, as are virtually all large organizations in modern society, such as the military, universities, and corporations. To a large extent, police agencies have similar structures and management processes. The major differences in agencies exist between the large and the very small agencies; the former will be more complex, with much more specialization, hierarchical structure and a greater degree of authoritarian style of command.

The administration of most police organizations is based on the traditional, pyramidal, quasi-military organizational structure containing the elements of a bureaucracy: specialized functions, adherence to fixed rules, and a hierarchy of authority. This pyramidal organizational environment is undergoing increasing challenges, especially by college-educated police personnel.

A simple structure indicating the traditional pyramidal chain of command is shown in Figure 1–1.

In the 1970s, experts on police organization such as Egon Bittner (1970:51) contended that the military-bureaucratic organization of the police was a serious handicap, creating obstacles to the development of a truly professional police system. The reasons for this disillusionment are several and include the

FIGURE 1-1. Traditional Pyramidal Chain of Command

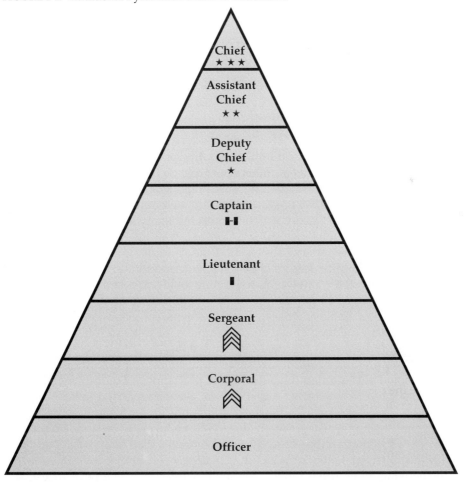

quasi-military structure and discipline of police organizations; the lack of opportunity by management to match talent and positions; the organizational restrictions on personal freedom of expression, association, and dress; communication blockage in the tall structure; the clinging to outmoded methods of operation within the organization; the lack of management flexibility; and the narrowness of job descriptions in the lower ranks of police organizations (Johnson et al., 1981:53).

Notwithstanding the growing disenchantment with the traditional bureaucratic structure of police organizations, this structure continues to prevail; for many administrators, it is still the best structure when rapid leadership and division of labor are required in times of crisis. The traditional school of thought—that each police supervisor can effectively supervise approximately seven employees—is part of the reason for the "tall" organizational structure. A number of agencies have experimented with other approaches, with mixed results (Alpert and Dunham, 1988:71). Indeed, where police agencies have attempted to flatten the organizational structure and replace paramilitary police uniforms with blazers, they have usually returned to the traditional style. An alternative is to keep a few features of the military model (e.g., police officers taking orders from superiors during critical incidents), a few features of the bureaucratic model, and go beyond these to create a reasonably professional organization. As policing enters the era of community policing and problem solving, the transition requires less bureaucracy and strong support on the part of supervisors.

Organizational Policies, Procedures, and Rules and Regulations

Policies, procedures, rules and regulations are very important in defining role expectations for police officers. Supervisors rely on these directives to guide officers' behavior and performance. Because police agencies are meant to be service oriented in nature, they must work within well-defined, specific guidelines designed to ensure that all officers conform consistently to behavior that will enhance public protection (Sheehan and Cordner, 1989:446–47).

The task for the supervisor is to find the "middle ground" between wide discretionary authority possessed by the police, and total standardization. The police role is much too ambiguous to become totally standardized, but it is also much too serious and important to be left completely to the total discretion of the patrol officer. Officers will often seek a supervisor's opinion and guidance in discretionary matters. This requires a supervisor to be well informed about all policies, procedures, and rules and regulations.

Policies are quite general and serve basically as guides to thinking rather than action. Policies reflect the purpose and philosophy of the organization and help interpret those elements to the officers. An example of a policy might be that all persons who are found to be driving while under the influence of drugs or alcohol shall be arrested, or that all juveniles who are to be detained must be taken to a specified facility. **Procedures** are more detailed than policies and provide the preferred methods for handling matters pertaining to investigation, patrol, booking, radio procedures, filing reports, roll call, use of force, arrest, sick leave, evidence handling, promotion, and many more job elements. Most police agencies are awash in procedures.

Rules and regulations are specific directives that leave little or no latitude for individual discretion. Some examples are requirements that police officers not smoke in public, check the operation of their vehicle and equipment before going on patrol, not consume alcoholic beverages within a specified number of hours before going on duty, or arriving in court or at roll call early. Rules and regulations are not always popular, especially if they are perceived as unfair or unrelated to the job. Nonetheless, the supervisor's responsibility is to ensure that officers perform these tasks with the same degree of diligence as other job duties. Thomas Reddin, former Los Angeles police chief, stated:

> Certainly we must have rules, regulations and procedures, and they should be followed. But they are no substitutes for initiative and intelligence. The more a [person] is given an opportunity to make decisions and, in the process, to learn, the more rules and regulations will be followed (Reddin, 1966:17).

Unity of Command

A related, major principle of hierarchy of authority is **unity of command,** an organizational principle that dictates that every officer should report to one and only one superior (follow the chain of command) until that superior officer is relieved.

Ambiguity over authority occurs frequently in police organizations. Detectives and patrol officers often dispute who has authority over a criminal case; officers in two different patrol beats may disagree over who has responsibility for a call for service that is located on a beat boundary line. There are numerous situations that result in conflict because the lines of authority are unclear, and as departments become larger and more complex, the amount of conflict naturally increases.

The unity of command principle also ensures that multiple and/or conflicting orders are not issued to the same police officers by several supervisors. For example, a patrol sergeant might arrive at a hostage situation and deploy personnel and give all the appropriate orders, only to have a shift lieutenant or captain come to the scene and countermand the sergeant's orders with his or her own orders. This type of situation is obviously counterproductive for all persons concerned. It is also important that all officers know and follow the chain of command at such incidents.

Span of Control

The term **span of control** refers to the number of persons one individual can effectively supervise. The limit is small, normally three to five at the top level of the organization and often broader at the lower levels, depending on factors such as the capacity of the supervisor and those persons supervised, the types of work performed, the complexity of the work, the area covered by it, distances between elements, the time needed to perform the tasks, and the types of persons served (Iannone, 1994).

The tendency in modern police operations is to have the supervisors spread too thinly. The supervisor can reduce his or her span of control by delegating work, but the tasks must be clearly defined for those persons who have to perform them.

ADVICE THAT HAS STOOD THE TEST OF TIME: SOME PRACTICAL COUNSEL

On Being Successful

The success of any organization is highly influenced by the quality of work within the agency. Peter Drucker, often referred to as a "business guru" (Lynch, 1986:5–6), observed that:

> Nothing quenches motivation as quickly as a slovenly boss. People expect and demand that [supervisors] enable them to do a good job. . . . People have . . . a right to expect a serious and competent superior (Swanson et al., 1993:127).

Unfortunately, as Drucker implied, there are good and bad supervisors, because many people—untrained, uncaring, unfit, or unwilling to have the mantle of responsibility thrust upon them—do not succeed (at least in the eyes of their subordinates).

Supervision may be defined simply as "getting things done through people"; supervision might also be defined as "the process of influencing organizational members to use their energies willingly and appropriately to facilitate the achievement of the [agency's] goals" (Eastman and Eastman, 1971:17). In more specific terms, the supervisor's work has been variously compared to that of being a "team captain, parent, steward, battle commander, fountain of wisdom, poker player, group spokesperson, gatekeeper, minister, drill instructor, facilitator, initiator, mediator, navigator, candy-store keeper, linchpin, umbrella-holder and everything else between nurse and Attila the Hun" (Swanson, et al., 1993:142). In these views, lie the essence of supervision.

Perhaps in the purest sense, a successful supervisor influences others by example—one who gains the willing obedience, confidence, respect, and loyalty of subordinates, displaying what we term in Chapter 3 as the art of leadership. This characteristic of leadership was recognized in the sixth century B.C. by Lao-Tzu, when he wrote:

> The superior leader gets things done
> With very little motion.
> He imparts instruction not through many words
> But through a few deeds.
> He keeps informed about everything
> But interferes hardly at all.
> He is a catalyst.
> And although things wouldn't get done as well
> If he weren't there.
> When they succeed he takes no credit.
> And because he takes no credit
> Credit never leaves him.
> (quoted in Bennett and Hess, 1996:77).

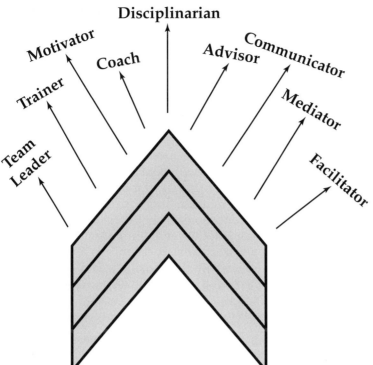

FIGURE 1-2. The Work of a Supervisor

Analects of Confucius and Machiavelli

A view of the historical writings of two other major figures might assist in developing a perspective on the role of supervisors. The analects (or brief passages) of Confucius (551–479 B.C.) and the maxims of Niccolò Machiavelli (1469–1527) are still quite popular today. Many college students in a variety of academic disciplines have been compelled to analyze the writings of both, especially Machiavelli's *The Prince* (1513). Both of these philosophers tended to agree on many points regarding the means of governance, as the following will demonstrate. Confucius often emphasized the moralism of leaders, saying:

> He who rules by moral force is like the pole-star. Govern the people by regulations, keep order among them by chastisements, and they will flee from you, and lose all self-respect. Govern them by moral force, keep order among them . . ., and they will . . . come to you of their own accord. If the ruler is upright, all will go well even though he does not give orders. But if he himself is not upright, even though he gives orders, they will not be obeyed (Waley, 1938:88, 173).

Confucius also felt that the persons the leader promotes is of no small importance: "Promote those who are worthy, train those who are incompetent; that is the best form of encouragement" (Waley, 1938:92). He also felt that leaders should learn from and emulate good administrators:

In the presence of a good man, think all the time how you may learn to equal him. In the presence of a bad man, turn your gaze within! Even when I am walking in a party of no more than three I can always be certain of learning from those I am with. There will be good qualities that I can select for imitation and bad ones that will teach me what requires correction in myself (Waley, 1938:105, 127).

Unlike Confucius, Machiavelli is often maligned for being cruel; the "ends justifies the means" philosophy imputed to him even today has cast a pall over his writings. However, although often as biting as the "point of a stiletto" and seemingly ruthless at times ["Men ought either to be caressed or destroyed, since they will seek revenge for minor hurts but will not be able to revenge major ones," and "If you have to make a choice, to be feared is much safer than to be loved" (Adams, 1992: xvii, 7, 46), Machiavelli, like Confucius, often spoke of the leader's need to possess character and compassion. For all of his blunt, management-oriented notions of administration, Machiavelli was prudent and pragmatic.

Machiavelli's counsel agreed with that of Confucius in the sense that leaders should surround themselves with persons both knowledgeable and devoted: "The first notion one gets of a prince's intelligence comes from the men around him" (Adams, 1992:63). But, again like Confucius, Machiavelli believed that supervisors should be careful of their subordinates' ambition and greed:

A new prince must always harm those over whom he assumes authority. You cannot stay friends with those who put you in power, because you can never satisfy them as they expected. The man who makes another powerful ruins himself (Adams, 1992:5, 11).

On the need for developing and maintaining good relations with subordinates, he wrote:

If . . . a prince . . . puts his trust in the people, knows how to command, is a man of courage and doesn't lose his head in adversity, and can rouse his people to action by his own example and orders, he will never find himself betrayed, and his foundations will prove to have been well laid. The best fortress of all consists in not being hated by your people. Every prince should prefer to be considered merciful rather than cruel. The prince must have people well disposed toward him; otherwise in times of adversity there's no hope (Adams, 1992:29, 60).

In a related, more contemporary vein, we might briefly note other writers' views of today's supervisors. For example, Peter Drucker, cited earlier, provided a compelling opinion of the importance of supervision: "Supervisors are, so to speak, the ligaments, the tendons and sinews of an organization. They provide the articulation. Without them, no joint can move" (quoted in Bennett and Hess, 1996:54). Similarly, the critical importance of supervisors was noted by Wally Bock (1993:39), who drew an analogy from the military:

The old saying, "Generals win battles but sergeants win wars," is true of military organizations—and of police departments. What a department is, to the officer on the street and the citizens of your community, is a direct result of what the sergeants are and do.

The fundamental responsibility of supervisors is to ensure that what needs to be accomplished in any given shift is accomplished, effectively and legally. They are concerned with the supervision of the day-to-day concerns of their subordinates. Sergeants are directly responsible for all nonranking employees in the agency. Among the functions they may perform are:

- Managing line personnel in the field.
- Executing agency objectives and work plans.
- Supervising patrol activities.
- Conducting inspections.
- Maintaining discipline.
- Conducting roll call.
- Enforcing laws and ordinances (Bennett and Hess, 1996:54).

However, supervisors must first *earn the right to supervise.* Jim Weaver (1990:47–49) argued that "Promotion to sergeant no more makes a cop a supervisor than walking in a hangar makes him [or her] a pilot." However, it has also been observed that supervisors are frequently not trained in the new skills they need. Chris Vail (1993:80) described the supervisors' training needs thusly:

> Initial training should precede promotion, or be initiated as soon as practicable. It should also always be job-related and relevant to the role of supervision. It should focus on the specific responsibilities of the supervisor and how he or she can obtain more and better performance from employees. Initial training should concentrate on the "people activities" performed by supervisors, with particular emphasis on motivating others.

Because we will elaborate on these concepts—the key functions of supervisors, assuming the supervisory position, the need for relevant training—we only treated them briefly here.

As police organizations struggle with the complexities of a rapidly changing world and ever demanding workforce, its supervisors might do well to heed the analects of Confucius, Machiavelli, and the other, more contemporary observers.

Cues for Supervisors

The implications for contemporary supervisors from the above philosophers and writers are several. First, supervisors must lead by example, including their appearance, and occupy several roles. Lao-Tzu tells us that the successful supervisor is one who keeps informed, does not rant and rave, and prefers to "condemn in private, praise in public." Confucius tells us that supervisors must above all be moral and upright; advance their subordinates—through means we might employ today as positive reinforcement and performance appraisals—and try to learn something from all of their human contacts.

Machiavelli also teaches us that supervisors should emulate successful leaders; recruit and train competent subordinates; be able, upon newly assuming a supervisory role, to maintain an adequate amount of professional distance between themselves and their subordinates—some of whom may have been good friends with the new supervisor and may now attempt to see how much they can get away with; and be able to say no to underlings while still being compassionate toward them.

SUMMARY

This chapter has set the stage for the study of police supervision, defining the book's purpose, intended audience, and key terms, and setting forth the book's organization. This chapter also defined organizations generally, then it placed police agencies within the context of organizational and bureaucratic structures. It also reviewed how supervisors can be successful, using the writings of Confucius and Machiavelli as guideposts.

The reader will now have a better frame of reference for understanding the always challenging, and at times very difficult, position of police supervisor. The important part supervisors play in human resource management is undisputed; they communicate, negotiate, train, evaluate, discipline, and deploy, and must be sensitive to subordinates' needs and administrative goals and objectives. It was also shown that supervisors, as first responder, must have a fundamental knowledge of a variety of major incidents and operations. These challenges are examined in the chapters that follow.

KEY TERMS

administration (p. 4)
management (p. 4)
supervision (p. 4)
police officer (p. 5)
law enforcement
  officer (p. 5)

peace officer (p. 5)
organization (p. 5)
policies (p. 8)
procedures (p. 8)

rules and regulations
  (p. 9)
unity of command (p. 9)
span of control (p. 9)

SOURCES

ALPERT, G. P., and DUNHAM, R. G. (1988). *Policing urban America.* Prospect Heights, Ill.: Waveland.

BENNETT, W. W., and HESS, K. (1996). *Management and supervision in law enforcement* (2d ed.). St. Paul, Minn.: West.

BITTNER, E. (1970). *The functions of the police in a modern Society.* Public Health Service Publication 2059. Washington, D.C.: U.S. Government Printing Office.

BOCK, W. (1993). "Generals Win Battles But Sergeants Win Wars," *Law and Order* (May): 39–40.

CONFUCIUS (1938). *The analects of Confucius.* A. Waley (trans.). London: Allen and Unwin.

EASTMAN, G. D., and EASTMAN, E. M. (eds.) (1971). *Municipal police administration.* 7th ed. Washington, D.C.: International City Management Association.

GAINES, L. K., SOUTHERLAND, M. D., and ANGELL, J. E. (1991). *Police administration.* New York: McGraw-Hill.

GUYOT, D. (1979). "Bending granite: Attempts to change the rank structure of American police departments." *Journal of Police Science and Administration* (7):253–84.

IANNONE, N. F. (1994). *Supervision of police personnel.* 5th ed. Englewood Cliffs, N.J.: Prentice Hall.

JOHNSON, T. A., MISNER, G. E., and BROWN, L. P. (1981). *The police and society: An environment for collaboration and confrontation.* Englewood Cliffs, N.J.: Prentice Hall.

LYNCH, R. G. (1986). *The police manager: Professional leadership skills.* 3d ed. New York: Random House.

MACHIAVELLI, N. (1992). *The prince.* R. M. Adams, (trans.) New York: Norton (Original work published 1513).

REDDIN, T. (1966). "Are you oriented to hold them? A searching look at police management." *Police Chief* (3):17.

ROBBINS, S. P. (1987). *Organizational theory: Structure, design and applications.* Englewood Cliffs, N.J.: Prentice Hall.

SHEEHAN, R., and CORDNER, G. W. (1989). *Introduction to police administration.* 2d ed. Cincinnati, Ohio: Anderson.

SWANSON, C. R., TERRITO, L., and TAYLOR, R. W. (1993). *Police administration.* 3d ed. New York: Macmillan.

TANSIK D. A., and ELLIOT, J. F. (1981). *Managing police organizations.* Monterey, Calif.: Duxbury.

VAIL, C. (1993). "Supervision Requires 'More' in Policing." *Law and Order* (May): 77–80.

WEAVER, J. (1990). "Supervising the Veteran Officer." *The Police Chief* (February): 47–49.

2

Supervisory Roles and Responsibilities

Surround yourself with the best people you can find, delegate authority, and don't interfere.

—RONALD REAGAN

A man is known by the company he organizes.

—AMBROSE BIERCE

Responsibility is the price of greatness.

—WINSTON CHURCHILL

INTRODUCTION

Now that we have obtained a fundamental understanding of supervision within organizations from Chapter 1, we know that the supervisor—directly and regularly in touch with those employees who actually do the work of the organization and interact with its customers and clients—is one of the most important members of an organization (Brown, 1992). If the supervisor fails to make sure that employees perform correctly, the organization will not be very successful.

This chapter continues that theme, identifying some important characteristics of policing and police organizations that make police supervision complex and distinctive. First, we discuss the supervisor's role and how it relates to management. Then we expand on the basic view of police organization presented in Chapter 1, setting supervisors in the larger context of an organizational structure. Next, we describe in broad terms how one goes about assuming the supervisory role; this section includes the various means by which patrol officers may be promoted, their new tasks, the influence of agency size, some considerations for supervising patrol officers and investigators, and the influence of the police culture. Two case studies are provided in this chapter.

THE SUPERVISORY ROLE

A Complex Position

The supervisor is caught in the middle; we will expand on that view in this chapter. The supervisor deals with working employees—labor—on the one hand, and middle or upper management on the other. The concerns, expectations, and interests of labor and management are inevitably different and to some extent in conflict (Reuss-Ianni, 1983). Labor and management are, respectively, at the bottom and the top of the organization. While management's job is to squeeze as much productivity as possible out of workers, labor's motivation often seems to be to avoid as much work as possible. Supervisors find themselves right in the middle of this contest. Their subordinates expect them to be understanding, to protect them from management's unreasonable expectations and arbitrary decisions, and to represent their interests. Management, though, expects supervisors to keep employees in line and to represent the interests of management and the overall organization.

The supervisor leads, directs, and controls employees while acting as mediator, mentor, coach, disciplinarian, and trainer. As such, no other position nor any higher rank in police management or administration will exert more direct influence over the employees' working environment, morale, and performance. Thus, the supervisor will in large measure determine the overall success of the organization.

In organizations that require supervisors to continue to perform actual work fairly regularly, the pull toward identifying with labor's interests may be particularly strong. Many police departments fit into this situation, with corporals and sergeants required to handle calls and investigate cases in addition to supervising subordinates.

Further adding to the complexity of the supervisor's role is the fact that the supervisor is generally in his or her first managerial position. A new supervisor, especially one who is young and new to the job, has to go through a transition phase to learn how to exercise command and get cooperation from subordinates (Bock, n.d.). The new supervisor is no longer responsible solely for her or his own personal behavior but is responsible, instead, for the behavior of several other employees. The step from worker to supervisor is a big step that calls for a new set of skills and knowledge largely separate from that learned at lower levels in the organization.

Even more complexity is created when the new supervisor is promoted from within the ranks and placed in charge of friends and peers. Longstanding relationships are put under stress when one party suddenly has official authority over former equals. Expectations of leniency or preferential treatment may have to be dealt with. When new supervisors attempt to correct deficient behavior, their own previous performance may be recalled as a means of challenging the reasonableness or legitimacy of their supervisory action.

Supervisors with any skeletons in their closets can expect to hear those skeletons rattling as they begin to use their new-found authority.

The supervisor's role, put simply, is to get subordinates to do their very best. This task involves a host of actions, including communicating, motivating, leading, team building, training, developing, appraising, counseling, and disciplining. Getting subordinates to do their very best includes figuring out their strengths and weaknesses, defining good and bad performance, measuring performance, providing feedback, and making sure that subordinates' efforts coincide with the organization's mission, values, goals, and objectives.

Supervising a group of subordinates is made more difficult because of the so-called human element. People are complex and sometimes unpredictable. Rules and principles for communicating, leading, and similar supervisory tasks are rarely hard and fast because different people react differently. What works for a supervisor in one situation may not work for that supervisor in another situation, much less for some other supervisor. Thus, supervisors have to learn to "read" subordinates and diagnose situations before choosing how to respond. Supervisors have to become students of human behavior and of behavioral science disciplines such as psychology and sociology. Unfortunately, these are inexact sciences.

Supervision is also tough because the job is dynamic, not static. Even without any turnover of personnel, a supervisor's subordinates change over time as they age, grow, mature, and experience satisfaction and dissatisfaction in their personal and work lives. In addition, turnover is common, so that new subordinates come under the supervisor's wing; the supervisor must learn the best way to handle these new subordinates and at the same time be attuned to their effects on other subordinates and on the work group as a whole.

It is not only one's subordinates that change; the organization and its environment change over time. Effective supervision over the long haul requires continuous monitoring and adaptation. The organization's rules and expectations may change. Clients and customers may make new demands. Societal values evolve. Certainly, new technologies come and go these days at the blink of an eye. Supervisors must be aware of these changing conditions if they are to be successful over time in getting their subordinates to do their very best. The organization expects the supervisor to keep up with such changes in order to keep subordinates on track; subordinates expect the supervisor to help them interpret and adapt successfully to such changes.

SUPERVISORS WITHIN THE ORGANIZATIONAL STRUCTURE

Purposes and Concerns

All organizations have a structure, be it written or unwritten, very basic or highly complex. Administrators, managers, and supervisors use this organizational chart or table of organization as a blueprint for action. The size of the organization depends on the demand placed on it and the resources available to it. Growth precipitates the need for more people, greater division of labor, specialization, written rules, and other such elements. Police administrators modify or design the structure of their organization to fulfill its mission.

An organizational chart reflects the formal structure of task and authority relationships determined to be best suited to accomplishing the police mission. The major concerns in organizing are (1) to identify what jobs need to be done, such as conducting the initial investigation, performing the latent or follow-up investigation, and providing for the custody of evidence seized at crime scenes; (2) to determine how to group the jobs, such as those responsible for patrol, investigation, and the operation of the property room; (3) to form grades of authority, such as officer, detective, corporal, sergeant, lieutenant, and captain; and (4) to equalize responsibility, illustrated by the example that if a sergeant has the responsibility to supervise seven detectives, that sergeant must have sufficient authority to discharge that responsibility properly or he or she cannot be held accountable for any results (Robbins, 1976).

Figure 2–1 provides an illustration of an organizational chart for a large police agency (Seattle, Washington), and shows the divisions of labor and responsibilities common to an agency of this size. The boxes show the separation of patrol, detectives, administration, and services. They also show lines of reporting and responsibility. Each of these areas may be further divided into smaller subunits. For example, a detectives bureau might typically be divided by crimes against people and crimes against property. Personal crimes may be subdivided into units such as robbery, homicide, sexual assault, and juvenile. Crimes against property could include burglary, fraud, and auto theft units, with each unit comprised of several detectives managed by a supervisor.

What distinguishes administrators from supervisors is that they also perform planning, organizing, staffing, and other managerial functions. Higher-ranking managers have executive as well as supervisory responsibilities. They are responsible for both organizationwide functions and the supervision of their immediate subordinates.

Because all managers, regardless of their levels in the organization, must supervise their subordinates, all are responsible for directing and controlling. However, because higher-level managers have so many other responsibilities, they generally are unable to devote as much attention as first-line supervisors to these two important tasks. Thus, the brunt of direction and control in most organizations, including police departments, usually falls on the shoulders of supervisors.

Subordinates and Units

So far we have distinguished supervision primarily in terms of directing and controlling immediate subordinates. In addition, it is not unusual for supervisors to be in charge of, or at least somewhat responsible for, initiatives, programs, and small units within the organization. In these capacities, a supervisor may not only be expected to direct and control subordinates but also may be responsible for program development, resource allocation, implementation, and related duties. Under these circumstances, supervisors may be held accountable for program or unit effectiveness as well as for the behavior of their subordinates.

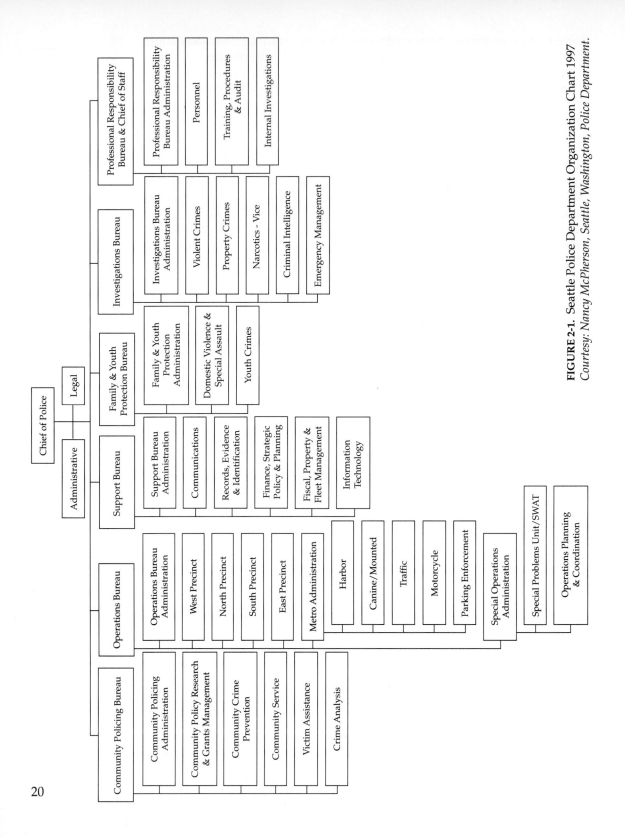

FIGURE 2-1. Seattle Police Department Organization Chart 1997
Courtesy: Nancy McPherson, Seattle, Washington, Police Department.

These additional duties reflect the fact that in many organizations some supervisors are also given managerial responsibilities. Supervisors who find themselves in charge of programs or small units should recognize that they have both supervisory and managerial responsibilities.

ASSUMING THE ROLE

In this section, we describe the means by which patrol officers are promoted to supervisory positions and assume the role. Then we examine the kinds of tasks and activities that are performed by police supervisors and discuss some of the more important aspects of policing and police organizations that distinguish police supervision from supervision in general. These include the wide variety of tasks found in police organizations, characteristics of police officers, the strength of the police culture, and the nature of police work itself.

Seeking the "Stripes"

For most rank-and-file officers, the opportunity to attain the rank of supervisor is an attractive one. Generally, lateral entry from agency to agency at the lower ranks does not exist; therefore, officers are not generally able to transfer to another police agency through promotion. Their promotional opportunities are limited to their present agency, and the waiting period for sergeant's vacancies to arise through retirement or otherwise—especially in smaller agencies—can seem to be an interminable one.

Another administrative consideration that can filter into the promotional process is the knowledge that good officers do not automatically become good supervisors. Many good officers who are promoted to the rank of sergeant can not divorce themselves from being "one of the troops" and are unable to flex their supervisory muscles when necessary (see Case Study 2–1). In short, a good sergeant must wear two hats, that of being a people-oriented, democratic leader with concern for subordinates, but one who also is task oriented and authoritarian when that style is called for.

Fuld (1909) argued many decades ago that the ideal supervisor needs to possess four qualifications: the ability to write, review, and prepare reports; a thorough knowledge of police business; a capacity for being discreet and intelligent; and a thorough knowledge of criminal law. Those qualities are still very much needed today.

Means for Getting Promoted

It is probably not uncommon for as many as 60 to 65 percent or more of eligible officers to take the supervisor's test. Competition for promotion in most police agencies is normally keen.

It should also be noted that, for several reasons, many excellent "street cops" simply do not wish to be promoted. Perhaps they want to remain one of the troops and do not feel that they could maintain the personal distance, perspective, or disciplinary authority needed at times. Or perhaps they prefer to remain in their current assignment, would lose a lot of overtime pay if promoted, or would be transferred to what they deem an undesirable shift.

Still, the opportunity to test for sergeant normally draws a crowd. Many officers test simply for the experience, because of pressure from peers, through curiosity, or just to get off the streets for a short while (Van Maanen, 1989). Most, however, seriously compete for the higher rank.

Becoming a sergeant in most agencies is governed by departmental and civil service procedures that are intended to guarantee legitimacy and impartiality for the process. In some jurisdictions, this is a fairly complicated process where each step is strictly governed by law or regulation. Larger departments generally use a multifaceted process where officers must compete in a series of tests or exercises. In smaller departments, the promotion examination may be nothing more than an interview by the mayor or city council. Supervisors are generally chosen from a final, rank-ordered list of names, often based on scores from written and oral tests. Some agencies include in the process such factors as seniority, performance evaluations, and experience.

One of the best methods for promoting the best personnel is the assessment center, which may include interviews; psychological tests; in-basket exercises (where, for example, job candidates are asked to act as a new sergeant who receives an abundance of paperwork and problems to be prioritized and dealt with in a prescribed amount of time); management tasks; group discussions;

Case Study 2–1
Adapting to the Responsibilities of the Role

Sergeant Tom Gresham is newly promoted and assigned to patrol on graveyard shift; he knows each officer on his shift, and several are close friends. Sgt. Gresham is an excellent patrol officer and prides himself on his reputation and ability to get along with his peers. He also feels this trait would benefit him as a supervisor. From the beginning, Sgt. Gresham has believed that he could get more productivity from his officers by relating to them at their level. He made an effort to socialize after work and took pride in giving his team the liberty of referring to him by his first name. Sgt. Gresham also believed that it was a supervisor's job to not get in the way of "good" police work. In Gresham's view, his team responded tremendously, generating the highest number of arrest and citation statistics in the entire department. Unfortunately, his shift also generated the highest number of citizen complaints, yet few complaints were sustained by internal affairs. It is Gresham's opin-

ion that complaints are the product of good, aggressive police work. He has quickly developed a reputation among subordinates as being "a cop's boss." One Monday morning, Sgt. Gresham is surprised to be called into his patrol captain's office; the internal affairs lieutenant is also present. They show Gresham a number of use-of-force complaints against his team over the past week when Sgt. Gresham was on vacation. Despite his captain's efforts to describe the gravity of the situation, Gresham fails to grasp the seriousness of the complaints and how his supervisory style may have contributed to them.

1. What do you feel are some of Sgt. Gresham's problems as a new supervisor?
2. As his captain, what kinds of advice would you give to Gresham?
3. What corrective action must Sgt. Gresham take immediately with his team of officers?

simulations of interviews with subordinates, the public, and news media; fact-finding exercises; oral presentation exercises; and written communications exercises. Individual and group role-playing provides a hands-on atmosphere during the process; candidates may be required to perform in simulated police-community problems, a major incident, a news briefing, or other such exercises. Although assessment centers are obviously more costly than conventional testing procedures, they are well worth the extra investment and can help to avoid promoting the wrong person while saving large dollar amounts in lawsuits and problems for many years to come.

After being promoted, several dynamics are at work that make the transition difficult. The new supervisor confronts a solitary process. Many departments provide new supervisors with training prior to or after promotion, and require that they complete a structured field training program similar to that given to new officers before being assigned supervisory responsibilities. In some states, training for various supervisory ranks is mandated by statute. In many agencies, however, training is simply not available; thus advice and counsel from peers must be relied upon.

Eventually, the new supervisor adapts to the role, developing an individual style that becomes very well known to the officers who are supervised.

A newly promoted sergeant. The rank of sergeant is one of the most difficult and challenging positions in a police organization.
Courtesy Washoe County, Nevada, Sheriff's Office Photo Unit.

Police Supervisory Tasks

Police supervision shares with general supervision an emphasis on the direction and control functions. By way of illustration, a job analysis of the sergeant's position in the 400 sworn-officer Lexington, Kentucky, Police Department found the following 10 tasks to have the greatest importance, according to incumbent sergeants. In decreasing order of importance, these are:

1. Supervises subordinate officers in the performance of their duties.
2. Disseminates information to subordinates.
3. Ensures that general and special orders are followed.
4. Observes subordinates in handling calls and other duties.
5. Reviews and approves various departmental reports.
6. Listens to problems voiced by officers.
7. Answers backup calls.
8. Keeps superiors apprised of ongoing situations.
9. Provides direct supervision on potential high-risk calls or situations.
10. Interprets policies and informs subordinates.

Tasks 1 and 9 on this list are global supervisory tasks that incorporate both direction and control. Tasks 2 and 10 are aspects of the directing function while tasks 3, 4, and 5 are elements of controlling. Thus, 7 of these top 10 sergeant's tasks involve directing and controlling. The remaining three tasks provide interesting glimpses into some of the other duties and responsibilities performed by police supervisors: listening to subordinates' problems, notifying superiors of problems, and directly assisting subordinates in performing their work. Police supervisors provide an important communications link in the hierarchy between workers and management as well as a sounding board for problems and grievances. They also get involved from time to time in performing street police work.

Supervisory tasks can range from the mundane (typing and filing reports, operating dictation equipment) to the challenging (assigning priorities to investigations, training personnel in forced-entry procedures and barricaded persons). Tasks may be administrative (preparing monthly activity reports, scheduling vacation leave), operational (securing major crime scenes, assisting stranded motorists), general (maintaining inventory of equipment, training subordinates), or specialized (conducting stakeouts, training animals for use in specialized units).

Obviously, police supervisors perform a wide range of duties requiring many different skills and a broad base of knowledge. We will elaborate on several of these duties in later chapters.

Differences by Agency Size

There is a great deal of variety among the 17,000 or so police departments in the United States (Reaves, 1993). Included in this group are general purpose police agencies, state police, sheriff's offices, highway patrols, state investigative agencies, campus police departments, and natural resources police. The agencies service small and large municipalities, merged metropolitan areas, counties, and entire states. Also included are federal law enforcement agencies and the police and security branches of the military.

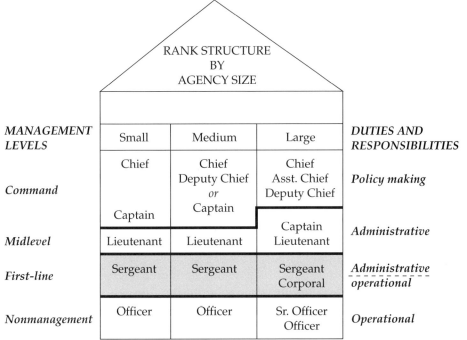

FIGURE 2-2. Rank Structure by Agency Size

Perhaps the greatest source of police organizational variation is size. Fully half of all American police agencies have fewer than 10 full-time sworn personnel (U.S. Department of Justice, Bureau of Justice Statistics, 1996). In many of these departments, especially those with five or fewer officers, the chief of police may be the only supervisor. In this kind of situation, the chief must fulfill all of the supervisory and managerial functions for the organization, a very tall order that is made even more difficult by the 24-hour-a-day, seven day-a-week nature of the police business. If the chief is the only supervisor and works a normal 40-hour week, then for 128 hours each week no supervisor is on duty. In other words, these chiefs are responsible for supervising their officers even though they are not usually on duty with the officers. Often, these chiefs also perform patrol activities while they are on duty and serve as follow-up criminal investigators.

In slightly larger police organizations, particularly those with 6 to 10 officers, the one or two sergeants are, for all intents and purposes, assistant chiefs. They typically share both supervisory and managerial duties with the chief of police and are in operational command of the department much of the time. Out of necessity, they usually perform patrol, investigative, and other direct service activities as well. Figure 2–2 shows the varying ranks and managerial and supervisory duties that may exist in departments of varying size.

The larger the police agency, the more likely that the duties of supervisors (usually sergeants, but sometimes corporals as well) will be focused on supervising their subordinates rather than on doing police work or helping the chief manage the agency. In larger agencies, supervisors will ordinarily have a sufficient number of subordinates so that the supervisor is not expected to do much of the work (handling calls, investigating crimes, and so forth). Overseeing subordinates is, in and of itself, a full-time job.

Another important difference between small and larger police agencies is in the degree of specialization that affects supervisors. In small agencies with one or two supervisors, the subordinates under their direction and control do everything—patrol, handle calls, investigate crimes, organize crime prevention groups, present school-based programs, and so forth. Supervisors in small departments, like their officers, have to be experts in all facets of police work. In larger agencies, a supervisor may be responsible only for a squad of detectives, or a squad of burglary detectives, or even a squad of residential burglary detectives. The range of activity under the supervisor's authority is generally narrower in larger agencies. On the other hand, the volume of work under the supervisor's control may be greater, as may be the number, expertise, and sophistication of subordinates.

One implication of these size differences is that in a small police agency all supervisors perform pretty much the same job, whereas in a large agency any two sergeants may have quite different jobs. Both probably are engaged primarily in directing and controlling their subordinates, but the kind of work performed by their subordinates may vary widely: general patrol, emergency operations, specialized investigations, crime analysis, and community relations. Also, the functions that supervisors are called upon to perform over and above directing and controlling will likely differ. Not all sergeants will be expected to maintain records on grant projects, but some will. Some will review accident statistics while others will not. Some, but not all, will have civilian subordinates. These and many other variables in larger police organizations create diversity among supervisory positions.

One final important source of variation in police supervision has to do with time and place. Police supervision is complicated by the 24-hour-a-day nature of the business and by the fact that the police still make house calls. Those fortunate supervisors who work at the same time and in the same place as their subordinates, such as a patrol team assigned to swing shift or a burglary unit in detectives, have a tremendous advantage over their colleagues who are separated from their subordinates by time, space, or both. Directing and controlling are much easier when one can continuously observe subordinates. Of course, the reality of most police supervision, especially in patrol and investigations, is that officers do their work alone and out of sight of supervisors (Van Maanen, 1989). For that reason police supervisors must find other methods for overseeing officers' performance. This fundamental aspect of policing will be explored further in a later section.

Supervision of Police Officers

One of the most influential situational theories of leadership holds that the nature of subordinates is the key determinant of which style of management will be most successful (Hersey and Blanchard, 1988). Every indication is that this situational or contingency theory is highly applicable to police supervision (Southerland and Reuss-Ianni, 1992), and we will examine it in detail in Chapter 3. Here we consider whether there are any general characteristics of

Supervisors are commonly responsible for directing and overseeing civilian units and personnel.
Courtesy New York Police Department Photo Unit.

police officers seeking promotion that might have a pervasive impact on police supervision.

Some early studies suggested that policing attracts certain kinds of people with distinct personalities and philosophies. It was believed that conservative, authoritarian individuals with a preference for uniforms, weapons, and discipline were drawn to police work. Later studies, however, found that new police recruits scored surprisingly "normal" and typical on psychological and intelligence tests. The most compelling characteristics that these recruits have in common are a desire to help others, an interest in job security, and perhaps some inclination toward risk taking and adventure. Otherwise, a police recruit class generally provides a good cross-section of the population at large (Burbeck and Furnham, 1985).

Veteran police officers clearly are different, however, from the general population. As recruits they may have started out much like their friends and neighbors, but police officers frequently become more rigid, more conservative, more cynical, and more suspicious as a result of adopting the police role and doing police work. This is understandable because they probably experience more anger, fear, and frustration than workers in most other fields. They see some of the worst things that people do to each other in the form of neglect, abuse, crime, and violence. And they have a good deal of lying, deception, suspicion, hatred, and violence directed at them. Given the rather dramatic and intense nature of policing and the police role, it would be odd if the personalities and viewpoints of police officers were not affected. One manifestation of these effects on police officers is stress, a topic that is addressed more fully in Chapter 7.

Second, and of equal importance, police supervisors must attend to the emotional and psychological development of their subordinates. In so doing, they counter the very occupational tendencies toward cynicism and stress-related mental and physical ill health described above. Perhaps the greatest responsibility given to police supervisors is guiding the moral and intellectual development of their subordinates (Muir, 1977). We discuss ethics, values, and liability issues in Chapter 8.

The supervisor's challenge is to restore a balance to the lives of officers, a balance which is often thrown out by the experience of policing. Today's supervisor cannot function like a military commander; the contemporary supervisor requires more than just unquestioned strength and toughness. Successful supervision utilizes such traditionally "feminine" attributes as empathy, caring, and nurturing, as well as such "masculine" attributes as decisiveness, boldness, and toughness.

This more balanced view of supervision has gained credence not only because it is obviously superior but also because of the increasing numbers of women and minority police officers and the higher levels of education officers possess today. A macho and overbearing style of police supervision that may have worked in the past is inappropriate for today's officers who are less responsive to paramilitary management styles.

The Police Culture

The role of the supervisor is also affected by the strength of the **police culture,** which is a determining factor in work behavior. For example, the number of traffic citations issued or the number of arrests by officers is frequently determined by norms established by the work group. And, on rare occasions, police cultures support flagrant forms of deviance: drinking on duty, brutalizing prisoners, selling drugs, and corruption (Kappeler et al., 1994; Kleinig, 1996). These behaviors do occur and are a major concern to supervisors. Nonetheless, some level of such activity can be expected in any cross-section of citizens.

Most police officers do not engage in flagrant deviance, of course, and not all police organizational cultures encourage or even allow such behavior. The police supervisor's responsibility is to be keenly familiar with the norms and values of his or her organization's culture; if these norms and values are consistent with official expectations, the supervisor can use the culture to direct and control subordinates' behavior. When the organizational culture supports unhealthy attitudes and deviant behavior, however, the supervisor's job is made much more difficult. Either subordinates must be convinced to reject the culture's deviant norms and values, or the culture itself must be changed. For example, in some departments speeding in marked patrol cars is routinely accepted by officers and the police culture. Yet, when officers speed but are not responding to an emergency call, it not only is dangerous but also undermines citizen satisfaction with the police. Citizens expect their police to abide by the same laws under which they themselves are held accountable. In this case, supervisors must be diligent in bringing police behavior into compliance with laws and larger societal expectations.

Other characteristics of the police role provide police supervisors with some opportunities to resist a deviant organizational culture. For example, if a group of officers is separated geographically from the rest of the organization or works at a different time from other officers, the impact of the organizational culture may be reduced and the supervisor's opportunity to develop an alternative culture is heightened. Indeed, it is quite common in police departments to find distinct behavioral styles among different squads, shifts, and units; these styles are frequently the result of supervisors' own varying philosophies, styles, and values. This not only applies to deviant behavior but also to day-to-day activities. Supervisors can have an impact on individual officers' priorities. If a sergeant thinks ticket writing is most important, then subordinates will very likely strive to write more tickets.

Patrol and Investigation

Major Aspects of Patrol

Because supervisors are principally concerned with assuring that subordinates do their work correctly, the nature of the work in an organization has considerable influence on the context and practice of supervision. The most common work assignments in police depa rtments are patrol and investigations. Patrol officers, the most numerous of all police personnel, are generalists who perform a wide variety of duties; thus, patrol supervisors must be generalists as well. Among the major aspects of patrol work that supervisors must oversee are:

1. *Call Handling.* Patrol officers handle the entire range of calls for service from crimes in progress to domestic disputes to parking complaints. The supervisor's responsibility is to ensure that these calls are handled efficiently and effectively. To do this, supervisors monitor police radio transmissions, review police reports, meet with officers, and, less frequently, observe officers firsthand. Supervisors also meet with citizens who complain about the way officers handle their calls, and sometimes proactively contact citizens to measure the level of "customer satisfaction" with police service.
2. *Investigations.* Police academies have historically stressed the importance of the first officer on the scene, including his or her observations and protecting the evidence thereon. Indeed, in some agencies patrol officers are expected to conduct complete investigations, turning to detectives only when

absolutely necessary. Here supervisors need to guide and oversee their patrol officers in evidence gathering, case preparation, and other truly investigative activities.

3. *Routine Patrol.* Most patrol officers spend more time "patrolling" than doing anything else, generally trying to be observant and seen by the public. The supervisor's primary responsibility is to ensure that officers use their free patrol time productively; at the least, patrol supervisors must see that officers remain in their assigned areas, answer their radios, do not abuse their free patrol time, and actively attend to issues and problems in beat areas. Detective supervisors should ensure that officers spend their time comprehensively following leads, while traffic supervisors should ensure that officers are enforcing traffic laws in areas with a high number of accidents.

4. *Targeted Assignments.* Police departments today, especially those with a **community policing and problem solving (COPPS)** orientation, would target recurring problems and assign patrol officers to that problem during their free patrol time. These assignments are usually based on information produced by crime analysis or dispatched calls for service data. These data help officers identify "hot spots" (locations), individuals (offenders and victims), or types of crime that occur with some frequency. In these situations, the supervisor's primary function is to reinforce the validity of the assignments and to ensure that officers are provided the time and tools necessary to develop reduction and prevention strategies.

   Along these same lines, investigative supervisors may have detectives target violent offenders or offenders who commit multiple crimes. Indeed, there are opportunities in every unit in the police department for supervisors to target problems and direct subordinates' activities.

5. *Emergency Situations.* Supervision is perhaps most critical in emergency situations. Supervisors and patrol officers are usually the first on the scene of serious traffic accidents, major fires, hostage situations, and similar emergencies. In many cases, responsibility for such emergencies eventually shifts to specialists (accident investigators, detectives, firefighters, SWAT teams, and so forth), but during the first few minutes, and sometimes for longer periods, supervisors and officers are responsible for life saving, protection of the scene, establishing a perimeter and communications, and related activities. During these emergencies, supervisors must assess the situation, make assignments, notify superiors, control the behavior of officers and others on the scene, and otherwise take command until relieved by specialists or higher authority. We will discuss supervisors' roles in special situations and critical incidents more fully in later chapters.

Overseeing Investigations

Investigative supervisors do not have to oversee as wide a range of activity as patrol supervisors, but their responsibilities are equally demanding. Their detective subordinates gather physical evidence, interview victims and witnesses, work with informants, interrogate suspects, write reports, prepare applications for arrest and search warrants, meet with prosecutors, and testify in court. Detectives may also work undercover, sometimes for extended periods of time, particularly to investigate vice- and drug-related crimes.

Detectives view a suspect photo lineup. Supervising a specialized unit in detectives, training, or administration requires additional skills, knowledge, and abilities.
Courtesy New York Police Department Photo Unit.

Three categories of investigative work that have somewhat differing implications for supervision are property crimes, personal crimes, and vice. Detectives tend to have heavy caseloads in property crime investigations—burglary, theft, fraud, and even robbery—making this a high-volume activity. A primary role for the supervisor of property crime investigators is caseload management—setting priorities, screening out low-priority cases, monitoring caseload sizes, and so forth. Also, these kinds of investigations frequently involve informants, so monitoring their detectives' relations with informants is an important concern for supervisors.

Crimes against persons, which include homicide, rape, child abuse, and child sex offenses, normally involve smaller caseloads, but each investigation tends to be more intensive, in-depth, and longer. Because these crimes are generally more serious than property crimes, more is at stake in their investigation. Detectives and their supervisors may have to withstand pressure from victims, family, friends, the media, politicians, and even police superiors. The chances of detectives becoming personally involved in individual cases is great, as is the possibility of burnout caused by repeated exposure to violence and human suffering. Thus, supervisors must give careful attention both to the details of particular investigations and to the emotional health and well-being of their detective subordinates.

Supervisors of vice, narcotics, and undercover investigators should have an even greater concern than supervisors of personal crime detectives for the well-being of their subordinates. Detectives who focus on vice and drugs and those who work undercover operate on the fringes of society and are exposed to a variety of temptations, including drugs, sex, and money. Undercover investigators sometimes become so immersed in lies and deception that they become confused about their occupational role and lose track of legal and professional ethics and responsibilities (Kleinig, 1996).

A different problem sometimes arises, particularly in narcotics investigation, when detectives feel so strongly about the evils of drugs and become so frustrated by the difficulty of making good cases that they may take the law into their own hands by fabricating evidence, planting drugs, using excessive force, and routinely lying in court (Barker and Carter, 1990; Kappeler et al., 1994). Although rare, supervisors of undercover and vice detectives must be alert to all these possibilities; besides overseeing the investigation of particular cases, they must be especially attuned to the moral and psychological health of their subordinates.

Other Supervisory Responsibilities

Supervisors must also direct and control their subordinates' use of discretionary authority. Supervisors must also make sure that when officers do stop, search, detain, and charge citizens that they do so using proper techniques and that they act within the law. This includes proactively observing and reviewing the actions of subordinates as well as responding to citizen complaints about the behavior of officers.

Supervisors must ensure that their officers are not prone to unnecessary or excessive use of force. Supervisors must carefully review each instance of a subordinate's use of force to make sure that it was proper, legal, and within departmental guidelines.

Police supervisors must enhance officer safety and help officers deal with the psychological effects of danger. Supervisors must also be wary of another reaction: Some officers see so much danger in every situation that their approach to citizens becomes uniformly heavy-handed and oppressive. Ultimately, police supervisors need to develop their officers into consistent and reliable decision makers.

Supervisors also need to ensure that their officers recognize and respect the varied functions of policing, and overcome the view that work relating to order maintenance and social services is "not real police work." Supervisors should use performance appraisals, assignments, commendations, and other rewards and punishments under their control to drive home the message that all the varied functions of policing are legitimate aspects of police work.

The Ideal versus the Real

We need to acknowledge the crucial difference between what experts and police administrators say supervisors should do and what these supervisors actually do. The most common complaint heard from police executives is that supervisors do not exercise enough control over subordinates. This may partially be a consequence of the strong emphasis within police administration over the last decade or two on the human relations approach to management (Cordner, 1994).

The introduction of more humane, tolerant, and participative forms of management was sorely needed in policing but, as with so many other things, police supervisors may have overcompensated in their zeal to atone for past mistakes. Today's police supervisors are sometimes so conscious of communications, perception, motivation, leadership, group dynamics, team building, participation, and similar human relations concerns that they ignore their other responsibilities to set standards, monitor behavior, correct errors, and impart discipline when substandard performance continues.

These kinds of complaints from police administrators should be taken with a few grains of salt, however. Senior practitioners in many fields, including policing, have historically bemoaned the perceived lack of toughness and discipline in their younger successors. On the other hand, police officers, like most workers, generally indicate that they would like to have greater say in decision making in their organizations and more control over their own work (Wycoff and Skogan, 1994).

How can these apparently contradictory views be reconciled? They mirror the competing interests of officers and administrators, reflective of more general labor-management conflict found in most organizations. And they are indicative of the inevitable conflict created by any kind of power and authority; just as conflict between citizens and police officers is inevitable, so too is conflict between police officers and their superiors. However, the reasons why police officers and police administrators have contradictory impressions of police supervision run even deeper. Police administrators realize how little actual control they have over police officers (Sykes, 1985) and thus rely very extensively on supervisors to keep things in check. Police officers, on the other hand, expect their supervisors to be kind and humane because the rest of police management often seems remote, impersonal, punitive, and unpredictable. Officers know that mistakes are easy to make in police work and they feel that administrators are out of touch with reality, so they pressure their supervisors to protect them. Any failure of supervisors to support the troops is regarded as treason by subordinates.

Police supervisors are thus caught in the middle, as always, and different supervisors react differently. Some lean clearly one way or the other, choosing to identify with the "street cops" or with the "management cops" (Reuss-Ianni, 1983). Others attempt to find a middle road, either by balancing the competing demands placed upon them or simply by doing as little as possible. The latter style, unfortunately, tends to be as common among supervisors as among police officers; both learn that the easiest path is not to rock the boat, not to make waves, not to ask questions, not to point out problems, not to take risks, and not to try out innovative ideas. Case Study 2–2 shows how one officer's emphasis on report writing affected the morale and response of his subordinates.

What should supervisors do to satisfy the competing demands put on them? The answer is that it all depends; in any particular situation, a more officer-oriented or a more management-oriented approach may be called for, depending on the specific background and characteristics of the situation. In general, though, a police supervisor must give substantial attention to both sides. Ultimately, the supervisor's primary allegiance must be to the organization rather than to subordinates, but neither the supervisor nor the organization can be successful without the cooperation and assistance of subordinates.

Case Study 2–2
Seeing the Big Picture

Sergeant Henry Garcia is a highly educated 18-year veteran, who came out near the top in his promotional exam. His career has essentially been spent in the planning/research and the training divisions. He also teaches report writing at the academy and at the local community college. Sgt. Garcia believes very strongly that officers are only as good as the reports they write. He feels his officers should be exceptional report writers, and devotes most of his time reviewing reports, counseling officers on report content, and recommending changes and revisions. His demands require officers to spend inordinate amounts of time with their report-related duties, where they accrue much overtime in the process. At the recruit academy, Garcia often uses his team's reports as examples of "good" police work. Arrests in his division are the worst in the agency, and his division has the highest number of reported offenses. Sgt. Garcia often asks his officers why the arrest and crime statistics are so poor, but they fail to respond to him. He's confused and seeks the input of his friend, a senior sergeant, to discuss the source of the problems.

1. As the senior sergeant, what is your advice to Sgt. Garcia about the reasons for the crime problem in his district and the relations with his team?
2. What might you suggest to rectify this situation?

SUMMARY

This chapter has focused on the complex demands and considerations of police supervision; several important characteristics of policing and police organizations were identified that compel police supervision to be a complex and unique role.

Supervision was set in the larger context of an organizational structure, and we described how one goes about assuming a supervisory position. Included were the various means by which patrol officers may be promoted, their new tasks, the influence of agency size, some considerations for supervising patrol officers and investigators, and the influence of the police culture.

Placed as they are in "in-between" kinds of positions, police supervisors need to maintain and improve their familiarity with the work done by their subordinates, with their own supervisory duties, and with the kinds of managerial-level responsibilities to which they might be promoted.

KEY TERMS

police culture   (p. 28)

community policing
and problem solving
COPPS   (p. 30)

ITEMS FOR REVIEW

1. Explain how the supervisor's role is uniquely difficult and complex.
2. Delineate the means by which one is promoted to a supervisory level, some of the factors that influence whether one is promoted, some reasons for an officer's refusal to be promoted, and some of the problems that one faces upon assuming the role.

3. What are the supervisor's tasks?
4. What are some of the major aspects of patrol work that supervisors must oversee?
5. Define what is meant by the "ideal" versus "real" supervision of patrol officers.

SOURCES

BARKER, T., and CARTER, D. (1990). "Fluffing up the evidence and covering your ass: Some conceptual notes on police lying." *Deviant Behavior* 11:61–73.

BOCK, W. (n.d.). "Briefing memo: On the transition to sergeant." Oakland, Calif. Mimeographed.

BROWN, M. F. (1992). "The sergeant's role in a modern law enforcement agency." *Police Chief* (May): 18–22.

BURBECK, E., and FURNHAM, A. (1985). "Police officer selection: A critical review of the literature." *Journal of Police Science and Administration* 13:58–69.

CORDNER, G. W. (1994). "Administration." In W. G. Bailey (ed.). *The Encyclopedia of Police Science.* New York: Garland.

FULD, L. F. (1909). *Police Administration.* New York: G. P. Putnam's Sons.

GOLDSTEIN, H. (1960). "Police discretion not to invoke the criminal justice process: Low visibility decisions in the administration of justice." *Yale Law Journal* 69 (March): 543–94.

GOLDSTEIN, H. (1977). *Policing a free society.* Cambridge, Mass.: Ballinger.

GULICK, L. (1937). "The theory of organization." In L. Gulick and L. Urwick (eds.). *Papers on the Science of Administration.* New York: Institute of Public Administration.

HERSEY, P., and BLANCHARD, K. H. (1988). *Management of organizational behavior: Utilizing human resources,* 5th ed. Englewood Cliffs, N. J.: Prentice Hall.

KAPPELER, V., SLUDER, R., and ALPERT, G. (1994). *Forces of Deviance: Understanding the Dark Side of Policing.* Prospect Heights, Ill. Waveland.

KLEINIG, J. (1996). *The ethics of policing.* Cambridge: Cambridge University Press.

MUIR, W. K., JR. (1977). *Police: Streetcorner politicians.* Chicago: University of Chicago Press.

REAVES, B. A. (1993). "Census of state and local law enforcement agencies, 1992." *Bulletin.* Washington, D.C.: Bureau of Justice Statistics.

REUSS-IANNI, E. (1983). *Two cultures of policing: Street cops and management cops.* New Brunswick, N.J.: Transaction Books.

ROBBINS, S. P. (1976). *The Administration Process.* Englewood Cliffs, N. J.: Prentice Hall.

SOUTHERLAND, M. D. and REUSS-IANNI, E. (1992). "Leadership and management." In G. W. Cordner and D. C. Hale (eds.). *What Works in Policing? Operations and Administration Examined.* Cincinnati, Ohio: Anderson.

SYKES, G. (1985). "The functional nature of police reform: The "myth" of controlling the police." *Justice Quarterly* 2(1): 51–65.

U.S. DEPARTMENT OF JUSTICE, (1996). "State and local police departments, 1990." *Bureau of Justice Statistics,* (February): 1.

VAN MAANEN, J. (1989). "Making rank: Becoming an American police sergeant." In R. G. Dunham and G. P. Alpert (eds.). *Critical Issues in Policing: Contemporary Readings.* Prospect Heights, Ill.: Waveland.

WYCOFF, M., and SKOGAN, W. (1994). "The effect of community policing management style on officer's attitudes." *Crime and Delinquency* 40(3): 371–83.

3

Leadership and Motivation Theories

Of the best leaders, when he is gone,
they will say: We did it ourselves.

—CHINESE PROVERB

It is time for a new generation of leadership,
to cope with new problems and new opportunities.
For there is a new world to be won.

—JOHN F. KENNEDY

Individual commitment to a group effort—that is
what makes a team work, a company work,
a society work, a civilization work.

—VINCE LOMBARDI

INTRODUCTION

In Chapter 1 we identified the first-line supervisor as one of the most important and influential members of the police organization whose primary functions involved directing and controlling the work of subordinates. But our discussion was limited to the functional duties and tasks, or the mechanics of the position. Here we go deeper, exploring the motivational side of supervision, or the "art of leadership." We will explore why some supervisors are capable of capturing the "hearts and minds" of their subordinates and arouse their passion to perform extraordinary tasks, while other supervisors struggle to gain officers' compliance to simple directions.

We begin with a discussion of several early management theories that have stood the test of time and are of primary interest to supervisors past, present, and future. We would do well to remember that behind every good practice lies a good theory. Theory and practice are inextricably intertwined. Thus, we look at the primary theories behind employee satisfaction, motivation, and leadership. We might also point out that many books have been written which examine leadership theories in length; thus, we will limit our coverage here to a brief overview of the theories most applicable to policing.

Included are discussions of the evolution of management from its beginning as a science through humanism and systems approaches. Then, general motivations theories are discussed along with a comparison of the concepts of management and leadership. Next, we examine leadership theories and the supervisor as leader, situational leadership, quality management, team building, and, finally, why leaders fail.

THE SUPERVISOR AS LEADER

A Problem of Definition

Leadership is the heart and soul of effective supervision. The idea of leadership has been with us for a long time, yet there continues to be widespread debate and disagreement about its characteristics and meaning. As Bennis and Nanus (1985:5) observed, there has been longstanding difficulty in defining leadership: "Like love, leadership . . . is something everyone knew existed but nobody could define." First, as we saw above, it was assumed that leadership skills were a matter of birth: the so-called Great Man theory of leadership. When this view failed to explain leadership, it was replaced by the notion that great events made leaders of certain people who excelled in extraordinary situations. Moses, Julius Caesar, Martin Luther, Martin Luther King, Jr., Winston Churchill, Harry Truman, Gandhi, and many others like them sought to assert their influence when time and social events intersected to make them great leaders. However, this—what has come to be called the "Big Bang" idea—proved to be another inadequate definition.

Many other theories of leadership have come and gone. Some looked at the leader, others looked at the situation. None, Bennis and Nanus (1985) argued, has stood the test of time. Now, they argued, we have an opportunity to appraise our leaders and ponder the essence of power. They maintained that the leadership environment of today must be examined in three major contexts: commitment (maintaining a strong work ethic, with employees working at full potential); complexity (keeping abreast of changes—legal, financial, technological, and so forth—that have profound effects on organizations); and credibility (surviving in a time when everyone is questioning and challenging authority).

The word *leadership* is widely used and has resulted in as many definitions as there have been studies of the subject. Some commonly used definitions include:

- "Leadership is the process of directing the behavior of others toward the accomplishment of some objective" (Certo, 1989:351).
- "The process of influencing the activities of an individual or a group in efforts toward goal achievement in a given situation" (Hersey and Blanchard, 1977).

- "The activity of influencing people to strive willingly for group objectives" (Bennett and Hess, 1992:61).
- "The exercise of influence" (Bennett and Hess, 1992:61).

In criminal justice organizations, **leadership** might be defined as "the process of influencing organizational members to use their energies willingly and appropriately to facilitate the achievement of the [agency's] goals" (Swanson et al., 1993:165).

The ability to influence people to do the work is a common thread throughout these definitions. As a result, leadership has been commonly described as more of an art than a science.

It is also clear that supervisors use various methods for motivating officers. There is no one best way to manage and lead people in every situation. Indeed, as will become more evident from the theories discussed in this chapter, supervisors may need to rely on a combination of strategies to become effective leaders.

EARLY MANAGEMENT THEORY AND EXPERIMENTATION

Scientific Management

Frederick Winslow Taylor, whom many consider to be the "father of scientific management," sought to refine management techniques by studying how workers might become more complete extensions of machines. Taylor (1911) was primarily interested in discovering the best means for getting the most out of employees—chiefly the blue-collar workers at the Bethlehem Steel works in Pennsylvania where Taylor worked as chief engineer in 1898. Taylor maintained that management knew little about the limits of worker production. He was the first to introduce time and motion studies to test his argument.

Taylor felt that by observing workers in action, wasted motions could be eliminated and production increased. He began by measuring the amount of time that workers required to shovel and carry pig iron. Taylor then standardized the work into specific tasks, improved worker selection and training, established workplace rules, and advocated close supervision of workers by a foreman.

The results were incredible and worker productivity soared; the total number of shovelers needed dropped from about 600 to 140, and worker earnings increased from $1.15 to $1.88 per day. The average cost of handling a long ton (2,240 pounds) dropped from $0.072 to $0.033. Although criticized by labor unions for his management-oriented views, Taylor nonetheless proved that administrators must know their employees. His views caught on and emphasis was soon placed entirely on the formal administrative structure. Later, terms such as *authority, chain of command, span of control,* and *division of labor* evolved in the workplace.

Government was highly skeptical of the scientific management movement, and unions also vigorously attacked the concept, describing it as mechanistic and totally ignorant of employee needs. Furthermore, while **scientific management** was never presented as a complete management theory, it was still the first scientific effort focusing on the individual task to be performed and it did attempt to learn about workers as individuals. It was embraced by some law enforcement agencies, but found greater acceptance in business and industry. It became a part of university curricula after 1900 (McFarland, 1986).

Gulick's POSDCORB

Later, the manager's task was clearly set forth in 1935 when Luther Gulick (1937) conceived the acronym **POSDCORB** (planning, organizing, staffing, directing, coordinating, reporting, and budgeting) to describe the elements that he felt formed the universal functions of managers in organizations (see Figure 3–1). Gulick was most interested in how organizations might be structured and the roles of managers within them. POSDCORB, in its simplicity, identified the key administrative activities that occupy the majority of a manager's time.

Gulick also emphasized the need for coordinating the work by dividing labor within formal organizations. The division of labor in police agencies is evident when looking at an organizational chart. (See Figure 2–1 in Chapter 2, an organizational chart for the Seattle, Washington, Police Department, which shows the divisions of labor and responsibilities common to an agency of its size.)

Gulick also saw the need for a hierarchy in organizations, whereby supervisors used a chain of command to coordinate orders and information from the top to the bottom of the organization. He also believed that work should be coordinated in groups with one supervisor in charge. This concept, referred to as **"span of control"** identified the number of persons reporting to a supervisor. Five to seven officers reporting to one supervisor is a commonly accepted span of control in policing.

Taylor's scientific management theory and Gulick's principles of administration, with their emphasis on the technical and engineering side of management, were quickly adopted by police in the first training schools in New York City and Berkeley, California, and influenced some of the most respected

FIGURE 3-1. POSDCORB

Planning—working out in broad outline the things that need to be done and the methods for doing them to accomplish the purpose set for the enterprise.
Organizing—establishment of the formal structure of authority through which work subdivisions are arranged, defined, and coordinated for the defined objective.
Staffing—the whole personnel function of bringing in and training the staff and maintaining favorable conditions at work.
Directing—the continuous task of making decisions, embodying them in specific and general orders and instructions, and serving as a leader of the enterprise.
Coordinating—the all-important duty of interrelating the various parts of the work.
Reporting—keeping those to whom the execution is responsible informed about what is going on, which includes keeping himself and his subordinates informed through records, research, and inspection.
Budgeting—all that goes with budgeting in the form of fiscal planning, accounting, and control.

Source: Luther H. Gulick and Lyndell Urwick, eds., *Papers on the Science of Administration* (New York: Institute of Public Administration, 1937) p. 13.

writers on police administration, including O. W. Wilson, V. A. Leonard, and August Vollmer. Even today, police administrators and supervisors use these concepts for performing their administrative functions and designing and redefining organizations.

The Emergence of Humanism

Humanism is the study of employee motivation and performance. The landmark research at the Hawthorne plant of the Western Electric Company in a suburb outside Chicago, by physicist Elton Mayo and sociologist Fritz Roethlisberger of the Harvard Business School, identified the important role of people in organizations (Homans, 1951). Their studies began as a scientific management experiment to evaluate whether altered working conditions involving work area lighting would affect productivity. Initial findings revealed that by increasing illumination, production would also increase.

Further testing showed that other working conditions, such as the number of breaks per day and hours of work per day, also had a positive effect on production. Most surprising to researchers was the discovery that production levels remained significantly higher than preexperimental levels, even after the study was completed and workers returned to their original working conditions. This important finding became known as the "**Hawthorne effect.**" Researchers determined that workers were motivated and responded positively to the additional attention and human contact during the experiments as much as the changed work environment. Simply put, people respond positively when they believe that others are interested in them. This is a basic precept of humanist thought.

During the 1940s and 1950s, this research led to the recognition by both private and public organizations of the strong effect of the working environment and informal structures on the organization. In policing, attention was paid to job enlargement and enrichment techniques to generate interest in the profession as a career. "Employee-centered" management approaches such as democratic and participatory management began to appear in police agencies. There was also a move away from the traditional pyramid-shaped organizational structure toward a more flattened structure with fewer midlevels of management. This has resulted in an increase in responsibilities for the first-line supervisor.

The human relations approach, however, is not without its critics. There is concern that shifting the emphasis away from an organization's administration and structure to social rewards for employees would distract from the accomplishment of organizational goals. Critics also argued that it led employees to expect more rewards for less effort (Lynch, 1986).

For all these reasons, the human relations movement had a limited impact. As a general rule the police profession found bureaucratic management to be more acceptable. In the first half of the 20th century, police managers were strongly influenced by the reform movement that swept the nation. Corruption was rampant and the key words for resolving the problems were "efficiency" and "change." The goal of progressive chiefs was to gain control of their departments and to reduce political influence. Human relations was viewed as being vague, and the military model with its rank and structure was regarded as the almost perfect panacea for resolving the problems of police managers (More and Wegener, 1992).

41

CHAPTER 3
Leadership and
Motivation Theories

A Systems Approach

By the mid-1960s, it was apparent that no single, best way to manage organizations existed. As a result, the **systems approach** to management evolved, essentially combining the features of the scientific management and human relations approaches.

The systems approach emphasizes the interdependence and interrelationship of each part to the whole. According to Luthans (1976:94), "A system is composed of elements or subsystems that are related and dependent upon one another. When these subsystems are in interaction with one another, they form a unitary whole."

The main premise of the theory is that to fully understand the operation of an entity, the entity must be viewed as a system or as a whole. The system must be modified only through changes in its parts. A thorough knowledge of how each part functions and the interrelationships between the parts must be present before modifications can be made (Certo, 1989).

This view is basically in opposition to the way in which law enforcement agencies have traditionally been organized and have functioned. For example, detective units often work apart from the remainder of the police department. It is not uncommon for other specialty units such as gangs, traffic, and street crimes to work in isolation as well. Functionally, what often occurs is that there are isolated subsystems with a limited interrelation. The systems approach to management attempts to deal with this problem by unifying management theory.

A systems-oriented supervisor and other leaders must look at the big picture and continually analyze and evaluate how the entire organization is performing with respect to its missions, goals, and objectives. In the case of a new policy regarding police pursuits, for example, a systems-oriented supervisor would be conscious of every impact the new policy might have on all pertinent organizational divisions, including patrol, investigations, administration, and training. A systems approach also takes into account the potential impact of decisions on external factors such as the general public, the political environment, and other criminal justice agencies. The goal is that all affected agencies and their units work together to resolve problems.

Motivation Theory

Motivation is the inner state that causes an individual to behave in a way that ensures the accomplishment of some goal (Berelson and Steiner, 1964). At its most fundamental level, motivation involves a needs-goal model, where an individual seeks to fulfill a need (see Figure 3–2). The need is then transformed into some behavior that is directed toward satisfying that need. For example, when one becomes hungry, behavior is directed toward buying, preparing, and eating food.

However, motivating employees on the job is not so simplistic. Therefore, motivation theory helps us to understand the "why" of people's behavior. It is

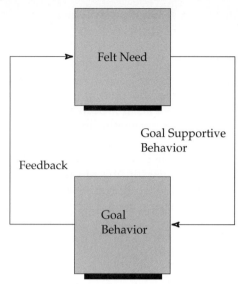

FIGURE 3-2. The Needs-Goal Model of
Motivation
Source: Samual Certo, *Principles of Modern
Management: Functions and Systems,* 4th ed.
(Needham Heights, Mass: Simon and
Schuster, 1989), p. 377.

often misunderstood as something that supervisors do to employees. In reality,
it is more internal and relates to an individual's needs, wants, and desires. But
what exactly sparks an employee's desire to achieve a higher level of performance is not easily identified. What is clear, however, is that what motivates one
employee to perform may not motivate another employee at all.

Motivation theory may be divided into two general categories: (1) content
theories and (2) process theories. Content theories focus on the individuals'
needs, wants, and desires, and attempt to explain what motivates people's behavior. Process theories attempt to explain how people are motivated and focus
more on the motivation process.

CONTENT THEORIES

Maslow's Hierarchy of Needs

Abraham H. Maslow founded the humanistic school of psychology during the
1940s. Maslow's (1954) work focused on human needs and wants. He viewed
people as perpetually "wanting" in nature, and described their needs as insa-
tiable. According to Maslow, people's needs are not random, but progress in a
hierarchy of needs (physical, safety, social, ego-esteem, and self actualization)
as shown in Figure 3–3.

Maslow asserted that people were motivated by their lowest level of unsat-
isfied need. Once a lower need is satisfied, higher needs are sought. An important implication to motivation theory lies in the understanding that a satisfied

FIGURE 3-3. Maslow's Hierarchy of Human Needs

Self-actualization Needs	Job-related Satisfiers
Reaching Your Potential	Involvement in Planning Your Work
Independence	Freedom to Make Decisions Affecting Work
Creativity	
Self-expression	Creative Work to Perform
	Opportunities for Growth and Development

Esteem Needs	Job-related Satisfiers
Responsibility	Status Symbols
Self-respect	Merit Awards
Recognition	Challenging Work
Sense of Accomplishment	Sharing in Decisions
Sense of Competence	Opportunity for Advancement

Social Needs	Job-related Satisfiers
Companionship	Opportunities for Interaction with Others
Acceptance	Team Spirit
Love and Affection	Friendly Coworkers
Group Membership	

Safety Needs	Job-related Satisfiers
Security for Self and Possessions	Safe Working Conditions
Avoidance of Risks	Seniority
Avoidance of Harm	Fringe Benefits
Avoidance of Pain	Proper Supervision
	Sound Company Policies, Programs, and Practices

Physical Needs	Job-related Satisfiers
Food	Pleasant Working Conditions
Clothing	Adequate Wage or Salary
Shelter	Rest Periods
Comfort	Labor-saving Devices
Self-preservation	Efficient Work Methods

Source: A. H. Maslow, *Motivation and Personality,* 2d ed. (New York: Harper & Row, 1970).

need is no longer a motivator of behavior. Simply stated, people who have their security needs met can only be motivated by higher needs.

What are the implications of this theory for supervisors? According to Maslow's hierarchy, a supervisor will better understand officers' performance and what motivates them by identifying their unfulfilled needs. There must also be a recognition that different officers may be at various levels in the hierarchy of needs and, therefore, are not necessarily motivated by the same wants. For example, a rookie officer may be most concerned with successfully completing the probationary period; therefore, safety and security are that officer's primary concern and motivator. Conversely, for the veteran officer interested in promotion, motivation may derive from esteem and status level. The supervisor may be successful in motivating this officer by delegating some team leader duties to the officer and assisting that officer in preparing for the sergeant's exam. Generally, officers will ascend in the hierarchy described by Maslow.

McGregor's Theory X and Theory Y

Douglas McGregor was a proponent of a more humanistic and democratic approach to management. His work was based on two basic assumptions about people: Theory X, which views employees in the negative sense and sees the need for structured organizations with strict hierarchal lines and close supervision; and Theory Y, which takes a more humanistic view toward employees, believing that they are capable of being motivated and productive. A further explanation of the assumptions about human nature and behavior that emerge from these divergent theories are as follows:

Theory X
- The average employee dislikes work and will avoid it whenever possible.
- People are lazy, avoid responsibility, and must be controlled, directed, and coerced to perform their work.
- People are inherently self-centered and do not care about organizational needs.
- People will naturally resist change.

Theory Y
- The average employee does not inherently dislike work.
- People will exercise self-control and are self-directed when motivated to achieve organizational goals.
- People are capable of learning and will not only accept but seek responsibility.
- People's capacity for imagination, ingenuity, and creativity are only partially utilized.

Theory X portrays a dismal view of employees and their motivation to work and supports the traditional model of direction and control. In contrast, Theory Y is more optimistic and leads one to believe that motivated employees will perform productively. Also, Theory Y assumes some responsibility on the part of managers to create a climate that is conducive to learning and achieving organizational goals.

While it may appear that Theory X managers are bad and Theory Y managers are good, McGregor did not support one style over the other. As noted by Fulmer (1983), administrators may need the flexibility of employing one or both theories, depending on the personnel involved and the situation. For example, a supervisor dealing with an officer resisting attempts to remedy unacceptable behavior may need to rely on a Theory X approach until the officer is corrected. On the other hand, a self-motivated and skilled officer given the task of developing a training lesson plan for briefing may require limited supervision and therefore, guided through the task by employing Theory Y.

Argyris's Maturity-Immaturity Theory

Chris Argyris's (1957) **maturity-immaturity continuum** also furnishes insight on human needs. According to Argyris, as people progress naturally from immaturity to maturity, they develop needs for more activity, a state of relative independence, many different ways of behavior, deeper interests over a relatively long time perspective, and more awareness of themselves and control of their own destiny. Unlike Maslow's needs, Argyris's needs are not arranged in a hierarchy.

Argyris viewed an effective organization as one requiring employees to be self-responsible, self-directed, and self-motivated. He argued that motivation

Many of the tasks performed by field officers are self-directed.
Courtesy New York Police Department Photo Unit.

can be maximized when each employee pursues goals and experiences psychological growth and independence (Argyris, 1957).

Herzberg's Motivation-Hygiene Theory

In 1968 Frederick Herzberg developed a motivation theory based on a study of 200 engineers who were queried about when they were satisfied and dissatisfied with their jobs. The findings led Herzberg to identify two vital factors that are found in all jobs: (1) factors that influence the degree of job dissatisfaction, called **maintenance** or **hygiene factors,** which relate mostly to the work environment, and (2) factors that influence the degree of job satisfaction, called **motivators,** which relate to the work itself (see Figure 3–4).

If hygiene factors are undesirable in a job situation, workers will become dissatisfied. Making these factors more desirable by increasing salary, for example, generally will not motivate people to do a better job, but it will keep them from becoming dissatisfied. In contrast, if motivating factors are high in a particular job situation, workers generally are motivated to do a better job. People tend to be more motivated and productive as more motivators are built into their job situation (Certo, 1989).

The process of incorporating motivators into a job situation is called job enrichment. The most productive employees are involved in work situations with desirable hygiene factors and motivating factors. This also relates to Maslow's hierarchy of needs; for example, hygiene factors (e.g., a pay raise) can help to satisfy physical, security, and social needs, while motivating factors (e.g., an award for outstanding performance) can satisfy employees' esteem and self-actualization needs.

According to Herzberg, hygiene factors may attract people to join an organization, but they do not provide the intrinsic satisfaction in the work itself that motivates people to perform. Intrinsic motivation can only come from what the individual does through job responsibilities and subsequent satisfaction gained from job accomplishment. It appears that people are influenced more by intrinsic motivators than by hygiene factors. Put simply, job satisfaction appears to be more important to most people than pay and benefits. Case Study 3–1 illustrates the motivation problems facing a newly promoted detective. A supervisor who conducts frequent team meetings to keep officers informed about

FIGURE 3-4. Herzberg's Hygiene Factors and Motivators

Dissatisfaction: Hygiene or Maintenance Factors	Satisfaction: Motivating Factors
1. Company policy and administration	1. Opportunity for achievement
2. Supervision	2. Opportunity for recognition
3. Relationship with supervisor	3. Work itself
4. Relationship with peers	4. Responsibility
5. Working conditions	5. Advancement
6. Salary	6. Personal growth
7. Relationship with subordinates	

departmental matters and to dispel rumors, who delegates additional duties to those officers ready to accept new challenges and compliments their work, and solicits officers' participation in decision making whenever possible, is appealing to their intrinsic motivators.

47

CHAPTER 3
Leadership and
Motivation Theories

PROCESS THEORIES

Expectancy Theory

In reality, the motivation process is much more complex than that depicted by the needs-goal model shown in Figure 3–2. The Victor Vroom (1964) expectancy theory was developed in the 1960s and addresses some of the complexities. **Expectancy theory** also holds that people are motivated primarily by a felt need that affects behavior; however, the Vroom model adds the issue of motivation *strength*—an individual's degree of desire to perform a behavior.

Vroom's expectancy model is shown in equation form in Figure 3–5. According to this model, motivation strength is determined by the perceived value of the result of performing a behavior and the perceived probability that the behavior performed will cause the result to occur. As both of these factors increase, the motivation strength, or desire to perform the behavior, will increase. Generally, individuals tend to perform the behaviors that maximize rewards over the long term.

Case Study 3–1
The "Rising Star" Who Falls Too Far

Detective Thurmond Thomas is a "rising star" in the Bently County Sheriff's Department. At age 25, he is the youngest officer ever to be promoted there to the rank of detective. Recently married, Thomas is excited about his new assignment and is looking forward to the day shift hours and weekends off.

Thomas begins his new assignment with great desire, often volunteering for the less popular cases and working a lot of overtime. He is doing everything possible to make a good impression on his more experienced peers.

Sergeant Wise takes a particular liking to Thomas and is making every effort to recognize his good work on the detective staff. He even suggests that Thomas consider being promoted at the earliest possible time and offers to coach him for the promotional exam. Everything appears to be going well for young Thomas.

After a couple of months, however, Sgt. Wise begins to notice that Thomas is using a lot of sick time and has lost much of his enthusiasm for the job. Wise

meets with Thomas to discuss the matter. Thomas explains that he is now very uncomfortable in the detective division and does not fit in with the rest of the detectives. He adds that the others simply ignore him, never inviting him to lunch or coffee.

Sgt. Wise decides that Thomas is simply lacking self-confidence because of his young age. He then discusses Thomas's concerns and his potential with the other detectives, with the hope of improving relations. Instead, matters only worsen, and now the lieutenant is directing Wise to investigate Thomas's sick time to determine whether he is abusing his leave time.

1. What is your assessment of this situation?
2. Does Sgt. Wise correctly understand the nature of the problem?
3. How would you describe Thomas's problem, using the motivation theories discussed in this chapter?
4. What could Sgt. Wise have done differently?

$$\text{Motivation strength} = \text{Perceived value of result of performing behavior} \times \text{Perceived probability that result will materialize}$$

FIGURE 3-5. Vroom's Expectancy Model of Motivation in Equation Form

Expectancy theory suggests that officers who experience success will feel more competent and therefore be more willing to take risks in improving performance levels. When officers know that certain behaviors will produce anticipated departmental rewards, they may be motivated based on expectancy theory. For example, an officer may be motivated to participate in a community policing project knowing that it could result in a higher performance rating, departmental letter of commendation, and improve promotional prospects.

For example, Sergeant Jones, who is very happy with her present rank, also understands that a promotion to lieutenant carries a $5,000 a year salary increase. Assuming that Jones needs the extra money, her motivation to seek the promotion will be determined by two major factors: her perceived value of $5,000, and the perceived probability that she can successfully compete for the promotion. As the perceived value of the $5,000 and the probability of promotion increase, so will Jones's motivation to seek promotion, and vice versa.

Equity Theory

From a motivation perspective, **equity** refers to the perceived fairness of rewards and of the reward system itself. J. Stacy Adams (1965) formulated one of the best-known equity theories. He contended that when people believe there is inequity in the way they are being treated, they will attempt to eliminate the discomfort in order to restore a sense of equity to the situation. Inequities exist because people believe the rewards or incentives they receive for their work are unequal to the rewards other workers appear to be receiving in proportion to their work. Everyone wants to be treated equitably (not equally), and will engage in some type of social comparison to determine whether equity exists.

For example, police officers often compare their work and treatment to that of other officers in the organization. Therefore, patrol officers might compare what they do with officers assigned to other units in the department whom they perceive as doing little or no "real" police work. Comparisons of this type can affect officer morale negatively, especially among veteran officers who see less experienced officers assigned to specialty units (e.g., traffic, training, and detectives) receiving additional pay, preferred work hours, and more recognition and prestige.

It does not matter what supervisors feel is fair and equitable because fairness and equity lie in the minds of those affected; in other words, "perception is reality." Even if sergeants and officers were rewarded in exactly the same way, inequities, caused by factors such as pay differentials, access to agency resources, preferential assignment, and promotion, would still be perceived (More and Wegener, 1992).

Organizations embarking on community policing and problem solving (COPPS), to be discussed in Chapter 13, must also be careful that they do not allow for officers engaged in COPPS activities to be held in higher esteem or receive benefits not available to other patrol officers. This can have a significant negative impact on officer morale.

The motivation theories discussed above help us to understand the many factors that influence workers' job satisfaction and willingness to perform their duties. It seems clear that employees want meaningful and challenging work. To deny this may result in frustration and poor performance. This is especially true of employees entering the workplace today. They are a new breed of worker: better educated, less resistant to change, motivated by varied job experiences and upward mobility, and less tolerant of military-style structure and controls. This presents a tremendous challenge for the supervisor to maintain the officers' interest in their work.

These theories may also tell us that the Theory X management style, as well as the conventional bureaucratic structures and administrative practices upon which most police agencies were built, may be outdated for today's officer. Attention must be paid to job enrichment, participation, and human resources. By doing so, it becomes easier for the supervisor to ensure that employees' personal goals coincide with those of the organization.

LEADING VERSUS MANAGING

Leading is related to managing. In this chapter, however, we maintain that effective leadership and supervision go well beyond the basic management functions described thus far. Bennis and Nanus (1985:21) help us to understand the broader role of supervision in their discussion of management and leadership: "To be a manager is to bring about, to accomplish, to have charge of responsibility for, to conduct. Leading, on the other hand, is influencing, guiding in direction, course, action, opinion." They add that managers are people who "do things right" and leaders are people who "do the right things." They summarize the distinction by explaining that managers are more efficiency driven and focus on mastering routine activities, while leaders are driven by vision and judgment and tend to issues of effectiveness.

In this regard, the following was developed by United Technologies Corporation, and provides much food for thought:

> People don't want to be managed. They want to be led. Whoever heard of a world manager? World leader[s], yes. They don't manage. The carrot always wins over the stick. Ask your horse. You can *lead* your horse to water, but you can't *manage* him to drink. If you want to manage somebody, manage yourself. Do that well and you'll be ready to stop managing. And start leading (quoted in Bennis and Nanus, 1985:22).

Another clear distinction between the leader and the manager is organizational consensus on overall goals—a vision. According to Bennis and Nanus, by focusing attention on a vision, the leader operates on the *emotional* and *spiritual resources* of the organization, on its values, commitment, and aspirations. The manager, by contrast, operates on the *physical resources* of the organization, its capital, human skills, raw materials, and technology. As they put it:

Any competent manager can make it possible for people to earn a living [and] see to it that work is done productively and efficiently, on schedule, and with a high level of quality. It remains for the effective leader, however, to help people in the organization know pride and satisfaction in their work (Bennis and Nanus, 1985:92).

They added: "The essential thing in organization leadership is that the leader's style *pulls* rather than *pushes* people on. Leading is a responsibility, and the effectiveness of this responsibility is reflected in the attitudes of the led" (Bennis and Nanus, 1985:80–81).

We concur that a successful police supervisor must be a good manager as well as a good leader. As Whisenand and Ferguson explained (1996:13), "If you're a competent manager, you are getting the most out of your resources. If you're a competent leader, you are pointing their energy in the right direction." It is therefore important that the supervisor manage departmental resources in as efficient a manner as possible while also motivating and inspiring employees to perform to the best of their ability. Therein lies the influential art of leadership that instills the sense of *esprit de corps* or common purpose found in successful cohesive organizations.

LEADERSHIP THEORIES

We begin this section with a view of the three essential skills that leaders should possess and then discuss the various leadership theories: trait, behavioral, situational, or contingency. Whereas trait theories attempt to explain leadership on the basis of what the leader is, behavioral theories try to do the same thing by concentrating on what the leader does (Dessler, 1976). Situational theories maintain that effective leadership is a product of the fit between the traits or skills required in a leader as determined by the situation in which he or she is to exercise leadership (Stogdill, 1974).

Developing Leadership Skills

Robert Katz (1975) identified three essential skills that leaders should possess: technical, human, and conceptual. Figure 3-6 illustrates these three essential skills and how they apply to supervisory ranks. Notice that technical skills are most important at the lower supervisory ranks while conceptual skills preoccupy the higher ranks in an organization. Katz defined a skill as the capacity to translate knowledge into action in such a way that a task is accomplished successfully (Katz, 1975:23). Each of these skills, when performed effectively, results in the achievement of objectives and goals, which is the primary nature of leadership.

Technical Skills. Skills that a leader needs to ensure that specific tasks are performed correctly are called **technical skills.** They are based on proven knowledge, procedures, or techniques. A leader's technical skills may involve knowledge in such myriad areas as high risk tactics, computer applications,

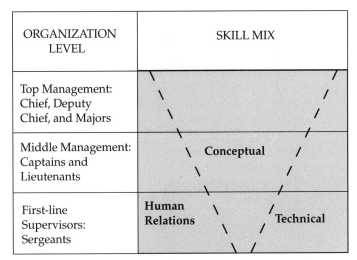

ORGANIZATION LEVEL	SKILL MIX
Top Management: Chief, Deputy Chief, and Majors	
Middle Management: Captains and Lieutenants	Conceptual
First-line Supervisors: Sergeants	Human Relations Technical

FIGURE 3-6. The Leadership Skill Mix in a Police Department
Source: Charles R. Swanson, Leonard Territo, and Robert W. Taylor, *Police Administration: Structures, Processes, and Behavior,* 3d ed. (New York: Macmillan, 1993), p. 169.

budgeting, strategic planning, labor relations, public relations, and personnel administration.

Human Skills. Skills that involve working with people, including thorough familiarity with what motivates employees and how to utilize group processes, are called **human skills.** Katz visualized human skills as including "the executive's ability to work effectively as a group member and to build cooperative effort within the team he leads" (Katz, 1975: 63). Katz added that the human relations skill involves (1) tolerance of ambiguity and (2) empathy. Tolerance of ambiguity means that the leader is able to handle problems where insufficient information precludes making a totally informed decision. Empathy is the ability to put oneself in another's place. An awareness of human skills allows a leader to provide the necessary leadership and direction, ensuring that tasks are accomplished in a timely fashion and with the least expenditure of resources (Higgins, 1982).

Conceptual Skills. Katz said that **conceptual skills** involve "coordinating and integrating all the activities and interests of the organization toward a common objective." Katz considered such skills to include "an ability to translate knowledge into action" and emphasized these skills can be taught to actual and prospective administrators (Katz, 1975: 65); thus, good administrators are not simply born but can be trained in the classroom.

Furthermore, all three of these skills are present in varying degrees for each organizational level. As one moves up the hierarchy, conceptual skills become more important and technical skills less important. The common denominator for all organizational levels is *human* skills. In today's unionized, litigious environment, it is inconceivable that a leader could neglect the human skills.

Trait Theories

Early leadership studies of the 1930s and 1940s focused on the individual and assumed that some people were born leaders, and that good leaders could be studied and compared with nonleaders to determine the special traits that only the leaders possess. From an organizational standpoint, **trait theory** had great appeal. For example, in the police field it was assumed that all that was needed was to identify leaders with these special traits and to promote them to managerial positions within the department.

For more than 50 years researchers have attempted to identify those special traits that separate successful leaders from poor leaders. For example, Ralph Davis (1940) found 56 different traits that he considered important. While admitting it was unlikely that any leader would possess all 56 traits, 10 were required for executive success: intelligence, experience, originality, receptiveness, teaching ability, personality, knowledge of human behavior, courage, tenacity, and a sense of justice and fair play.

The age-old assumption that leaders are born and develop their technical, human, and conceptual skills as described by Katz (1975) was completely discredited because researchers have been unable to agree or present empirical evidence to support its claims (Tannenbaum and Weschler, 1961). Consequently, it is now believed that certain traits and skills increase the *likelihood* that a given person will be an effective leader, but there are no guarantees.

Behavioral Theories

The behavioral approach focused on a leader's behavior and direction of employees in relation to their environment. Studies at the University of Michigan, Ohio State University, and Blake and Mouton's "Managerial Grid" led the early research of behavioral theories of leadership. These studies were important because they studied leadership in real situations. These theories are discussed more below.

Leadership Styles

When researchers could not agree on universally accepted leadership traits, they began to study the style approach to leadership. An early focus of the style theory of leadership resulted in the adoption of a single style, based on a manager's position in regard to initiating structure (discussed below) and consideration. Three pure leadership styles were thought to be the basis for all managers: autocratic, democratic, and laissez-faire.

Autocratic Leadership. Autocratic leaders are leader centered and have a high initiating structure. They are primarily authoritarian in nature and prefer to give orders rather than invite group participation. They have a tendency to be personal in their criticism. This style works best in emergency situations in which there is a need for strict control and rapid decision making. The problem with autocratic leadership is the inability of an organization to function when the leader is absent. It also stifles individual development and initiative because subordinates are rarely allowed to make an independent decision (Holden, 1986).

Democratic Leadership. The democratic, or participative, leadership style tends to focus on working within the group and striving to attain cooperation from group members by eliciting their ideas and support. People tend to view democratic leaders as consideration oriented, who strive to attain mutual respect with subordinates. Democratic leaders operate within an atmosphere of trust and delegate considerable authority. This style is useful in organizations where the course of action is uncertain and problems are relatively unstructured. The decision-making ability of subordinates is often tapped. However, in emergency situations requiring a highly structured response, democratic leadership may prove too time consuming and awkward to be effective. Thus, although the worker may appreciate the strengths of this style, its weaknesses also must be recognized (Holden, 1986).

Laissez-Faire Leadership. The third leadership style, laissez-faire, is a hands-off approach where the leader is actually a nonleader. The organization in effect runs itself, with no input or control from the manager. This style has no positive aspects because the entire organization is soon placed in jeopardy. In truth, this may not be a leadership style at all but an abdication of administrative duties (Holden, 1986).

Style theory assumes that each administrator will adopt one of the styles—autocratic, democratic, or laissez-faire—almost exclusively. Further, the style theory assumes that all administrators will select a style that they believe works and stay with it. This assumption has led many researchers to abandon its tenets for one that is more flexible: situational leadership. This subject is discussed later in the chapter.

University of Michigan and Ohio State Studies

Researchers at the Survey Research Center at the University of Michigan conducted a series of studies of leadership behavior in relation to job satisfaction and productivity in business and industrial workgroups. They determined that leaders must have a sense of the task to be accomplished as well as the environment in which the followers worked. Researchers found the following beliefs as those of a successful leader:

1. The leader who assumes the leadership role is more effective.
2. The closeness of supervision will have a direct bearing on the production of employees. High-producing units had less direct supervision; highly supervised units had lower production. Conclusion: Employees need some area of freedom to make choices. Given this, they produce at a higher rate.
3. Employee orientation is a concept whereby the manager takes an active interest in subordinates. It is the leader's responsibility to facilitate employee accomplishment of goals (Bennett and Hess, 1992:65–66).

The Bureau of Business Research at Ohio State University began its study of leadership in 1945 and later identified leadership behavior in two dimensions: "initiating structure" and "consideration." Initiating structure referred to supervisory behavior that focused on the achievement of organizational goals and included such characteristics as assigning subordinates to particular tasks, holding subordinates accountable for following rules and procedures, and informing subordinates of what is expected of them. Consideration was directed toward a supervisor's openness concerning subordinates' ideas and respect for their feelings as persons. It included such characteristics as listening to subordinates, willingness to make changes, and being friendly and approachable. It was assumed that high consideration and moderate initiating structure yielded higher job satisfaction and productivity than did high initiating structure and low consideration (Sales, 1969).

The Managerial Grid

The **Managerial Grid,** developed by Robert R. Blake and Jane S. Mouton (1962), has received a great deal of attention since its appearance and is based on the previous research conducted at Ohio State and Michigan State universities.

The Managerial Grid (see Figure 3–7) has two dimensions: (1) concern for production and (2) concern for people. Each axis or dimension is numbered from 1, meaning low concern, to 9, indicating a high concern. The horizontal axis represents the concern for production and performance goals, and the vertical axis represents the concern for human relations or empathy. The way in which a person combines these two dimensions establishes a leadership style in terms of one of the five principal styles identified on the grid. A questionnaire establishes a numerical score that determines the quadrant into which a person would be placed: 1,9, 9,1, 9,9, 1,1, and 5,5. The grid is read to the right and upward.

The points of orientation are related to styles of management. The lower left-hand corner of the grid shows the 1,1 style (representing a minimal concern for task or service and a minimal concern for people). The lower right-hand corner of the grid identifies the 9,1 style. This type of leader would have a primary concern for the task or output and a minimal concern for people. Here, people are seen as tools of production. The upper left-hand corner represents the 1,9 style, often referred to as "country club management," with a minimum of effort given to output or task. The upper right-hand corner, 9,9, indicates high concern for both people and production—a team management approach of mutual respect and trust. In the center—a 5,5, "middle-of-the-road" style—the leader has a philosophy of "give a little, be fair but firm," providing a balance between output and people concerns (Favreau and Gillespie, 1978).

These five leadership styles can be summarized as follows (Bennett and Hess, 1992:66):

- Authority-compliance management (9,1).
- Country club management (1,9).
- Middle-of-the-road management (5,5).
- Impoverished management (1,1).
- Team management (9,9).

Transformational Leadership

A more recent development in leadership theory is called **transformational leadership,** which is an employee-centered approach to leadership that seeks to elevate employees' levels of performance by teaching and articulating

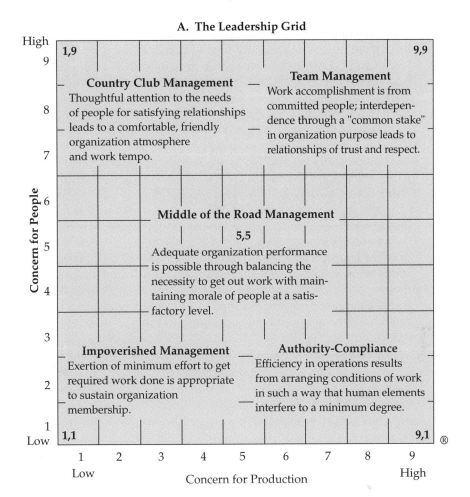

A. The Leadership Grid

High

1,9

Country Club Management
Thoughtful attention to the needs of people for satisfying relationships leads to a comfortable, friendly organization atmosphere and work tempo.

9,9

Team Management
Work accomplishment is from committed people; interdependence through a "common stake" in organization purpose leads to relationships of trust and respect.

Concern for People

Middle of the Road Management

5,5

Adequate organization performance is possible through balancing the necessity to get out work with maintaining morale of people at a satisfactory level.

Impoverished Management
Exertion of minimum effort to get required work done is appropriate to sustain organization membership.

Authority-Compliance
Efficiency in operations results from arranging conditions of work in such a way that human elements interfere to a minimum degree.

1,1
Low

9,1 ®

Low 1 2 3 4 5 6 7 8 9 **High**

Concern for Production

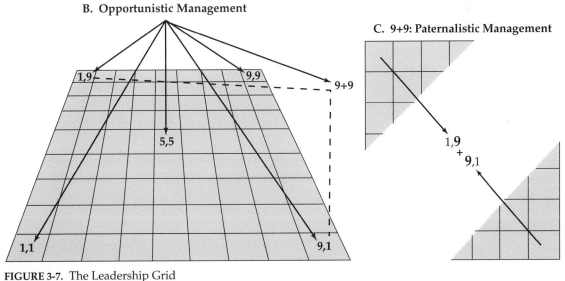

B. Opportunistic Management

C. 9+9: Paternalistic Management

FIGURE 3-7. The Leadership Grid
Source: The Leadership Grid® figure, Paternalism Figure and Opportunism from *Leadership Dilemmas—Grid Solutions,* by Robert R. Blake and Anne Adams McCanse (Formerly the Managerial Grid by Robert R. Blake and Jane S. Mouton). Houston: Gulf Publishing Company, (Grid Figure: p. 29, Paternalism Figure: p. 30, Opportunism Figure: p. 31). Copyright 1991 by Scientific Methods, Inc. Reproduced by permission of the owners.

organizational values. It has also been stated that transformational leadership occurs when leaders and followers interact in such a way that they are elevated and committed to some great cause external to the relationship (Swanson et al., 1993). An example is the transformational role played by Martin Luther King, Jr., in leading millions of Americans of all races to support the civil rights movement of the 1960s.

Transformational leadership is dynamic because leaders enter into a purposeful and mutually supportive relationship with followers who are activated, motivated, and sustained by it. In the police field, the challenge for the police chief executive is to help police officers redefine their role and accept responsibility for following in a constantly changing, transformational environment. The key ingredients in developing an effective leadership/followership strategy are genuine participation, communication, shared decision making, equity, self-control, and interdependence.

The transformational approach emphasizes the importance of people, commitment, leadership, and empowerment. Here leadership is not the exercise of power, but the empowerment of others to help set and achieve mutually acceptable goals or objectives. Good police supervisors and administrators cultivate effective followership by creating and nurturing collective ownership of the enterprise based on a common culture, shared values, mutual respect, trust, problem solving, and collaborative risk taking (Rippy, 1990).

Situational Leadership

Situational leadership recognizes that the workplace is a complex setting subject to rapid changes. Therefore, it is unlikely that one best way of managing these varying situations would be adequate. Simply, the best way to lead depends on the situation.

Paul Hersey and Kenneth A. Blanchard (1977) presented a model of situational leadership that has been used in training by many major corporations and the military services. Their model emphasizes the leader's behavior in relationship to followers' behavior (see Figure 3–8). The **situational leadership** approach requires the leader to evaluate follower responsibility in two ways: willingness (motivation) and ability (competence).

Situational leadership takes into account worker maturity; maturity is defined as the capacity to set high but attainable goals, the willingness to take responsibility, and the education and/or experience of the individual or the group. Figure 3–8 depicts the situation leadership model; the various levels of follower maturity are defined as:

M1: The followers are neither willing nor able to take responsibility for task accomplishment.

M2: The followers are willing but unable to take responsibility for task accomplishment.

M3: The followers are not willing but are able to take responsibility for task accomplishment..

M4: The followers are willing and able to take responsibility for task accomplishment (Hersey and Blanchard, 1977).

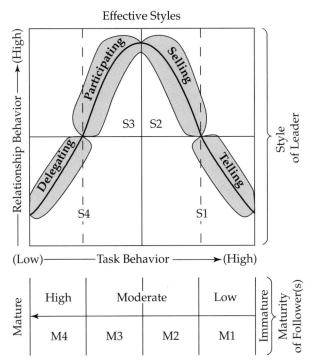

FIGURE 3-8. The Situational Leadership Model
Source: Paul Hersey and Kenneth H. Blanchard, *Management of Organizational Behavior:
Utilizing Human Resources,* 3d ed., © 1977, p. 170. Reprinted by permission of Prentice
Hall, Inc., Englewood Cliffs, N.J.

Task behavior, shown in Figure 3–8, is essentially the extent to which a
leader engages in one-way communication with subordinates; relationship behavior is the extent to which the leader engages in two-way communication by
providing positive reinforcement, emotional support, and so on.

Four basic styles of leadership are associated with task accomplishment; the
definition of these four operate similarly to the Managerial Grid. They are characterized as follows:

S1: *Telling.* High task–low relationship style characterized by one-way
communication in which the leader defines the roles of followers and
tells them what, how, when, and where to do various tasks.

S2: *Selling.* High task–high relationship behavior is provided by two-way
communication and socioemotional support to get followers to voluntarily buy into decisions that have been made.

S3: *Participating.* High relationship–low task behavior indicates both leader
and follower have the ability and knowledge to complete the task.

S4: *Delegating.* Low relationship–low task behavior gives followers the opportunity to "run their own show" with little supervision (Swanson et
al., 1993).

The bell-shaped curve in the style-of-leader portion of Figure 3–8 means that as the maturity level of followers develops from immaturity to maturity, the appropriate style of leadership moves correspondingly (Hersey and Blanchard, 1993). For example, a police supervisor who has a subordinate with a maturity in the M3 range would be most effective employing an M3 style of leadership.

Hersey and Blanchard asserted that leaders could reduce their close supervision and direction of individuals and increase delegation as the readiness of followers to complete tasks increased. The difficulty of this style of leadership is its dependence on leaders to diagnose follower ability and then adjust their leadership style to the given situation. This is often easier said than done (see Case Study 3–2).

Contingency Theories

During the late 1950s and early 1960s, several researchers (Burns and Stalker, 1961; Woodward, 1965) attempted to show that no single leadership style was appropriate for all job situations. Then, the publication of Harvey Sherman's *It All Depends* in 1966 made a major statement. Sherman believed that "There can be no ideal design that will fit all times, all situations, all objectives, and all values. These forces are in constant flux" (Sherman, 1966:57). Therefore, situational

---

Case Study 3–2
Where to Begin When a Veteran Comes In

Officer Maria Sanchez has 17 years of experience, mostly in undercover narcotics and vice in detectives. She is a capable officer with numerous departmental commendations and awards for her work. As a result, Sanchez was selected to be a member of an elite multiagency vice and narcotics task force.

On the first day of her new assignment, Sanchez met with her new supervisor, Sgt. Webster. He is from another agency and did not know Sanchez outside the selection interview process and review of her personnel file.

Sgt. Webster was also assigned recently to the unit from patrol division where he gained a reputation as a perfectionist and detail-oriented person. Webster assumed responsibility for breaking in all new team members to ensure they knew exactly what, when, where, and how they should perform their tasks. Webster had developed a four-week orientation for all new members.

After two weeks of basic orientation, including an elementary review of drug law, raid procedures, vice laws, and so on, Sanchez has become extremely frustrated with Sgt. Webster and asks why she is not allowed to participate in drug and vice raids with the rest of her team. She argues that she has worked with the task force on many occasions, is very familiar with operational procedures, and could demonstrate her abilities if Webster would only allow her to work with the rest of the team. Webster denies her request.

The next day, Sanchez submits a memo to the lieutenant in charge of the task force, requesting reassignment back to her previous agency. In the memo, Sanchez states that she believes Sgt. Webster is treating her differently from other people in the unit and does not have any respect for her past experience and work. She does not believe she can work under these conditions where she is "treated like a child."

1. Could this problem have been avoided? How?
2. What situational style of leadership was Sgt. Webster employing?
3. How would you assess the maturity level of Officer Sanchez?
4. Discuss what style of situational leadership would be more appropriate for this situation.

theories of leadership are based on the concept of leader flexibility—that successful leaders must change their leadership style as they confront different situations. But can leaders be so flexible as to employ all major styles? Obviously, not all leaders are capable of, or willing to do so; there are numerous obstacles to leader flexibility.

Fred Fiedler (1965) developed a strategy for overcoming these obstacles. Fiedler's contingency theory was to change the organizational situation to fit the leader's style, and not vice versa. According to Fiedler, leader-member relations (the degree to which the leader feels accepted by the followers), task structure (the degree to which the work to be done is outlined clearly), and position power of the leader (discussed below) should be used for moving leaders into situations appropriate to their leadership styles.

The basic components of the **contingency theory** are that (1) people have a central need to achieve a sense of competence; (2) the ways that people fulfill this need will vary from person to person; (3) competent motivation is most likely to be fulfilled when there is a fit between task and organization; and (4) a sense of competence continues to motivate people even after competence is achieved (Plunkett, 1983).Contingency theory argues that Theory X organizations are more conducive to persons performing structured and organized tasks. Theory Y is best suited for those persons performing unstructured and uncertain tasks. Understanding this distinction requires that supervisors tailor jobs to fit people or to give people the skills, knowledge, and attitudes they will need to become competent (Plunkett, 1983).

Fiedler's work helped destroy the myth that there is one best leadership style and that leaders are born, not made. His work also supports the theory that almost every manager in an organization can be a successful leader if placed in a situation appropriate for the person's leadership style (Certo, 1989).

LEADERSHIP THEORIES IN APPLICATION

Station House Sergeants and Street Sergeants

To learn the differences in leadership style as a function of the workplace, we consider John Van Maanen's (1984) study of a 1,000-officer police department in which two contrasting types of police sergeants were identified: "station house" and "street." Station house sergeants had been out of the "bag" (uniform) prior to their promotion to sergeant and preferred to work indoors in an office environment once they won their stripes. This preference is clearly indicated by the nickname of "Edwards, the Olympic torch who never goes out" given to one sergeant. Station house sergeants immersed themselves in the management culture of the police department, keeping busy with paperwork, planning, record keeping, press relations, and fine points of law. Their strong orientation to conformity also gave rise to nicknames such as "by the book Brubaker."

In contrast, Van Maanen found that street sergeants were serving in the field when promoted; consequently, they had a distaste for office procedures and a strong action orientation which nicknames such as "Shooter McGee" and "Walker the Stalker" suggested. Moreover, the concern of street sergeants was not with conformity, but with "not letting the assholes take over the city."

Station house and street sergeants were thought of differently by those whom they supervised: station house sergeants "stood behind their officers," whereas street sergeants "stood beside their officers." Station house sergeants might not be readily available to officers working in the field but could always be located when a signature was needed and were able to secure more favors for their subordinates. Street sergeants occasionally interfered with the autonomy of their subordinates by responding to a call for service previously assigned to a subordinate and "interfering" in other ways.

Van Maanen has allowed us to speculate that station house sergeants are learning routines, procedures, and skills that will improve future promotional opportunities. Furthermore, they are making contacts with senior police commanders who can give them important assignments and possibly influence future promotions. In contrast, street sergeants may gain some favorable publicity and awards for their exploits, but they are also more likely to have citizens complain about them, be investigated by internal affairs, or be sued. Consequently, street sergeants are regarded by their superiors as "good cops" but difficult people to supervise. In short, the action-oriented street sergeant may not go beyond a middle-manager's position in a line unit such as patrol or investigation (Swanson et al., 1993).

Power and Leadership

Another aspect of leadership that is important to understand concerns *power*. To successfully lead others, supervisors must understand what power is, as well as the steps they can take for increasing their power over subordinates as it becomes necessary.

Perhaps the two most often confused terms in leadership are *power* and *authority*. **Authority** is the right to command or give orders; the extent to which an individual is able to influence others so they respond to orders is called **power.** The greater this ability, the more power an individual is said to have.

The total power a leader possesses consists of two kinds of power: position power and personal power. **Position power** is power derived from the position a person holds in the organization. In general, moves from lower-level supervisor to upper-level administrator accrue more position power. **Personal power** is power derived from a leader's human relationships with others (Certo, 1989).

Leaders can increase their total power by increasing their position power or their personal power. Position power can generally be increased by a move to a higher organizational position, but leaders usually have little personal control over moving upward in an organization. They do, however, have substantial control over the amount of personal power they hold over other organization members (Certo, 1989). To increase personal power, a leader can attempt to develop the following:

1. *A sense of obligation in other organization members that is directed toward the leader.* If a leader is successful in developing this sense of obligation, other workers think they should rightly allow the leader to influence them, within certain limits. Doing personal favors for others is a basic strategy.

2. *A belief in other organization members that the leader possesses a high level of expertise within the organization.* To increase the perceived level of expertise, the leader must quietly make significant achievement visible to others and rely heavily on a successful track record and respected professional reputation.
3. *A sense of identification that other organization members have with the leader.* The leader can strive to develop this identification by behaving in ways that other organization members respect and by espousing goals, values, and ideals commonly held by them.
4. *The perception in other organization members that they are dependent on the leader.* Here, the main strategy the leader should adopt is a clear demonstration of the amount of authority that he or she possesses over organizational resources. This is aptly reflected in the leadership version of the Golden Rule: "He who has the gold makes the rules" (Kotter, 1977).

WHEN LEADERS ADOPT A CUSTOMER FOCUS

The most successful organizations today employ a variety of systematic improvement methods to reengineer their organizations around a concept that has many names, but which is often termed **total quality management,** or **TQM.** TQM is now an increasingly dominant practice and a concept that can assist an organization in several ways. As demands mount for less bureaucratic red tape and better services, police supervisors and other leaders must mentally shift to a *customer focus,* which means realizing that the customer or client is the most important ingredient in the feedback loop of all organizational processes.

Entrepreneurial governments that have adopted the TQM concept are driven by their goals instead of their rules and regulations. They espouse participatory management and less bureaucracy, pushing organizational power and decision making downward, delegating authority, and encouraging problem solving at the lowest appropriate levels. In TQM, supervisors listen to the voices of their subordinates, including dissenters, and are always open to ideas for improvement from all sources.

In *The Seven Habits of Highly Effective People,* Steven Covey (1989) provided a list of principles and advice on leadership, management, and organizational relationships that are important to a leader's effectiveness. As Covey explained:

> When one of our governing values is total quality, we will care not only about the quality of our products and services, but also about the quality of our lives and relationships. Total quality is a total philosophy. And it is sequential; if you don't have it personally, you won't get it organizationally.

The total quality, entrepreneurial spirit of government can be adapted to public safety. Following are some examples of how many of these principles can be implemented when police leaders begin to "reinvent" their organizations:

- *Tulsa, Oklahoma.* The police studied arrest trends and school dropout statistics. They concluded that teenagers from one section of town—containing a major public housing development—were creating most of the city's drug problems. They organized residents and together they prosecuted and evicted drug dealers; they created an antidrug education program and established job placement and mentoring programs; they set up a youth camp for teenagers; and they worked with the schools to develop an antitruancy program (Osborne and Gaebler, 1992:50).

- *Sunnyvale, California.* The city developed performance measures for all municipal departments. In each program area, the city articulated a set of goals, objectives, and performance indicators. For example, one objective was to keep the city "within the lowest 25 percent of Part I crimes [the group of offenses, called "major offenses," for which the F.B.I. publishes annually in a Uniformed Crime Report (UCR).] for cities of comparable size, at a cost of $74.37 per capita" (Osborne and Gaebler, 1992:143–44.)

- *Paulding County, Georgia.* The county built a 244-bed jail when it needed only 60 extra beds, so it could charge other jurisdictions $35 a night to handle their overflow. In the first year of business, the jail brought in $1.4 million, $200,000 more than its operating costs (Osborne and Gaebler, 1992:197).

- *California.* Some enterprising police departments are earning money renting out motel rooms as weekend jails. They reserve blocks of rooms at cheap motels, pay someone to sit outside to ensure inmates stay in their rooms, and rent the rooms to convicted drunk drivers at $75 a night (Osborne and Gaebler, 1992:197).

These examples clearly demonstrate what can happen when police leaders begin to think like entrepreneurs rather than strict bureaucrats. Obviously, this is unlike conventional police work; a different mind-set is required to think and act in this fashion.

Another means of addressing customer needs is through community surveys. Today's police agencies must attempt to "feel the pulse" of their communities. Public opinion surveys can provide vital information and feedback for assessing public perceptions of officer performance, assess the effectiveness of police communication with the public, and assist police leaders making public policy decisions (White and Menke, 1982). These surveys can ask citizens to rate their police in areas such as concern, helpfulness, fairness, knowledge, quality of service, professional conduct, how well they solved the problem, and whether they put the person at ease (Osborne and Gaebler, 1992:173).

TEAM BUILDING

Why Teamwork?

Millions of Americans were riveted to their television sets hoping for the unthinkable—and it happened. In 1980 at Lake Placid, New York, the United States Olympic Hockey Team beat the heavily favored Russians for the Gold Medal. A decisive goal by team Captain Mike Eruzioni stunned the Russian team and proved to the world the awesome potential of teamwork.

Why do we think in terms of teams? Teamwork is not only vital to an organization for accomplishing its goals, but also it is an important responsibility of the supervisor. There is a synergy about leadership, motivation, and teamwork that often results in the accomplishment of great things. Four important factors have been identified that relate to police effectiveness: (1) synergy, (2) interdependence, (3) a support base for community-oriented policing, and (4) total-quality police services.

Synergy. "What energy is to the individual, synergy is to the groups." Synergy is premised on the assumption that the combined efforts of the group are greater than the individual. When thinking about synergy, we take a systems approach to managing and leading organizations, as discussed above.

Interdependence. The combined efforts of highly interdependent individuals with various specialized abilities make up effective teams. For example, a SWAT entry team may be comprised of four members, each with specific specialized responsibilities, including a team leader (supervisor), entry officer, and rear guard. Each team member is dependent on the other for safe team movement and completing the task.

Support for Community-Oriented Policing. A team concept is a natural fit for community policing (discussed in depth in Chapter 13). Decentralized teams of officers working in neighborhoods for extended periods of time will learn more about the problems and be capable of building trust and collaborative efforts to reduce crime and disorder than if they were deployed under conventional practices.

Total Quality Services. A total quality service is a product of teamwork. Total quality service supports innovation and self-initiation among employees. It means that the entire organization is working toward a common vision of continuous improvement (adapted from Whisenand and Ferguson, 1996:143).

Building a Successful Team

Team building requires leadership at the supervisory level. Effective team leaders display the following traits (Hellriegel et al., 1983):

1. Ability to focus continuously on a goal.
2. Participate in the group and at the same time observe the activities of the group as detached leaders.
3. Acknowledge the need for assuming primary responsibility for controlling the relationships between the group and other units or individuals.
4. Facilitate group members in the assumption of leadership roles when the situation dictates because of changing group needs.

Team building means that supervisors seek to create a work environment that brings officers together to pursue organizational goals. It also means that the supervisor works to improve the talents of each individual but keeping the team's overall effectiveness in mind. For example, a patrol sergeant with five officers assigned to a district would want all officers to be capable of handling routine calls for service. The supervisor may also want to have officers capable of handling more difficult tasks, including crime scene investigation, injury accident

Supervisors are often responsible for coordinating the responses of patrol and specialized units, such as detectives and crime scene technicians at crime scenes. *Courtesy Washoe County, Nevada, Sheriff's Office Photo Unit.*

investigation, and tactical situations. In this case the supervisor would make sure that officers with an interest in these areas received the proper training so that the team may function more effectively when confronted by problems in the area assigned.

Teamwork is a strong motivational factor in policing. Team development transforms a group of independent people into an interdependent entity. It feels good for the members to be a part of a winning team or a successful organization, even if an employee is not directly involved in the work. Our sense of belonging is a strong motivational factor, as Maslow (1954) pointed out. Team building assumes that (1) individuals are technically competent, (2) the staff knows what they should do, (3) the human limitations are merely perceived and not real, (4) police work is exciting (Whisenand and Ferguson, 1996).

Policing is a field that is naturally composed of teams. Most police organizations divide patrol into teams of officers who are supervised by a sergeant and assigned to different areas in a community. For example, the detective division is divided into teams of officers working fraud, robbery/homicide, juvenile, burglary, and auto theft. Usually there also are many specialized functions in police agencies that involve teams of officers assigned to gang, traffic, crime prevention, training, and so on. Each of these teams would have a supervisor assigned to them, and that supervisor assumes the ominous task of channeling each individuals talents and energies into organizational efforts.

The above discussions of theories and methods of leadership—some developed several decades ago—were intended to help supervisors and other leaders to avoid failure. In today's stop-and-go, ever dangerous, litigation-vulnerable world of policing, the price paid for incompetent supervision by workers and supervisors alike is too high; there is little room for on-the-job training.

During the 1984 Olympics in Los Angeles, a police officer planted a bomb in the wheel of a bus; he was apprehended, fired, and prosecuted. When asked why he committed this act, he said, "My sergeant was driving me nuts, and I had hoped the situation would get me transferred" (quoted in Whisenand and Ferguson, 1996:398–99). Obviously this officer overreacted to the situation, but it underscores the lengths to which an employee can attempt to sever him- or herself from a poor supervisor.

Some supervisors are too preachy, rigid, cold and uncaring, and vindictive. A number of books and articles discuss the proper ways a supervisor, manager, or administrator should think and behave. However, it is also helpful to examine how a leader should *not* conduct business. Space limitations preclude our covering the many possibilities of supervisory failure that can come to mind; however, we offer a few types of "problem bosses" below:

1. *Ticket Puncher.* One who maneuvers daily to advance in status, power, and rank. Promotion is paramount, and a ticket puncher will do whatever is necessary to get ahead.
2. *Spotlighter.* Requires attention and center stage, demanding recognition for all of the positive results. When things go awry, a spotlighter is quick to disappear. At the same time, however, a spotlighter shares any successes with others.
3. *Megadelegator.* A person who seldom does real work and views him-or herself as a "participative manager." A megadelegator accomplishes nothing, while everyone else is working hard.
4. *Micromanager.* This boss is either insecure, a perfectionist, or needs to control every aspect of work. A micromanager seeks feedback incessantly and requires frequent reporting.
5. *One Best Style.* This type of manager believes there is only one style of managing that guarantees success. In other words, if you mimic this person's style, you're a winner.
6. *Control Taking.* This person craves power. Force is foremost, control is critical, and being correct is imperative.
7. *The Phantom.* This person is uncomfortable with social interaction, preferring to remain invisible. A phantom is uneasy empowering others but is usually an excellent test-taker and thus is able to attain a position of command (adapted from Whisenand and Ferguson, 1996:399–401).

Finally, Steven Brown (1989) provided a list of 13 fatal errors that can erode a leader's effectiveness.

1. Refuse to accept personal accountability.
2. Fail to develop people. Operations should function successfully in your absence.

3. Try instead to control results.
4. Join the wrong crowd.
5. Manage everyone the same.
6. Forget the importance of service.
7. Concentrate on problems, not objectives.
8. Be a buddy, not a boss.
9. Fail to set standards.
10. Fail to train your people.
11. Condone incompetence.
12. Recognize only top performers.
13. Try to manipulate people.

SUMMARY

This chapter has examined several leadership theories that are of primary interest to supervisors, what motivates employees, how managers are distinguished from leaders, theories of leadership, and quality leadership and team building. In addition to covering these theories that have withstood the test of time, we pointed out several theories and approaches that have not succeeded. One can learn much from a failed approach or even from a poor boss who failed to appreciate and understand subordinates and practiced improper, few, or no motivational techniques.

It should be remembered that all of these elements and issues of supervision revolve around one very important feature of the workplace: people. Perhaps the major point emphasized in this chapter is that supervisors must know their people and how to motivate them. To be effective in the labor-intensive field of policing, supervisors should first learn all they can about this most valuable asset, just as much as they must learn about agency policies and procedures, and new technology. Effective leaders are made, not born; thus they must also receive the requisite training and education for performing well. An educated approach is far better than simply marching the new supervisor off the plank, to either sink or swim in an ocean of alligators.

KEY TERMS

leadership   (p. 38)
scientific management
   (p. 38)
POSDCORB (planning,
   organizing, staffing,
   directing, coordinating,
   reporting and
   budgeting)   (p. 39)
humanism   (p. 40)
"Hawthorne effect"   (p. 40)
systems approach   (p. 41)
motivation   (p. 41)
hierarchy of needs   (p. 42)
maturity-immaturity
   continuum   (p. 45)

maintenance factors
   (p. 46)
hygiene factors   (p. 46)
motivators   (p. 46)
expectancy theory   (p. 47)
equity   (p. 48)
technical skills   (p. 50)
human skills   (p. 51)
conceptual skills   (p. 51)
autocratic leadership
   (p. 52)
democratic leadership
   (p. 53)
laissez-faire leadership
   (p. 53)

Managerial Grid   (p. 54)
transformational
   leadership   (p. 54)
situational leadership
   (p. 56)
contingency theory   (p. 59)
power   (p. 60)
authority   (p. 60)
position power   (p. 60)
personal power   (p. 60)
Total Quality Management
   (TQM)   (p. 61)
team building   (p. 63)

ITEMS FOR REVIEW

1. Describe scientific management theory, including its problems and contributions to the field.
2. Explain what Maslow's hierarchy of needs teaches us about people's needs.
3. Compare Theory X and Theory Y, and what each tells us about motivating employees.
4. Summarize Vroom's expectancy theory of motivation.
5. Contrast what is meant by "leader" versus "manager."
6. Describe situational leadership and how it applies to the leader.
7. Review some of the ways in which a leader can increase his or her personal power.
8. Explain the concept of equity as it applies to motivating employees, and its importance for employees.

SOURCES

ADAMS, J. S. (1965). "Inequity in social exchange." In L. Berkowitz (ed.), *Advances in Experimental Social Psychology.* Vol. 2. New York: Academic Press.

ARGYRIS, C. (1957). *Personality and organization.* New York: Harper.

BENNETT, W. W., and HESS, K. (1992). *Management and supervision in law enforcement.* St. Paul, Minn.: West.

BENNIS, W., and NANUS, B. (1985). *Leaders.* New York: Harper and Row.

BERELSON, B., and STEINER, G. A. (1964). *Human behavior: An inventory of scientific findings.* New York: Harcourt, Brace, and World.

BLAKE R. R., and MOUTON, J. S. (1962). "The developing revolution in management practices." *Journal of the American Society of Training Directors* 16:29–52.

BROWN, S. B. (1989). "Fatal errors managers make: And how you can avoid them." The National Law Enforcement Leadership Institute. Police Leadership Report, 1(3):6–7.

BURNS, T., and STALKER, G. M. (1961). *The management of innovation.* London: Tavistock.

CERTO, S. C. (1989). *Principles of modern management: Functions and systems.* 4th ed. Boston: Allyn and Bacon.

COVEY, S. R. (1989). *Seven habits of highly effective people.* New York: Simon and Schuster.

DAVIS, R. C. (1940). *Industrial organization and management.* New York: Harper.

DESSLER, G. (1976). *Organization and management: A contingency approach.* Englewood Cliffs, N.J.: Prentice Hall.

FAVREAU, D. F., and GILLESPIE, J. E. (1978). *Modern police administration.* Englewood Cliffs, N.J.: Prentice Hall.

FIELDLER, F. (1965). "Engineer the job to fit the manager." *Harvard Business Review* 43 (September–October): 115–22.

FIEDLER, F. (1967). *A theory of leadership effectiveness.* New York: McGraw-Hill.

FULMER, R. M. (1983). *The new management.* New York: Macmillan.

GAINES, L. K., SOUTHERLAND, M. D., and ANGELL, J. E. (1991). *Police administration.* New York: McGraw-Hill.

GULICK, L., and URWICK, L. (1937). *Papers on the science of administration.* New York: Institute of Public Administration.

HELLRIEGEL, D., SLOCUM, J. W., JR. , and WOODMAN, R. W. (1983). *Organizational behavior.* 3d ed. St. Paul, Minn.: West.

HERSEY, P., and BLANCHARD K. H. (1977). *Management of organizational behavior.* Englewood Cliffs, N.J.: Prentice Hall.

HERZBERG, F. (1968). "One more time: How do you motivate employees?" *Harvard Business Review* (January–February):53–62.

HIGGINS, J. M. (1982). *Human relations: Concepts and skills.* New York: Random House.

HOLDEN, R. (1986). *Modern police management.* Englewood Cliffs, N.J.: Prentice Hall.

HOMANS, G. C. (1951). "The Western Electric researches." In D. H. Schuyler (ed.), *Human Factors in Management.* New York: Harper.

KATZ, R. L. (1975). "Skills of an effective administrator." *Harvard Business Review* (52):23.

KOTTER, J. (1977). "Power, dependence, and effective management." *Harvard Business Review* (July–August):128–35.

LYNCH, R. G. (1986). *The police manager: Professional leadership skills.* Englewood Cliffs, N.J.: Prentice Hall.

LUTHANS, F. (1985). *Organizational behavior.* New York: McGraw-Hill.

MCFARLAND, D. E. (1986). *Management principles and practices.* 4th ed. New York: Macmillan.

MCGREGOR, D. (1960). *The human side of enterprise.* New York: McGraw-Hill.

MASLOW, A. H. (1954). *Motivation and personality.* New York: Harper and Row.

MORE, H. W., and WEGENER, W. F. (1992). *Behavioral police management.* New York: Macmillan.

OSBORNE, D., and GAEBLER, T. (1992). *Reinventing government: How the entrepreneurial spirit is transforming the public sector.* Reading, Mass.: Addison-Wesley.

PLUNKETT, W. R. (1983). *Supervision: The direction of people at work.* Dubuque, Iowa: William C. Brown.

RIPPY, K. M. (1990). "Effective followership." *Police Chief* (September):45.

SALES, S. M. (1969). "Supervisory style and productivity: Review and theory." In Larry Cummings and William E. Scott (eds.), *Readings in Organizational Behavior and Human Performance,* Homewood, Ill.: Richard D. Irwin.

SHERMAN, H. (1966). *It all depends: A pragmatic approach to organizations.* Tuscaloosa: University of Alabama Press.

STOGDILL, R. M. (1974). *Handbook of leadership: A survey of theory and research.* New York: Free Press.

SWANSON, C. R., TERRITO, L., and TAYLOR, R. W. (1993). *Police administration.* 3d ed. New York: Macmillan.

TANNENBAUM, R., and WESCHLER, I. R. (1961). *Leadership and organization: A behavioral science approach.* New York: McGraw-Hill.

TAYLOR, F. W. (1911). *The Principles of Scientific Management.* New York: Harper.

VAN MAANEN, J. (1984). "Making rank: Becoming an American police sergeant." *Urban Life* 13 (2–3): 155–76.

VROOM, V. H. (1964). *Work and motivation.* New York: Wiley.

WHISENAND, P. M., and FERGUSON, F. (1996). *The managing of police organizations.* Upper Saddle River, N.J.: Prentice Hall.

WHITE, M. F., and MENKE, B. A. (1982). "On assessing the mood of the public toward the police: Some conceptual issues." *Journal of Criminal Justice* 10(1): 120–31.

WOODWARD, J. (1965). *Industrial organization: Theory and practice.* London: Oxford University Press.

4

Communication, Negotiation, and Conflict Management

The difference between the right word and the almost right word is the difference between lightning and lightning bug.

—Mark Twain

Grow antennae, not horns.

—James R. Angell

The right of every person "to be let alone" must be placed in the scales with the right of others to communicate.

—Chief Justice Warren Burger

INTRODUCTION

Communication is one of the most important dynamics of an organization. Therefore, communications skills are perhaps the most important skills a supervisor can possess. A sergeant may be a good planner and be decisive in critical situations, but he or she will be ineffective in most situations without adequate communications skills to impart information effectively to others in the organization. Communication is how tasks come to be accomplished in police organizations, and the supervisors are responsible for ensuring that subordinates complete work assignments and accomplish the agency's objectives, as well as effectively communicating directives, policies, assignments, and information to their officers.

In addition to being skilled communicators, supervisors must also possess negotiation and conflict management skills. Along with the ability to "negotiate" satisfactory outcomes to the day-to-day problems they confront with the public, it is just as important that supervisors are capable of dealing effectively with subordinates and superiors. Thus, solid communications, negotiation, and conflict management skills are prerequisites for the supervisor to effectively deal with people and conflict.

This chapter explores the communication, negotiation, and conflict management processes. The focus is on how supervisors can effectively interact with work groups and individuals to gain higher levels of compliance with organizational requirements. We begin with a look at communication process generally; then we consider barriers to effective communication and methods for improving communication in police agencies. Then we examine the art of negotiating, including various approaches and tactics. We conclude the chapter with a discussion of the nature and levels of conflict within police organizations, including its nature, sources, and management. The role of police supervisors vis-à-vis these processes is covered throughout the chapter.

THE ACT OF COMMUNICATING

We now communicate by means of facsimile machines, e-mail, cellular telephones, and so on. We converse orally in written letters and memos, through our body language, over television and radio programs, through newspapers and meetings. Even private thoughts—which take place four times faster than the spoken word—are communication. Every waking hour, our minds are full of ideas and thoughts. Psychologists say that nearly 100,000 thoughts pass through our minds every day, conveyed by a multitude of media (Bennett and Hess, 1992).

Communication is an extremely complex process. Indeed, communications—formal or informal, written or verbal—serve to link people and activities. Yet people seldom give much thought to how they communicate and to the content of their communications. When there are errors in communication or when information is not communicated effectively, there is a greater probability that subordinates will not fully grasp the meaning of the communication, and mistakes can result. From the supervisor's viewpoint, proper communication essentially serves to make a group of workers into a team and provides a means to coordinate people and work. Next, we define this complicated process.

The Communication Process

Communication has been defined as "the process by which the sender—a person, group, or organization—transmits some type of information (the message) to another person, group, or organization (the receiver)" (Greenberg and Baron, 1995). Thus, the act of communicating is a complicated transaction between two or more parties. In reality, communicating is a complicated process fraught with pitfalls which can lead to mistakes or ineffective communications. Figure 4–1 provides a detailed schematic for communicating and shows how complicated communications really are.

The process begins when the communicator or sender wishes to communicate an idea or information to another person(s) or organization. The first step in the communication process is to *encode* the idea or information—the sender translates information and ideas into a form that can be reduced to writing, lan-

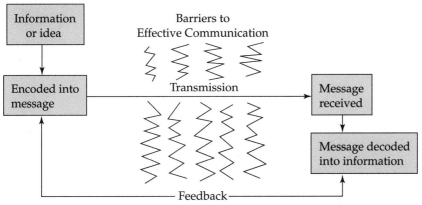

FIGURE 4–1. The Communications Process

guage, or nonverbal communications. The encoding process can be difficult, especially if the sender is attempting to communicate a set of complex ideas. Although people may have little difficulty in conceptualizing complex ideas, they sometimes have difficulty in putting them into the proper words or language so that others can understand the full meaning of their idea. In other instances the communicator may have difficulty in communicating; that is, some people are restricted by a limited vocabulary or their understanding of language. Successful supervisors are those who can successfully encode their ideas into some form of communications.

Once a message has been encoded, the sender must select a communications *channel*, or the medium through which a message is transmitted to the recipients. The primary communications channels are formal and informal. Within these two channels, communications can be written, verbal, and nonverbal. **Formal communications** are the official transmission of information in the organization. Generally, they follow the police department's chain of command or organizational chart. Managers and other members of police departments use formal communications to transact official business. Formal communications generally are written in the form of letters, memoranda, or orders. **Informal communications** are generally oral.

Once information is transmitted to a recipient, the recipient must *decode* the message, or conceptually translate the information into meaningful knowledge or information. When people receive new information, they typically give it meaning by comparing it with past experiences and information, which can be either a help or a hindrance. The receiver may have difficulty internalizing its full implication or, in the worst case, may reject it entirely.

Once information is decoded, it should agree with the sender's information prior to encoding. If inconsistencies occur, then the desired information has not been fully internalized. One way of ensuring full internalization is **feedback:** the process whereby the sender initiates additional two-way communications to test the receiver's comprehension of the information communicated. Feedback serves to ensure that everyone received the proper or correct information. The level of feedback should increase (1) as the content of messages becomes more complex, (2) when it is critical that receivers have the information, (3) when the information is drastically different from past information or operating procedures, and (4) when there are disruptions in the communications process itself. Case Study 4–1 illustrates the consequences of a communications breakdown. The supervisor has the responsibility for ensuring that information is properly exchanged.

Formal and Informal Communication

Formal and informal communications, discussed briefly above, can be written or oral. Generally, however, formal communications are reduced to writing, while informal communications are oral. Written communications allow all participants to have a permanent record of the communication. Sometimes this is important at a future time when the persons involved in the communications must refresh their recollection of the transaction. Also, as an official document, written communications have weight or authority requiring a measure of action or response. The problem with written communication is that it is sometimes difficult for people to reduce complex issues into writing.

Informal communications are generally accomplished by means of conversations and informal notes. For example, a supervisor on a shift may leave a note for a supervisor on the following shift to have the officers check a residence

---

Case Study 4–1
Giving the "Bum's Rush" to City Problems

Urban City's downtown district recently witnessed a serious increase in panhandling, inebriated individuals, and various types of crime. The mayor and council voice concern about these problems and their impact on the coming summer tourist season. A day-long planning session is held involving city officials, the police chief, and business owners, and a comprehensive plan of action is developed. The chief of police delivered the plan to his command staff for implementation. The downtown watch commander, Lieutenant Jennings, met with the supervisors and explained that "the administration" is upset with the "bums" and wants the downtown cleaned up in two weeks. Sgt. Washington, the swing shift supervisor downtown, met with his team to convey the lieutenant's orders. The officers became upset and began to argue about how busy they were already. Washington quickly cut them off, stating the issue was not negotiable and that he expected them to "handle it as ordered." Two weeks later, Washington is pleased to see that the area is largely free of transients; indeed, he and his team are praised by the lieutenant for their efforts. However, at a recent regional law enforcement executives' meeting, a sheriff from a neighboring county complains to the chief that his deputies have noticed a major influx of transients in that county; furthermore, the transients are telling his deputies that they were dumped outside the city limits by Urban City officers. The chief is horrified and demands an investigation. When questioned, Washington's officers defend their actions, stating that "The sergeant told us to clean up the downtown; we simply followed orders . . . this is what the chief and mayor wanted."

1. Discuss how the communications process broke down in this case.
2. Did the officers simply do what the chief and mayor wanted?
3. Despite the breakdown of communications, what could Sergeant Washington have done to prevent this situation from occurring?

where prowlers or suspicious persons were reportedly seen. Although the note in this example is a form of informal communications, it is being used in an official capacity. By leaving a note, the supervisor is able to communicate rapidly and effectively. On the other hand, instead of leaving a note the supervisor could have waited to tell the next shift supervisor directly about the problem. This face-to-face conversation would have allowed the sergeant to fully explain what had happened and what actions the sergeant took. In essence, informal communications can be used for formal or informal purposes. Informal communications allow officers to communicate rapidly without going through the chain of command.

Informal communications typically do not follow the chain of command, and they consist of "interpersonal networking" (Schermerhorn et al., 1994) and quasi-formal exchanges of information between co-workers. Such exchanges typically use verbal and nonverbal communications. Often members of an organization find that formal organizations are inadequate for accomplishing communications activities. When this occurs, people tend to use informal networks where they contact people to obtain official information, or they work unofficially with others to solve problems.

Informal communications essentially allow information to flow more freely and rapidly. Peters and Waterman (1983), in their review of excellent organizations, found that increased levels of informal communications were associated with organizational success. Indeed, supervisors who can rapidly gain larger amounts of information or discuss problems with subordinates and managers throughout the police department would have an important advantage.

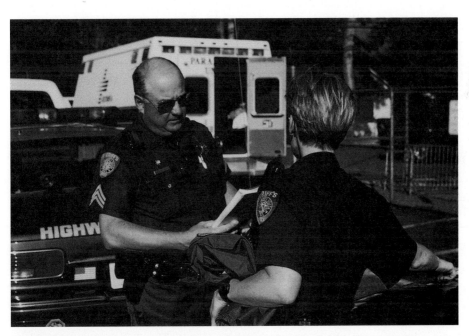

Establishing two-way communication with officers is essential for the supervisor.
Courtesy Washoe County, Nevada, Sheriff's Office Photo Unit.

Another type of informal communication are rumors, or the **grapevine,** so termed because it zigzags back and forth like a grapevine across organizations. There is probably *no* type of organization in our society that has more grapevine information than that which exists in police agencies. Departments even establish "rumor control" centers during major riots. Adding to the usual barriers to communication is the 24-hour, 7-day nature of policing, so that rumors are easily carried from one shift to the next as officers discuss issues such as pay raises, assignments, new policies or procedures, and other matters that affect them at work or at home.

Although it may carry many falsehoods, cynicism, and employee malice, the grapevine has several potential benefits for the supervisor. The grapevine's most effective characteristics are that it is fast, it operates mostly in the workplace, and it supplements regular, formal communication. It can be a tool for management to get a feel for employee attitudes, to spread useful information, and to help employees vent their frustrations. Without a doubt, the grapevine is a force for supervisors to reckon with on a daily basis. Some officers introduce false information into the grapevine to cause dissension or disruption in the formal organization. Supervisors must make a special effort to monitor the information communicated informally in the work group and take measures to ensure that false information does not result in problems in work group performance.

Barriers to Effective Communication

The act of communicating occurs under a variety of circumstances. For example, supervisors sometimes perform tasks at drunk-driving checkpoints, where officers are out of their vehicles stopping and checking motorists. It is extremely difficult for the sergeant to effectively communicate to all the officers in this type of situation, so the sergeant must take care to ensure that all the officers receive any orders or directions. Distractions can occur in almost any situation. These distractions are commonly referred to as **noise,** which is anything that disrupts the communications process (Van Fleet and Peterson, 1994). Supervisors should be aware of a number of different types of noise when communicating. These are discussed in the following sections.

Perceptual Problems

Perceptual problems arise when the perceptions of either the sender or receiver of the other affect how the message is sent or received. One perceptual problem is status. To a great extent, people judge the significance and accuracy of information by the status and ability of the sender. Information from an assistant chief will be received differently than information given by a lieutenant, even though both officers provide their receivers with accurate information. All information should be evaluated on its face. Another perceptual problem is stereotyping, where judgments are made about communications because of the sender's traits or qualities. For example, a police union leader and a police commander would be likely to interpret the same information differently because of their relative orientations about the department. The information should be given due consideration, regardless of where it emanated from.

A third perceptual problem is the value judgments people make about information. If the information is consistent with old information or values, it generally is given more credibility. On the other hand, if the information is inconsistent, receivers sometimes have difficulty accepting or internalizing it. Supervisors should take extra precautions when attempting to communicate new or radically different information.

A fourth perceptual problem is semantic problems, in which the receiver decodes a message improperly because the sender's symbols or verbiage are interpreted differently by the receiver. Certain words have different meanings to different people. Semantic problems can be overcome through the feedback process or by restating the same information several times. Semantic problems perhaps are the most difficult problems to detect in the communication process.

Physical Barriers

Physical barriers to communication refer to those attributes and activities in the immediate environment that interfere with or detract from the communications process. For example, if police officers are spread over a wide area, a supervisor will find it more difficult to communicate effectively with them; and it is physically distracting when a supervisor attempts to counsel subordinates in an office while attempting to answer the telephone. Every effort should be made to ensure that communications are free of such barriers and, when barriers exist, the sender should delay communicating or take special precautions to ensure that receivers receive the correct information.

Improving Communication in Police Agencies

As has been shown, the act of communicating, although seemingly a straightforward process, can be troublesome because of the many inherent problems that can occur. The most effective way to communicate is to be aware of potential pitfalls and take action to counteract them when they occur. The following section provides information that the supervisor can use to overcome many communication problems. First, face-to-face communication is the most effective way of communicating because it can maximize the feedback between the sender and receiver.

Furthermore, many police departments are investing in computer network systems and in-car computers or terminals which facilitate the communications process. These systems also allow officers to communicate through electronic mail (E-mail), which can substantially enhance formal and informal communications throughout a police department. It allows officers to communicate at any time and encourages feedback through its messaging system.

Another method of enhancing communications is **empathy.** Empathy is the act of putting oneself in another's position. The communicator should be receiver oriented and consider how the message will affect the receiver. If a supervisor understands how information will affect the listener, then he or she can better organize and present the message so that it has a greater chance of being accepted by the listener. At the same time, the sender should participate in **active listening,** where the listener coaxes or assists another to communicate. This is accomplished by asking questions, providing comments, and being especially

Supervisors are often challenged to motivate officers who are assigned to the less prestigious functions of traffic control.
Courtesy New York Police Department Photo Unit.

attentive when information is provided. When supervisors actively listen to subordinates, especially when they have provided them with information such as policies or directives, supervisors actively engage the subordinates in feedback to ensure that they comprehend the information.

Communication by Police Supervisors

In our earlier discussions of the communications process and its inherent problems, we provided a number of examples of how supervisors "fit" into this arena, as well as the kinds of problems they may confront. Clearly, the act of communicating with individuals or groups of individuals is an indispensable part of the supervision process. Indeed, a large percentage of the police supervisor's job consists of involvement in some form of communications. Supervisors usually spend about 15 percent of their time with superiors, 50 percent with subordinates, and 35 percent with other managers and duties. These estimates emphasize the importance of communications in everyday operations (Bennett and Hess, 1992).

Another study found that supervisors spend about 80 percent of their time communicating. The percent of time engaged in various types of communication is 45 percent listening, 30 percent talking, 16 percent reading, and 9 percent writing (Von der Embse, 1987). It appears that supervisors are communicating to others about 39 percent of the time and someone is communicating to them about 61 percent of the time. Clearly, supervisors spend more time receiving information than providing it.

Supervisors communicate with a variety of people at all levels of the department. More and Wegener (1996) reported that about 55 percent of a supervisor's communications is with subordinates. Approximately 26 percent of their communications is with superiors in the department, while only 4 percent is with other supervisors. Finally, only 15 percent of a supervisor's communications are with the public. More and Wegener (1996) also examined the tasks performed by first-line supervisors. They found that 51 percent of the tasks involved some form of communicating. These statistics indicate that supervisors spend most of their time working with and supervising subordinates.

THE ART OF NEGOTIATING

Definition and Function

Negotiation is a form of communicating. The ability to effectively negotiate with others is an important characteristic or trait. Essentially, it consists of effectively communicating with other people. For example, negotiations play a key role when management and employees attempt to agree on a new contract or working conditions. In this instance the two sides communicate until an agreement is reached. When the two sides communicate effectively, they are more likely to arrive at an agreement. Negotiations have been defined as "the collaborative pursuit of joint gains and a collaborative effort to create value where none previously existed existed" (Donnelly, Gibson, and Ivancevich, 1995:433).

When there is a group of people, there very likely will be conflict, such as officers jockeying for power and recognition. For example, officers often disagree with departmental policies regarding pursuit driving, arrest procedures, or how to deal with citizens.

One can easily see the need for negotiation skills when dealing with the public. For example, when a police officer encounters a domestic violence situation or a barroom fight, the best way for the officer to handle the situation is to "talk" the combatants into submission.

Approaches to Negotiating

Effective negotiations occur when the issues of substance are resolved and the working relationships between the negotiating parties is improved or at least not harmed (Schermerhorn, 1996). Because negotiations may take a long period of time, it is critical that the parties attempt to maintain good working relationships. It is not in the interest of a particular side to destroy the other side, since they very likely will meet again.

There are three criteria by which to judge the quality of negotiations: quality, cost, and harmony (Schermerhorn, 1996). First, quality refers to attempts by both sides to come to a win-win solution. In some cases one side may be more interested in using the negotiations as a form of disruption. For example, when officers lodge complaints about minor issues and reject honest efforts to resolve them, they are probably attempting to be disruptive as opposed to pursuing legitimate concerns.

Cost does not refer to the amount of money involved in negotiations but to the time and energy spent negotiating. When two sides have a disagreement, it is in everyone's best interest to resolve it as soon as possible. When supervisors allow a problem to drag on and worsen, they very likely will cause the unit to suffer in terms of lost effectiveness.

Finally, harmony refers to the feelings of personnel about the department and its members after the conflict or problem is resolved. If a supervisor orders subordinates to conform to a departmental policy or order without giving the subordinates due consideration, then work group harmony is damaged or lost. Furthermore, it may take a considerable amount of time for the supervisor to recapture the collegiality that was destroyed.

The Prenegotiation Stage

Negotiation is a process that occurs in steps, the first being the prenegotiation stage. Negotiators must prepare themselves in advance. There are three important elements in the prenegotiation stage. First, the negotiator must fully understand what is at issue. In some cases this is rather simple, such as whether there is space in the training schedule for personnel to receive training. But when the issues are complex, as is often the case in collective bargaining, it may be a fairly difficult task to come to some understanding about what is at stake. The successful negotiator is able to ferret out the real issues when conflict occurs.

Second, it is important for the negotiator to be empathetic and understand the other side's position. In some cases officers may make demands that are totally out of the question or infeasible because of budget constraints or personnel limitations. In other cases, however, officers may make demands as a result of a problem that adversely affects their ability to get the job done. For example, officers may complain about how beats are configured. Some officers may be overworked as a result of beat boundaries while others have too little to do. Thus, it is important for the supervisor to become thoroughly familiar with officers' concerns before attempting to address them.

Third, the successful negotiator understands all the options before sitting down to negotiate. For example, if a sergeant is aware that officers are upset about a particular policy, the sergeant should research it prior to discussing it with subordinates. Or a new departmental policy may prohibit officers from eating meals outside their beats. For graveyard shift officers, this policy might pose a major problem if no restaurants are on their beat and their homes are far from the beat area. Here, the graveyard shift supervisor might need to study the situation independently and recommend a policy change to the chief executive.

Negotiation Tactics

A number of tactics are available to the negotiator. If all the information about the other side and options have been collected, the negotiator is better able to select a set of tactics that will result in a desired outcome. The negotiator can select from a number of tactics (Donnelly et al., 1995).

1. *Good-guy/bad-guy team.* The good-guy and bad-guy ploy has long been used by the police when interrogating suspects. The bad-guy tends to be a hardliner who refuses to give an inch. The good-guy comes in later after the op-

ponent has had time to reflect on the extreme position and makes several accommodations. This ploy helps negotiations to move the other side toward
the middle, especially when the other side is intransigent.

2. *The nibble.* The nibble is a small concession made to facilitate movement on
   the other side. Generally, a nibble will give the negotiator leverage in negotiating for a greater concession. The nibble usually is the first step to a series
   of concessions on both sides to come to an agreement.
3. *Joint problem solving.* Joint problem solving occurs when both sides recognize the need to identify an acceptable solution. If at all possible, this is the
   method to use, but in most circumstances other tactics are required to get
   the parties to the point where they will engage in joint problem solving.
4. *Power of competition.* The threat of going someplace else may cause the other
   side to be more accommodating. For example, if a precinct commander is experiencing a crime problem, he or she may call on detectives, crime prevention, or tactical units to attack the problem. The threat of working with another unit may cause an intransigent opponent to rethink his or her position.
5. *Splitting the difference.* Splitting the difference refers to both sides moving simultaneously toward a mutually acceptable position. Splitting differences
   can be effective only after each side has become thoroughly familiar with
   the other side's negotiating position.
6. *Lowballing.* Lowballing takes place when one side makes a ridiculously low
   offer in an effort to scare the other side into a negotiating position. Lowballing also disguises the real distance between the two sides. Lowballing is
   also used to try to get the other side to move substantially as a result of negotiating. The best reaction to lowballing is to hold one's position until the
   offerer reshapes his or her negotiating position.

Guidelines for Conducting Negotiations

Although every negotiation proceeds differently, some general guidelines may
be helpful (adapted from Stoner and Freeman, 1992):

1. Have and understand your objectives. This includes the rationale for having the objectives and their relative importance.
2. Do not hurry when negotiating. Information is far more important than
   time, and information is lost when negotiating is done hastily.
3. When there is doubt, consult others for the facts. It often is extremely difficult to break agreements that are the result of negotiations.
4. Make sure that you have access to supporting documentation and data as
   the negotiations become more formal.
5. Maintain some measure of flexibility in your position.
6. Attempt to discover the driving force behind the other side's request.
7. Do not become deadlocked over minutiae or some singular point.
8. Allow room for your opponent to save face. Total defeat of an opponent
   leads to long-term resentment and future problems.
9. Focus on listening throughout the negotiating, and pay close attention to the
   other side.
10. Make sure that your emotions are controlled, regardless of how the negoti-
    ations proceed.

11. During the negotiation process, make sure that you listen and consider every word. Nail down statements into precise, understood language.
12. Try to understand your opponents.

These guidelines can assist a supervisor in negotiating with subordinates, peers, or superiors.

Negotiation by Police Supervisors

Although we have mentioned police supervisors in the foregoing discussion of negotiations, here we focus more specifically on their unique role.

Police supervisors must constantly negotiate with their subordinates, and be able to ensure their maximum compliance with orders, directives, and assignments. Although the sergeant can "order" his or her subordinates to perform certain tasks, it is generally more effective if a consensus is reached—and a consensus can normally be reached only through negotiation. A supervisor is better able to induce voluntary compliance when he or she is able to negotiate effectively.

Police supervisors also must often negotiate with their superiors. They must argue their case when there are personnel shortages or when members of the unit are given too many responsibilities. Conflict between units over assignments sometimes occur, resulting in the supervisor having to negotiate with peers about working conditions.

Thus, it is evident that negotiation becomes particularly problematic when we consider the nature of police work. Police officers are often called upon to engage in activities that are perceived as being less important or not as prestigious as other tasks. For example, most police officers would rather investigate a homicide or robbery than direct traffic after a high school football game. Directing traffic is not as interesting, nor will it reap the same amount of prestige or publicity, that a successful homicide investigation might bring to the officer. Nonetheless, directing traffic is a vital function that the police department performs. Indeed, there are many more mundane tasks than exciting ones for officers. Yet, all of these tasks must be performed and be performed well.

COPING WITH CONFLICT

The Nature of Organizational Conflict

Conflict is a natural phenomenon, occurring in all organizations. Conflict is a situation in which two or more people disagree over issues of organizational substance and experience some emotional antagonism with one another (Schermerhorn et al., 1994). Conflict has four key elements: (1) individuals or groups with opposing interests; (2) acknowledgment that opposing viewpoints or interests exist; (3) the belief by parties that the other will attempt to deny them their goal or objective; and (4) one or both sides of the conflict have overtly attempted to thwart the others' goals and objectives (Greenberg and Baron, 1995). These elements require overt action to have occurred, but conflict may exist prior to any overtness. If the level of antagonism between the antagonists is substantial, then conflict will exist without any action by one of the parties.

Conflict should be viewed as a continuous process, occurring against a backdrop of relationships and events. There will inevitably be conflict when there are people, relationships, and activities. Thus, conflict is not an isolated, short-term event, but something that supervisors will encounter on a continuing basis. Conflict as a process also affects and involves a variety of people and activities within the organization. It tends to spread and cut across other activities. Finally, it can result from a variety of reasons, ranging from personal to professional; personal conflict affects professional relationships just as professional conflict affects personal relationships (Thomas, 1992).

The nature of police work often leads to conflict. Few citizens are pleased when they encounter a police officer, regardless of the nature of the encounter. Such encounters often require intervention and negotiation by a supervisor. Also, in many instances the police supervisor is perceived as the person in the middle who must mediate the impact of departmental policies on subordinate officers. Officers tend to expect supervisors to make policies realistic in their application, while administrators expect supervisors to follow the letter of the law with regard to policies and procedures.

Levels of Conflict

Conflict can occur throughout an organization. For example, two precinct commanders may develop a conflict over resources (e.g., whether new resources should be given to the patrol or to the jail function), or conflict may develop between detectives and patrol officers as a result of both attempting to solve the same case. Supervisors should be aware of the conflict swirling around them, since this conflict very likely will have some eventual impact on them or their units. With this in mind, conflict can occur at four levels within the agency:

1. *Intrapersonal,* where an individual has conflict within him- or herself.
2. *Interpersonal,* where individuals have conflict with others in the unit or department.
3. *Intergroup,* where work groups within the organization develop conflict.
4. *Interorganizational,* where different organizations are at odds as the result of some issue or event.

Intrapersonal conflict is a situation where the individual is not content or satisfied with what is occurring in his or her life. The conflict may be work related, where the individual is not satisfied with his or assignment or potential for being promoted. It may also be related to the individual's personal life. An officer may be experiencing problems at home or in some other part of his or her life (we discuss police officer stress and wellness in Chapter 7). Such conflict generally manifests itself in withdrawal or aggression. When a supervisor observes unusual changes in a subordinate's demeanor or personality, the supervisor should attempt to provide support to the officer. The supervisor may also attempt to indirectly discern the problem, for example, by keeping in contact with officer's peers. In any event the supervisor should try to work more closely with the officer who demonstrates personal problems, so that the problem does not affect the officer's work or result in overly aggressive behavior in dealing with the public.

Interpersonal conflict occurs when members of the work group have personal disagreements and conflict with one another. Whenever several people are working together, conflict is inevitable. Again, the conflict can be the result of the job or personal in nature. For example, some officers may become agitated because they perceive that their work schedule or assignments are not as desirable as those given to others. They may become jealous of other officers' productivity. Interpersonal conflict must be addressed. Too often supervisors fail to deal with it, hoping that it will dissipate. In most cases, however, interpersonal conflict will only worsen if not addressed.

Intergroup conflict occurs when officers in one unit have conflict with officers in another unit. A good example of intergroup conflict took place on the popular television show "NYPD Blue." A homicide occurred on the street that separated two precincts. Detectives from one precinct moved the body to the other side of the street, forcing detectives from the other precinct to investigate the case. Needless to say, when the latter learned what the other detectives had done, a significant confrontation ensued. Supervisors must carefully watch work activities and be ready to mediate any possible conflicts with other work groups. The sergeant must be prepared to intervene and mediate such disputes. In some cases it may entail taking the issue to commanders. Regardless, the supervisor must not allow the conflict to manifest itself in aggressive, unprofessional acts. Decisive action is required.

Finally, **interorganizational conflict** occurs when problems arise between the police department and other organizations. Unfortunately, law enforcement is not always the united, amicable, cooperative "family" that outsiders perceive it to be. It is not at all uncommon for, say, a county sheriff's office and a municipal police department in the county to fail to get along with each other because of professional jealousy or for reasons relating to "turf protection." Indeed, long-standing turf battles and refusal to communicate and cooperate between certain federal law enforcement agencies are well known in police circles. These interdepartmental problems are often due to a rift between the respective agency administrators, and do not directly involve supervisors or their responsibilities; nevertheless, the supervisor can easily be caught up in this discord and attempt to ameliorate any resulting problems.

As another example, a judge may require officers to not wear their uniforms to court. Most police officers would be highly offended by such a requirement. Nonetheless, it is a requirement that must be followed. In this case the supervisor must counsel officers about the possible impact of not following the judge's directive, and emphasize that the object of going to court is to present the evidence in the best possible manner. In other words, the officers must get beyond the order and attend to the business at hand.

Sources of Conflict in Police Organizations

Conflict can occur for a variety of reasons. Most often, conflict can be categorized as organizational or interpersonal. Greenberg and Baron (1995) have identified a number of causes of conflict which are addressed in Figure 4–2.

One source of conflict is competition over resources, which occurs when units or sections within a police department compete for personnel, responsibilities, equipment, and other tangibles related to the job. Indeed, if managers

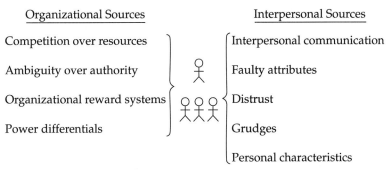

FIGURE 4–2. Causes of Conflict in Organizations

and supervisors are doing their job, they will constantly strive to obtain greater amounts of personnel or equipment. When resources become available, everyone generally attempts to garner as many resources as possible. Competition for resources inevitably leads to conflict, especially when the parties resort to political measures to obtain their objectives.

A second source of conflict is ambiguity over authority, which refers to instances where two units or supervisors believe they have authority over a situation or personnel. It is very similar to a breach in the span of control (see Chapter 1).

Third, organizational reward systems cause conflict. Organizational reward systems consist of tangible and intangible benefits. Tangible benefits include extra pay in the form of overtime or specialists' pay, new equipment, and new vehicles. Intangible benefits include prestige and public exposure. Detectives frequently receive vast amounts of publicity when they solve a major case, while other units, even though they may have been central to the investigation, may receive little if any recognition. Because of the nature of their work, some units have more equipment; and some units, such as traffic, may be given substantial amounts of overtime. As perceptions of inequality increase as a result of a department's reward system, so will job dissatisfaction and conflict. It is almost impossible to have all rewards distributed evenly within a police agency because of the nature of the work.

Fourth, conflict results when a power differential exists within a police department. A power differential refers to some members having more power within the department than others. It usually occurs as a result of "nonlegitimate" power; for example, the chief may have spent most of his or her career in the traffic unit, and now favors that unit over others. Individuals in the organization—because of their assignment, past work record, or personal relationships—may have closer ties with the chief or other high-ranking commanders, affording them higher levels of power and access. Each of these instances can cause animosity and conflict within a police organization.

Problems of power differential occur at lower levels of an organization as well as across units. When people at the lower levels, such as an officer or sergeant, feel that they have little input into decision making and believe that they are not appreciated by the department, they will become frustrated and be more likely to engage in conflict.

Interpersonal Causes

The *failure to properly communicate* is a common interpersonal cause of conflict. The information or message may be incomplete, contain faulty information, or be communicated in a way that antagonizes the receiver. Supervisors sometimes do not take the time to ensure that their message is complete or obtain suitable feedback to ensure that the receiver clearly understands the message. Or the supervisor may be curt or discourteous when communicating to subordinates. The supervisor may also give the subordinate unwarranted or inappropriate criticism. In either case the subordinate becomes frustrated, which ultimately leads to conflict.

A second interpersonal cause of organizational conflict is *faulty attribution*, where the intentions or rationale for an action is misunderstood by someone who is directed to complete some task. In such cases the assignment is seen as an act of malevolence rather than a legitimate request. For example, when a detective supervisor requests that a detective recontact some witnesses in a case, the detective may see the request as harassment, while the supervisor may believe that the detective's report contained insufficient information. Faulty communications often lead to faulty attributions in the workplace.

Third, *distrust* creates a great deal of conflict. Police officers and groups of officers in specific units have a great deal of experience with other officers and units within a department. Over time, officers come to trust or distrust these other units or officers. Some units, such as patrol and investigations, are constantly thrust into potential conflict situations because of the way police departments are organized and the nature of the job. Patrol officers see detectives "stealing" their cases once they complete their initial investigation, while detectives complain of patrol officers' failure to cooperate with them. Along these same lines, officers may come to distrust superiors or other officers. For example, an officer may distrust a sergeant because the sergeant fails to communicate adequately, back the officer when there is a problem, or keep a promise about an assignment. There are innumerable situations that can result in officers coming to distrust one another. Seldom, however, are the situations addressed openly.

Fourth, people develop and tend to *hold grudges* against others in the department. Grudges may be personal in nature, such as an attempt by two officers to date the same person or the sale by one officer to another of an automobile that turns out to be a lemon. Grudges also can be professional in nature, such as an officer who withholds information in a case so he or she can make the arrest, or an officer who reports another officer's deviant or improper behavior to superiors. Grudges may occur for a variety of reasons. It is important to understand that they may last a number of years, and in some cases, officers never forgive the person for whom they hold a grudge.

Finally, an officer's *personal characteristics* may lead to conflict. Personal characteristics refer to such attributes as curtness, the inability to communicate clearly, a need to pry into the business or affairs of other officers, or being disorganized and commonly failing to perform adequately. All sorts of people can be labeled as difficult or uncooperative. Generally, it is the nature of their personality that causes them to have difficulties with others. These people are frequently difficult to work with, and the reactions of others to them often antagonizes, rather than appeases, them.

Supervisors' Roles in Conflict Management

Supervisors can use a variety of strategies to deal with conflict. There is no one way to deal with conflict because it manifests itself in many ways and there are always different factors contributing to it. It is important, however, for a supervisor to be able to recognize conflict when it occurs and quickly take action. As noted above, negotiation skills play a key role in conflict resolution. Such skills are necessary to mediate between the combatants when conflict occurs. The goal of conflict resolution is to eliminate the causes of conflict and reduce the potential for additional conflict in the future.

Intervention in conflict essentially involves two supervisory skills: cooperativeness and assertiveness (Schermerhorn, 1996). **Cooperativeness** refers to instances where the supervisor attempts to cooperate with the conflicting parties and work toward a solution. **Assertiveness** occurs when the supervisor orders or directs combatants to behave in a certain manner, usually in accordance with departmental policies and procedures. Assertiveness does not attempt to alleviate the conflict, but to remove its manifestations from the workplace.

Figure 4–3 shows the conflict management grid, containing the five means of addressing conflict.

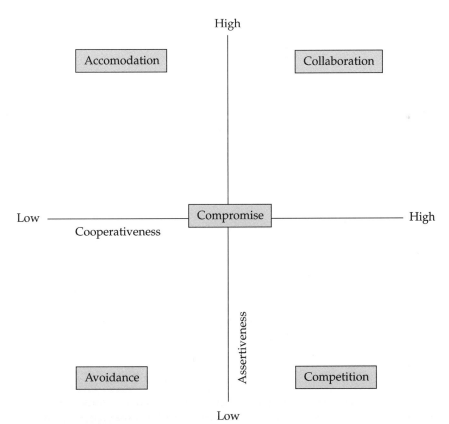

FIGURE 4–3. Conflict Management Grid

Avoidance. Perhaps the most common supervisory reaction to conflict is **avoidance,** where the supervisor refuses to recognize the existence of conflict, hoping that it simply will go away. However, conflict is seldom resolved without intervention on a timely basis. When conflict is left unresolved, it probably will have a negative impact on the conflicting parties and their associates in the work group. Obviously, avoidance does not involve cooperativeness or assertiveness on the part of the supervisor. Supervisory intervention into such matters is generally extremely difficult, personal, and uncomfortable, and it can be a highly emotional ordeal that could lead to additional conflict between the negotiator and the parties involved. Thus, the natural tendency is to avoid dealing with conflicts. This, of course, is a mistake since the problem is very likely to worsen.

Accommodation. A second strategy for handling conflict is called **accommodation,** or smoothing. Accommodation involves minimum intrusion on the part of the supervisor. Here the supervisor attempts to smooth over differences between those engaged in the conflict. Accommodation represents a high level of cooperativeness and a low level of assertiveness on the part of the supervisor. The supervisor asserts his or her authority, only to induce a higher level of cooperativeness. Actual differences are avoided so that harmony can be maintained. A sergeant involved in accommodation would attempt to work more closely with the officers engaged in the conflict. The sergeant would attempt to become more personable, engaging the officers in conversation about departmental and extradepartmental issues. Here the sergeant would attempt to make the issues central to the conflict a low priority.

Competition. A third conflict resolution strategy is **competition,** where the supervisor intervenes and meets with the combatants, forcing them to present all the facts about the situation, and then making a decision. Here, the conflict becomes a competitive situation where there is a clear winner. In other words, competition results in definite winners and losers. It involves a maximum degree of assertiveness with little or no cooperation on the part of the supervisor. Obviously, this strategy does not resolve the underlying cause of the conflict, and it could result in the conflict recurring at a later time.

An example of competition is a dispute between patrol officers and detectives about cases or arrests. Upon completing preliminary investigation, patrol officers generally turn the case over to detectives. However, when patrol officers make an arrest or are close to making an arrest in a high-profile case, they resent giving the case, and its inherent credit, to detectives. Thus, case assignment becomes a "winner take all" proposition unless other accommodations are made. Some departments have resolved this type of situation by allowing patrol officers to work with detectives throughout the follow-up investigation so that credit is shared. This arrangement also provides invaluable experience and training to patrol officers which ultimately results in improved investigative skills.

Compromise. A fourth strategy to resolve conflict is **compromise,** which involves a mix of cooperation and assertiveness on the part of the intervening supervisor. Here the supervisor searches for a solution that satisfies all parties to the conflict. It is a process whereby everyone generally gains something, but at the same time accommodates others. It is essentially a search for the middle ground. Supervisors frequently use compromise when they make the work schedule. They attempt to divide days off and hours worked so that everyone is accommodated to some extent. At the same time, few officers are totally happy with the arrangement. In a compromise strategy, the supervisor determines the compromise.

Problem Solving. Finally, conflict resolution can involve **problem solving.** Here the supervisor attempts to work through problems to fully address everyone's concerns. When people work cooperatively, it is much easier for them to see other perspectives and to develop an appreciation for the other side. Once this occurs, people are more willing to work with each other toward a solution. In the compromise strategy the sergeant determined a solution while in the problem solving strategy those enmeshed in the conflict arrived at a solution.

Whenever there is conflict, there usually will be winners and losers. Avoidance and accommodation generally result in lose-lose outcomes to conflict resolution; when avoidance or accommodation are used, the conflict is never really addressed and no one really attains his or her objectives. If the conflict is allowed to continue, it will ultimately result in ill feelings that will affect work relations

---

Case Study 4–2
The Case of "Superman" on Patrol

Officer "Spike" Jones recently transferred back to the patrol division after three years in a street crimes unit where he was involved with numerous high-risk arrests of dangerous offenders. He has a reputation within the department as a highly skilled tactical officer. He is team leader of the agency's special operations (SWAT) team and also a trainer in special operations and tactics at the regional police academy. For these reasons, Jones's supervisor was pleased to have him assigned to the team so he could impart his knowledge and experiences to the other officers. Indeed, when Jones first comes to the team, the supervisor praises his accomplishments in front of the other officers. Within a month, however, the supervisor begins to notice a wide rift developing between Jones and the rest of the team. Jones is overheard on several occasions discussing the menial work of patrol, saying it's not "real" police work. He is always trying to impress other officers with his experiences and says he cannot wait to get out of patrol and into another specialized, high-risk assignment. The team members complain to the supervisor that Jones does not fit in. After two months this rift has grown much wider, and the supervisor notices that other officers are slow in backing up Jones at calls. On questioning some of the team members, the supervisor hears that "Superman Jones doesn't need our help anyway."

1. As the supervisor concerned, how would you mediate the conflict developing within your team?
2. What kinds of strategies can the supervisor employ to reduce or eliminate the rift that has developed within the team?
3. What does the supervisor need to do with the other team members? What kinds of compromises or adjustments do the team members need to make in order to include Jones as part of their team?
4. What does the supervisor need to do with Jones? What kinds of compromises or adjustments does Jones need to make in order to become a good team member?

for some time. Competition and compromise strategies generally result in win-lose outcomes, where one side wins and the other side loses. Again, this ending will have negative effects on at least one side of the conflict. Competition and compromise fail to address the root causes of conflict and even though a temporary solution might be found, the conflict is likely to recur. Only collaboration attempts to seek solutions whereby all sides win. Collaboration attempts to impress upon all the parties that it is mutually beneficial for a solution to be identified that is acceptable to everyone. Collaboration attempts to engage people in problem solving and it encourages them to work out differences.

A supervisor may use all of these strategies in dealing with the unit. Obviously, collaboration results in the best outcome, but in some cases the situation and the people involved in the conflict may prohibit the use of a collaborative strategy. Jealousies and dislikes among the parties involved in the conflict may be too deeply engrained.

The supervisor must collect information and develop a thorough understanding of the conflict prior to intervention. The facts of the situation dictate the degree of assertiveness and cooperativeness in the supervisor's strategy.

SUMMARY

This chapter has addressed the interpersonal dynamics surrounding organizational communication, negotiation, and conflict management. These three supervisory activities must be mastered if the supervisor is to supervise subordinates effectively. Supervision is about people, and good supervisors possess good people skills.

As stated in the introduction, communication skills are perhaps the most important skills a supervisor can possess. Communications, formal or informal, written or oral, serve to link people and activities. In reality, communications is the means by which tasks are accomplished in police organizations. A supervisor cannot negate the importance of the ability to communicate.

Likewise, negotiations play an important role in one's success as a sergeant. To a great extent, successful policing involves reaching a consensus about police goals and objectives. However, not everyone agrees with what should be done or how it should be done. Supervisors must use negotiation skills to make officers see the importance of following departmental procedures.

Finally, conflict is a natural phenomenon that occurs in all organizations. A substantial amount of conflict is the result of poor communication skills; effective negotiation skills are frequently called upon to resolve conflict. A supervisor must understand that conflict is almost always present, recognize conflict, and take definitive action to resolve it.

KEY TERMS

formal communications (p. 71)	informal communications (p. 71)	noise (p. 74)
feedback (p. 71)	grapevine (p. 74)	physical barriers to communication (p. 75)

empathy (p. 75)
active listening (p. 75)
intrapersonal conflict (p. 81)
interpersonal conflict (p. 82)

intergroup conflict (p. 82)
interorganizational conflict (p. 82)
cooperativeness (p. 85)
assertiveness (p. 85)

avoidance (p. 86)
accommodation (p. 86)
competition (p. 86)
compromise (p. 86)
problem solving (p. 87)

ITEMS FOR REVIEW

1. Describe the communication process.
2. Define formal and informal communications.
3. Explain barriers to effective communications.
4. Describe how police supervisors communicate.
5. How do supervisors negotiate? Review the tactics they use and the guidelines that apply to successful negotiation.
6. Define organizational conflict, its levels, and sources.
7. Explain how supervisors can engage in conflict resolution.

SOURCES

BENNETT, W. W., and HESS, K. (1992). *Management and supervision in law enforcement.* St. Paul, Minn.: West, 1992.

DONNELLY, J. H., GIBSON, J. L., and IVANCEVICH, J. M. (1995). *Fundamentals of management.* 9th ed. Burr Ridge, Ill.: Richard D. Irwin.

GREENBERG, J., and BARON, R. A. (1995). *Behavior in organizations.* 5th ed. Englewood Cliffs, N.J.: Prentice Hall.

MORE, H. W., and WEGENER, W. F. (1996). *Effective police supervision.* 2d. ed. Cincinnati, Ohio: Anderson.

PETERS, T. J., and WATERMAN, R. H. (1983). *In search of lessons from America's best-run companies.* New York: Warner Books.

SCHERMERHORN, J. R. (1996). *Management.* 5th ed. New York: John Wiley.

SCHERMERHORN, J. R., HUNT, J. G., and OSBORN, R. N. (1994). *Managing organizational behavior.* 5th ed. New York: John Wiley.

STONER, J. A., and FREEMAN, R. E. (1992). *Management.* 5th. ed. Englewood Cliffs, N.J.: Prentice Hall.

THOMAS, K. W. (1992). "Conflict and negotiation processes in organizations." In M. Dunnette and L. Hough, eds. *Handbook of Industrial and Organizational Psychology.* 2d ed., Vol. 3. Palo Alto, Calif.: Consulting Psychologists Press.

VAN FLEET, D. D., and PETERSON, T. O. (1994). *Contemporary management.* 3d. ed. Boston: Houghton Mifflin.

VON DER EMBSE, T. J. (1987). *Supervision: Managerial skills for a new era.* New York: Macmillan.

Supervising Human Resources: Training, Evaluation, and Discipline

Part Two

Supervising Human Resources: Training, Evaluation, and Discipline

5

Training and Professional Development

*A man can seldom—very, very seldom—fight a winning fight against his
training: the odds are too heavy.*

—Mark Twain

Knowledge is the food of the soul.

—Plato

The secret of education lies in respecting the pupil.

—Ralph Waldo Emerson

If you think education is expensive, try ignorance.

—Derek Bok

INTRODUCTION

Training is one of the most critical issues facing police departments today as well
as a primary function and responsibility of supervisors. Our nation's growing
social, economic, and legal problems challenge the police to acquire and maintain the knowledge, skills, and abilities necessary to cope with an ever-changing
world. Proper training also provides a vital link to employee performance and
accountability and may protect the agency from unnecessary litigation.

We begin this chapter by discussing the various types of training available
to police officers and supervisors, followed by the component parts of a police
training program.

Although we realize that many readers of this text are not yet supervisors
or are newly promoted in that position, this is the age of computers, electronic

mail, and the Internet, all of which are readily available to everyone, including supervisors. These resources provide a wealth of information about training, whether one is engaged in the work of patrol, investigation, traffic, or some other assignment. Also, these resources provide access to supervisors in other agencies, allowing them to share information. Therefore, we deem it important to include in this chapter a discussion of the types of training materials and several means by which supervisors can keep abreast of developments in their field.

Then we examine the subject of supervisors as trainers, arguably an area where the supervisor can make the greatest contribution to the organization. We conclude the chapter with a review of training and liability issues.

CONTEMPORARY POLICE TRAINING

Training is a critical function of police agencies generally, and supervisors specifically. Unfortunately, it is also a function that is often subject to the political winds, holding a lesser priority than other functions and ofttimes lacking sufficient resources (e.g., in time, money, and personnel) to influence the professional development of officers.

A study by the U.S. Bureau of Justice Statistics (1993) examined police training nationwide. This study found that the average number of training hours required of new police recruits ranged from over 1,100 in departments serving a population of 100,000 or more, to less than 500 hours in agencies serving fewer than 2,500 residents.

Once a recruit officer graduates from an academy, the state's commission or board of **Peace Officers Standards and Training (POST)** awards a basic certificate of completion. Over the years POSTs have also developed intermediate, advanced, managerial, and executive certificates for police officers; above the basic level, these certificates are generally categorized as "advanced" certificates. Each certificate requires a specified number of hours of training and/or higher education in various areas such as investigation, management, and operations.

The purpose of advanced certification programs is to enhance lifelong learning and career development for the officer. Over the years advanced POST certification and higher education have also become popular bargaining issues for police unions and associations. Some agencies offer as much as a 5 percent pay increase for an advanced certificate or a combination of advanced certificates and a four-year college degree. These incentives provide strong motivation for officers to continue their education and training.

National standards for police training have also been promoted in recent years. In 1983 the **Commission on Accreditation for Law Enforcement Agencies, Inc. (CALEA),** became the only national accrediting body for police; it has developed approximately 1,000 standards reflecting every aspect of the profession under six major topics: agency role and responsibility, organization and administration, personnel administration, operations and support, prisoner- and court-related issues. An entire chapter containing 45 standards is dedicated solely to training.

The benefits of accreditation through CALEA include more effective administrative systems, reduced liability potential, greater supervisory accountability, and greater governmental and community support. Standards are applicable to agencies based on their mission and size. An estimated 18 percent of the nearly 600,000 full-time police officers in the United States at the city, county, and state levels, and 10 percent of Canadian officers, are employed by agencies involved in the accreditation process through CALEA (Doughtry, 1996).

TYPES OF TRAINING

The training of police officers occurs in five general categories: basic academy, field training, roll-call, in-service training, and specialized. We briefly discuss these types of training and see how the roles and responsibilities of the supervisor in each area are vital to the success of the officer and organization.

Basic Academy Training

A new recruit officer's career begins with academy training. This is one of the largest investments in training for police departments. Academy training usually involves three to six months of classroom instruction on a variety of topics. In the past most larger agencies administered their own academies and utilized their own staff as instructors. However, this is not generally the case today. The high costs of administering and staffing an academy have led agencies to seek less expensive alternatives, such as regional training centers. These training centers have changed the environment of police academy training.

The traditional "high stress" military training model is no longer recommended and has been largely replaced by one that promotes academics and adult learning. In many states, selected community colleges are the sites for regional police academy training. Commonly, a number of positions in each class are reserved for persons not yet hired but who are interested in becoming police officers; these students pay their own expenses and associated fees and receive a certificate of completion, but they are not guaranteed employment. POSTs also provide basic police academy training in many states and are usually attended by personnel from smaller rural departments as well as agencies that have officers with police officer status, including adult and juvenile parole and probation officers, school police, airport police, and fire marshals.

As our society and culture change, so must the police adjust academy training to meet these changes and the needs of the public and police. Some examples of subjects added to police department curriculums during recent years include:

- *Community policing and problem solving,* which provides officers with new skills and tools to conduct in-depth analysis of persistent crime conditions and to pursue collaborative, tailor-made responses with other government organizations, businesses, social service agencies and the community at large. We discuss community policing and problem solving in detail in Chapter 13.
- *Stress training,* because police officers are confronted with the dual problem of managing their own stress as well as the stress of others in difficult situations. Teaching officers how to manage stress under difficult circumstances

A recruit officer receives instruction in the proper use of the police baton. The improper use of weapons and defense techniques can result in personal injury to officers and citizens, as well as litigation.
Courtesy Washoe County, Nevada, Sheriff's Office.

is critical to their personal safety and long-term health. We discuss stress in detail in Chapter 7.

- *American Disabilities Act (ADA),* which mandates certain services that must be provided to persons with disabilities. ADA requires that organizations provide a "reasonable accommodation" for disabled employees.
- *Blood-borne pathogens,* which present a major threat to police who frequently come in contact with blood and other body fluids during the course of their duties. The federal Occupational Safety and Health Administration (OSHA) has developed strict workplace and training requirements that outline measures of prevention.
- *Cultural diversity,* because we live in an increasingly diverse society of many cultures and languages that pose new challenges for police. Police officers must acquire new skills when working in these environments. Brown and Hendricks (1996:60) stated that "cultural awareness training embraces the

future of policing." Our increasingly diverse society and the evolution of community policing and problem solving serve to legitimize cultural diversity training for police officers.

- *Domestic terrorism,* because the United States realized after the bombings of the World Trade Center in New York City and the Murrah Federal Building in Oklahoma City that this country is no longer immune from terrorism. As we increasingly become a global village, the threat of domestic violence by radical religious and antigovernment groups will elevate the concern and present new challenges to federal, state, and local police agencies.
- *Computer-related crimes,* because of their spreading incidence and the fact that even the average home personal computer with a telephone modem is capable of being used in the most sophisticated of credit card and other fraudulent schemes.
- *Ethics,* due to the ethical issues that arise daily in policing. The Rodney King incident of 1991 was an extreme example of police brutality, and it reminds us how important it is to teach officers proper ethical behavior. Supervisors must accept and perform the difficult task of overseeing officers' behavior. Ethics courses are becoming more common in both academy and in-service training. We discuss ethics in Chapter 8.
- *Youth gang violence,* because few violence-related problems are of greater concern to the police and public than youth gangs. Gangs are proliferating across the nation. Police must continually learn new strategies for detection, prevention, and diversion to effectively deal with youth gang issues.

It is extremely important that supervisors keep abreast of new and developing areas in the field in order to adequately train new and veteran officers.

Field Training Officer Programs

Following the completion of studies at a basic academy, a patrol officer is normally assigned to a **field training officer (FTO)** program in a uniformed patrol division, where the probationary officer can put his or her newly acquired classroom academy classroom knowledge into practice. As we will see below, the supervisor assumes a tremendous responsibility at this stage of the probationary officer's career.

Most larger and progressive police agencies have adopted an FTO program based on a model designed in the early 1970s by the San Jose, California, police department. The time when a new officer was simply issued a gun, badge, and a map of the city and then sent to work on a beat is mostly gone. By 1986 a national survey of field training programs in police departments revealed that 64 percent (188) of the 288 responding agencies had formal FTO programs. The advantages of field training programs include reductions in civil liability complaints, the development of standardized training processes, and improved documentation for new officers (McCambell, 1986).

A typical FTO program is about 14 weeks' duration and divided into four phases. Each phase is designed to help the recruit learn a particular set of tasks. The first three phases are about four weeks' duration, and the last phase consists of a final two-week evaluation. The trainee is normally assigned to a different

FTO and different shift during each of the first three phases. This provides the officer with maximum exposure and experience before returning to the original FTO for the final phase. The content of each phase of training is as follows:

Phase I. This is the introductory phase in which the trainee is taught certain basic skills, including officer safety and other areas of potential liability to the organization and trainee. An important element of this phase is the trainee's acceptance of training and willingness to learn from experienced officers. A great deal of the trainee's success may hinge on how well he or she accepts the training and is willing to learn.

Phase II. The training becomes more difficult in this phase. Here the trainee begins to apply some mastery to basic skills. Report writing, traffic enforcement, and crime scene investigations become routine for the trainee during this phase. Therefore, the FTO will begin to share more workload and decision-making responsibilities with the trainee.

Phase III. This is the last phase of directly supervised formal training. It is characterized by advanced skills training and polishing those skills already learned. During this phase, the FTO has an opportunity to review those tasks previously accomplished and to make sure that the trainee is prepared for the final phase. By the completion of this phase, the trainee should be able to assume responsibilities in the most difficult situations, including shootings, robberies in-progress, and so on, and to do so with little assistance from the FTO.

Phase IV. This phase is the final evaluation period, and the trainee returns to the original FTO. In this phase the trainee assumes the role of primary officer while the FTO might wear civilian clothes and only observe. The purpose of Phase IV is to evaluate whether the trainee is capable of functioning without the direct supervision of an FTO.

Field training programs are labor intensive and require a great deal of administration and management. FTOs complete a comprehensive **daily observation report (DOR)** form, as shown in Figure 5–2. The DOR is a permanent record of the trainee's progress as well as any remedial efforts and identified problems. The form shown in Figure 5–2 is composed of five major performance areas—appearance, attitude, knowledge, performance, and relationships—which are divided into 30 rating categories. These categories address a range of skills necessary for an officer to become proficient. The FTO observes and evaluates the trainee in each applicable area during a shift, using a rating scale of 1 to 7. A narrative explanation is required in every area where the trainee is rated below average (less than 4) or exceptional (more than 5).

The selection of good officers as FTOs is critical because they have a long-term impact on the behavior and performance of new and often very impressionable trainees. Criteria should include their education, experience, police skills, and ability and interest in training. The role of the FTO is similar to that of a supervisor. Guidance, counseling, and remediation of minor mistakes are required daily. (See Case Study 5–1.)

DATE_____   DAILY OBSERVATION REPORT NO._____

_____   _____
TRAINEE'S LAST NAME FIRST (MI) NO.   FTO'S LAST NAME FIRST (MI) NO.

RATING INSTRUCTIONS: RATE OBSERVED BEHAVIOR WITH REFERENCE TO THE SCALE BELOW. COMMENT ON THE MOST AND LEAST SATISFACTORY PERFORMANCE OF THE DAY. A SPECIFIC COMMENT IS REQUIRED ON ALL RATINGS OF "2" OR LESS AND "6" AND ABOVE. CHECK "N.O." IF NOT OBSERVED. IF TRAINEE FAILS TO RESPOND TO TRAINING, CHECK "N.R.T." BOX AND COMMENT.

WATCH WORKED_____
FTO PHASE _____
ASSIGNMENT_____

			NOT ACCEPTABLE BY FTO STANDARDS			ACCEPTABLE LEVEL	SUPERIOR BY FTO STANDARDS					
			1	2	3	<4>	5	6	7			
R.T.										N.O.	N.R.T.	
												APPEARANCE
[ ]	[ ]	1.	1	2	3	4	5	6	7	[ ]	[ ]	GENERAL APPEARANCE
												ATTITUDE
[ ]	[ ]	2.	1	2	3	4	5	6	7	[ ]	[ ]	ACCEPTANCE OF FEEDBACK-FTO
[ ]	[ ]	3.	1	2	3	4	5	6	7	[ ]	[ ]	ATTITUDE TOWARDS POLICE WORK
												KNOWLEDGE
												DEPARTMENT POLICIES AND PROCEDURES REFLECTED IN:
[ ]	[ ]	4.	1	2	3	4	5	6	7	[ ]	[ ]	VERBAL/WRITTEN TESTING
[ ]	[ ]		1	2	3	4	5	6	7	[ ]	[ ]	FIELD PERFORMANCE
												CRIMINAL STATUTES REFLECTED IN:
[ ]	[ ]	5.	1	2	3	4	5	6	7	[ ]	[ ]	VERBAL/WRITTEN TESTING
[ ]	[ ]		1	2	3	4	5	6	7	[ ]	[ ]	FIELD PERFORMANCE
												MUNICIPAL ORDINANCES REFLECTED IN:
[ ]	[ ]	6.	1	2	3	4	5	6	7	[ ]	[ ]	VERBAL/WRITTEN TESTING
[ ]	[ ]		1	2	3	4	5	6	7	[ ]	[ ]	FIELD PERFORMANCE
												TRAFFIC ORDINANCES REFLECTED IN:
[ ]	[ ]	7.	1	2	3	4	5	6	7	[ ]	[ ]	VERBAL/WRITTEN TESTING
[ ]	[ ]		1	2	3	4	5	6	7	[ ]	[ ]	FIELD PERFORMANCE
												PERFORMANCE
[ ]	[ ]	8.	1	2	3	4	5	6	7	[ ]	[ ]	DRIVING SKILL: NORMAL CONDITIONS
[ ]	[ ]	9.	1	2	3	4	5	6	7	[ ]	[ ]	DRIVING SKILL: STRESS CONDITIONS
[ ]	[ ]	10.	1	2	3	4	5	6	7	[ ]	[ ]	ORIENTATION/RESPONSE TIME
[ ]	[ ]	11.	1	2	3	4	5	6	7	[ ]	[ ]	ROUTINE FORMS: COMPLETE/ACCURATE
												REPORT WRITING
[ ]	[ ]	12.	1	2	3	4	5	6	7	[ ]	[ ]	ORGANIZATION/DETAILS
[ ]	[ ]	13.	1	2	3	4	5	6	7	[ ]	[ ]	GRAMMAR/SPELLING/NEATNESS
[ ]	[ ]	14.	1	2	3	4	5	6	7	[ ]	[ ]	APPROPRIATE TIME USED
[ ]	[ ]	15.	1	2	3	4	5	6	7	[ ]	[ ]	FIELD PERFORMANCE: NON-STRESS
[ ]	[ ]	16.	1	2	3	4	5	6	7	[ ]	[ ]	FIELD PERFORMANCE: STRESS
[ ]	[ ]	17.	1	2	3	4	5	6	7	[ ]	[ ]	INVESTIGATIVE SKILL
[ ]	[ ]	18.	1	2	3	4	5	6	7	[ ]	[ ]	INTERVIEW/INTERROGATION
[ ]	[ ]	19.	1	2	3	4	5	6	7	[ ]	[ ]	SELF-INITIATED FIELD ACTIVITY
[ ]	[ ]	20.	1	2	3	4	5	6	7	[ ]	[ ]	OFFICER SAFETY: GENERAL
[ ]	[ ]	21.	1	2	3	4	5	6	7	[ ]	[ ]	OFFICER SAFETY: SUSPECTS/PRISONERS
[ ]	[ ]	22.	1	2	3	4	5	6	7	[ ]	[ ]	VOICE COMMAND
[ ]	[ ]	23.	1	2	3	4	5	6	7	[ ]	[ ]	PHYSICAL SKILL
[ ]	[ ]	24.	1	2	3	4	5	6	7	[ ]	[ ]	PROBLEM SOLVING/DECISION MAKING
												RADIO
[ ]	[ ]	25.	1	2	3	4	5	6	7	[ ]	[ ]	USE OF CODES/PROCEDURES
[ ]	[ ]	26.	1	2	3	4	5	6	7	[ ]	[ ]	LISTEN AND COMPREHEND
[ ]	[ ]	27.	1	2	3	4	5	6	7	[ ]	[ ]	ARTICULATION/TRANSMISSION
												RELATIONSHIPS
[ ]	[ ]	28.	1	2	3	4	5	6	7	[ ]	[ ]	CITIZENS IN GENERAL
[ ]	[ ]	29.	1	2	3	4	5	6	7	[ ]	[ ]	ETHNIC GROUPS OTHER THAN OWN
[ ]	[ ]	30.	1	2	3	4	5	6	7	[ ]	[ ]	OTHER DEPARTMENT MEMBERS

_____MINUTES OF REMEDIAL TIME

FIGURE 5–1. Daily Observation Report

The Supervisor's Role

The role of the supervisor is equally vital to a new trainee's success. The supervisor's responsibility is to ensure that the standards and objectives of the agency's field training program are met. The supervisor must pay close attention to the training activities of the FTO and seek periodic feedback on the new trainee as the FTO program progresses.

When assigned a trainee, supervisors should periodically observe the trainee's handling of calls and the interaction between trainee and FTO, and conduct periodic informal meetings to discuss the progress of training. The supervisor also should ensure that necessary corrective actions are taken so that the trainee has every opportunity to complete the program or that the proper documentation exists in case the trainee is recommended for termination from employment.

The supervisor also will be responsible for the collection, review, and approval of all DOR forms completed by the FTO. The forms are reviewed to ensure that they are consistent with program goals and guidelines. A supervisor also should complete a weekly supervisory observation report (SOR), which is the supervisor's evaluation of the trainee's performance. Information for the SOR is obtained by a variety of means, including reviewing crime reports, listening to the radio, ride-alongs, field visits, and weekly conferences with the FTO and trainee.

Case Study 5–1
An FTO Who "Drives" Her Points Home

Six months have passed since the Arturo Hills Police Department lost its first officer to a traffic accident. A probationary officer was killed when his vehicle collided at an intersection with a passenger vehicle, killing the female driver and her two children. An investigation of the accident determined that the officer was responding to a business alarm and ran through a stop sign at 50 miles per hour. It was determined that the circumstances did *not* warrant the speed involved and that the accident was avoidable.

A lawsuit quickly ensued, and lawyers representing the family of the woman and her two children began by reviewing the department's training files. They learned that 54 percent of the agency's accidents involved probationary officers, and that 90 percent of those employees were trained by the same field training officer (FTO): Nancy Banks.

Banks is a veteran officer with 12 years of patrol experience; she is the department's pursuit driving instructor. She tells probationary officers assigned to her shift that she loves working nights because of its freedom from the administrative "brass hats" and the boring school and shoplifting calls that are so common on the day shift. For Banks, stop signs and stoplights don't exist on the graveyard shift, because "only 'cops and crooks' are out." Banks is hard on the recruits and pushes their driving skills to the limit during in-progress calls. A few recruits have complained about the dangers involved with the driving style that she teaches and requires, but their concerns are ignored.

1. What lessons can be learned from this case?
2. Could the department have done anything different in the administration of their FTO program to keep this tragedy from developing?
3. Should a supervisor have known about the potential problems and intervened? How?

Upon completing the FTO program, the trainee is usually assigned to uniformed patrol to serve the remainder of a probationary period, which will vary in length between agencies. Once the employee completes probation, roll call, in-service, and specialized training contribute mainly to an officer's career development.

Roll Call Training

Roll call is that period of time—15 to 30 minutes prior to the beginning of a tour of duty—used by supervisors to prepare officers for patrol. Roll call sessions usually begin with a supervisor assigning the officers to their respective beats. Information about wanted and dangerous persons and major incidents on previous shifts is usually disseminated. Other matters may also be addressed, such as issuing officers court subpoenas, explaining new departmental policies and procedures, and discussing shift and beat-related matters.

However, roll call meetings also afford an excellent opportunity for supervisors to update officers' knowledge and to present new ideas and techniques. This is particularly advantageous for smaller police agencies that have limited training staff and resources.

In-Service Training

Changes in departmental policies and procedures, court decisions, and operational strategies and techniques demand that training be an ongoing process throughout a police officer's career. It is simply unreasonable to expect that the knowledge gained during academy or specialized training can serve an officer for an entire career. **In-service training** is the most commonly utilized method for maintaining and improving officer performance and competency, and may also reduce the likelihood of citizen complaints and future litigation. In-service training is also used to recertify, refresh, or provide new information to officers in the most critical areas of their job, including weapons qualification, driving, defensive tactics, first aid, and changes in the law (Moore and Stephens, 1991).

Creating an effective in-service training program presents many challenges for both the administrator and supervisor. First, few departments have adequate funds to provide training beyond that mandated by law or that which creates the greatest public concern or liability. Scheduling training can also be a nightmare. In-service and specialized training often result in staffing shortages in areas where officers attending the training are assigned. Labor agreements can also hinder training; contracts may prohibit agencies from moving officers off an evening shift to train on day shift without compensation at an overtime rate. Agencies may also be required by contract to maintain certain established staffing levels, further complicating the supervisor's task of ensuring that officers are properly trained.

As officers gain experience and are selected for specialized assignments (e.g., detectives, narcotics, traffic, and gangs), the need for training emerges. Here the supervisor who is in charge of the specialized unit is responsible for providing the officers with an initial orientation and for locating a school to provide more in-depth training.

COMPONENTS OF A TRAINING PROGRAM

Training evolves from a logical and cyclic process. The training cycle contains five interrelated components: assessing training needs, establishing objectives, program development, delivering training, and assessing training effectiveness.

Assessing Training Needs

Training must be based on organizational goals and employee needs, the latter being determined by surveys and interviews with officers, supervisors, citizens, and elected officials; reviewing lawsuits and citizen complaints; and looking at what other agencies are doing (Rossett, 1987). A **training needs assessment** is the foundation for developing a training curriculum. It ensures that the training will meet the needs of the organization and employees. The failure to conduct a needs assessment may result in the training having no practical application in the minds and functions of the officers.

Training objectives identify what the trainer hopes to accomplish during the course of a session. They are based on the needs assessment and should clearly define for the trainee the intended outcome of the training. It also should address what the trainee is expected to learn. Objectives relate directly to expected performance and are excellent for testing purposes.

After needs and objectives have been established, the training can be developed. This is where the trainer decides the who, what, when, where, why, and how of the course. The information is assembled and developed into a structured lesson plan that serves as a guide for the instructor to present the information. Time, available resources, costs, and type of audience are all factors requiring consideration in the development of training.

Assessing Training Effectiveness

After the training has been presented, an evaluation of its effectiveness should follow. Training that is currently successful and applicable may soon become outdated. The two most common methods of assessing training are examinations and student evaluations. The Federal Bureau of Investigation's Instructor Development Course recommends four steps to complete a total course assessment:

1. Evaluation reaction. How well did the trainee like the training?
2. Learning evaluation. What principal facts and techniques were learned?
3. Behavior evaluation. What job behavior resulted from the training program?
4. Results. What were the tangible results of the program—reduced costs, improved performance, reduced liability?

These questions may be answered in a well-constructed evaluation form; a sample training evaluation form is shown in Figure 5–2. Student examinations and course evaluations provide important and necessary feedback mechanisms to evaluate the effectiveness of both the instructor and the curriculum. With this information the trainer can revamp and update courses and/or change methods of instruction to better meet officer and organizational needs.

Instructor: _____   Course: _____

In an effort to improve this course, we would appreciate your candid comments concerning the following items. Thank you for your cooperation.

1. How would you rate the content of this course in terms of its value to you?

   Poor   Average   Excellent
    1   2   3   4   5

2. Do you believe the course objectives were met by the instructor?

    Yes   No   Partially

   Comments:

3. What topical area covered was of most benefit to you?

4. Identify the weak areas of the course that either need to be strengthened or eliminated.

5. How would you rate the overall performance of the instructor?

   Poor   Average   Excellent
    1   2   3   4   5

6. Was the instructor prepared, with adequate material, and utilize a lesson plan?

7. Can you offer any suggestions to help the Instructor improve?

8. Please offer any other comments or suggestions you think will improve the quality of this course.

FIGURE 5–2. Sample Training Evaluation Form

TRAINING MATERIALS

A variety of instructional materials are available to improve a training curriculum. Those conducting training should consider a range of different training tools and materials to make the training more meaningful and lasting, such as the following:

Visual Aids

The old adage "a picture is worth a thousand words" is very true where training is concerned. Visual aids can greatly enhance a presentation and help reduce the gap between speaking and listening. The most common and simplest types of visual aids are overheads, computer graphics, films, videotapes, chalkboards, and flip charts.

Audio- and Videocassettes

As training requirements continue to increase, police departments are finding it more difficult to free personnel to attend mandated annual training because of scheduling concerns and the lack of personnel to cover shifts while officers attend training. Short videotapes and audiotapes are excellent methods of delivering training during roll call sessions. They also provide supervisors the

104

*PART TWO
Supervising Human
Resources: Training,
Evaluation, and
Discipline*

flexibility of assigning one officer at a time to review a videotape or listen to an audiotape during nonpeak hours of a shift, or to take training videos home to review on their own time. However, the Fair Labor Standards Act (FLSA) and employee contracts may prohibit home checkout, or at least require the department to compensate employees for the time devoted for this purpose.

Video Simulation

Interactive **video simulation** adds realism to police training in a variety of areas, including driver's training, domestic violence, and firearms. Several companies offer "shoot-don't-shoot" simulators that present 40 or more scenarios involving night vehicle stops, drug deals, domestic violence, armed robberies, and hostage situations; these often challenge the officer to make a deadly force decision and add stress and realism to the training. The instructor can use the computer to change the scenario. The system evaluates the officer's decision to shoot, shooting technique, and accuracy. Most systems offer a variety of realistic guns that shoot plastic bullets at a 10–20 foot screen. The system's computer logs every shooting exercise for records detention purposes and examines previous reaction times and decision-making ability.

Computer-Assisted Training

Today's police recruits are more comfortable and skilled with computer technology than officers who entered policing in the 1970s or 1980s. According to a national study (LEMAS, 1993) of local police departments, nearly all departments serving a population of more than 10,000 residents were using one or more types of computers in their operations. Many courses are being adapted to the personal computer for instruction purposes. This affords students the opportunity to engage in learning at their own pace and the department the flexibility of providing training in a format that may have the least impact on scheduling.

Teleconferencing

The advancement and availability of communications satellite technology during the past few years has made **teleconferencing** more available to departments. Through interactive teleconferencing, colleges, universities, and government agencies can transmit a training session from one site to an unlimited number of sites across the country. Unlike videotapes, teleconferencing allows for two-way conversation between the presenter and viewers. Most important, it allows a variety of training opportunities with minimal costs and coordination (Gilman, 1997).

Television Programming

The **Law Enforcement Television Network (LETN)** is policing's answer to Cable Network News (CNN). LETN provides a 24-hour-a-day television schedule of programming on various police issues. Agencies pay a monthly fee for satellite connection. Programs can be taped and shown at the convenience of the agency and offer an excellent tool for agencies that cannot afford training and struggle with state-mandated requirements. LETN's short format makes it well suited for roll call and in-service courses. It is important to note that supervisors should review all such outside training materials to ensure they do not present any liabilities. For example, methods for conducting high-risk vehicle stops and weaponless defense procedures may vary greatly between jurisdictions.

Internet

Use of the Internet has greatly expanded in recent years. An increasing number of police and other government agencies have developed their own "home page" containing volumes of information. For a very low cost, the Internet allows police officers to communicate with their colleagues across the nation or abroad about policies and programs, and to exchange ideas and information. The Internet is becoming an invaluable research and communication tool for the trainer and supervisor. Following are some Internet addresses where trainers and supervisors can conduct research and gain information about virtually anything about law enforcement.

National Criminal Justice Research Service. A clearinghouse of publications and on-line reference service about a broad range of criminal justice issues. http://www.ncjrs.org

National Law Enforcement and Corrections Technology Center. Provides information about new equipment and technologies to federal, state, and local law enforcement and corrections officials. http://www.nlectc.org

U.S. Department of Justice. Includes information about a wide range of research, training, and grants. http://www.usdoj.gov

Community Policing Consortium. A compendium of information about community policing and problem-solving training and funding under the crime bill. http://www.community policing.org

Bureau of Justice Statistics. Includes a variety of information about Criminal Justice Statistics and provides links to other research Web sites. http://www.ojp.usdoj.gov/bjs

Law Enforcement Sites on the Web. Lists all Federal, State, and Local Agencies on the Web. http://www.ih2000.net/ira/ira.htm

COPNET. Myriad information about police training, job opportunities, links to other agencies, and chat rooms to various subjects. http://police.sas.ab.ca/

E-Mail

Electronic mail (E-mail) is becoming a common means of communication in police agencies and has replaced the traditional paper memorandum system. Through a local area network (LAN), E-mail links an entire organization

106

PART TWO
Supervising Human
Resources: Training,
Evaluation, and
Discipline

through personal computers. Within seconds, a simple message between employees or a lengthy new policy, training bulletin, or document can be sent to an entire agency.

THE SUPERVISOR'S OWN PROFESSIONAL DEVELOPMENT

Requisite Skills

Once police officers are promoted to a supervisory position, an entirely different world of policing emerges for them. Supervisors are the backbone of an organization. Promotion forces them into situations they probably have never experienced. The dual demands of operations and administration are overwhelming at times and require an entirely new set of knowledge and skills to be successful.

The IACP (1985:81) noted that promotion "represents probably the most critical and challenging adjustment for the employee who must, for the first time, supervise the performance of others in the agency." These special supervisory skills require most agencies to look outside their departments for relevant training. Commonly, agencies depend on state POSTs to provide such training.

While a specialized course on supervision will provide the new supervisor with needed professional management skills and knowledge, the application of new knowledge may be provided through a field training program similar to that discussed above for patrol officers. For example, some agencies require that new supervisors complete a structured field training program of up to six or more weeks before being assigned to supervise a team of officers. A shift lieutenant assumes the role of FTO and utilizes a critical task manual to evaluate the newly promoted supervisor's field performance. A number of supervisory dimensions are evaluated, including role identification, leadership, employee performance appraisal, discipline, employee relations, training, report review, and critical incident management. Then, upon completion of the field training program, the supervisor is assigned to manage a team of officers in a uniformed patrol division. Figure 5–3 is an example of the training and critical incident sections of a critical task manual for supervisors.

A number of sources of information and skills are also relevant to police supervision. Probably the three most important subject areas pertinent to police supervision are police work, supervision, and management. Police supervisors need to continually maintain and enhance their knowledge and skills relating to the business they are supervising (police work), their current responsibilities (supervision), and those responsibilities to which they may soon advance (management). In addition to these three subjects, and in some ways overlapping them, police supervisors should continually seek to improve their skills in oral and written communication, reasoning, analysis, and human relations.

Next, we discuss other related aspects of a supervisor's professional development in the three areas of police work, supervision, and management: training, education, literature, professional and civic organizations, and assignments.

	Instructed by Trainer Trainer's Initials/Date	Satisfactorily Understood Trainee Initials
Training: The supervisor will understand the responsibilities of being a trainer		
1. Understands the instructional role of the supervisor.		
2. Understands the elements of the agency's FTO program and supervisory responsibilities.		
3. Understands the need to plan, schedule, and conduct roll call training.		
4. Understands the need to evaluate the training subordinates received:		
a. To ensure it meets their needs.		
b. To ensure they are applying what they learned.		
5. Is aware of the training resources that are available within the agency.		
6. Understands the career development process and provides subordinates proper guidance.		
7. Understands the concepts of *vicarious liability* and *failure to train.*		
8. Critical Incident Management: The supervisor will demonstrate an understanding of the agency's procedures in managing critical incidents utilizing the critical Incident Checklist:		
a. Bomb threats		
b. Barricaded suspect		
c. Command post operations		
d. Hazardous materials spills		
e. Use of SWAT/Hostage Negotiations		
f. Multiagency operations		
g. Officer-involved shootings		
h. Other disasters		

UPON COMPLETION PLACE IN MASTER TRAINING FILE

FIGURE 5–3. Supervisor's Critical Task Guide

Training

One obvious route to supervisory professional development is training. Whenever possible, new supervisors should receive basic supervisory training on their promotion or, at the latest, very soon thereafter. This type of training typically lasts for a week or longer and generally is provided, or at least certified, in each state by the Peace Officer Standards and Training (POST) Commission or a similar entity. Larger police departments often conduct this training themselves for their own supervisors and sometimes make spaces available to personnel from other agencies.

In states that mandate annual in-service training for all police personnel, the annual training of supervisors should be geared toward developing their police, supervision, and management knowledge and skills. Refresher courses, updates, and training in new subjects should all contribute to the supervisor's professional development. One noteworthy example is the Law Enforcement Management Institute of Texas (LEMIT). The core program within LEMIT is the Graduate Management Institute (GMI), comprised of a one-week and three two-week modules. The modules focus on developing writing and analytical skills (including computer skills) and on three substantive topics: business management, Texas government and politics, and police administration. Each module is scheduled several times a year and held at various locations throughout the state. LEMIT also offers a variety of shorter executive issues seminars and special topics programs each year.

At the national level, several highly regarded institutions offer professional development courses appropriate for police supervisors and/or higher-ranking police executives. Among the best known of these are the Federal Bureau of Investigation's National Academy, the Police Executive Research Forum's Senior Management Institute for Police, the Southwestern Law Enforcement Institute's Command and Management College, and the long courses offered by the Northwestern University Traffic Institute and the Southern Police Institute. Shorter courses are offered by the International Association of Chiefs of Police, the Federal Law Enforcement Training Center, and the Institute for Police Technology and Management, among others.

Supervisors should also be aware of training opportunities outside the police industry. Local and state governments, the federal government, universities, private companies, and private vendors often offer a variety of general supervision, management, and administration courses.

Higher Education

The purposes of higher education are broader and more general than those of training, although the line gets harder to draw as training becomes more sophisticated and education seeks to become more practical (Haley, 1992). Police officers and supervisors can benefit from education in many subjects beyond police administration or criminal justice: psychology, sociology, political science, public administration, history, business, and the humanities, to name a few. Any education that broadens one's outlook and contributes to police supervisors' reading, writing, reasoning, and management skills and their understanding of people, organizations, and society is likely to be beneficial to them individually and to their departments.

Higher education seems a logical necessity to prepare rank-and-file officers and supervisors and middle managers to cope effectively with the difficult demands of police work. Yet, higher education continues to be one of most controversial and debated issues among academics and police administrators alike. There is increasing empirical evidence supporting the need for higher education for police officers and supervisors. Studies have found that educated officers:

- Have significantly fewer citizen complaints than their non-college-educated counterparts (Kappeler et al., 1992).
- Have better peer relationships and are likelier to take a leadership role in the organization (Weirman, 1978).
- Tend to be more flexible (Trojanowicz and Nicholson, 1976).
- Are less dogmatic and authoritarian (Dalley, 1975).
- Have lower absenteeism, take less time off, and are involved in fewer traffic accidents (Cascio, 1977).
- Have a greater ability to analyze situations and make judicious decisions, and have a more desirable system of personal values consistent with the police function in a modern society (Sterling, 1974).
- Are less insubordinate (Lynch, 1987).

The emergence of community-oriented policing and problem solving (COPPS) has also been cited to argue the need for higher education of police officers (Carter and Sapp, 1992). The knowledge and skills required of officers under COPPS—to be an effective decision maker, service provider, communicator and problem solver—makes college education even more critical.

Literature

One mark of professionals is that they keep up with developments in their fields, largely by reading their field's professional literature. Police supervisors should pursue this approach to professional development by keeping up with books, government publications, and periodicals pertinent to policing and police supervision. This is difficult to do, of course, because dozens of books on police topics and enormous numbers of government documents are published every year, and since police supervisors have many other demands on their time.

The most feasible approach involves two methods. The first is to register with the National Criminal Justice Reference Service (NCJRS), a no-cost federally funded service that notifies criminal justice professionals each month of relevant new publications. Perusing the monthly *NCJRS Bulletin* is a quick way to identify new publications of interest and to determine how to obtain them (some are free).[1]

The other key method for keeping up with the literature is to rely on periodicals: newsletters, magazines, and journals. These periodicals, because they

---

[1]To register with the NCJRS, call 1-800-851-3420 or 1-301-251-5500. It is easy to register and it really is free.

110

PART TWO
Supervising Human
Resources: Training,
Evaluation, and
Discipline

come out several times a year, are generally more current than books and they also present information in a more condensed format. In addition, they frequently contain reviews of recently published books.

The police field now has a surprising number of periodicals. Some contain advertising, but many do not. Some cater more to an audience of police practitioners while others aim more toward policy makers and police educators. Some of the better known police periodicals are briefly described below.

FBI Law Enforcement Bulletin. A magazine-style periodical published monthly by the FBI. Contains articles on various police-related issues, legal analyses, book reviews, and regular features. Readable and informative.

Law & Order. A privately published monthly magazine that contains extensive advertising, short articles describing contemporary police practices, and opinion pieces.

Law Enforcement News. A newspaper-style periodical published every two weeks by the John Jay College of Criminal Justice in New York City. Contains news items, short articles, and interviews with police officials. Very useful for keeping up with current events in the police field.

Police Computer Review. A quarterly newsletter/bulletin devoted to computer applications in the police field. Contains short articles and regular features such as product updates, tips and tricks, and training calendars.

Police Forum. A quarterly newsletter of the Police Section, Academy of Criminal Justice Sciences. Contains short articles and book reviews.

Police Liability Review. A quarterly newsletter published by Alpha Enterprises of Richmond, Kentucky. Contains short articles and extensive excerpts from state and federal court decisions pertaining to police civil liability.

Subject to Debate. A quarterly newsletter of the Police Executive Research Forum. Contains short articles, organization news, legislative updates, and other regular features.

The Police Chief. A monthly magazine of the International Association of Chiefs of Police. Contains extensive advertising, legal notes, short articles describing contemporary police practices, organization news, and regular features such as positions open.

Professional Organizations

Another mark of professionals is that they organize to share information and further their interests. There are no organizations focused exclusively on police supervision, but there are several prominent national organizations for police specialists and police managers. Regular or associate membership in these organizations would generally be open to police supervisors. Among the many specialized professional organizations are the American Society of Law Enforcement Trainers, the International Association of Crime Analysts, and the International Association of Computer Investigative Specialists. Seven more general purpose professional organizations are briefly described below.

International Association of Chiefs of Police. The primary membership organization of police chief executives. Provides publications, training, consulting, and other membership services and holds a major annual conference.

International Association of Law Enforcement Planners. A membership organization catering to police planners, analysts, and middle managers. Provides a newsletter, certifies police planners, maintains a database of police programs, and holds an annual conference.

National Organization of Black Law Enforcement Executives. A membership organization that represents and gives a voice to African Americans in policing. Develops new programs and provides various membership services.

National Sheriffs Association. The primary membership organization for sheriffs, an often overlooked group of law enforcement executives. Provides publications, training, consulting, and other membership services and holds an annual conference.

Police Executive Research Forum. A membership organization for police chief executives of larger jurisdictions. A college degree is also required for membership. Conducts studies; develops new programs; provides publications, training, and consulting; and holds an annual meeting.

National Association of Field Training Officers. A membership organization comprised of Field Training Officers.

Police Section, Academy of Criminal Justice Sciences. The Academy of Criminal Justice Sciences is the primary membership organization for faculty teaching criminal justice in colleges and universities. The Police Section of the Academy provides a newsletter for its members and helps organize the police portion of the annual conference. Among its members, the Academy has many police and criminal justice practitioners and students in addition to teachers and researchers.

Assignments

In larger police organizations, an important element in the professional development of supervisors involves assigning them in such a way that they acquire a broad base of experience and understanding. This inevitably requires a balancing act between specialized expertise and generalized knowledge. For example, if a narcotics detective is promoted to sergeant and left in the narcotics unit, he or she will have the advantage of in-depth familiarity with the specialized work performed in the unit. On the other hand, if this supervisor remains in the narcotics unit for an extended period, he or she will become increasingly inexperienced and unfamiliar with the work done in the rest of the police department. This would in turn have three important consequences: the supervisor would become less qualified to perform other supervisory functions in the agency, reducing assignment options; the supervisor would become a less attractive candidate for promotion, since jobs farther up the ladder require broader rather than narrower expertise; and the supervisor's allegiance would likely focus more on the special unit rather than on the whole organization, thus ultimately impeding the achievement of overall goals and objectives.

In a larger police agency, any supervisor or manager who becomes too closely identified with any specialized activity runs the risk of short-circuiting his or her career opportunities, for the reasons outlined above. This is especially dangerous for certain combinations of officers and assignments: women officers and women supervisors, for example, must avoid becoming stereotyped as clerical or administrative personnel and minority officers should avoid being labeled solely as community relations officers. These observations are made not because administrative duties and community relations are any less important elements of the police business than other activities, but because one's career options could become limited because of overspecialization in those areas.

Again, balance is the key, both for the individual supervisor and for the police organization. Individuals must take what opportunities are available, but whenever possible they should seek assignments that correct weaknesses or lack of experience in certain aspects of policing. The police department should make supervisory assignments that lead to the grooming of future executives while also ensuring that the organization's work gets done efficiently and effectively.

THE SUPERVISOR AS TRAINER

The supervisor's primary function is to obtain results through people. They are judged on their ability to get those persons who work for them to accomplish their agency's mission, goals, and objectives. Training is a very important tool in obtaining the desired results. As More and Wegener (1996:435) observed:

> Everything a supervisor does in directing the work force has some element of training in it; conversely, every training activity involves an element of supervision. Supervision and training are inherent in the sergeant's role. [He or she makes] an incalculable contribution to the growth and development of the department's human resources.

Furthermore, Whisenand and Rush (1993) noted that the supervisor's job is to create opportunities, release potential, remove obstacles, encourage growth, and provide guidance.

In this same vein, we also know that "good teaching does not just happen—it is not accidental. It is a result of careful preparation. Success or failure in any instruction program is seldom due to the efforts of the learner alone. The major portion of the responsibility rests upon the individual instructor . . ." (Barlow, 1951:iii).

Much of the success and failure of an organization rests with the supervisor's ability to guide and train officers to perform their duties within the law and in accordance with departmental goals and objectives. An officer's attitude, performance, perceptions, motivation, stress, and job satisfaction are strongly influenced by the supervisor. Most of the training provided by supervisors is informal and involves daily interaction with subordinates, conducting roll call training, and continuous counseling, advising, guiding, and coaching on proper police procedures and difficult field situations. The result of this close working relationship is a trust and respect that does not exist between other ranks in the organization.

A unique aspect of the supervisor's role as trainer concerns the successful implementation of community policing and problem solving (COPPS), discussed above and more fully in Chapter 13. One of the most difficult hurdles for supervisors to overcome with COPPS is the idea that giving officers the opportunity to be creative and take risks does not diminish the supervisor's role or authority. Risk taking and innovation require mutual trust between supervisors and line officers. Supervising in a COPPS environment means taking on the role of "facilitator" and "coach" for officers. Supervisors must learn to encourage innovation and risk taking among their officers, and they must be well skilled in problem solving, especially in the analysis of problems and evaluation of efforts. Conducting workload analysis and finding the time for officers to solve problems and engage with the community is an important aspect of supervision. A supervisor must also be prepared to intercede and remove any roadblocks to officers' problem-solving efforts.

Obviously, the training of subordinates is not an easy task, and it cannot be assumed that every newly promoted supervisor will succeed as a trainer. But as supervisors gain experience and develop their interpersonal skills, they should find their training role much easier to perform. Any group of police officers will be composed of individuals with varying skills, knowledge, and abilities. To correctly assess their individual needs, the supervisor must first consider the officer's career background, previous training, educational level, and career aspirations.

The attributes needed for one to become a good supervisor-trainer include strong interpersonal skills, such as coaching, mentoring, and an interest in human resource development. Patience is also required, because employees learn at different rates and the trainer must determine the best approach and methods to employ.

It is also important to note that correcting an officer's behavior also serves a training purpose. Discipline, where applied correctly, teaches the officer what is unacceptable behavior. Thus, training and discipline often accomplish the same objective—a change in employee behavior. For this reason training is often a recommendation in the disciplinary process (see Chapter 9).

These are several benefits that training offers for the supervisor (More and Wegener, 1996):

1. *Getting to know subordinates.* Training helps to understand their needs, wants, and potential. This information can be factored into decisions concerning discipline, transfers, promotions, and pay raises.
2. *Promoting good human relations.* Through training, police officers gain self-confidence, pride, and a sense of security. The supervisor's actions give subordinates reasons to cooperate with their peers and the administration. Training helps establish unity of purpose, trust, and mutual respect.
3. *Feeling good about accomplishments.* Training subordinates to do a good job produces a good feeling and motivates the supervisor to put forth more effort.
4. *Furthering one's own career.* As subordinates grow in abilities, expertise, and reputation, so will the supervisor. As subordinates look better, feel better, and perform better, they enhance one's reputation as a supervisor.

The supervisor must be a trainer, coach, and mentor. Here a supervisor trains SWAT officers in team movement.
Courtesy of Reno Police Department, Nevada

5. *Gaining more time.* Training helps to make subordinates more confident and self-sufficient. As their performance improves, the supervisor spends less time correcting their behavior. This time can be invested in other supervisory functions, such as planning, organizing, and coordinating.

TRAINING AND LIABILITY ISSUES

In Chapter 8 we will discuss the broad issue of liability. Federal and state laws hold agencies and their supervisors liable for acts of negligence. The importance of training from a liability perspective cannot be overemphasized. The failure to train officers and supervisors in this regard has resulted in costly litigation against departments; furthermore, the negligence of police supervisors is currently one of the most frequently litigated areas of liability. The public's inclination to sue individual officers, supervisory personnel, and chiefs of police is quite strong. The courts have sent a clear message: Supervisors may be held accountable for the negligence and wrongful acts of their subordinates.

Supervisors are expected to keep their personnel properly informed and trained and to take necessary action to correct problems and prevent future harm. The failure to do so may result in a lawsuit for failing to act or properly train personnel. Case Study 5–2 illustrates the importance of proper training procedures without which police officers and supervisors could face liability charges. The following checklist should help agencies and supervisors guard against liability (Thibault et al., 1995):

Case Study 5–2
The "Too Cool for School" Supervisor, or How to Conduct Training in Absentia

Sergeant Arnold Kazinsky has been with the state police for nearly 30 years. His reputation is legendary for being a no-nonsense, hard-nosed veteran, as are stories about the record number of citations he has written over the years. Kazinsky often yearns for a return to the days when troopers were hired and given a map, citation book, the keys to a cruiser, and assigned to work by their sergeant. Kazinsky does not agree with the contemporary emphasis on trooper training, and feels that the troopers' time can be better spent on the road instead of in the classroom.

When state headquarters issues a series of officer safety videos to be shown at briefings, in typical fashion Kazinsky does not take the training seriously. He plays the videotapes during briefings as told, but turns down the volume so low that it is almost impossible to hear them. Furthermore, he does not distribute the accompanying handout materials for discussion, and even leaves the room while the training video is playing, allowing the troopers freedom to banter among themselves at will.

Meanwhile, Trooper Benjamin Scott, who has just completed the nine-month basic training academy, is assigned to work for Sgt. Kazinsky. Scott idolizes the legendary Kazinsky and wants to do his best to please his first supervisor. At briefing, even with the training video sound turned low,

Scott strains to watch and hear the video intently, in hopes of picking up some new methods for performing his job better.

That evening Scott is dispatched to a suspicious person call at a highway truck stop. Scott uses a frisk technique he saw earlier that day on the briefing video, patting the suspect down with one hand while holding his shotgun in the other. The shotgun accidentally discharges, killing the suspect. Internal Affairs later discovers that the video was actually a demonstration on how *not* to frisk a suspect. The discussion during the video and the handout materials made that very clear, and a training staff member was supposed to be present to emphasize the point. However, without any training or supervisory personnel making it clear to all who saw the video, this major point obviously was lost to the viewers.

1. Did Kazinsky err? If so, how? Is he civilly liable?
2. Do you feel Trooper Scott is blameworthy?
3. In this chapter we discussed many different types of training. How can training create liability for supervisors?
4. How can training that is national in scope be in conflict with local ordinances or policies? What should an agency do to ensure that the wrong training information is not distributed to officers?

1. Do not allow untrained officers to perform any field police duties.
2. Official department policies should be reflected in training. Critical issues such as deadly force, pursuit driving, arrest procedures, and weaponless defense should be carefully outlined in the context of academy and updated in-service training courses.
3. All lesson plans, policies, training bulletins, and instructional techniques should be reviewed periodically and updated.

SUMMARY

This chapter has examined many aspects of police and supervisory training, which occupies a central position in contemporary supervision. The changing nature of U.S. society and its laws, coupled with increasing technology and

116

PART TWO
Supervising Human
Resources: Training,
Evaluation, and
Discipline

diversity, places incredible demands on officers and supervisors to maintain the skills, knowledge, and abilities to perform their duties proficiently. Supervisors fill a unique position in an organization's structure to assess officers' training needs and to provide employees with the necessary instruction and guidance. We also noted that training is very important for supervisors themselves; among the avenues of professional growth for police supervisors are training, education, literature, professional and civic organizations, and assignments that contribute to career development.

This chapter pointed out that training begins in the academy and continues through a variety of means including roll call, in-service, and specialized training formats. The success of the supervisor as a trainer is often directly related to the success of officers and the organization in carrying out their goals and objectives.

We also saw that the failure of supervisors to properly train or recognize the need for training can create tremendous liability for an organization. Liability alone requires that agencies take training seriously and obligate the necessary people and resources to organize, plan, and document all courses taught.

KEY TERMS

Peace Officers Standards and Training (POST) (p. 94)

Commission on Accreditation for Law Enforcement Agencies (CALEA) (p. 94)

field training officer (FTO) program (p. 97)

daily observation report (DOR) (p. 98)

roll call (p. 101)

in-service training (p. 101)

training needs assessment (p. 102)

video simulation (p. 104)

teleconferencing (p. 104)

Law Enforcement Television Network (LETN) (p. 104)

ITEMS FOR REVIEW

1. Explain the status and types of police training.
2. Describe what is meant by field training officer (FTO) programs.
3. What is the supervisor's role in police training?
4. Delineate the components of a police training program. What instructional materials are needed?
5. Outline the steps involved in a supervisor's professional development program.
6. Describe the benefits that accrue to the supervisor who provides training.
7. Explain how supervisors may be liable for inadequate training of their subordinates.

SOURCES

BARLOW, M. (1951). *Instructor's guide for roll call training.* Los Angeles: Los Angeles Police Department.

BROWN, M. P., and HENDRICKS, J. E. (1996). "The future of cultural awareness training." *Police Chief* (November): 56–60.

CARTER, D. L., and SAPP, A. D. (1992). "College education and policing: Coming of age." *FBI Law Enforcement Bulletin* 1: 8–14.

CASCIO, W. F. (1977). "Formal education and police officer performance." *Journal of Police Science and Administration* 5: 89–96.

DALLEY, A. F. (1975). "University and non-university graduated policemen: A study of police attitudes." *Journal of Police Science and Administration* 3: 458–68.

DOUGHTRY, S. (1996). "Time to take another look at law enforcement accreditation." *Police Chief* (November): 20–23.

GILMAN, D. (1997). "Satellite televideo training: Access made easy." *Government Technology* 10(4): 64–65.

HALEY, K. N. (1992). "Training." In G. W. Cordner and D. C. Hale, (eds.). *What Works in Policing? Operations and Administration Examined.* Cincinnati, Ohio: Anderson.

INTERNATIONAL ASSOCIATION OF CHIEFS OF POLICE (1985). *Police supervision.* Arlington, Va: IACP.

KAPPELER, V. E., SAPP, A. D., and CARTER, D. E. (1992). "Police officer higher education, citizen complaints and departmental rule violations." *American Journal of Police* (November): 37–54.

LYNCH, G. W. (1987). "Cops and college." *America* (April 4):274–75.

MCCAMBELL, M. S. (1986). *Field training for police officers: State of the art.* Research in Brief. Washington, D.C.: National Institute of Justice.

MOORE, M. H., and STEPHENS, D. W. (1991). *Beyond command and control: The strategic management of police departments.* Washington, D.C.: Police Executive Research Forum.

MORE, H. W., and WEGENER, W. F. (1996). *Effective police supervision.* 2d ed. Cincinnati, Ohio: Anderson.

ROSSETT, A. (1987). *Training needs assessment.* Englewood Cliffs, N.J.: Educational Technology Publications.

STERLING, J. W. (1974). "The college level entry requirement: A real or imagined cure-all?" *Police Chief* (8): 28–31.

THIBAULT, E. T., LYNCH, L. M., and MCBRIDE, R. B. (1995). *Proactive police management.* 3rd ed. Englewood Cliffs N.J.: Prentice Hall.

TROJANOWICZ, R., and NICHOLSON, T. (1976). "A comparison of behavioral styles of college graduate police officers v. non-college going police officers." *Police Chief* 43 (August): 58–59.

UNITED STATES DEPARTMENT OF JUSTICE, BUREAU OF JUSTICE STATISTICS (1993). *Local police departments.* Executive Summary, Washington, D.C.: U.S. Department of Justice.

UNITED STATES DEPARTMENT OF JUSTICE, BUREAU OF JUSTICE STATISTICS (1993). *Local police departments.* Law Enforcement Management Administration Statistics (LEMAS) report. Washington, D.C.: U.S. Department of Justice.

WEIRMAN, C. L. (1978). Variances of ability measurement scores obtained by college and non-college educated troopers. *The Police Chief* (May): 34–36.

WHISENAND, P. M., and RUSH, G. E. (1993). *Supervising police personnel,* 2d ed. Englewood Cliffs, N.J.: Prentice Hall.

6

Evaluation and Performance Appraisal

Excellence is to do a common thing in an uncommon way.
—Booker T. Washington

Excellent firms don't believe in excellence, only in constant improvement and constant change.
—Tom Peters

INTRODUCTION

As we have noted so far in this book, police supervisors have the very important responsibility of ensuring that officers effectively perform tasks, diligently attend to responsibilities, and work toward the department's goals and objectives. Supervisors are responsible for coordinating officers' activities and ensuring that their activities meet organizational expectations. Supervisors must also hold officers accountable by reviewing their activities and providing them feedback when their activities are deficient.

These are not easy tasks; many supervisors, both new and old, find the obligation to evaluate and appraise the performance of their subordinates an intimidating exercise. But for most supervisors, this is a "make or break" component of supervision. One can hardly be called a supervisor if not fairly and accurately rating subordinates.

This chapter explores several issues surrounding police officer evaluation and appraisal. The chapter is divided into two primary sections: productivity measurement and management and performance appraisal. The productivity measurement and management section addresses how supervisors should collect information about subordinates' activities, how this information should be utilized, and how supervisors should go about improving subordinates' performance. Performance appraisal refers to the formal process police departments establish to measure officers' performance and to provide them with feedback on it. Most departments perform this activity on an annual or semi-annual basis.

PRODUCTIVITY MEASUREMENT

Productivity measurement is an important supervisory activity because supervisors must make judgments about the relative success of their subordinates. This generally entails comparing their productivity to some standard. In some cases officers are compared with each other, while in others they are compared with some universal department or unit standard. Departmental or unit standards are inherently superior to the comparison of averages for two reasons. First, if averages are used, half of the officers, regardless of productivity, will always be below the average. Second, if averages are used, it means that the work group, rather than supervisors or administrators, are setting productivity levels. Regardless of the method used, supervisors are faced with the prospect of developing productivity measures to accomplish this function.

A host of potential measures exists; that is, every activity a police officer performs can be measured. It is critical that supervisors focus on the correct measures, because officers pattern their behavior and activities on prescribed performance standards. For example, if a patrol sergeant emphasizes traffic citations, officers will tend to write more tickets and possibly neglect other activities. If the same sergeant fails to comment about or investigate officers' performance at domestic violence calls, officers may develop the attitude that such calls are unimportant and feel free to deal with them as they please. Thus, productivity measurement is very important in molding police officer behavior and contributes heavily to overall departmental effectiveness.

What Is Productivity?

Theoretically, **productivity** refers to how well the police provide services to citizens. It is the relationship between the resources used by a police department and the amount or level of services provided (Kuper, 1970). The National Commission on Productivity (1973:1) has defined productivity as "the return for a given unit of input." These definitions point to four general concerns when attempting to measure productivity: efficiency, effectiveness, equity, and accountability (Gaines et al., 1991). We will briefly discuss each concern.

Efficiency refers to the cost of accomplishing a given task with a minimum expenditure of resources. Constituents want to minimize inputs (resources devoted to the task) while maximizing outputs (desired outcomes). The supervisor must consider various strategies and implement those that not only achieve desired agency objectives, but also do so at the lowest cost. Also, once a program is implemented, it should be examined periodically to determine whether it can be made more efficient.

The calculation of efficiency measures is no easy task; costs of activities are generally computed by examining the number of personnel, amount of

120

PART TWO
Supervising Human
Resources: Training,
Evaluation, and
Discipline

equipment and staff support, and the number of noncapital supplies (e.g., gasoline, paper, and electricity consumed by the program). The cost of outputs, on the other hand, is either very difficult or impossible to compute; for example, how can a supervisor determine how many accidents or deaths were prevented by setting up a drunk-driving check lane?

Supervisors can maximize efficiency through assignment and supervision. For example, should detectives or patrol officers be assigned partners or should they work singly? How many patrol units should be assigned to calls? Can the department take some reports by telephone? All police activities should be monitored to ensure that only those resources necessary for the job are expended.

Effectiveness refers to how well the task is performed, regardless of cost, as a result of program activities: Were program goals met? The calculation of measures of effectiveness requires the identification of goals and goal-achievement strategies. If objectives were not completely met, how close did the program come to doing so? For example, a police supervisor might decide to implement a problem-solving initiative in an area with low-income housing that has had high numbers of **calls for service (CFS)** during the past six months. A goal might be set to, say, reduce the number of CFS by 25 percent in the next two months. Here, the objectives might include increased patrol, increased citizen contacts, conducting crime prevention activities, and neighborhood cleanups. Or, if officers are given an assignment or dispatched to a call, did they satisfactorily resolve the situation? For example, if officers must return repeatedly to family disturbance calls, it may indicate that they are taking inappropriate measures on the first occasion. Supervisors must follow up calls and activities to ensure that officers make every effort possible to adequately manage situations.

Equity is another important productivity measure. It refers to the quality of police services delivered to various groups in the community (see Hepburn, 1981). This refers to the notion that all citizens' problems should receive the same level of concern. This is accomplished through operational planning. Equity in police services frequently becomes a political focal point. Citizens are concerned with the number of patrol units in their area, the probability of being victimized, and the response time of the police. If police services in their area are perceived to be consistent with those of other areas, citizens are more likely to have a positive image of the police.

Supervisors must ensure that officers do not discriminate on the basis of race, gender, economic class, religion, national origin, or any other human characteristic. Our democratic values dictate that we treat all citizens equally. The police, as guardians of the Constitution, must ensure that all people are treated accordingly.

Finally, the idea of **accountability** refers to whether inputs are used for proper purposes, and infers that the police are public servants and, consequently, should provide services that meet public concerns and needs (see Murphy, 1975). Police officers too often see their role as "crime fighters" and want to relegate other responsibilities. However, research indicates that the public consistently requests the police to be more involved in peacekeeping and service activities than in law enforcement activities (Lab, 1984; Wilson, 1968). Supervisors must ensure that officers meet these citizen demands.

Traditional Views

Historically, the police have been more concerned with efficiency than effectiveness, equity, or accountability. Police managers and supervisors have been primarily concerned with the number of activities generated by officers or units. Such measures include the number of citations issued, number of arrests, percentage of cases cleared by arrest, number of citizen complaints about police services and conduct, conviction rates, and amount of stolen property recovered. These conventional measures, collected by most agencies, have been used as the primary source of officer performance criteria; however, they do not indicate that the department, unit, or officers are striving to achieve specified goals and objectives or that they have achieved these goals or objectives. For example, police officers may write large numbers of traffic citations, but if they are written at locations where there are few accidents or for violations other than those that contribute to accidents at specific locations, the officers' efforts will not contribute to the objective of reducing traffic accidents.

Patrol, the backbone of any police department, has been examined in a variety of ways to generate productivity measures. Mastrofski (1984) discussed measuring patrol productivity in terms of individual officers' knowledge of their patrol areas. Knowledge of the patrol beat is of critical importance and a prerequisite to effective policing (Van Maanen, 1974; Rubinstein, 1973). Unfortunately, police departments seldom measure what officers know about the area

The number of reports, citations, and arrests by officers are traditional performance measures still in use by many police agencies.

122

PART TWO
Supervising Human
Resources: Training,
Evaluation, and
Discipline

or people they police. Thus, there is no organizational reason for officers to attempt to learn their beats. Officers without adequate knowledge of their beats tend to be reactive and to deal superficially with calls and problems.

Others have proposed more traditional measures for patrol productivity. The National Commission on Productivity (1973) considered the availability of patrol to be the most critical factor. The commission advocated increasing the number of officers assigned to patrol, use of special tactical units to assist with directed patrol activities, flexible scheduling, and simplification of administrative chores. The thrust of the commission was to reemphasize patrol over specialized units, to maximize patrol officer time spent with patrolling, and to focus on the deterrence of crime, apprehension of criminal offenders, and the provision of noncrime services. The commission viewed efficiency as the first step in improving police patrol.

Others have taken productivity a step further and conceptualized it in terms of outputs (Hatry, 1975; Hirsch and Riccio, 1974). These researchers advocated factors such as the number of arrests surviving the first judicial screening relative to the number of patrol hours for each arrest; convictions relative to arrests; the number of patrol officers relative to the total number of sworn personnel in the department; patrol response time; and the amount of sick time taken in relation to the number of available officers. These researchers attempted not only to examine critical patrol areas, but also to place them in a context that would allow for comparisons over time and across departments. For example, the number of felony convictions divided by the number of felony arrests provides information well beyond what the number of arrests provide. It describes the "quality" of investigations and cases. When examined in terms of individual officers, it identifies officers who are not proficient in investigations and court presentations.

Research indicates that there is substantial variation among officers. Walsh (1985) examined the arrests for one precinct in New York City in 1980 and found varying rates of felony arrests across patrol officers. He found that 63 officers did not make a felony arrest during the year, 59 officers had 1 to 8 felony arrests, 19 officers had 9 to 20 felony arrests, and 15 officers had 25 to 69 felony arrests. Walsh's data demonstrate the importance of monitoring productivity. Every critical area of police work can be examined similarly.

Planning and Problem Solving

The above section addresses some of the traditional views of productivity measurement, especially as applied to police patrol. These views focus on internal uses and considerations, but fail to link them to external needs and requirements. Longmire (1993) has referred to this problem as the "activity trap." An activity trap is an easily quantifiable activity that police managers remain content to measure instead of examining the effects of the activity on problems. Measurement of police activities must go beyond efficiency and focus on effectiveness, accountability, and equity. Police supervisors and managers must think beyond bean counting—measuring police productivity by counting activities.

If a police agency is to be productive, a large percentage of its officers' activities must relate to solving some community problem or helping citizens. Po-

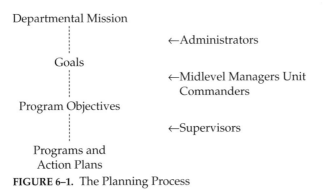

FIGURE 6–1. The Planning Process

lice departments have attempted to accomplish this objective through **planning,** which may be defined as "an orderly, systematic, and continuous process of bringing anticipations of the future to bear on present decisions" (Department of Justice, Law Enforcement Assistance Administration, 1975). Planning is also, roughly stated, deciding what the police agency should be doing; it is the linking of current activities to future conditions. It is decision making regarding operational activities based on anticipated contingencies (Gaines et al., 1991).

As Figure 6–1 shows, top-level administrators monitor and evaluate the environment or community and identify police department goals; midlevel managers break these goals down into unit-level objectives and develop programs to accomplish the objectives; and finally, supervisors are charged with ensuring that officers perform according to operational plans and achieve the desired objectives. The planning process becomes the link between internal measures or productivity and external needs.

This planning model has a number of problems. First, police departments have difficulty in identifying overall goals for the department and, as such, often resort to general statements that provide little direction for lower-level managers and supervisors (Hoover, 1993). Second, when goals are identified, it becomes difficult to make adjustments when changes take place in the environment. This inflexibility results in discrepancies between services provided by the department and actual community need. Third, supervisors have little input into the system. They are not involved in designing work activities or performance measures; furthermore, they are provided little opportunity to criticize or make adjustments in organizational activities that are not working properly.

Formal planning has been abandoned in some departments in favor of management systems that focus on productivity and, therefore, the correction of some of these problems. Swanson, Territo, and Taylor (1993) advocated the use of total performance management (TPM) in policing. TPM consists of three principles:

1. The collection of data from customers and employees to provide information about both positive and negative aspects of performances, along with data about productivity.
2. Playing back the data in summarized forms to both managers and employees.
3. Managers and employees develop action plans to build on strengths and eliminate or reduce weaknesses (Swanson, et al., 1993:634).

124

PART TWO
Supervising Human
Resources: Training,
Evaluation, and
Discipline

With TPM, action planning is vested at lower levels of the police department which allows officers and supervisors to provide feedback into the planning process. In addition, because it involves obtaining data from citizens, it allows the department to understand and respond to community problems more rapidly. TPM constructs a management structure that is conducive to productivity. It is a bottom-up planning process whereby planning originates and is conducted at lower levels of the organization.

Another similar organizational form to enhance police productivity is community policing and problem solving (COPPS), first mentioned in Chapter 2 and to be discussed in detail in Chapter 13. Essentially, COPPS focuses on concerns in the community. Problem solving is the primary tactic used in this strategy, with the police department attempting to identify problems and then developing a plan to solve the problem. Each problem is handled differently, depending on the nature of the problem, and the police department works with other units of government or private agencies in deploying solutions.

The evaluative criteria employed in the traditional policing model, such as crime rates, clearance rates, and response times, have been problematic when applied to the professional model itself and are even less appropriate for the COPPS model. Geller and Swanger (1995) argued for a marriage between the quality and quantity of performance criteria, noting "who cares how many coffee beans we have got if the java tastes nasty!" These measures also fail to gauge the effect of crime prevention efforts. Under a COPPS philosophy, the department must change its criteria for determining the quality of officer performance. Following are some of the kinds of criteria that might be used in this appraisal:

- Identifying and solving local crime and disorder problems through a police-community consultation process.
- Higher reporting rates for both traditional crime categories and for nontraditional crime and disorder problems.
- Reducing the number of repeat calls for service from repeat addresses.
- Improving the satisfaction with police services by public users of those services, particularly victims of crime.
- Increasing the job satisfaction of police officers.
- Increasing the reporting of information of local crime and disorder problems by community residents and increasing the knowledge of the community and its problems by local beat officers.
- Decreasing the fear of personal victimization (Peak and Glensor, 1996:127).

Productivity is an important issue in policing. Too often, managers and supervisors fail to measure and take steps to improve productivity. When this occurs, the department is usually stagnant and ineffective in meeting the needs of the community. Every manager and supervisor in the police organization should constantly evaluate productivity so that they know where they stand and what changes must be made to get there.

PERFORMANCE APPRAISAL

Simply stated, performance appraisal is an evaluation of how employees do their jobs. Departments have used a variety of names to refer to the performance appraisal process: performance evaluation, activity audit, employee rating, or performance review. Generally, **performance appraisal** is a formal process whereby supervisors examine and rate subordinates' performance and provide them with feedback about their behavior. It is a formal process because departments generally have a system in which all officers are evaluated at the same time and by the same rating form and system.

A department's formal performance appraisal process should coexist and parallel the informal evaluation that supervisors constantly make of their subordinates' behavior and performance. The informal process allows supervisors to collect information for the performance appraisal and to take action and change subordinates' behavior that fails to comply with departmental expectations. Neither the formal nor informal process should supplant the other.

We provide examples of performance appraisal categories and forms later in this chapter.

Rationale and Purposes

Police departments generally identify three reasons for a formal performance appraisal:

1. Standardize the nature of the personnel decision-making process so that the rights of the job incumbent are fully represented.
2. Assure the public that the agency representatives are fully qualified to carry out their assigned duties.
3. Give the job incumbent necessary behavior modification information to maintain appropriate behaviors (Landy and Goodin, 1974:167).

Performance appraisal, in essence, is an accountability and control process. It is a system for ensuring accountability because the results can be used to evaluate individual officers, units within the police department, or the department as a whole. Administrators are able to make a number of comparisons by examining the results of performance appraisals. It is a control process because managers can use the results to direct and change the behavior of their subordinates. Supervisors can counsel individual officers who do not perform at expected levels, and managers can discuss results with supervisors and unit commanders when unit productivity does not reach expected levels.

More specifically, the performance appraisal serves a number of organizational purposes: formalized feedback to employees, recruitment and selection, training, field training evaluation, horizontal job changes, promotions, compensation management, and discipline. We will briefly discuss each of these in turn.

Formalized Feedback to Employees

Police supervisors should constantly provide their subordinates with feedback about their performance at timed intervals. This activity is the very essence of supervision. The quality and quantity of this feedback varies tremendously even within a given police department. Some supervisors will closely supervise their subordinates and constantly counsel them about their performance while others may only discuss performance occasionally with their subordinates. The department should provide the structure—a minimum agenda—to guide the

126

PART TWO
*Supervising Human
Resources: Training,
Evaluation, and
Discipline*

evaluation and the resulting feedback session. Also, the department establishes policy that dictates the time and frequency of appraisals. A formal feedback session for subordinates is the most important purpose of performance appraisals.

Recruitment and Selection

As a formal process, performance appraisal provides a structure whereby supervisors can have collective input into recruitment and selection criteria. Personnel specialists should examine performance appraisals to identify personnel weaknesses or deficiencies. As problems are identified, they should be used to target pools of people for recruitment and to develop selection tests and criteria.

Training

The performance appraisal process should identify deficiencies or problems with officers' performance. In some instances these deficiencies are the result of improper training or the lack of it. The training staff should review the results of each annual performance evaluation to identify training deficiencies. Adjustments can then be made in the recruitment or basic training program for police officers or to provide veteran officers with in-service training programs.

Field Training Evaluation

As discussed in Chapter 5, most police departments have a probationary period for their new officers. The probationary period is designed to allow the department to evaluate officers' performance and to determine whether they should be retained as police officers. These field training evaluations are extremely important because if the officer is retained after the probationary period, he or she can be dismissed only by showing cause. This creates a situation that forces departments to retain officers who are mediocre in their performance or who constantly cause minor problems. Below-average or problem-causing officers should be dismissed during the probationary period.

Horizontal Job Changes

An accurate performance appraisal system will document each officer's strengths and weaknesses. Many police departments have specialized units such as traffic, criminal investigation, or planning which require officers to have a variety of skills and different levels of job knowledge. Commanders of these units can review performance appraisal information to identify those officers who possess the best skills and capabilities for these units. The performance appraisal can provide invaluable information when making decisions about lateral transfers.

Promotions

The performance appraisal is one of the most common measures used in the promotion process. For example, a survey by the International Association of Chiefs of Police (IACP) and the Police Foundation (PF) showed that 32 percent of the departments surveyed used performance evaluations in their promotion system (IACP and PF, 1973). Only written tests and oral boards were used more frequently. The performance appraisal allows the department to consider the past behavior of officers when making promotional decisions. Generally, past behavior is the best predictor of future behavior.

When performance is used for promotions, police departments should use promotability ratings (Cederblom, 1991). The difference between promotability ratings and performance appraisals is that the former concentrate on job dimensions that are important for the supervisory position while the latter focus on important job behaviors for the current position.

Compensation Management

A number of departments base annual salary increments on the performance appraisal. For example, officers in the Lexington, Kentucky, police department must have a minimum of 70 percent on their annual performance appraisal to receive their annual increment. Other departments provide merit raises for officers who receive high rankings. For example, the 10 officers who receive the highest performance appraisal scores for the department might receive an extra 5 percent merit raise. Performance appraisals are used extensively in determining raises for police officers.

Disciplinary Actions

In some instances the performance appraisal can be used as a basis to discipline officers. This is especially applicable when an officer fails to meet departmental expectations but otherwise does nothing that violates policies or lies outside the bounds of acceptable behavior. Performance that is consistently below average or otherwise deficient can be documented on the performance appraisal form. If an officer fails to correct the behavior and receives several deficient evaluations, the department might take disciplinary action. The performance appraisal formally documents unacceptable behavior and provides a record of the feedback to the officer.

Overview of Performance Appraisals

One problem with performance appraisals is that police managers attempt to use them for too many purposes. The purpose of the ratings generally affects how supervisors rate their subordinates. For example, supervisors tend to be more lenient when ratings are used for promotions than when they are used strictly for counseling. Consequently, when a department attempts to use a single set of ratings for multiple purposes, it tends to distort the ratings and create a variety of problems. Given that performance appraisal is such a critical part of supervision, police departments should consider developing a number of rating schemes.

It should also be understood that performance appraisal is not an event but functions as a process. Even though the performance appraisal may be administered only once or twice a year within a given department, a great deal of activity precedes it and occurs after its administration. Adequate attention must be given to these details if the performance appraisal process is to effectively accomplish its objectives.

When developing or implementing a performance appraisal system, supervisors should take great care to ensure that the system meets the needs of the

128

PART TWO
Supervising Human
Resources: Training,
Evaluation, and
Discipline

department. Four overarching criteria should be considered for the successful implementation of a performance appraisal system: (1) relevancy, (2) sensitivity, (3) reliability, and (4) acceptability (Cascio, 1982). In terms of **relevancy,** the system must force supervisors to make judgments about subordinates' performance on critical or important work behaviors. If an activity is unimportant, it should not be measured or included on the performance appraisal. In terms of **sensitivity,** the system should distinguish and separate workers according to the quality and quantity of their work. In essence, there must be variability in the ratings. A system that fails to classify or identify the gradations separating employees is of little utility to the department or to individual employees. **Reliability** infers that the ratings should accurately measure subordinates' performance. Subordinates must be able to have confidence in their scores. Finally, the system should possess **acceptability** for the organization and the personnel being rated. Acceptability refers to how the results are used. If the results are used incorrectly, the system will not be acceptable to employees. If the system is unacceptable, it could result in internal turmoil and conflict.

Defining Rating Criteria

Defining rating criteria is a three-step process. First, the job is studied in an attempt to identify what should be measured by the performance appraisal system. This includes reviewing job descriptions, job-task analysis information, and other job-related information, such as departmental policies and procedures, to identify the critical and most important activities associated with the position. This process ultimately should provide a listing of job activities and measures of their relative importance. Hence, the most important job components can be identified for measurement.

Once this is accomplished, performance standards must be established; that is, at what level must subordinates perform these tasks or activities for their behavior to be deemed unacceptable, acceptable, or above average. When rating subordinates' work behavior, supervisors must have fairly specific standards to guide their decision making. Furthermore, subordinates must be made aware of standards so that they can evaluate their own work. These performance standards must then be captured on the performance appraisal rating form.

Performance standards are usually articulated by using some form of the critical incident method (Flanagan, 1949; Henderson, 1984). The critical incidents or important tasks as identified by the job analysis are reviewed by supervisors and incumbent officers. Here, they are asked to describe the worst, average, and best examples of how each task has been performed by fellow officers. These examples are then studied and condensed into short descriptions for inclusion in the rating system.

Job criteria and performance standards must be articulated within the performance appraisal system; that is, the department must develop rating forms and guidelines which are provided to everyone prior to their usage. Every officer must be trained on the system prior to implementing it. Police administrators cannot expect subordinates to perform at acceptable levels unless the subordinates have been informed of the standards. See Figure 6–2.

| Job Elements | $\longrightarrow$ | Performance Standards | $\longrightarrow$ | Evaluation Criteria |

FIGURE 6–2. Defining the Rating Criteria

For example, when Bradley and Pursley (1987) developed a performance appraisal system for the North Little Rock, Arkansas, police department, they identified 202 unique tasks that were critical or frequently performed by the officers. They also identified 23 **skills, knowledge, and abilities (SKAs)** that were necessary to perform the tasks. The 23 SKAs were then grouped into eight general categories: job knowledge, decision making, dependability, initiative, equipment use, communication, demeanor, and relations with others. The performance appraisal system was then developed around these eight dimensions.

A system does not necessarily have to concentrate on SKAs. For example, the Ohio Highway Patrol implemented a performance rating system that focused on critical job tasks (Rosinger et al., 1982). For example, sergeants rated officers on "stopping vehicles for violations," "detecting intoxicated drivers," and "securing accident scenes."

Finally, it should be noted that performance appraisal ratings represent unique measures of officer performance. Falkenberg, Gaines, and Cordner (1991) investigated the constructs or dimensions used in performance appraisals and found that the measurements were distinctive from other psychological dimensions or scores on management tests. They concluded that performance appraisals provided productivity information that could not be obtained through other means.

Choosing among Rating Forms

Managers have a variety of rating forms from which to choose when developing a performance appraisal system. Each form has its strengths and weaknesses. The purposes of the performance appraisal should dictate the type of form used by a department. The following sections examine the various forms.

Perhaps the simplest rating form is that shown in Figure 6–3.

Graphic Rating Form

The graphic rating form lists the job dimensions to be rated and provides a space for the rater to select a numerical rating. When using the rating form in Figure 6–3, the supervisor would merely place an "X" or a check mark in the column that best describes the officer's performance. For example, if the officer's performance in public relations was only "good," it would be so noted. The supervisor would make this determination by considering the officer's behavior and citizen input (both complaints and commendations).

A variation on the graphic rating form is the numerical rating form. The only difference between these two forms is that the descriptive adjectives at the top of the form in Figure 6–3 are replaced by numbers, generally ranging from 0 to 10 or 50 to 100. A numerical rating form allows the rater to have a wider range of possible scores. For example, the rating "fair" may be replaced by a range of 61 to 70. The rater can then give the fair officer a score within this range.

130

PART TWO
Supervising Human
Resources: Training,
Evaluation, and
Discipline

Dimension	Unsatisfactory	Fair	Good	Superior	Exceptional
Relationship with others					
Quantity and quality of work					
Communications skills					
Attendance and punctuality					
Public relations skills					

FIGURE 6–3. Graphic Form for Rating Police Officers

The foremost difficulty with graphic rating forms is their lack of reliability. Police departments generally have several people involved in rating. Supervisors from each shift or unit are responsible for rating their subordinates. The difficulty arises in interpreting the descriptive adjectives or numbers used in the scale. For example, one supervisor may rate a subordinate "good" on a particular dimension while another supervisor will rate the same employee "superior." As the number of supervisors involved in the rating process increases, so does the number of errors or inconsistencies. The problem is that each supervisor has associated different meanings with the adjectives. The form does not provide the raters with information to assist in giving the ratings any meaning.

Behaviorally Anchored Rating Scale

Another variation of the graphic rating scale is the **Behaviorally Anchored Rating Scale (BARS)** (Bradley & Pursley, 1987). The BARS attempts to provide the rater with more information about performance standards and, therefore, leads to more accurate and reliable ratings. Figure 6–4 provides an example of a BARS for rating officers in the handling of domestic violence situations. Notice that in addition to a numerical rating scale and an adjective rating scale, the form includes weighted descriptions of police officer behavior or performance when handling these situations. The form contains "fixed standard" information. When rating a subordinate, a supervisor attempts to select the description that best describes how the officer typically handles family disturbances. The primary advantage of BARS is that the descriptions assist the supervisor in making better ratings and to be more consistent when rating several subordinates.

Mixed Standard Scale

The mixed standard scale (see, Blanz & Ghiselli, 1972; Rosinger et al., 1982) is a variation of the BARS. The **mixed standard technique** involves developing a number of ordered statements, similar to the ones used in the BARS. The statements are then randomly ordered and the supervisor reviews each statement and indicates whether the officer's performance is better ($+$), about the same (0), or not as good ($-$) as the performance described in the statement. An officer's score is tabulated by adding the pluses, zeros, and minuses.

Extremely good	+ 7	Uses good judgment in determining proper action. Always considers what performance is best for the victim. Will also attempt to discover a workable solution for the aggressor. Will consider actions for the short term as well as the long term.
Good performance	+ 6	Generally uses good judgment in determining proper action. Always considers what is best for the victim but does not necessarily take action that considers the aggressor or a long-term solution.
Slightly good performance	+ 5	Responds to calls. Generally collects information that is helpful in deciding on what action to take. Sometimes considers both the victim and the perpetrator. Usually makes the correct decision.
Adequate performance	+ 4	Responds to calls. Attempts to collect information that is helpful in deciding on what action to take. Attempts to help the victim but usually does not consider the perpetrator. Sometimes makes the correct decision.
Slightly poor	+ 3	Responds to the calls and takes information from the complainant and other witnesses. Usually will only do the minimum necessary action. Not interested in problem solving at all.
Poor performance	+ 2	Only interested in answering the call and taking the action that is the most expedient for the officer. Always does the absolute minimum. Sometimes takes action that escalates the situation.
Unacceptable	+ 1	Responds to calls because he or she has to. Sometimes becomes embroiled in the conflicts and too frequently leaves the situation worse than before police intervention.

FIGURE 6–4. Behaviorally Anchored Rating Scale

The mixed standard technique has a number of advantages. First, like the BARS, it provides raters with more information by which to make better ratings. Second, it is constructed and administered in a fashion that forces raters to give more time and consideration to each rating. Raters must consider each statement individually when conducting a performance appraisal. Finally, it provides a mechanism for administrators to verify the consistency of each rater's ratings. This is accomplished by reviewing the statements and scores associated with each rating dimension.

For example, consider the following two statements:

1. Uses good judgment in determining proper action. Always considers what is best for the victim. Will also attempt to discover a workable solution for the aggressor. Will consider actions for the short term as well as the long term.

2. Generally uses good judgment in determining proper action. Always considers what is best for the victim but does not necessarily take action which considers the aggressor or a long-term solution.

132

PART TWO
Supervising Human
Resources: Training,
Evaluation, and
Discipline

If the statements in Figure 6–4 were used and a supervisor rated an officer a plus for the first statement and a zero on the second statement, there would be an inconsistency.

Inconsistencies can be checked by administrators. Too many inconsistencies indicate that the rater did not exercise due care in assigning the ratings. This evaluation component in the mixed standard technique allows for more reliable ratings.

Forced Choice Evaluation Method

The **Forced Choice Evaluation Method (FCEM)** was developed to force raters to evaluate their subordinates in the blind; that is, supervisors using the FCEM system do not know whether they are rating subordinates high, low, or somewhere in the middle. This method was developed to eliminate or at least reduce rater biases and other rater errors that commonly occur in ratings.

The FCEM incorporates a series of items consisting of four statements, such as those found in Figure 6–5. The rater is asked to select the two statements that best describe the officer being rated. Two of the statements in Figure 6–5 are more important and weighted while the other two are not. If the rater selects the one or both of the "important" statements, the officer being rating receives points. If the "important" statements are not selected, the officer receives no points.

The statements used in the FCEM are taken from a job analysis. The job analysis is used to identify the most important and frequently performed tasks for a given job or position. Important or critical tasks are paired with less important task statements. The less important task statements may appear to be important to the casual observer, but they are not rated highly as a result of the job analysis. This method essentially forces raters to describe officers by means of predetermined statements. The raters are not told which statements are weighted. If officers' performance does not match or associate with the critical statements, they do not receive points.

The above performance appraisal forms and techniques represent those that are most commonly used in law enforcement, but police managers are constantly experimenting with innumerable other forms and systems. Interestingly, police departments tend to borrow systems from other police agencies. Walsh (1990) found that 79 percent of the 122 police agencies he surveyed used forms that were obtained from some other department. Regardless, research tends to indicate that it really does not matter what form or system is used because the

FIGURE 6–5. Example of the Forced Choice Evaluation Method
Select two of the following statements that best describe the officer being rated.

1. The officer always does a comprehensive job of completing his or her reports and seldom has any mistakes.
2. The officer gets along with his or her fellow officers and superiors.
3. The officer ensures that departmental equipment in his or her control is well cared for.
4. The officer writes a substantial number of traffic citations each month, and always is a leader in productivity.

outcome is usually the same (Guion and Gibson, 1988; Giffin, 1989). Case Study 6–1 considers officers' performance in relation to the district of the city in which they serve.

IMPROVING RATER PERFORMANCE

Perhaps the most notable problem associated with performance appraisals is the raters' ability to accurately evaluate subordinates. For example, DeNisi, Cafferty, and Meglino (1984) described the rating process as a complicated operation where supervisors should constantly collect, encode, store, and retrieve information for rating purposes. However, many personnel experts believe that this process results in more problems than the form or system utilized. The following sections expound on rating problems and possible solutions.

Case Study 6–1
Knowing Your People, or Searching for Hidden Meanings

You are a supervisor in Bay City, recently transferred from the robbery/homicide section of detectives to day shift patrol. You begin your new assignment by reviewing crime reports and calls for service data for the area and meeting with each of your officers to discuss their view of the area's problems and their work productivity.

The south area of the district is divided geographically into five beats consisting of single-family homes, small commercial businesses, and several large apartment complexes. Approximately 50,000 citizens, mostly middle-class whites and Hispanics, live and work in the area. Crime analysis data reveal that the most prevalent crimes are daytime burglaries and thefts of property from the apartment complexes, juvenile drinking, and vandalism. The vandalism is not gang related, and is mostly spray paint tagging of schools and businesses. There are three main thoroughfares through the area, but traffic accidents are low compared with the rest of the city.

You review three of your officers' past performance evaluations:

Officer Stengel leads the patrol division in felony arrests. Her follow-up investigations have led to the identification of two groups of daytime burglars who were truants from the local school. A review of other performance areas shows similar good effort.

Officer Robbins has just completed his probationary period. Troubled by the vandalism, he began working with the city attorney and local business owners on an ordinance that would ban the sale of spray paint to juveniles. Robbins makes every effort to work on this project between calls for service, but some of his fellow officers have complained about having to handle some of his calls.

Officer Franklin has 10 years' experience and would like to work a motorcycle traffic assignment. Selections will be made in six months. To demonstrate his interest in that assignment, Franklin currently leads the department in the number of citations written. He also leads the department in citizen complaints of rude behavior, but only 2 of 10 complaints in the past three months were sustained.

Assume that you are about to engage in an annual performance appraisal for each officer.

1. Discuss your observations of each officer's performance.
2. Do you have any concerns about any of the behaviors demonstrated by any of the officers?
3. Do the officers satisfactorily address the district's problems?
4. Do any other issues require your attention? If so, how would you handle those issues?
5. Which performance appraisal system described in this chapter would you opt to use?

Rater Errors

Rater errors refer to problems which potentially occur any time superiors rate subordinates. Errors occur for a variety of reasons, and they must be controlled if the department is to have an effective performance appraisal system. The following is a discussion of some of the most common rater errors.

Halo Effect

The **halo effect** occurs when a rater evaluates a subordinate high or low on all rating dimensions because of one dimension. For example, a sergeant may believe that patrol officers should write a generous number of traffic citations. Officers who tend to write more citations receive high ratings, while those who write fewer numbers of tickets receive only average or below average ratings. In this example, the sergeant allows the number of citations written by officers to cloud his or her judgment about other rating dimensions.

Recency Problem

The recency problem refers to the undue effect that a recent event, negative or positive, has on an officer's ratings. For example, immediately prior to the end of the rating period an officer may make a traffic stop that results in the seizure of several pounds of cocaine and the arrest of several midlevel drug dealers. The sergeant making the ratings may give this arrest undue weight and rate the officer high. It may not matter that the arrest was the only felony arrest made by the officer during the rating period or that the officer's overall performance was less than average. Ratings should represent the average performance during the total rating period.

Rater Bias

Rater bias is the distortion of ratings caused by raters' values or prejudices. People have all sorts of biases that can affect ratings: religion, race, gender, appearance, existence of a disability, prior employment history, or membership in civic clubs and organizations. Biases can help or detract from an officer's ratings. Biases are one of the most difficult rater errors to overcome.

Constant Error Problem

Some raters are too strict, others too lenient, while still others tend to rate everyone in the middle. For example, a new sergeant may rate all subordinates lower so that they can show improvement in the next rating period. These rating patterns affect the outcome of rating combinations of several different raters. When ratings are combined, some officers have a distinct advantage or disadvantage over other officers.

Unclear Standards

Unclear standards is a problem when there is little agreement among the rating officers about the rating dimensions or associated standards. For example, sergeants may be asked to rate their subordinates on productivity. One sergeant may define productivity one way, while another may define it differently. Varying interpretations of rating dimensions substantially affect ratings. If sergeants are to have consistent ratings, they must have clear, consistent understandings of the standards in use.

These five errors represent the most common rating errors, but raters can make a number of other mistakes. For example, raters tend to value officers who are more like themselves and dislike those who are different. This can apply to a person's appearance, background, education, hobbies, and so on. First impressions by new officers may also have an undue impact on subsequent ratings. Finally, officers who previously had high profile assignments may have an advantage over other officers because they are perceived as being better. Finally, a large number of factors have nothing to do with officers' performance but can affect their performance appraisal ratings. Case Study 6–2 discusses one officer's performance evaluation method.

Rater Training

One of the most important methods for controlling rater errors is rater training. Too often, supervisors are given performance appraisal forms and expected to complete them accurately. However, research indicates that the rating process is extremely complicated (DeNisi et al., 1984) and that rater training is one of the better administrative mechanisms for improving ratings. Bernardin and Buckley (1981) identified three key performance appraisal areas that require training: enhanced observational skills, a common frame of reference for raters, and training raters to be critical.

Enhanced Observational Skills

As noted above the rating process results in raters performing several steps: collecting information, encoding the information into a meaningful form, storing the information, and, finally, retrieving the information for rating purposes.

Case Study 6–2
Seeing the World—and Subordinates—through Rose-Colored Glasses

Sergeant Wilcox is a 10-year veteran of the police force where she has worked mostly in the fraud section of detectives. She is recently assigned to the day shift patrol division and assumes responsibilities for a team of mostly experienced and capable officers. Wilcox believes in a participative management style and therefore feels that her officers should help set their work goals and objectives, and participate in the performance evaluation process.

Wilcox meets with her team and outlines her approach to performance evaluations. Believing that this should be a positive and participative experience for all, she instructs her officers to keep an individual log of their more notable achievements during the performance period. At the end of the rating period, Wilcox uses their top five accomplishments as a basis for their annual evaluation. When the first rating period is completed, Wilcox is pleased to find that her officers received some of the highest performance ratings in the department. However, she recently learns from her lieutenant that other supervisors are voicing criticisms of her evaluation methods. She is now confused and upset about this criticism.

1. What, if any, do you perceive to be the good aspects of Wilcox's personal method of evaluation?
2. What problems might arise from Sgt. Wilcox's rating system?
3. What rater errors are being committed, if any? What might be the basis for the peer supervisors' criticisms?

136

PART TWO
*Supervising Human
Resources: Training,
Evaluation, and
Discipline*

Raters must be taught to gather and store pertinent information in a fashion that enhances the rating process.

When faced with the prospect of having to complete performance appraisal forms for their subordinates, supervisors often hurriedly ponder past activities, make judgments about those activities, and prepare to complete the required forms. This haste generally results in the consideration of only partial data and leads to errors such as halo effect or recency.

Raters can be trained on how to collect and store information for the rating process. Supervisors should be taught how to observe and critically analyze subordinates' performance. The key is to focus on critical job events. They also should be trained to keep diaries of subordinates' behavior and activities throughout the rating period. To ensure that all pertinent information is considered, raters should retain both positive and negative information, regardless of its magnitude. A few exceptional examples of work behavior should not counterbalance an otherwise below-average performance period. Likewise, one or two mistakes should not overly blemish a productive work period.

Common Frame of Reference

To reduce the error of unclear standards, training should be provided to all raters to ensure that they clearly understand, accept, and adhere to the rating standards. Raters must use a common frame of reference when completing performance appraisals. For example, if sergeants are rating subordinates on interpersonal relationships, each sergeant doing ratings should have the same understanding of what interpersonal relationships mean. If variation occurs among the sergeants, some officers will be treated unfairly, departmental morale will be affected, and the intended purposes of the performance appraisals will not be fulfilled. Behavioral anchors such as those found on a BARS are helpful in eliminating this problem, but a training program in which all raters are exposed to thorough and complete discussion of the rating dimensions, their meanings, and expected behavior will substantially reduce rater error. A training program can provide raters with video-recorded examples or vignettes comprising critical incidents of the job. Supervisors' ratings can be analyzed and discussed in a classroom atmosphere to foster more accurate ratings.

Critical Appraisal of Subordinates

As mentioned earlier, one of the major problems associated with performance appraisals is that raters are often too lenient and put too high a rating on all or most of their subordinates. They fail to critically appraise subordinates' activity and behavior, and their ratings reflect that appraisal. A number of reasons explain this occurrence. For example, it is a natural behavioral reaction because almost everyone attempts to avoid confrontations. Or supervisors may fail to properly supervise subordinates, so they feel unable to explain or defend lower ratings adequately. Raters may evaluate everyone high because low ratings might cast a doubt on the rater's ability to supervise. Another reason is that supervisors may not properly understand departmental expectations and therefore cannot accurately distinguish poor performance from good performance.

A training program can emphasize the standards used to evaluate officers, and it can be used to underscore the importance of making accurate ratings which distinguish good, average, and below-average performers. Training can indoctrinate raters on how ratings are used and the importance of making distinctions in ratings. In the end, training is one of the most important mechanisms that a department can use to enhance the accuracy of ratings.

DIFFERENT APPROACHES TO APPRAISAL

Using Peer and Self-Evaluations

For the most part, performance appraisals in policing have been viewed as a management prerogative; that is, performance appraisals have been used almost exclusively by management to evaluate subordinates. Very few departments have experimented with or used peer evaluations (Falkenberg and Gaines, 1991; Love, 1981a, 1981b) or subordinate evaluations of superiors (McEvoy, 1987).

Peer evaluations comprise a system whereby officers complete performance appraisal forms for the other officers within their work group. One supposed benefit of peer evaluations is that closer working relationships enable officers to

It is important that officers are evaluated on their individual assignments. A footbeat officer would not necessarily be evaluated on the exact same criteria as one who is assigned to detectives, traffic, or training.
Courtesy New York Police Department Photo Unit.

possess more information about their colleagues than supervisors; consequently, officers can make better appraisals. It is questionable whether officers have more knowledge than supervisors about their peers, but they unquestionably have different information. The circumstances in which police work is conducted among peers is probably very different than the interactions between police officers and their supervisors. The inclusion of this information in the performance appraisal process could be very beneficial.

Love (1981a, 1981b) noted that the primary concerns with peer evaluations are reliability, validity, friendship bias, and negative user reactions. However, Love's research indicated that peer evaluations were just as reliable and valid as performance appraisals. Furthermore, he did not find that friendship bias affected ratings. When placed in a position of rating peers, officers would attempt to consider only those aspects of a peer's performance that related to the rating dimensions. Finally, they, like many supervisors, found performance rating to be a negative experience. It seems that whoever is involved in ratings will find it to be a negative experience.

Falkenberg and Gaines (1991) investigated peer evaluations to determine what they measured. They examined the relationships between peer ratings and a number of psychological dimensions, management qualities, and departmental performance appraisals. No consistent relationships were identified. They concluded that peer evaluations represent unique measures of performance which provide information that otherwise would not be included in performance appraisals.

Finally, self-evaluations must also be considered. It may be very beneficial to a department to have officers complete self-evaluations to identify their own strengths and deficiencies. Supervisors could compare the department's performance appraisal with the individual's self-evaluation to identify areas of agreement, blind spots, and areas of overevaluation. The self-evaluation also could serve as an excellent catalyst when discussing performance with subordinates.

The extent to which agencies are using peer, subordinate, or self-evaluations is not known. Police managers should be open minded and use the type of rating system that best meets the needs of the department.

Subordinate Appraisal of Supervisors

McEvoy's (1987) investigation of subordinate appraisals of managers came up with the following findings:

1. Subordinate appraisals frequently have been used for management development rather than evaluation purposes, but anecdotal reports of their use for both purposes are generally positive.
2. Managers report that subordinate feedback is very helpful in improving their performance.
3. A substantial amount of "halo" exists in subordinate appraisals of managers because subordinates tend to rate superiors on only one dimension rather than differentiating on the multiple dimensions commonly used on the rating forms.

4. A modest positive correlation exists between ratings by subordinates and ratings of the same individuals by superior officers, indicating some level of concurrent validity.

McEvoy's research revealed that subordinate ratings were very effective in predicting manager success. In his study he compared the results of subordinate appraisals to the results of an assessment center and found that subordinate appraisals predicted future performance appraisal scores more effectively. He also found that regardless of the number of dimensions used in such ratings, subordinates tended to rate superiors on one universal dimension.

PROVIDING APPRAISAL FEEDBACK

A critical component of the performance appraisal process is subordinate feedback. As noted above, the most important purpose for conducting performance appraisals is formalized feedback to employees. Substantial efforts should be exerted to ensure that this purpose is effectively achieved. The above sections addressed a number of mechanical aspects of performance appraisal, including how to prepare raters for rating. It is just as important for supervisors to prepare for feedback sessions. There are a number of steps in this process.

1. Prior to a feedback session, supervisors should refresh their memories regarding the ratee's productivity record. Departmental printouts, other productivity records, and the completed performance appraisal form should be reviewed. This information should be discussed as a supplement to the performance appraisal.
2. Supervisors should know what they are going to say or the major points they will cover before the interview. Furthermore, the supervisor should ensure that the feedback session does not become sidetracked; the officer's performance should remain the focal point at all times. These interviews should be planned or mapped out prior to the interview. Supervisors should even rehearse interviews when possible.
3. Both positives and negatives should be discussed. Positive reinforcement of good work habits are just as important as eliminating negative ones.
4. Force the ratee to discuss his or her performance. This can be accomplished by asking questions or requesting the ratee to comment about his or her performance. This helps force the subordinate to evaluate his or her behavior realistically.
5. Force the ratee to develop a performance plan. If an officer's performance is substantially below expectations, require the officer to present a plan explaining how he or she will improve on it. The plan can be verbal or written, but it is critical that a plan be presented. The plan can be used in subsequent counseling sessions if necessary.
6. Leave the subordinate with a clear understanding of what is expected. This can be accomplished by providing the officer with goals and objectives, and discussing overall departmental goals. Regardless of the method used, subordinates must have clear ideas of what is expected of them if they are to be good employees.

140

PART TWO
Supervising Human
Resources: Training,
Evaluation, and
Discipline

No matter what methods a department uses to evaluate police officer performance, the system will be only as good as the feedback sessions that supervisors provide subordinates. Unfortunately, many supervisors take this responsibility too lightly and do only a mediocre job during the performance appraisal feedback session. Police managers must ensure that supervisors conduct effective feedback sessions.

EFFECTIVENESS OF PERFORMANCE APPRAISALS

As we stated above, the performance appraisal is an important supervisory tool. Theoretically, it should assist in increasing productivity and contribute to a police department's overall performance. Sometimes, however, the performance appraisal is not used effectively, and the police department fails to reap its benefits. For example, Walsh (1990:101) surveyed 122 police sergeants from several small- and medium-size police departments and found that 87 percent reported that the performance evaluation was of little help to them in their job as supervisors. The most common reasons given for their ineffectiveness were:

1. The performance criteria are subjective.
2. The systems lack managerial control. This creates rater inconsistency and favoritism.
3. Supervisors have very little input into the process but are its major users.
4. The forms are filed and mean nothing.
5. Management is not concerned with performance but only with making sure that things run smoothly.
6. The supervisor's performance assessments are changed by administrators who have not observed the officer perform on a daily basis.

Walsh's findings clearly indicate that police departments must pay more attention to how their performance appraisal systems function. The problems voiced by the supervisors in Walsh's study are the result of deficiencies or problems that are addressed above. Such problems also indicate that departments are failing to use the information produced through performance appraisals. Police managers must put forth the effort to ensure that performance appraisals are functioning as envisioned by the department.

SUMMARY

This chapter has addressed two important issues in police supervision: productivity measurement and performance appraisals. Supervisors are primarily responsible for a department's productivity. They supervise line personnel and must ensure that officers are not only productive, but that their activities have a demonstrable effect on community problems. Balancing these two perspectives is an extremely difficult and time-consuming task.

One way for supervisors to manage this chore is through performance evaluations. Performance evaluations are formalized feedback sessions where supervisors advise officers about the quantity and quality of their activity. One purpose of the performance appraisal is to use it as a supervisory tool to direct officers' behavior. Supervisors should use it to move officers toward recognized objectives.

Performance appraisals also serve a variety of other departmental functions. When they are used for more than one function, the process becomes complicated and stated objectives may not easily be accomplished. The critical aspect about performance appraisals is that they represent a system; as such every aspect of the system from developing rating forms, to training supervisors, to rating and providing feedback to officers must be managed properly. If any one link in the system is defective, the total system will be damaged.

KEY TERMS

productivity   (p. 119)
efficiency   (p. 119)
effectiveness   (p. 120)
equity   (p. 120)
accountability   (p. 120)
calls for service (CFS)
   (p. 120)
planning   (p. 123)

performance appraisal
   (p. 125)
relevancy   (p. 128)
sensitivity   (p. 128)
reliability   (p. 128)
acceptability   (p. 128)
skills, knowledge, and abilities (SKAs)   (p. 129)

Behaviorally Anchored
   Rating Scale (BARS)
   (p. 130)
mixed standard technique
   (p. 130)
Forced Choice Evaluation
   Method (FCEM) (p. 132)
halo effect   (p. 134)

ITEMS FOR REVIEW

1. Define productivity measurement, and why it is so important for supervisory personnel.
2. Explain how efficiency, effectiveness, equity, and accountability are of concern in measuring productivity.
3. Describe how to evaluate criteria employed in the traditional policing model—such as crime rates, clearance rates, and response times—have been problematic when applied to community oriented policing and problem solving (COPPS) strategy.
4. Define performance appraisal and describe its purposes and uses.
5. Describe the various rating forms that supervisors can employ in a performance appraisal system. What are some of the strengths and weaknesses of each?
6. Delineate some of the problems and errors that exist when raters attempt to evaluate subordinates.
7. Explain some of the advantages, disadvantages, and problems in having subordinates rate their supervisors.

SOURCES

BERNARDIN, H. J., and BUCKLEY, M. R. (1981). "Strategies in rater training." *Academy of Management Review* 6(2):205–12.

BLANZ, F., and GHISELLI, E. E. (1972). "The mixed standard scale: A new rating system." *Personnel Psychology* 25:185–99.

BRADLEY, D. E., and PURSLEY, R. D. (1987). "Behaviorally anchored rating scales for patrol officer performance appraisal: Development and evaluation." *Journal of Police Science and Administration* 15(1):37–44.

CASCIO, W. F. (1982). "Scientific, legal, and operational imperatives of workable performance appraisal systems." *Public Personnel Management Journal* 11(4):367–75.

142

PART TWO
*Supervising Human
Resources: Training,
Evaluation, and
Discipline*

CEDERBLOM, D. (1991). "Promotability ratings: An underused promotion method for public safety organizations." *Public Personnel Management Journal* 20(1):27–34.

DEPARTMENT OF JUSTICE, LAW ENFORCEMENT ASSISTANCE ADMINISTRATION, 1975. *Criminal Justice Planning Institute*, Training Workbook, October 19.

DENISI, A., CAFFERTY, T. P., and MEGLINO, B. M. (1984). "A cognitive view of the performance appraisal process: A model and research propositions." *Organizational Behavior and Human Performance* 33:360–96.

FALKENBERG, S., GAINES, L. K., and CORDNER, G. W. (1991). "An examination of the constructs underlying police performance appraisals." *Journal of Criminal Justice* 19: 351–59.

FLANAGAN, J. C. (1949). "A new approach to evaluating personnel." *Personnel* (January–February): 42.

GAINES, L. K., SOUTHERLAND, M. D., and ANGELL, J. E. (1990). *Police administration*. New York: McGraw-Hill.

GELLER, W. A., and SWANGER, G. (1995). *Managing innovation in policing: The untapped potential of the middle manager.* Washington D.C.: Police Executive Research Forum.

GIFFIN, M. E. (1989). "Personnel research on testing, selection and performance appraisal." *Public Personnel Management* 18(2): 127–37.

GUION, R. M., and GIBSON, W. M. (1988). "Personnel selection and placement." *Annual Review of Psychology* 39:349–74.

HATRY, H. P. (1975). "Wrestling with police crime control productivity measurement." In J. Wolfle and J. Heaphy (eds.). *Readings on Productivity in Policing*. Washington, D.C.: Police Foundation.

HENDERSON, R. I. (1984). *Performance appraisal.* Reston, Va: Reston.

HEPBURN, J. R. (1981). "Crime control, due process, and measurement of police performance." *Journal of Police Science and Administration* 9(1):88–98.

HIRSCH, G. B., and RICCO, L. J. (1974). "Measuring and improving the productivity of police patrol." *Journal of Police Science and Administration* 2(2):169–84.

HOOVER, L. T. (1992). "Police mission: An era of debate." In L. Hoover (ed.). *Police Management: Issues and Perspectives*. Washington, D.C.: Police Executive Research Forum.

INTERNATIONAL ASSOCIATION OF CHIEFS OF POLICE AND THE POLICE FOUNDATION (1973). *Police personnel practices in state and local governments*. Washington, D.C.: Police Foundation.

KUPER, G. H. (1975). "Productivity: A national concern." In J. Wolfle and J. Heaphy (eds.). *Readings on Productivity in Policing*. Washington, D.C.: Police Foundation.

LAB, S. P. (1984). "Police productivity: The other eighty percent." *Journal of Police Science and Administration* 12(3):297–302.

LANDY, F. J. and GOODIN, C. V. (1974). Performance appraisal. In O. G. Stahl and R. A. Staufenberger, eds., *Police Personnel and Administration* (North Scituate, Mass.: Duxbury, pp. 180–181.

LONGMIRE, D. R. (1992). "Activity trap." In L. Hoover (ed.). *Police management: Issues and perspectives*. Washington, D.C.: Police Executive Research Forum.

LOVE, K. G. (1981a). "Accurate evaluation of police officer performance through the judgment of fellow officers: Fact or fiction?" *Journal of Police Science and Administration* 9(2): 143–49.

LOVE, K. G. (1981b). "Comparison of peer assessment methods: Reliability, validity, friendship bias, and user reaction." *Journal of Applied Psychology* 66(4):451–57.

MASTROFSKI, S. (1984). "Police knowledge of the patrol beat as a performance measure." In G. Whitaker (ed.). *Understanding Police Agency Performance*. Washington, D.C.: National Institute of Justice.

MCEVOY, G. M. (1987). "Using subordinate appraisals of managers to predict performance and promotions: One agency's experience." *Journal of Police Science and Administration* 15(2):118–24.

MURPHY, P. V. (1975). "Police accountability." In J. Wolfle and J. Heaphy (eds.). *Readings on Productivity in Policing.* Washington, D.C.: Police Foundation.

NATIONAL COMMISSION ON PRODUCTIVITY (1973). *Opportunities for improving productivity in police services.* Washington, D.C.: National Commission on Productivity.

PEAK, K. J., and GLENSOR, R. W. (1996). *Community policing and problem solving: Strategies and practices.* Upper Saddle River, N.J.: Prentice Hall.

ROSINGER, G., MYERS, L. B., LEVY, G., LOAR, M., MOHRMAN, S. A., and STOCK, J. R. (1982). "Development of a behaviorally based performance appraisal system." *Personnel Psychology* 35: 75–88.

RUBINSTEIN, J. (1973). *City police.* New York: Farrar, Straus, and Giroux.

SWANSON, C. R., TERRITO, L., and TAYLOR, R. W. (1993). *Police administration: Structure, processes, and behavior.* New York: Macmillan.

VAN MAANAN, J. (1974). "Working the street: A developmental view of police behavior." In H. Jacob (ed.). *The Potential for Reform of Criminal Justice.* Vol. 3, *Criminal Justice System Annals.* Beverly Hills: Sage.

WALSH, W. F. (1985). "Patrol officer arrest rates: A study of the social organization of police work." *Justice Quarterly* 2(3): 271–90.

WALSH, W. F. (1990) "Performance evaluation in small and medium police departments: A supervisory perspective." *American Journal of Police* 9(4): 93–109.

WILSON, J. Q. (1968). *Varieties of police behavior.* Cambridge, Mass.: Harvard University Press.

7

Stress, Wellness, and Employee Assistance Programs

There are two ways of meeting difficulties: you alter the difficulties or you alter yourself meeting them.

—PHYLLIS BOTTOME

When a person is down in this world,
an ounce of help is better than a pound of preaching.

—EDWARD G. BULWER-LYTTON

Health is a state of complete physical,
mental and social well-being,
and not merely absence of disease or infirmity.

—HEAVE

INTRODUCTION

Employees represent an important and invaluable asset to the police organization, which invests large amounts of money in their training and future development. Therefore, employers are becoming increasingly concerned about the health and welfare of their people. Administrators have come to realize that they must develop an organizational setting and atmosphere that is conducive to work and productivity, and also ensure that employees are mentally and physically prepared for the challenges of the workplace.

Supervisors, with virtual daily contact with officers, are probably the first persons other than the officers themselves to recognize that a problem exists. Supervisors are thus in the best position to observe the effects of stress and to take action to reduce its effects on their subordinates. Supervisors are also uniquely situated to assess overall employee wellness and to encourage—or force—subordinates to seek assistance from formal programs. For these reasons, stress, wellness, and employee assistance programs (EAPs) directly affect and involve supervisors.

This chapter focuses on the supervisor's role in dealing with three vital human resource areas that affect the workplace: employee stress, including understanding stress and its sources; employee wellness, which looks at programs for fitness and wellness and related legal considerations; and employee assistance programs, where we examine what can be done to address officer stress in general as well as alcohol, drug abuse, and other personal problems. Two related case studies are contained within the chapter.

UNDERSTANDING POLICE STRESS

Dimensions and Process

Police work is very different from most other occupations in U.S. society. Our police system is society's primary mechanism for controlling aberrant and illegal behavior. As such, society vests police officers with a substantial amount of authority—a level of authority possessed by no other occupation, including the right to employ deadly force.

This work environment can have adverse effects on police officers. It creates **stress,** which is anything that places an adjustive demand on the individual (Selye, 1981). We would also define stress as a force that is external in nature which causes physical and emotional strain on the body from its normal processes. Succinctly, **stressors** are situations or occurrences outside of ourselves that we allow to turn inward and cause problems.

Stress has two dimensions. First, it can be positive or negative. Positive stress is referred to as **eustress,** while negative stress is called **distress.** Generally, when people think about stress, they focus on negative stress and negative situations. However, positive events in our lives can create stress, too. For example, the promotion of an officer to sergeant is a very positive experience, but at the same time it creates stress. The officer has to react and adjust to the new position. Although positive for the officer's career, the promotion is somewhat psychologically disruptive.

Second, stress has a magnitude dimension. For example, Sewell (1983), using a list of 144 stressful events, surveyed 250 police officers in a Federal Bureau of Investigation (FBI) National Academy class and found the three most stressful events reported by officers were (1) the violent death of a partner in the line of duty, (2) dismissal from the force, and (3) taking a life in the line of duty. Although few police contacts are of this magnitude, police officers are confronted with a variety of situations daily, and each stressful situation affects the officer differently.

Stress should be viewed as a process rather than as a singular event. When an event or series of events occur, the individual reacts to the events. The reaction may be of short or long duration. Selye (1981) formulated the **General Adaptive Syndrome (GAS)** to describe the stress process. GAS consists of three

146

PART TWO
Supervising Human
Resources: Training,
Evaluation, and
Discipline

stages: (1) alarm, (2) resistance, and (3) exhaustion. The alarm stage develops when the stressful event occurs and the individual becomes aware of the event. Generally, psychological and physiological reactions occur. A variety of psychological reactions can surface, including fear, anxiety, depression, apprehension, or aggressiveness. Physiological reactions include an increase in the heart rate and a release of adrenaline into the blood stream. If the threat subsides, the individual ultimately will return to a normal state.

Resistance is the process whereby the individual attempts to cope or coexist with the stress. The threat remains but the individual continues to muster the strength to contend with it. Resistance is characterized by continued psychological and physiological changes or adaptations in the individual. Exhaustion is the point at which the individual is no longer able to effectively cope with the stressful situation. At this point, if the stressful event continues, the individual experiences physical or mental problems. Physiological responses can be as severe as a heart attack. Psychologically, an individual may reach the point that he or she cannot function mentally.

Effects during an Officer's Career

Stress does not affect everyone in the same way. Some people are more resistant while others are more susceptible to its effects. Some officers appear to be shaken by even the most minor incident while others appear unruffled. Like-

---

Case Study 7–1
Near Shootout at K-9 Corral

The headlines read, NEAR SHOOT-OUT AT K-9 CORRAL. The department is stunned by the events of Sunday evening. During a weekly training session, K-9 Officer Tom Watson pointed his duty weapon at Officer Jack Connolly and threatened to shoot him during an argument. Fortunately no one was injured, but Watson is under investigation for assault.

Officer Watson's friends were not surprised. Since joining the K-9 Unit three months ago, he had been the subject of intense teasing, especially by Connolly, who liked to imitate Watson's stuttered speech. Watson was extremely sensitive about his speech and had attended three years of therapy at the local university before he gained enough confidence to take the police officer's examination.

Lately, Connolly's teasing became more personal: He imitated Watson's stutter over the police radio. When other officers and dispatchers began to join in, Watson asked Sgt. Aldous to speak with Connolly. Aldous explained that all new guys got teased and warned him not to make the situation worse by complaining. For the next two weeks, Watson called in sick on the six days that he and Connolly were scheduled to work together.

Watson had broken up with his fiancée earlier in the day the incident occurred. He was in no mood for teasing and, when Connolly started it, Watson burst into a rage of vulgarities and threats. He then drew his service revolver and pointed it at Connolly before other officers tackled and disarmed him.

1. What were some of the issues and precipitating factors leading to this incident?
2. Were there any warning signs? If so, what were they?
3. Could this incident have been avoided? If so, how?
4. What were Sgt. Aldous's responsibilities in this matter? Did he meet those responsibilities?

wise, some people are more prone to experience stress over one type of event, while others find other types of events to cause anxiety. For example, Gaines and Van Tubergen (1989) found that older officers experienced more stress over the actions of their younger counterparts, while younger officers became stressed about things that occurred in the department and the job itself. Thus, it is difficult to accurately predict stress in individuals.

There has been a limited amount of research examining stress patterns in police departments. Dietrich (1989) and Violanti (1983) attempted to articulate police officer stress patterns based on years of service, and identified several stages of stress (see Figure 7–1).

Alienation

As shown in Figure 7–1, the first five years of a police officer's career can be described as a period of alienation and alarm. Officers essentially experience a re-

Painful sights on the ocean floor overcome police divers searching the wreckage of TWA flight 800.
Courtesy New York Police Department Photo Unit.

Author	Stages			
Niederhoffer (1967) and Violanti (1983)	Alarm stage (0–5 yrs.)	Disenchantment stage (6–13 yrs.)	Personalization stage (14–20 yrs.)	Introspection stage (20+ yrs.)
Dietrich (1989)	Alienation from nonpolice world (0–5 yrs.)	Emotional shutdown (5–10 yrs.)	Emotional unsureness (10–15 yrs.)	Namelessness (15–20 yrs.)	Maintaining the status quo (20–35 yrs.)

FIGURE 7–1. Stress Patterns by Years of Service

ality shock; they discover that the job is substantially different from what they first imagined. They also discover that they are bureaucrats who engage in numerous mundane activities; a police officer's career is quite different from the exciting portrayals of it on television and in novels. As a result of the many negative situations in which they intervene while on the job, officers come to view citizens as the enemy. Police officers generally have a very negative outlook on life during this phase of their careers.

Disenchantment

The second phase of an officer's career may be characterized as the disenchantment phase. Violanti postulated that this phase generally lasts from years 6 through 13, while Dietrich divided this time into two different phases: emotional shutdown and emotional unsureness. Regardless, many officers become bitterly disappointed in their careers during this period. They become emotionally detached and bitter about the job. To a great extent, they withdraw because they cannot reconcile the realities of police work with their perceptions of "how the world ought to be." These feelings often spill over into family life, causing additional stress. This is the peak period for police officer stress.

Getting Back on Track

It appears that police officers' stress is lower during years 14 through 20. During this period officers become interested in their families and outside activities. They may engage in hobbies and second jobs to occupy their free time. It is a period when police work begins to become secondary; that is, during this phase officers realize that their jobs are not their lives and that there are other, more important things in life. Negativism tends to subside during this phase. In some cases officers remain detached and noncommittal, but they are less bitter and cynical about the job and the citizens they serve. They often become more helpful and engaging when they respond to calls or become involved in other job-related activities. They come to realize that police work is nothing more than a job.

Introspection

Finally, as their careers approach 20 years, police officers become introspective about their jobs; that is, they typically do their jobs and avoid worrying about job-related problems such as failing to get promoted and not meeting citizen expectations or the demands of their superiors. They tend to take life in stride, realizing that there are more important things in life besides work.

These stress phases have two implications for supervisors. First, supervisors are not immune to this stress paradigm. They frequently develop stress symptoms that affect their own performance. Supervisors must remain focused and exert every effort possible to ensure that they and their subordinates work uninhibited by needless stress. Second, supervisors must be able to recognize the symptoms and stages of stress and help officers deal with them. In essence, they must provide social support, training, and counseling; and when necessary, they should ask for outside intervention to help reduce the debilitating effects of stress on officers.

SOURCES OF POLICE STRESS

Police officers can experience job stress as the result of a wide range of problems and situations. Next, we examine these sources of stress which we have categorized into four general areas: (1) organizational and administrative practices, (2) the criminal justice system, (3) the public, and (4) stress intrinsic to police work itself.

Organizational Sources

Studies of police stress have consistently found that the primary source of stress is the police organization itself. One survey of police officers in eight medium-sized departments found that organization-based problems were the most stressful for police officers (Crank and Caldero, 1991). Other researchers, examining stress in the Cincinnati police department, found that department administration was the second highest stressor, with 51 percent of the officers affected by it (Kroes et al, 1974). Police departments typically are bureaucratic, authoritarian organizations (Harrison and Pelletier, 1987; Franz and Jones, 1987; Langworthy, 1992); this situation creates a substantial amount of stress for officers. Police agencies are unique in their operation and consequently place a number of restrictions on how police officers conduct their daily activities.

Authoritarian Nature of Police Departments

A police department's authoritarian nature creates stress for individual officers in at least four ways. First, police departments are generally characterized by strict rules and regulations, dictated by top administration. Line officers seldom have direct input into their formulation, which results in a feeling of powerlessness and alienation on the part of officers toward the decisions that directly affect their jobs.

Second, these rules and regulations dictate how officers should perform many of their duties and responsibilities. While they are created to provide officers with helpful guidance, police officers sometimes see them as mechanisms used by management to restrict their freedom and discretion or to punish them. Officers also view rules and regulations as protection for the department when they make incorrect decisions or errors. In these instances departments may rely on rules and regulations to mitigate the liability incurred from officers' actions.

Third, police departments typically are characterized by close supervision. Sergeants frequently monitor police officer activities, check their work for completeness and deficiencies, and take control of the more serious calls or situations. In some instances officers are allowed to make decisions in only the most mundane calls or activities. Finally, many police departments have extensive chains of commands that require officers to use formal memorandums when communicating with superiors. This formalization can strain relations between officers and administration.

Police officers perceive these working conditions negatively. For example, Franz and Jones (1987) found that officers believed that the military model, when implemented in police organizations, impaired communications and departmental performance and resulted in distrust for superiors and low levels of morale. Talarico and Swanson (1982) also found that this organizational model affected police officer perceptions of the department and their work. Research tends to support the conclusion that the police organization, especially when it mirrors a bureaucracy, creates stress for police officers.

Because of their position in the organization, supervisors can directly influence officers' behaviors and, ultimately, their levels of stress. To some extent the supervisor is a buffer between officers and top administration. Supervisors must help officers to understand the reasons for administrative actions. They must play a key role in providing a social support system for subordinates when they encounter problems or have difficulty with departmental requirements. They must also use discretion when applying rules and regulations to police officers. Rules should not be applied aimlessly, but they should be enforced when substantive or "real" problems exist. Whenever possible, corrective action, counseling, and training should all be used before initiating disciplinary action.

Women on the Force

We must also discuss some of the exceptional problems faced by female police officers, who now compose 10 percent of sworn police personnel in the United States (U.S. Department of Justice, Federal Bureau of Investigation, 1996:278). It is important to remember that policing is a male-dominated occupation and that female officers do not have the same standing in a number of police agencies. Studies tend to indicate that the primary sources of stress for female officers are sexual harassment and treatment different than that of male officers (Morash and Haarr, 1991; Wexler and Logan, 1983). Women officers report that they are treated differently, given different assignments, are the object of jokes (especially those with a sexual orientation), are propositioned by male officers, and generally victimized by gender stereotyping in the department. Many such behaviors are prohibited by sexual harassment statutes, and any other behavior of this nature is totally unprofessional. Supervisors must ensure that female officers are treated equally in the workplace and are not sexually harassed from both a humanitarian and legal standpoint. This is best accomplished by taking action at the slightest provocation. This "no tolerance" stance is important to promoting equity and teamwork among officers.

The Criminal Justice System

Stress as a result of the criminal justice system refers to instances where officers have difficulty coping when they interact with other components of the criminal justice system or with the decisions and actions made by other criminal justice agencies. Each component of the criminal justice system affects the other components. For example, if a state is experiencing prison overcrowding and prematurely releases large numbers of inmates, it will affect police officers who most certainly will have repeated contact with some of the same criminals again. Individual participants in the criminal justice system can also cause stress for police officers. For example, some judges have required that police officers only wear business suits in court. In other situations judges have openly displayed hostile attitudes toward the police.

There have been limited studies examining the effects of the criminal justice system on police stress. However, one study found that 56 percent of the police officers reported stressful experiences with the courts (Kroes et al., 1974). In the criminal justice system, the courts have a direct impact on police officers and are probably one of their greatest sources of stress.

It is important that supervisors help police officers understand their role within the criminal justice system. The American system of justice dictates that when investigating crimes, the role of police is to determine whether probable cause exists to make an arrest; and if it does, to bring the suspect along with any evidence before the court for adjudication. Quite plainly, this is the primary role of police in the criminal justice system.

Police officers must not allow themselves to become consumed with anger or blame when they lose cases or if they are overturned on appeal. While their dissappointment is understandable, it must not be allowed to degenerate to the point of unprofessional behavior.

The Public

Most citizens recognize that the police perform an important function in our society. Indeed, a Gallup poll reported that 60 percent of Americans have "a great deal/quite a lot" of confidence in the police (Maguire and Pastore, 1995:133). In addition to combating criminal activities, the police provide many important services to the public, which otherwise would be unavailable. When police officers perform these services, however, they become involved in conflicts or negative situations. They arrest citizens, they write them tickets, and they give citizens orders when intervening in situations of domestic violence or disorder. Often, to resolve problems, they make half of the participants happy, but the other half are unhappy because of the outcome. Even though the end result of their work is generally positive, the activities of policing are very stressful for the officers.

Unfortunately, the problem is that police officers develop unrealistic or inaccurate ideas about citizens as a result of their negative encounters (Albrecht and Green, 1978) and, in some cases, form extremely negative attitudes toward citizens (Van Maanen, 1978). To reduce stress in this area, officers must keep their

152

PART TWO
Supervising Human
Resources: Training,
Evaluation, and
Discipline

relationship with citizens in proper perspective. This may be achieved by open, straightforward discussions of public attitudes and positive encounters with citizens. Supervisors may assist in this regard by assigning officers under their command periodically to assignments or events where positive contact with citizens is expected. These activities could help to mediate the effects of negative encounters with citizens and reduce stress.

Stressors Intrinsic to Police Work

Police work is fraught with situations that pose physical danger to officers. Anytime officers confront a felon, especially if drugs are involved, there exists the potential for physical violence. Domestic violence, disorders, and fight calls often require that officers confront suspects physically. Police work itself, because it includes dealing with dangerous activities and people, would seem to be the most stressful part of police work. Research, however, tends to indicate that the actual work of policing may not be excessively stressful for officers. Crank and Caldero (1991) found that organizationally induced stress was a far greater problem. Similarly, a survey of five suburban police departments found that police officers did not believe physical injury to be a frequent occurrence in police work (Cullen et al., 1983). Police officers seem to understand that the job has some dangers, but they do not see them as overpowering problems.

The supervisor's role is to ensure that police officers view their jobs and responsibilities realistically. On the one hand, police officers cannot be complacent when confronting potentially hazardous situations. Police officers can become careless—for example, using a poor defensive posture when talking with a subject who is standing near the officer or sitting in his or her vehicle—substantially increases the probability of physical injury. On the other hand, police officers should not overemphasize the danger of the job. Dwelling on physical danger affects officers' mental health and how they treat or interact with citizens. With regard to physical danger and injury, supervisors must ensure that officers maintain a delicate balance in their daily lives. While officers should be ever vigilant and wary of dangers of the job and the likelihood of injury, at the same time they must keep the job in proper perspective.

DEALING WITH STRESS

The preceding sections described the sources of stress and some of the resulting problems. Given that stress is a significant problem in policing, departments and supervisors must endeavor to reduce and, where possible, eliminate stress. A number of actions may be taken to accomplish this objective.[1]

---

[1]In March 1997, the National Institute of Justice (NIJ) published a monograph, *Developing a Law Enforcement Stress Program for Officers and Their Families.* From this, interested parties may learn how to plan, structure, staff, and market such a program, how to establish a referral network and manage program costs, and many other key elements of initiating this service (NIJ, 1997).

Social Support Systems

Social support is communications and actions that lead individuals to believe that they are cared for, important, and an integral part of a network of mutual obligations. Social support can be emotional in nature, whereby people let others know that they care for them, and it can be instrumental, which is the providing of assistance, such as money or doing another's work (House, 1981). Social support buffers working conditions, thus making work less stressful (Kaufmann & Beehr, 1989). Thus it can be an important factor in mediating stress in policing.

It is questionable if enough support for officers exists in police departments. For example, McMurray (1990) surveyed 161 Washington, D.C., and Newark, New Jersey, police officers who had been assaulted in the line of duty. He inquired about the level of support the officers received from their departments immediately after the assault. Sixty percent of the officers indicated that their department did not provide adequate support. However, 82 percent of the officers indicated that their supervisor was supportive. Assaults are visible, traumatic events, and one would expect supervisors to be attentive to officers experiencing assaults, but it is disappointing that the officers believed their agency provided them with inadequate support.

Given this information, one might wonder about support mechanisms and the level of assistance that exists for lesser events or even routine daily activities. You have read earlier that working conditions and relationships in the police organization are the most stressful for police officers, indicating that little support exists on a daily basis. Support may exist only for the occasional dramatic event while police officers' daily activities receive little attention.

Supervisors and departments in general must increase their ability to provide support services to officers, not only in traumatic situations, but also on a daily basis. Officers constantly need support and encouragement. In this vein Graf (1986) has identified three strategies to increase organizational support for officers. First, departments should attempt to reduce officer cynicism, which is most pronounced during the first 10 years of an officer's career. This involves direct intervention by supervisors to correct behavior and change officer attitudes. It also means increased involvement of supervisors in a wider range of officer problems. Supervisors should be supportive but also they must ensure that officer behavior is within acceptable boundaries. On a departmental level, officers should play a larger role in decision making, especially on matters that directly affect them.

Second, departments should provide counseling services. Psychologists and other professionals should be available to counsel officers who are experiencing problems. Some problems can be effectively dealt with only by professionals. At the same time, however, psychologists should not be used to supplant supervisors' efforts and responsibilities.

Third, actions should be taken to strengthen the support skills of agency personnel. Individual police officers should receive social support from their fellow officers and from their superiors. Both groups should be targeted for social support training. If a more supportive environment can be achieved, everyone would be less stressed.

154

PART TWO
Supervising Human
Resources: Training,
Evaluation, and
Discipline

It cannot be overemphasized that the supervisor plays an important role in reducing police officer stress. A police department can have the best programs and training available, but their effectiveness depends on the supervisor to implement them. The supervisor must take action to prevent job stress in the first place; if this fails, the supervisor must diagnose the problem and ensure that the proper assistance is provided.

Reduction through Training

Training is an effective way to combat stress, and a variety of training programs are available that departments can implement to help reduce it. To begin, training programs help officers understand their jobs and job requirements. This could assist in reducing officer cynicism and negativism. Social support and coping training could also help officers to deal with job stress and enable them to assist other officers who experience stress-related problems. Departments can also implement family orientation programs which help spouses understand and cope with job-related stress problems. Also, supervisory training is a fundamental necessity. Supervisors must be able to identify officers displaying symptoms of stress and be familiar with the department's resources and programs with which to competently respond to the problems. Finally, stress-reduction training should be a part of every department's basic and in-service training curriculum.

EMPLOYEE WELLNESS PROGRAMS

Definition of Wellness

Historically, the term *health* referred to the absence of disease; that is, if an individual was not sick or afflicted with some illness, he or she was deemed healthy. However, in 1947 the World Health Organization redefined the term **health** as "a state of complete physical, mental, and social well-being, and not merely the absence of disease or infirmity" (p. 29). The World Health Organization's definition added a new dimension to "health" by placing it on a continuum whereby one could be "healthy" or ill. This definition has continually been refined to the point that today many people in our society approach health "holistically"; that is, they not only consider disease but also assess diet, mental outlook, and social integration and skills. This approach is characterized in Figure 7–2.

This approach has come to be known as wellness. **Wellness** has also been defined as "an integrated and dynamic level of functioning oriented toward maximizing potential, dependent upon self-responsibility" (Robbins et al., 1991:8). This definition implies that individuals will adopt a lifestyle in which they attempt to achieve the highest level of well-being. This does not mean that everyone must achieve perfect wellness, but everyone should constantly be aware of the implications of their actions and strive for a more healthy lifestyle. People must examine every facet of their lives and, if necessary, select alternatives that are most conducive to health and wellness. This not only includes physical exercise, but also other activities such as diet, consumption of alcohol or drugs, use of tobacco products, or even the use of a seatbelt in a vehicle.

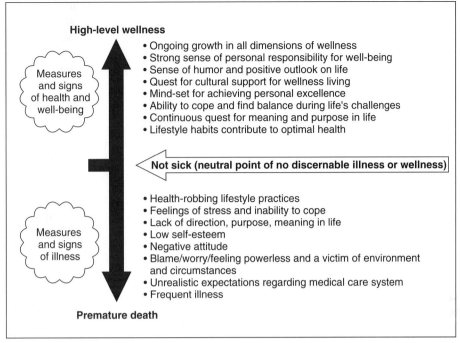

FIGURE 7–2. Illness-Wellness Continuum
Source: Robbins, G., D. Powers, and S. Burgess (1997). *A Wellness Way of Life* 3d ed.
Brown and Benchmark: Madison, Wis., p. 8

Dimensions of Wellness

Wellness includes a broad range of activities and considerations that touch every facet of our lives. Specifically, however, five important dimensions are subsumed within wellness (Anspaugh et al., 1991). To move toward optimal health or wellness, individuals must improve their lifestyle in each area.

1. *Spiritual.* Spirituality refers to an individual's belief in some force, such as religion, science, nature, or a higher power. It includes the individual's ethics, values, and morals. It provides people with direction and enables them to discover and act out their basic purposes in life.
2. *Social.* Social skills are extremely important in life. People must have the ability to interact with others in their environment, and they must have the ability to form intimate relationships with significant others. Individuals must be socially mature to the point that they are tolerant of ideas and opinions that differ from their own.
3. *Emotional.* Emotional health is the individual's ability to express his or her feelings and to understand the feelings and emotions of others. One must be able to control stress and deal with people and situations under adverse conditions.
4. *Intellectual.* People must be able to continuously learn and use newly acquired information. This is a necessary component for coping with the job, environment, and life in general. People who fail to absorb new information have difficulty keeping up with our ever-changing society.

156

PART TWO
Supervising Human
Resources: Training,
Evaluation, and
Discipline

5. *Physical.* The physical dimension implies that individuals not only maintain an adequate level of physical ability to perform a job, but also that they strive to achieve physical well-being. This ability is measured in terms of cardiovascular capacity, body fat, and nutrition. It also means that individuals will avoid tobacco products and drugs and other things and activities that adversely affect their health.

Each of these dimensions is important to a healthy life. An overcommitment to one area and the neglect of others will not result in any appreciable improvement in a person's life or wellness. Individuals must examine their lives with respect to each of these dimensions.

There are specific actions that an individual should take to achieve a maximum level of wellness. Figure 7–3 provides a rating scale for activities that police officers should consider in order to achieve wellness. The higher the rating, the more important the activity.

It is not a simple task to adopt the activities and goals supported in Figure 7–3. But the achievement of wellness requires a planned program, commitment, and support and encouragement from family members and people in the workplace.

POLICE FITNESS AND WELLNESS PROGRAMS

Police administrators have long been concerned with the physical ability of their officers. Only recently, however, have police departments, government, and industry become concerned with their employees' wellness. The following sections will examine physical fitness or ability and police wellness programs.

Finding an Acceptable Test: Practical and Legal Considerations

Physical Requirements: Height and Weight

Historically, police departments used height and weight requirements as a measure of police physical fitness. It was commonly believed that police officers had to be brutish and capable of handling any physical confrontation. For example, O. W. Wilson (1963:139), former Chicago police chief and one of the early founders of the police professionalism movement in the United States, noted:

> The patrolman is frequently called upon to display both strength and agility, and it is desirable that the standards for all police officers be worked out in such a way that there will be more officers in the upper height range. The small man is at a disadvantage in dealing with a crowd or with an unruly individual. The larger man is better able to observe in a crowd, and his size tends to instill a respect not felt toward the smaller person. One good-sized policeman, when asked whether there were any advantages in being so large replied that it saved a lot of fighting.

Wilson's view dominated policing into the early 1970s. Police officers had to be big, and size was associated with ability. No consideration was given to how *effectively* large- or small-statured persons could handle themselves in confrontations or when performing other police functions.

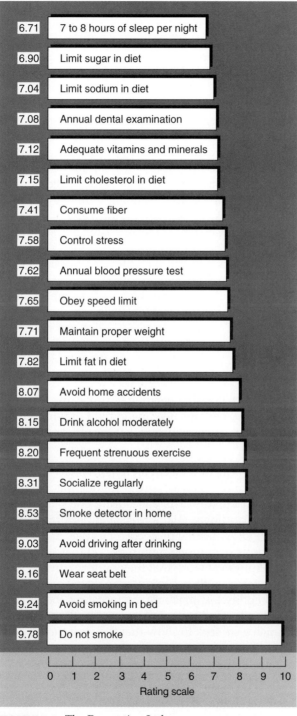

Rating	Behavior
6.71	7 to 8 hours of sleep per night
6.90	Limit sugar in diet
7.04	Limit sodium in diet
7.08	Annual dental examination
7.12	Adequate vitamins and minerals
7.15	Limit cholesterol in diet
7.41	Consume fiber
7.58	Control stress
7.62	Annual blood pressure test
7.65	Obey speed limit
7.71	Maintain proper weight
7.82	Limit fat in diet
8.07	Avoid home accidents
8.15	Drink alcohol moderately
8.20	Frequent strenuous exercise
8.31	Socialize regularly
8.53	Smoke detector in home
9.03	Avoid driving after drinking
9.16	Wear seat belt
9.24	Avoid smoking in bed
9.78	Do not smoke

Rating scale: 0 1 2 3 4 5 6 7 8 9 10

FIGURE 7–3. The Prevention Index
Source: Anspaugh, D., M. Hamrick and F. Rosoto (1991)
Concepts and Wellness Applications, Mosby: St. Louis p. 23

158

PART TWO
Supervising Human
Resources: Training,
Evaluation, and
Discipline

Title VII of the 1964 Civil Rights Act prohibited the use of selection criteria that discriminated against protected classes. Consequently, the height and weight requirements which many departments used until the 1970s were deemed illegal by the federal courts as discriminating against women. After that time police departments, in an effort to produce acceptable physical standards, developed a variety of job-related tests.

Physical Abilities Requirements and Testing

Today about 80 percent of large police departments and state police agencies use qualifying strength and agility tests (Ash et al., 1990). In the past these tests—and some still remain in effect today—have ranged from a minimally acceptable number of push-ups to timed running and jumping tests, including dragging weights, pushing cars, leaping over six-foot walls, walking on horizontal ladders, crawling through tunnels, and negotiating monkey bars. The problem of course is that police officers very seldom perform any of these feats. How often does a police officer do push-ups on the job? Walk on beams in an attic? Jump over six-foot walls?

Obviously, an entry-level physical abilities test has been sorely needed that fairly tests people in terms of the demands of policing, as well as one that promises an ability to successfully withstand legal challenges. One such test is the **Police Officers Physical Abilities Test (POPAT),** developed by a Canadian and now used by the Royal Canadian Mounted Police and several agencies in the United States (see Peak et al., 1992). In brief, the POPAT is based on the theory that police officers must be able to perform three basic, job-related physical functions:

1. *Getting to the problem,* possibly needing to run, climb, vault, and so forth.
2. *Resolving the problem,* perhaps needing to fight or wrestle with an offender.
3. *Removing the problem,* often requiring that the officer carry heavy persons or objects.

This timed test normally includes a circuit that involves running, climbing, and jumping; pushing and pulling on a "power training machine" that provides resistance; vaulting with squat thrusts (measuring one's ability to perform work while under maximal cardiovascular stress); and perform a weight carry.

To establish the POPAT testing protocol for a given jurisdiction, the agency's officers complete forms over a one-month period that solicit information concerning the kinds of physical work that they perform during their workday. Information from the forms is then computer analyzed and the data are used to develop a physical agility test that actually measures the recruit's ability to do the kinds of work performed by police officers in that specific locale. If challenged in court, such tests seek to show that they test for the actual job requirements of that jurisdiction and are not discriminatory against anyone—male or female, short or tall, small or large.

An Overview of Wellness Programs

Police departments throughout the United States have developed a variety of physical maintenance programs. Some departments have developed voluntary programs while others have implemented mandatory programs in which officers are disciplined if they fail to maintain a specified level of physical fitness. Still other agencies have adopted an incentive-based approach where officers who maintain an acceptable level of physical fitness are provided rewards such as a pay supplement or a bonus.

There is also substantial variety in how departments provide physical fitness facilities. Some departments pay officers' membership fees in health clubs while others have constructed training and health maintenance facilities available only to police officers. Still other departments have implemented requirements and provided no facilities whatsoever. These departments believe that physical readiness is a job requirement and the department does not have an obligation to support officers in maintaining their fitness. Finally, in order to facilitate physical fitness programs a number of agencies give officers time off to participate in fitness programs.

One type of physical fitness program—weight control—was introduced by the Kansas City, Missouri, police department (North, 1993). In 1991 the department spent $18,000 for workout equipment, but it had no mandatory fitness programs until May 1993, when the department implemented mandatory weight standards for its 1,150 employees. Former Chief of Police Steve Bishop carried out the program not only for health reasons, but also because he believed that slimmer, fitter officers would be better able to handle calls and gain respect from citizens. He also supported the program because of anticipated reductions in sick leave and medical expenses.

As noted above, most police physical fitness programs attempt to go beyond simple weight control and to evaluate officers' physical health. This is generally accomplished by a battery of tests which comprehensively evaluate an individual's strength and agility. The most common test consists of the following:

1. *Cardiovascular efficiency,* which is measured by a one and one-half mile run, a step test, or a treadmill test.
2. *Body fat composition,* which is measured with calipers or by weighing the individual in a tank of water. An individual's total weight is not as important as the percent of body fat.
3. *Flexibility,* which is measured by a reaching exercise similar to touching one's toes.
4. *Upper-body strength,* which is measured by a bench press or by push-ups.
5. *Abdominal strength,* which is measured by sit ups.

Individual test results are compared with the test scores for others of the same gender and age group. Generally, if a person tests in the upper 50 percentile he or she is deemed to be fairly physically healthy.

Other departments have chosen a more comprehensive physical maintenance program. The California Highway Patrol implemented a two-phase program. The first phase consisted of medical screening in which officers were given complete physical examinations. Once an officer successfully passed the medical screening, he or she progressed to phase two, physical agility screening (Craig, 1981). The medical phase was initiated to ensure that officers were capable and would not be harmed when involved in physical fitness testing. The combined results of the tests provided an accurate profile of each officer's health.

Wellness programs have been touted by unions and employers alike. Unions have supported them as employee benefits while employers have extolled them because they believe that such programs lead to an increase in productivity, a reduction in the use of sick leave, and a reduction in medical and insurance costs. Although wellness programs are definitely an employee benefit, it is questionable whether they provide enough benefits to offset their costs to the employer. For example, police agencies often must purchase equipment and a facility or provide one and give officers time off to participate in a program. This can be expensive.

A number of studies have examined wellness programs. Specific evaluations have shown that these programs can be successful. For example, a Johnson & Johnson Company study of more than 11,000 employees showed that a wellness program could reduce hospital admissions and the number of hospital days per admission (Bly et al., 1986). Similarly, wellness program users at Coors Brewing Company have medical claims that are 13 percent lower than those of employees who do not use the program (Kertesz, 1993).

Case Study 7–2
Lean Gene Has No Steam

Officer Gene Jennings is impressive. At 6 feet 5 inches tall and 310 pounds, few people dare challenge his authority. His size and strength are the reasons that Sgt. Joe Lyle selected him to be a member of the Hill City police department's Repeat Offender Program (ROP). In the ROP, officers engage in forced entry into apartments and houses, serving search warrants on the "worst of the worst" wanted felons. Their work is dangerous and physical, and that is why all officers selected by Lyle are nearly as big as Jennings and in top physical condition.

Lyle was a weight trainer prior to joining the force, and he has developed an equally impressive training regimen for the other ROP officers. They usually work out as a team at least once a week and pride themselves on never losing a suspect or a physical confrontation. To "blow off steam" they also frequently party together.

One day, while attempting to serve a robbery warrant at a local motel, the suspect escaped through a rear window and led officers on a foot pursuit. As the new member of the team, Jennings was assigned to cover the rear of the building, so he participated in the foot pursuit. After three blocks

Jennings and his two partners were exhausted and unable to maintain their chase.

The following week, the same suspect attempted to rob a fast-food market, where he killed a clerk and seriously wounded a police officer. Irate because the ROP team failed to catch the suspect earlier, Hill City patrol officers begin to criticize the ROP officers and challenge their claims of superior fitness. In one instance, a fight nearly ensues. The chief of police, concerned about the original incident and confrontations between the officers, asks the patrol commander to conduct an investigation to determine if any procedural or training issues require the department's attention.

1. As the patrol commander, what is your assessment of the situation?
2. Sgt. Lyle adamantly defends his officers as the most fit in the department. What kinds of inquiries might you make to determine whether this is the case, and to see if the officers are up to the demands of the job?
3. What are Sgt. Lyle's responsibilities in this role? Does he appear to have failed?

The best wellness programs are comprehensive compared with programs that focus only on one or a few areas. A police department wellness program should be flexible and attempt to assist officers in each of the above areas. It is important that departments develop individual programs for officers instead of depending on some kind of predetermined standard program. It is also important that officers receive continuous feedback about their wellness and progress toward becoming well (Erfurt, Foote, and Heirich, 1992).

Finally, it should be noted that the supervisor plays a significant role in wellness programs, whether they are formal programs or programs developed by the officers themselves. Supervisors must first be familiar with wellness and what it means. Then, supervisors will be able to identify subordinates who maintain healthy lifestyles and those who have problems. If the department has a formal program, supervisors should encourage officers to participate in it. If no program exists, supervisors should encourage officers to join a fitness facility or seek professional assistance depending upon the seriousness of the problem. In either case, the supervisor should take an active role in their subordinates fitness.

EMPLOYEE ASSISTANCE PROGRAMS

A Positive Response

The term **employee assistance program (EAP)** is relatively new, especially in policing. Historically, police officers were considered to be immune from stress and other personal problems, and, indeed, personal problems were not allowed or recognized by departments or officers. A few departments, however, became involved in various forms of employee assistance fairly early.

Early Initiatives

In the past, police departments hired or sought the volunteer services of ministers and priests to serve as department chaplains. Chaplains and spirituality were seen as the primary tool by which to deal with human problems. When formal programs were developed, they involved alcohol counseling for police officers with drinking problems. For example, the Chicago Police Officers' Fellowship began in 1955 to work with alcoholism, the New York City Alcohol Program was started in 1966, and Boston assigned an officer full-time to a departmental alcohol program in 1959.

Implementation of Employee Assistance Programs (EAPs)

Not until the 1970s and 1980s, when increasing numbers of departments began to implement EAPs, was employee assistance recognized as an important human resource tool. In addition to alcohol rehabilitation programs, some departments hired departmental psychologists or counselors. The psychologists not only worked with the alcohol-dependent officers but also with officers who were suffering from stress or had been involved in critical incidents such as shootings. Finally, the drug epidemic of the 1990s created a need for drug counseling. A number of departments started drug testing and counseling programs, which were housed within EAPs.

162

PART TWO
*Supervising Human
Resources: Training,
Evaluation, and
Discipline*

Police officers experience a number of problems that may necessitate their use of an EAP. As noted, police agencies should have a comprehensive wellness program to assist officers in coping with stress, but if that fails or if the department does not have a wellness program, an EAP should be available to assist officers who experience significant amounts of stress or whose health is jeopardized by it. This is especially true when job stress results in problem drinking, substance abuse, mental problems such as depression, or family problems.

Advocates of EAPs note that such programs assist the organization by helping employees who are responsible for disrupting the organization and by reducing the amount of time supervisors must spend dealing with problem employees. Basically, EAPs are a step toward humanizing the organization and increasing productivity (Perry and Cayer, 1992). Problem employees deplete significant amounts of organizational resources. The primary function of an EAP is to reduce employee absenteeism, accidents, terminations, and compensation claims and to enhance the organization's overall productivity.

Even though police supervisors are generally charged with intervening in employee problems, EAPs provide more professional services. EAPs can also help educate supervisors on how to identify and respond to employees' problems. One of the major organizational quandaries with problem employees is getting supervisors to take action. Supervisors too often ignore the troubled employee or attempt to handle it themselves. In most cases, formal intervention by an EAP is much more effective and beneficial to the employee and the agency, especially if done early.

Alcohol Abuse and Counseling

Drinking and alcoholism have always been a problem in policing as the following incidents taken from newspaper reports demonstrate:

- A Baton Rouge police supervisor was suspended without pay following a traffic accident. The supervisor crashed his unmarked police vehicle into a ditch. A subsequent breath test found the officer had a .23 percent alcohol level.
- A sheriff from De Queen, Arkansas, remains on the job after being fined $750 and having his license suspended after pleading no contest to a drunk driving charge.
- A Ritzville, Washington, police chief was given a work release sentence stemming out of a conviction for robbery. The lenient sentence was attributed to the chief's history of alcoholism.

Furthermore, evidence suggests that drinking problems are pervasive among police officers. In a study of police alcohol usage, Van Raalte (1979) found that two-thirds of the officers in his sample reported that they drank on duty. Kroes (1976) estimated that 25 percent of all police officers are alcohol dependent.

Police officers are a close-knit group who work and relax together, often in isolation from other people. Generally, when they unwind they use alcohol. When officers' drinking becomes excessive, other officers—and frequently supervisors ignore that a problem exists. In the end, however, covering up officers'

drinking only aggravates the problem. And drinking behavior that remains un-
treated frequently leads to more serious departmental problems.

Officers with drinking problems often display symptoms that can alert the supervisor. They tend to deny that they have a drinking problem; they often drink alone; they cannot control the amount of alcohol they consume; they crave alcohol; they have an increased tolerance to its effects; they have memory blackouts; and they develop a physical dependence on alcohol. Officers with drinking problems also tend to use more sick leave and have other personal problems as a result of their drinking.

Alcoholics Anonymous (AA) is the most effective program in dealing with alcoholism. Its group sessions not only assist officers to deal with their problem, but its long-term support helps officers remain sober. Unfortunately, it is often difficult to get police officers involved in AA or other self help programs attended by the general public. Consequently, a number of police departments have implemented their own programs. It does not matter which form of counseling the department uses as long as officers have services available and are willing to use them.

Drug Abuse and Counseling

Drug use in policing is not as pervasive as alcohol abuse. However, it does pose a serious problem. Kraska and Kappeler (1988) found that 20 percent of the police officers in one agency had used illegal drugs on duty at one time or another. Police drug-testing programs have identified problems. A study of the New Jersey State Police found that only five officers—.02 percent—tested positive for drug use (Burden, 1988). The substantial differences between these two studies point to an important factor: Drug testing appears to reduce the incidence of drug use among police officers. If officers know they are going to be tested, they are less likely to use drugs.

Drug testing takes many forms. Figure 7–4 shows how 24 police agencies approach drug testing. Seventy-five percent of the departments require officers suspected of drug usage to submit to drug testing while only one department

FIGURE 7–4. Drug-Testing Procedures in 24 Police Agencies

Job Category and Event Tested	Number of Departments	Percent
Job applicant	15	62.5%
Probationary officers	5	20.8
Officers seeking transfer to sensitive jobs	3	12.5
Officers in sensitive jobs	4	16.7
Officers suspected of drug use	18	75.0
After auto accidents	2	8.3
Scheduled testing	1	4.2

Source: J. T. McEwen, B. Manili, and E. Connors. *Employee Drug Testing Policies in Police Departments* (Washington, D.C.: National Institute of Justice, Research in Brief, 1986).

164

PART TWO
Supervising Human
Resources: Training,
Evaluation, and
Discipline

has scheduled testing. A number of departments require officers in selected assignments, such as narcotics or the special response team, to submit to periodic drug testing, and some departments require officers being transferred to such units to be tested prior to beginning their new assignment. It seems that departments have selected testing procedures that meet their needs and are acceptable to the department's personnel and leadership.

If an officer is found to be under the influence of illegal drugs, the police department is faced with a difficult decision: What should be done with the employee? There are a number of arguments for immediate termination. First, the police officer has committed a crime. Second, the officer has associated with known criminals when obtaining the illegal drugs. And third, the officer's drug use poses a liability problem for the police department.

However, immediate termination is counter to a humane view of personnel administration. It should be realized that job stress may be the primary contributing factor to the drug usage. Second, the department has a significant investment in each of its officers, and a decision to terminate should not be made lightly. Finally, problem officers can be salvaged and returned to work as productive officers. Thus, termination, although an acceptable choice for officers with chronic drug problems, may not be the best solution for officers who had not previously caused the department any problems or otherwise been in trouble.

Police officers who are found to be under the influence of illegal drugs should be investigated and sent to a departmental EAP. The EAP staff, in conjunction with internal affairs staff, should be charged with the responsibility of determining if an officer should be terminated or disciplined and rehabilitated. Employee names should remain confidential until the department decides to pursue formal termination charges. Factors considered in making this decision include the severity of the offense (i.e., the type and amount of drug used and whether the officer went beyond mere usage), prior drug and disciplinary problems, and the probability of the officer being rehabilitated.

If a rehabilitation program is recommended, all activities should remain confidential. The EAP should be charged with determining the effectiveness of any rehabilitation program, when an officer is to be reassigned to police duties, and any type of follow-up testing or treatment. The officer is not stigmatized by the event if these activities are vested with the EAP.

Finally, the EAP should be available to assist officers who voluntarily seek assistance with drug problems. If an officer voluntarily seeks counseling, the EAP should keep the information confidential unless the officer's behavior poses a threat to the department (e.g., the officer is using drugs while on duty). The EAP should determine a treatment program, follow-up testing program, and follow-up treatment if necessary.

General Counseling and the EAP

EAPs also handle a number of problems in addition to alcohol and substance abuse, including psychological problems, marital problems, and police officer shootings.

Psychological Counseling

It is not commonly recognized that police officers experience psychological problems that require intervention. Police officers are typically viewed as physically and psychologically strong and resistant to any form of personal problems. Police officers experience a number of psychological problems, including depression, sleep deprivation, hypertension, feelings of persecution, inferiority complexes, and dealing with failure when they cannot meet personal goals. Many of these problems are brought on by stress while others are the result of police officers being human and possessing human failings. In some cases these psychological problems result in physiological problems which can only be effectively dealt with through some form of counseling or rehabilitation.

Marital Counseling

Moreover, officers frequently encounter marital problems. Officers often place the job before their families. Their spouses often feel that the department expects them to adjust to the demands of the job, rather than the department making allowances for problems and conflicts; spouses also often feel that police work inhibits them from making long-range family plans. Thus, the job-related stress of officers affects their family life, which in turn creates additional stress that then affects the officer on the job—a vicious cycle which must be confronted by the officer and spouse. EAPs usually have counselors available not only to police officers, but also to family members who should be encouraged to make use of their services.

Police Shootings

Police shootings are extremely traumatic for police officers. They exact a profound psychological and physiological impact on them. For example, four out of five officers experience perceptual distortions and about two out of three officers experience auditory distortions after being involved in a shooting incident (Solomon, 1988). Officers may also experience tunnel vision or a heightened sense of detail. These physiological manifestations are the consequences of the body attempting to cope with a stressful event.

An officer involved in a shooting will psychologically progress through several phases once the shooting is over (Lippert and Ferrara, 1981). First is the denial phase, where the officer often is overcome with shock and disbelief and attempts to deny the shooting took place. Once the officer comes to grips with the shooting, the information-gathering phase begins. Here the officer realizes the magnitude of the act and attempts to gather as much information as possible about it. The motivation at this point is to prove that the shooting was justified.

The next phase is the reporting phase. This represents the official investigation. The officer, acting on instinct and training, will attempt to provide the facts to investigators. Physical anxiety sets in shortly after the shooting when the officer feels the full brunt of the stress. The officer is unable to sleep, is tense, and begins to question whether he or she should be a police officer.

Within 48 hours, most officers seek peer group support. They discuss the event with their fellow officers and seek their assurance that the shooting was

166

PART TWO
Supervising Human
Resources: Training,
Evaluation, and
Discipline

The death of a fellow officer is one of the most traumatic experiences that officers face during their career.
Courtesy Washoe County, Nevada, Sheriff's Office

justified and that everything will turn out all right. After two or three days, the officer engages in moral self-questioning. The officer relives the shooting, questioning its morality. At this point, the officer may believe that he or she cannot endure the stress of the situation. It is critical that officers involved in shootings be required to see counselors who have the experience and expertise to deal with the problem.

Obviously, police officers who have been involved in a shooting or who are experiencing other serious personal problems must be encouraged to use EAP services; however, police officers will not use the EAP voluntarily unless every aspect of their contact is confidential. Therefore, it is crucial that the EAP be physically located away from the department and that all EAP records (except those associated with disciplinary actions) remain confidential. Generally, it takes a considerable amount of effort to get officers to use the EAP, and a single breach of confidentiality will have a substantial prohibitive effect. Widespread utilization will come only after experimentation and officers begin to trust the program, staff, and department.

HOW SUPERVISORS CAN HELP

Stress is obviously a complex problem for supervisors to address. If stress is not dealt with, it eventually will lead to more severe problems. To some extent stress is the source of many behavioral problems among police officers. Thus, if supervisors can deal effectively with job stress, many other problems can be avoided.

The manner in which the supervisor responds to officer stress creates the norm to which other officers will later react. It is recommended that supervisors consider the following practices for helping patrol officers deal with their stress (adapted from Anderson et al., 1995):

- *Use listening skills.* Supervisors should make sure they are accurately hearing the facts and tuning into the right emotions.
- *Read people, including their body language and what is not expressed.*
- *Be supportive.* Supervisors should actively let the officers know they want to help and are available.
- *Reward good work.*
- *Use discipline fairly.* For discipline to work, it must be applied predictably and appropriately, across officers, and across time.
- *Encourage the development of support groups.* Officers will learn to give and receive support, express themselves, develop strong team discussions, and increase trust.
- *Reflect on your own style and relationships.* Supervisors develop new values, priorities, and style of relating, and they should periodically reflect on what is important, how the job is changing, and the kinds of relationships and professionalism that are imparted.

STUDIES PROVIDE CAUSE FOR HOPE

This chapter has discussed a dour subject and contained a considerable amount of gloomy information. However, several studies have indicated policing is not as dismal as it seems for its personnel.

For example, a 1994 study examined the National Mortality Detail Files to determine whether police officers had a higher rate of suicide than members of the public. The researchers concluded that when controls are added for differences in socioeconomic variables such as age, race, gender, and place of employment, "being a police officer is not significantly associated with the odds of death by suicide" (Stack and Kelly, 1994:84). Research also has generally indicated a small proportion of drug use by officers (Kappeler et al., 1996). And, while some older studies reported a high rate of police divorce (Durner et al., 1975), the majority concluded that the level of divorce is far lower than commonly assumed and is no higher than the national average. "The reality is that the overwhelming majority of police officers have families and stable marriages" (Kappeler et al., 1996:227).

Finally, while police stress has been linked to many psychological, performance, and health problems, there is no empirical support for the myth that police officers have a shorter life expectancy after retirement than that found in civilian populations (Kappeler et al., 1996).

SUMMARY

This chapter has addressed police officer stress, wellness, and employee assistance programs. These three areas represent critical issues in police personnel administration. Police departments must plan for meeting the needs of their human resources just as they plan operations or the purchase of capital equipment. Because police officers represent a significant investment, resources must be expended to ensure that they are cared for and can operate effectively.

Stress occurs in all jobs, but it is particularly troublesome in policing. Police officers must contend with problems arising from the organization, the public they serve, the criminal justice system, and the job itself. For the supervisor, stress often multiplies with the added administrative and operational responsibilities that accompany promotion. Officers must be able to receive assistance from the department—particularly when the stress level affects their work, family life, or personal well-being.

Police agencies, as part of their obligation to employees, should implement full-service employee assistance programs. If departments weigh the costs of attending to veteran employees against the cost of continually hiring new ones, it clearly is less expensive and more humane to provide employees with the assistance necessary to resolve their problems.

Finally, this chapter demonstrated that the supervisor plays a key role in employee stress reduction and wellness. Supervisors must constantly evaluate their subordinates and make judgments about their stress and wellness. If problems are detected, the supervisor must encourage officers to seek help. If they refuse to obtain assistance, the supervisor must in some cases force them to do so, for the good of the individual officer, the agency, and the community at large. Furthermore, the supervisor must be available to encourage and counsel subordinates as they work through their problems. This is a key function of supervision.

KEY TERMS

stress   (p. 145)
stressors   (p. 145)
eustress   (p. 145)
distress   (p. 145)

General Adaptive Syndrome (GAS)   (p. 145)
health   (p. 154)
wellness   (p. 154)

Police Officers Physical Abilities Test (POPAT) (p. 158)
employee assistance program (EAP)   (p. 161)

ITEMS FOR REVIEW

1. Explain the dimensions and process of stress.
2. Describe the typical stress pattern according to years of police service.
3. Examine the four general areas of police work that contribute to stress.
4. Explain how police personnel can try to manage their stress levels.
5. Describe the kinds of affirmative measures supervisors can take to assist officers in dealing with stress.
6. Define and explain employee wellness programs.
7. Explain the function of an employee assistance program.

SOURCES

169

CHAPTER 7
Stress, Wellness, and
Employee Assistance
Programs

ALBRECT, S., and GREEN, M. (1977). "Attitudes toward the police and larger attitude complex and implications for police-community relationships." *Criminology,* 15:67–86.

ALDAG, R. J., and BRIEF, A. P. (1978). "Supervisory style and police role stress." *Journal of Police Science and Administration* 6(3):362–67.

ANDERSON, W., SWENSON, D., and CLAY, D. (1995). *Stress management for law enforcement officers.* Englewood Cliffs, N.J.: Prentice Hall.

ANSPAUGH, D. J., HAMRICK, M. H., and ROSATO, R. D. (1991). *Wellness: Concepts and applications.* St. Louis: Mosby.

ASH, P., SLORA, K. B., and BRITTON, C. F. (1990). "Police agency officer selection practices." *Journal of Police Science and Administration* 17 (December):259–64.

BLY, J. L., JONES, R. C., and RICHARDSON, J. E. (1986). "Impact of worksite health promotion on health care costs and utilization." *Journal of the American Medical Association* 256(23):3235–40.

BURDEN, O. P. (1986). "The hidden truths about police drug use." *Law Enforcement Times* (March 10):1, 4.

CRAIG, G. (1981). "Physical maintenance project: California highway patrol develops physical maintenance standards." *Police Chief* 48(11):26–27.

CRANK, J. P., and CALDERO, M. (1991). "The production of occupational stress in medium-sized police agencies: A survey of line officers in eight municipal departments." *Journal of Criminal Justice* 19:339–49.

CULLEN, F. T., LINK, B. G., TRAVIS, L. F., and LEMMING, T. (1983). "Paradox in policing: A note on perceptions of danger." *Journal of Police Science and Administration* 11(4):457–62.

DIETRICH, J. F. (1989). "Helping subordinates face stress." *Police Chief* 56(11):44–47.

DURNER, J., KROEKER, M., MILLER, C., and REYNOLDS, C. (1975). "Divorce—another occupational hazard." *Police Chief* 62(11):48–53.

ERFURT, J. C., FOOTE, A., and HEIRICH, M. A. (1992). "The cost-effectiveness of worksite wellness programs for hypertension control, weight loss, smoking cessation, and exercise." *Personnel Psychology* 45(1):5–27.

FRANZ, V., and JONES, D. (1987). "Perceptions of organizational performance in suburban police departments: A critique of the military model." *Journal of Police Science and Administration* 15(2):153–61.

GAFFIN, J. W., and LOGAN, D. D. (1983). "Sources of stress among women police officers." *Journal of Police Science and Administration* 11(1):46–53.

GAINES, L. K., and VAN TUBERGEN, N. (1989). "Job stress in police work: An exploratory analysis into structural causes." *American Journal of Criminal Justice* 13(2):197–214.

GRAF, F. A. (1986). "The relationship between social support and occupational stress among police officers." *Journal of Police Science and Administration* 14(3):178–86.

GEISEL, J. (1992). "Wellness impact uncertain." *Business Insurance* (April 20):1, 29.

HARRISON, E. F., and PELLETIER, M. A. (1987). "Perceptions of bureaucratization, role performance, and organizational effectiveness in a metropolitan police department." *Journal of Police Science and Administration* 15(4):262–70.

KAPPELER, V. E., BLUMBERG, M., and POTTER, G. W. (1996). *The mythology of crime and criminal justice.* 2d ed. Prospect Heights, Ill.: Waveland.

KAUFMANN, G. M., and BEEHR, T. A. (1989). "Occupational stressors, individual strains, and social supports among police officers." *Human Relations* 42(2):185–97.

KERTESZ, L. (1993). "Preventive maintenance pays off: Employers tout health care savings from wellness program." *Business Insurance* (February 1):14.

KRASKA, P. B., and KAPPELER, V. E. (1988). "A theoretical and descriptive study of police on duty drug use." *American Journal of Police* 8(1):1–36.

KROES, W. (1976). *Society's victim, the policeman: An analysis of job stress in policing.* Springfield, Ill.: Charles C. Thomas.

170

PART TWO
Supervising Human
Resources: Training,
Evaluation, and
Discipline

KROES, W., MARGOLIS, B., and HURRELL, J. (1974). "Job stress in policemen." *Journal of Police Science and Administration* 2(2):145–55.

LANGWORTHY, R. H. (1992). "Organizational structure." In G. W. Cordner and D. C. Hale (eds.). *What Works in Policing?* Cincinnati: Anderson.

LIPPERT, W., and FERRARA, E. R. (1981). "The cost of 'coming out on top': Emotional responses to surviving the deadly battle." *FBI Law Enforcement Bulletin* (December):6–10.

MAGUIRE, K., and PASTORE, A. L. (eds.) (1996). *Sourcebook of criminal justice statistics, 1995.* U.S. Department of Justice, Bureau of Justice Statistics. Washington, D.C.: U.S. Government Printing Office.

McMURRAY, H. L. (1990). "Attitudes of assaulted officers and their policy implications." *Journal of Police Science and Administration.* 17(1):44–48.

MORASH, M., and HAARR, R. (1991). "Gender, workplace problems, and stress in policing." Paper presented at the Annual Meeting of the Academy of Criminal Justice Sciences, Nashville, Tenn.

NATIONAL INSTITUTE OF JUSTICE (1997). *Developing a law enforcement stress program for officers and their families.* Washington, D.C.: U.S. Government Printing Office.

NORTH, J. (1993). "KC police fight fat along with crime." *Kansas City Star* (February 3):B–1.

PEAK, K., FARENHOLTZ, D., and COXEY, G. (1992). "Physical abilities testing for police officers: A flexible, job related approach." *Police Chief* (January):51–56.

PERRY, R. W., and CAYER, N. J. (1992). "Evaluating employee assistance programs: Concerns and strategies for public employers." *Public Personnel Management* 21(3):323–33.

POGREBIN, M. R., and POOLE, E. D. (1991). "Police and tragic events: The management of emotions." *Journal of Criminal Justice* 19:395–403.

REISER, M. (1978). "Some organizational stresses on policemen." In L. Gaines and T. Ricks (eds.). *Managing the Police Organization.* St. Paul, Minn.: West.

ROBBINS, G., POWERS, D., and BURGESS, S. (1991). *A wellness way of life.* Dubuque, Iowa: William C. Brown.

SELYE, H. (1981). *Stress without distress.* Philadelphia: Lippincott.

SEWELL, J. D. (1983). "The development of a critical life events scale for law enforcement." *Journal of Police Science and Administration* 11(1):109–16.

SOLOMON, R. (1988). "Post-shooting trauma." *Police Chief* 55(10):40–41.

TALARICO, S. M., and SWANSON, C. R. (1982). "An analysis of police perceptions of supervisory and administrative support." *Police Studies* 5(1):47–54.

UNITED STATES DEPARTMENT OF JUSTICE, FEDERAL BUREAU OF INVESTIGATION. *Crime in the United States, 1995.* Washington, D.C.: U.S. Department of Justice.

VAN MAANEN, J. (1978). "The asshole." In P. Manning and J. Van Maanen (eds.). *Policing: A view from the street.* Santa Monica. Calif.: Goodyear.

VAN RAALTE, R. C. (1979). "Alcohol as a problem among officers." *Police Chief* 44:38–40.

VIOLANTI, J. M. (1983). "Stress patterns in police work: A longitudinal study." *Journal of Police Science and Administration* 11(2):211–16.

VIOLANTI, J. M., and MARSHALL, J. R. (1983). "The police stress process." *Journal of Police Science and Administration* 11(4):389–94.

WEXLER, C. and LOGAN, D. (1983). "Sources of stress among women police officers." *Journal of Police Science and Administration,* 11(1), pp. 46–53.

WOOD, S. D., KREITNER, R., FRIEDMAN, G. M., EDWARDS, M., and SOVA, M. A. (1982). "Cost-effective wellness screening: A case study of 4,524 law enforcement officers." *Journal of Police Science and Administration* 10(3):273–78.

WORLD HEALTH ORGANIZATION. (1947). "Constitution of the world health organization." *Chronicle of the World Health Organization* 1:29–43.

WRIGHT, J. (1984). "EAP: An important supervisory tool." *Supervisory Management* 29(2):15–23.

8

Ethical Issues, Values, and Liability

He that would govern others, first should be the master of himself.
—Philip Massinger

We are discussing no small matter, but how we ought to live.
—Socrates, Plato's *Republic*

If he really does not think there is no distinction between virtue and vice,
why sir, when he leaves the house, let us count the spoons.
—Samuel Johnson, *Letters*

INTRODUCTION

For the most part supervision is about people and activities. Supervisors must ensure that essential activities are completed by individuals who are in their charge. This requires that supervisors have a firm understanding of their unit's duties and responsibilities; in the end, the primary responsibility of the supervisor is to monitor subordinates' activities to ensure that duties and responsibilities are conducted in an acceptable and effective manner. Thus, supervision is about monitoring and controlling other people's behavior.

This chapter is concerned with what constitutes "correct" behavior. Individuals and organizations have standards of conduct. In order to understand organizations, it becomes important to comprehend these standards and their

172

PART TWO
Supervising Human
Resources: Training,
Evaluation, and
Discipline

etiology. First, we consider standards of behavior in policing, beginning with how behavioral decisions are made with respect to ethics and values, both generally and then with specific regard to supervisors. Then, we examine inappropriate or aberrant police behavior—including police lying and deception; gratuities and corruption; use of force; verbal, psychological, and legal abuse; and sexual misbehavior—and discuss it in terms of its effects on the individual, the police organization, and the public. Finally, we address the liability of police supervisors in terms of holding police officers and supervisors accountable for their actions.

TO FRAME THE QUESTION OF ETHICS: AN OPENING SCENARIO

It might be beneficial to commence this chapter with a related scenario: Assume that the police have multiple leads that implicate Mr. Smith as a pedophile, but they have failed in every attempt to obtain a warrant to search Smith's car and home where evidence might be present. Officer Jones feels frustrated so, early one morning, uses his baton to break a rear taillight on Smith's car. The next day he stops Smith for operating his vehicle with a broken taillight; Jones impounds and inventories the vehicle and finds evidence leading to Smith's conviction on 25 counts of child molestation and possession of pornography. Jones receives accolades for the apprehension.

Was Officer Jones's action regarding the taillight legal? Should his actions, even if improper or illegal, be condoned for "serving the greater public good"? Did Jones use the law properly? Assume that a supervisor observed Jones breaking the taillight; what actions, if any, should follow?

We invite the reader to keep this scenario and these questions in mind as we discuss ethics and ethical dilemmas throughout this chapter.

ETHICS IN POLICING

Philosophical Foundations

The term *ethics* is rooted in the ancient Greek idea of character. **Ethics** involves doing what is right or correct, and is generally used to refer to how people should behave in a professional capacity. However, many people would argue that there should be no difference between one's professional and personal lives. Thus, ethical conduct essentially should transcend everything a person does.

A central problem with understanding ethics is that there is always the question of "whose ethics" or "which right." This becomes evident when one examines controversies such as the death penalty, abortion, use of deadly force, or gun control. How individuals view a particular controversy largely depends on their ethics, values, and character. Both sides to these types of controversies believe they are morally right. These issues demonstrate that to understand behavior, the most basic ethics and values must be examined and understood.

Another area for examination is that of **deontological ethics,** which does not consider consequences but instead examines one's duty to act. The word *deontology* comes from two Greek roots, *deos* meaning duty, and *logos* meaning study. Thus, deontology means the study of duty. When police officers observe a violation of law, they have a duty to act. Officers frequently use duty as a reason for issuing traffic citations. Even though in some cases, they may have little utility other than punishing the violator. For example, when an officer writes a motorist a traffic citation for making a prohibited right turn at two o'clock in the morning when no traffic is around, the officer is fulfilling a duty to enforce the law. From a utilitarian standpoint (where we judge an action by its consequences), however, one may argue that little if any good was served. Here, duty prevailed over good consequences.

Immanuel Kant, the 18th-century philosopher, expanded the ethics of duty to include the idea of "good will." When people act, their actions must be guided by good intent. In the above example, the officer who wrote the traffic citation for an improper right turn would be acting unethically if the ticket was a response to a quota or some irrelevant reason. On the other hand, if the citation was issued because the officer truly believed that it would result in some good (e.g., reduction of accidents), the action would have been ethical.

Some people have expanded this argument even further. Kania (1988) argued that police officers should be allowed to freely accept gratuities because such actions would constitute the building blocks of positive social relationships between the police and the public. In this case, duty is used to justify an action that under normal circumstances would be considered unethical. Conversely, if the officers take the gratuity for self gratification rather than to form positive community relationships, then many people would consider the action unethical.

Types of Ethics

Ethics usually involves standards of fair and honest conduct, and what we call the conscience, the ability to recognize right from wrong, and acting in ways that are good and proper. There are *absolute* ethics and *relative* ethics. **Absolute ethics** has only two sides; something is either good or bad, black or white. The original interest in police ethics focused on such unethical behaviors as bribery, extortion, excessive force, and perjury.

Relative ethics is more complicated and can have a multitude of sides with varying shades of gray. What one person considers ethical behavior may be deemed highly unethical by another. However, not all police ethical issues are clear cut, and communities *do* seem willing at times to tolerate extralegal behavior when there's a greater public good, especially in dealing with problems such as gangs and child molesters. This willingness on the part of the community can be conveyed to the police.

As a community accepts relative ethics as a part of community policing, it may send the wrong message to the police: that there are few boundaries placed on police behavior and that at times "anything goes" in their fight against crime. As Kleinig (1996:55) pointed out, giving false testimony to ensure that a public

174

PART TWO
Supervising Human
Resources: Training,
Evaluation, and
Discipline

menace is "put away" or undertaking the illegal wiretap of an organized crime figure's telephone might sometimes be viewed as "necessary" and "justified" though wrong. Another example is that many police feel they are compelled to skirt the edges of the law—or even to violate it—in order to arrest drug traffickers. The ethical problem is that the action remains illegal even though it might be justified as morally proper. For many people, however, the protection of society overrides other concerns. As a Philadelphia police officer put it, "When you're shoveling society's garbage, you gotta be indulged a little bit" (U.S. Department of Justice 1997:62).

This viewpoint—the "**principle of double effect**"—holds that when one commits an act to achieve a good end, and an inevitable but intended effect is negative, then the act might be justified. There has been a long-standing debate concerning how to balance the rights of individuals against the community's interest in calm and order.

These areas of ethics can become problematical and controversial, particularly when police officers use excessive force, or lie and deceive people in the course of their work. One could rationalize a whole range of police activities that others may term unethical simply because the consequences resulted in the greatest good for the greatest number. If the ends justified the means, perjury would be ethical when committed to prevent a serial killer from being set free to prey on society. In our democratic society, however, the means are just as important, if not more important, than the desired end.

As we noted previously, the community appears to be more tolerate of certain kinds of extralegal police actions when public safety is at stake. For example, the police department in New York City is now enjoying the popular sup-

Imprisoned corrupt Officer Michael Dowd is highlighted during an NYPD internal affairs workshop.
Courtesy New York Police Department Photo Unit.

port of many citizens for "taking back the streets" and reducing the number of murders by 56 percent from 1990 to 1997 (Reibstein, 1997:64). But the New York Police Department (NYPD) is also being castigated by some citizens for its heavy-handed police tactics. Many citizens feel they have paid a price for the reduction in murders. From 1994 to 1996 complaints of police abuse rose by more than 50 percent. George Kelling, stated, "There's an enormous potential for abuse" (Reibstein, 1997:68). He criticized the NYPD for encouraging officers to demand identification from residents or conduct neighborhood drug sweeps, indiscriminately stopping and frisking people—and too often using excessive force. A long standing debate has been how to balance the rights of individuals against the community's interest in calm and order.

It is no less important today than in the past for police officers and supervisors to display proper ethical and moral behavior. Indeed, in the last few years ethical issues in policing have been affected by three critical factors (O'Malley, 1997):

1. The growing level of temptation stemming from the illicit drug trade.
2. The potentially compromising nature of the police organizational culture—a culture that exalts loyalty over integrity, with a "code of silence" that protects unethical, corrupt officers.
3. The challenges posed by decentralization (flattening the organization and pushing decision making downward) through the advent of community oriented policing and problem solving (COPPS). The latter concept is characterized by more frequent and closer contacts with the public, resulting in the minds of many observers in less accountability and, by extension, more opportunities for corruption.

Although perhaps small in comparison with the numbers of federal, state, and local police officers, incidents of police criminal behavior, corruption, brutality, or misuse of authority are not uncommon today; these accounts might lead one to believe that American policing is experiencing an ethical and moral crisis. Is there a significant problem of police ethics? That is a relative question; however, it is clear that the behavior of police officers is an issue of great concern among police agencies and the public they serve.

ESTABLISHING BEHAVIORAL GUIDELINES

Codes of Ethics and Conduct

Fair and Pilcher (1991) argued that one of the primary purposes of ethics is to guide police decision making. Ethics provide more comprehensive guidelines than the law and police operational procedures, and it answers questions that may otherwise go unanswered. When in doubt, police officers should be able to consider the ethical consequences of their actions or potential actions to evaluate how they should act or proceed. It is impossible for a police department to formulate procedures that address every possible situation an officer may encounter. Therefore, other behavioral guidelines must be in place to assist officers in making proper decisions.

Police officers are expected to adhere to the law and departmental policies to guide their behavior. This does not mean that if a particular behavior is not prohibited by law or policy, then it is permissible. Neither does it mean that if actions are not mandated, they merely represent an option. When police officers draw the line between acceptable from unacceptable behavior, they must do so with the intention of performing at a level that is ethical. Their actions should be guided by what is "right" for the situation and individuals involved, not what is required or prohibited.

Police supervisors obviously play a key role in ethics. Supervisors must not only enforce and uphold ethical standards, they also must guide and instruct officers in the ethical conduct of police business.

Toward this end, the law enforcement profession has adopted a Code of Ethics (see Figure 8–1). The **Code of Ethics** was originally adopted by the California Peace Officers Association, and then later by the International Association of Chiefs of Police (IACP) in 1957. It was believed that the police, like other professions such as medicine and law, would need such a code to achieve professional status. In 1989 the IACP included a **Police Code of Conduct** with the Code of Ethics. (see Figure 8–1). This code was broader, incorporating value statements that expressed more contemporary police administrative concerns. The Police Code of Ethics and the Police Code of Conduct are taught in most training academies and in some departments reinforced through in-service training. It is questionable, however, if either code has had any appreciable impact on police behavior. The codes provide the trappings of professionalism, but may in fact exert little control over police officer behavior. Generally, state statutes and departmental policy, which are more specific and less theoretical, better govern police behavior.

Professionalism and Ethics

Since August Vollmer administered the Berkeley and Los Angeles Police Departments during the early part of the 20th century, the police field has been pursuing professional status. This pursuit stems largely from the police belief that the public does not sufficiently recognize their importance in and contribution to society. The police also believe that once professional status is achieved, the public will be more willing to cooperate in addressing police problems. In essence, the bestowing of professional status to the police would serve as a seal of approval for America's police agencies.

Early police administrators attempted to articulate the elements of professions and to use these elements as guideposts for administrative decisions. For example, Greening (1939) identified five elements composing the police profession:

1. An organized body of knowledge, constantly augmented and refined, with special techniques based thereon.
2. Facilities for formal training in this body of knowledge and procedure.
3. Recognized qualification for membership in, and identification with, the profession.

4. An organization which includes a substantial number of members qualified to practice the profession and to exercise an influence on the maintenance of professional standards.
5. A code of ethics which, in general, defines the relations of the members of the profession to the public and to other practitioners within the group and normally recognizes an obligation to render services on other than exclusionary economic considerations.

Later, it was thought that professionalism could be attained by organizational efficiency. Beginning with Vollmer and extending through O. W. Wilson and the Chicago Police Department in the 1950s, police administrators attempted to introduce organizational efficiency through bureaucratization. Organizational control was seen as a method to eliminate problems with the community.

This approach to professionalism has a number of critics. Steinman and Eskridge (1985) referred to the police pursuit of professionalism as little more than rhetoric. They noted that the rhetoric allows administrators to achieve some degree of internal control while at the same time engendering public support for the police. It also gives the appearance that police administrators are upgrading their agencies. Manning (1978) noted that police departments developed mandates, strategies, and appearances as substitutes for real or meaningful police goals.

To a great extent, the police focus on technology, status, secrecy, and other internal mechanisms worked to the detriment of public security. Means, the appearances and strategies, become the desired ends, with operational efficiency being the means and end. Thus, professionalism was defined through bureaucracy rather than how well the police served the public.

The attainment of professional status is not contingent on the organization's appearance, but on the values of the officers in the agency and the ethics they practice. Rhoades (1991) advocated that the police, to be professional, must adhere to democratic values. The United States Constitution, especially the Bill of Rights, should guide police behavior. The Constitution is the foundation for our very existence.

The police as a government entity have a political obligation to serve the public in a democratic manner. Citizens give up the right to enforce or take the law into their own hands, instead vesting substantial law enforcement authority with the police. The police, in essence, bear substantial responsibility by accepting this authority. As representative agents of the government, they are duty bound to represent the interests of all citizens in a democratic fashion. This means that they must respect citizens' rights, attempt to serve their best interests, and take actions that affect or help people positively.

Although this is a relatively straightforward process, it is not simple to enact. Perhaps C. B. Klockars best characterized the problem when he examined police ethics and operational problems. Klockars asked, "When and to what extent does the morally good end warrant or justify an ethically, politically, or legally dangerous means to its achievement?" (Klockars, 1980:35). Circumventing constitutional guarantees to apprehend a wicked criminal is not acceptable—nor legal. Do good intentions justify bad means? From an ethical or

FIGURE 8-1. Law Enforcement Code of Ethics

All law enforcement officers must be fully aware of the ethical responsibilities of their position and must strive constantly to live up to the highest possible standards of professional policing.

The International Association of Chiefs of Police believes it is important that police officers have clear advice and counsel available to assist them in performing their duties consistent with these standards, and has adopted the following ethical mandates as guidelines to meet these ends.

PRIMARY RESPONSIBILITIES OF A POLICE OFFICER

A police officer acts as an official representative of government, and is required and trusted to work within the law. The officer's powers and duties are conferred by statute. The fundamental duties of a police officer include serving the community, safeguarding lives and property, protecting the innocent, keeping the peace, and ensuring the rights of all to liberty, equality and justice.

PERFORMANCE OF THE DUTIES OF A POLICE OFFICER

A police officer shall perform all duties impartially, without favor or affection or ill will and without regard to status, sex, race, religion, political belief or aspiration. All citizens will be treated equally with courtesy, consideration and dignity.

Officers will never allow personal feelings, animosities, or friendships to influence official conduct. Laws will be enforced appropriately and courteously and, in carrying out their responsibilities, officers will strive to obtain maximum cooperation from the public. They will conduct themselves in appearance and deportment in such a manner as to inspire confidence and respect for the position of public trust they hold.

DISCRETION

A police officer will use responsibly the discretion vested in the position and exercise it within the law. The principle of reasonableness will guide the officer's determinations and the officer will consider all surrounding circumstances in determining whether any legal action shall be taken.

Consistent and wise use of discretion, based on professional policing competence, will do much to preserve good relationships and retain the confidence of the public. There can be difficulty in choosing between conflicting courses of action. It is important to remember that a timely word of advice rather than arrest—which may be correct in appropriate circumstances—can be a more effective means of achieving a desired end.

USE OF FORCE

A police officer will never employ unnecessary force or violence and will use only such force in the discharge of duty as is reasonable in all circumstances.

Force should be used only with the greatest restraint and only after discussion, negotiation, and persuasion have been found to be inappropriate or ineffective. While the use of force is occasionally unavoidable, every police officer will refrain from applying the unnecessary infliction of pain or suffering and will never engage in cruel, degrading, or inhuman treatment of any person.

CONFIDENTIALITY

Whatever a police officer sees, hears, or learns of, which is of a confidential nature, will be kept secret unless the performance of duty or legal provision requires otherwise.

Members of the public have a right to security and privacy, and information obtained about them must not be improperly divulged.

INTEGRITY

A police officer will not engage in acts of corruption or bribery, nor will an officer condone such acts by other police officers.

The public demands that the integrity of police officers be above reproach. Police officers must, therefore, avoid any conduct that might compromise integrity and thus undercut the public confidence in a law enforcement agency. Officers will refuse to accept any gifts, presents, subscriptions, favors, gratuities, or promises that could be interpreted as seeking to cause the officer to refrain from performing official responsibilities honestly and within the law. Police officers must not receive private or special advantage from their official status. Respect from the public cannot be bought; it can only be earned and cultivated.

COOPERATION WITH OTHER OFFICERS AND AGENCIES

Police officers will cooperate with all legally authorized agencies and their representatives in the pursuit of justice.

An officer or agency may be one among many organizations that may provide law enforcement services to a jurisdiction. It is imperative that a police officer assist colleagues fully and completely with respect and consideration at all times.

PERSONAL/PROFESSIONAL CAPABILITIES

Police officers will be responsible for their own standard of professional performance and will take every reasonable opportunity to enhance and improve their level of knowledge and competence.

Through study and experience, a police officer can acquire the high level of knowledge and competence that is essential for the efficient and effective performance of duty. The acquisition of knowledge is a never-ending process of personal and professional development that should be pursued constantly.

PRIVATE LIFE

Police officers will behave in a manner that does not bring discredit to their agencies or themselves.

A police officer's character and conduct while off duty must always be exemplary, thus maintaining a position of respect in the community in which he or she lives and serves. The officer's personal behavior must be beyond reproach.

Source: Adopted by the Executive Committee of the International Association of Chiefs of Police on October 17, 1989. Used with permission.

180

*PART TWO
Supervising Human
Resources: Training,
Evaluation, and
Discipline*

professional standpoint, the answer has to be no. When police officers decide to break the law or use unethical behavior to arrest a suspect, it becomes questionable if the police are any better than the suspects they are attempting to bring to justice. Police actions should serve to accomplish good, and good means should be used to accomplish good ends.

VALUES AND POLICING

Articulating Police Ethics

To this point we have identified a number of complex issues associated with ethics and the pursuit of professionalism by police. While the IACP combined its Code of Ethics and Police Code of Conduct into more broad value statements for the field, the new Code of Ethics that evolved still did not seem to have any appreciable impact on policing. Felkenes (1984) observed that the professional ethics statements generated by the IACP and other police groups were too broad and often failed to provide officers with adequate guidance. Perhaps what agencies needed was to replace this broad national Code of Ethics with value statements that employees could embrace as theirs. Simply, these personalized values would articulate proper ethical behavior and guide employees in the performance of the duties (Wasserman and More, 1988).

With the advent of community policing, an increasing number of departments are developing value statements (Wasserman and Moore, 1988). They provide officers with general direction when performing their duties. They also can be viewed as goals and objectives; that is, they attempt to define or describe outcomes as the result of the police interacting with the community and citizens.

Values, from an organizational perspective, serve to provide a general understanding and commitment to a police department's mission (Covey, 1991). If everyone has a full understanding of the department's position relative to a given issue or problem, officers have better parameters to guide their decisions and actions. Therefore, it is critical for supervisors to comprehend their department's values and ensure that they are enforced and reinforced. If supervisors fail to accomplish this task, it is very likely that officers will fail to act consistently or according to the best interests of the department.

Value statements for police departments are not new. O. W. Wilson wrote value statements for the Wichita Police Department and the Chicago Police Department when he was chief in the 1950s. More recently, the Hayward, California, police department adopted a mission statement and organizational values to reflect its commitment to COPPS:

> We, the members of the Hayward Police Department, are committed to being responsive to our community in the delivery of quality services. We recognize our responsibility to maintain order, while affording and respecting dignity of life through a community partnership which promotes safe, secure neighborhoods.

This mission statement embraced the department's "Statement of Organizational Values," which incorporated the principles of SERVICE:

S trong planning and decision making involving employee participation to the greatest extent possible.

E xcellence in delivery of service to the public.

R espect for dignity of all employees and recognition of individual contributions and initiative.

V igorous pursuit of competency and responsibility in performance of our work.

I ntegrity and honesty in all aspects of service.

C ommunication achieved and information shared in a constructive, open and supportive manner.

E quitable treatment and opportunity for all employees (California Department of Justice, 1992).

The Hayward Police Department's value statements provide its employees with guidance in their thinking and behaviors expected in the delivery of police services. The Hayward Police Department's values promote (1) community involvement in police decision making is important, (2) the department should adhere to democratic values, (3) service delivery is a critical police function, and (4) employee participation in decisions is an important element in effective policing. If the Hayward Police Department is successful in incorporating these values into the police culture, the department should be more responsive to citizen needs, be more effective in combating crime, and treat people more humanely.

If a police department fails to competently integrate its values into the organization's culture, officers may be misled or confused. For example, Sherman (1982:14–15) identified a number of *inappropriate* behaviors that might be taught to rookies:

1. *Enforcement decisions.* Decisions about enforcing the law should be governed by the law and who the suspect is.
2. *Disrespect.* Disrespect for police authority should be punished by arrest or the use of force.
3. *Use of force.* Use of force should be used on those who need it and when it is helpful in solving a crime.
4. *Due process.* Due process only protects criminals and can be bypassed when necessary to solve a crime.
5. *Deception.* Lying and deception are important to police work and should be used when they lead to a conviction or the apprehension of a suspect.
6. *Responding to calls.* You cannot go too fast when chasing a perpetrator nor too slow when responding to a service call.
7. *Rewards.* Police work is very dangerous and police officers are paid very little, so it is acceptable for officers to take anything offered by the public.
8. *Loyalty.* An officer's most important duty is to protect his or her fellow officers.

Thus, it becomes very problematic when police departments fail to convey and enforce an adequate value system within the agency.

Supervisory Values

The values displayed by a supervisor are just as important as a line officer's values. Values affect how a supervisor manages subordinates and situations.

182

PART TWO
Supervising Human
Resources: Training,
Evaluation, and
Discipline

Von der Embse (1987:66) has identified several areas in which supervisory values affect work and workers:

1. Supervisory perceptions of individuals and groups.
2. Supervisory perceptions of specific problems and their solutions.
3. A supervisor's ethics relative to the job.
4. The correctness of decisions and judgments of others.
5. A supervisor's appraisal of success or failure.

A supervisor's value system must also be consistent with the department's if the supervisor is to assist the department effectively in the pursuit of its mission.

The preceding section delineated the importance and status of police ethics and values. The importance of ethics and values cannot be overemphasized. They are the organization's primary tool for ensuring that officers adhere to standards of acceptable conduct. If officers' behavior strays from departmental standards, then as Sherman indicates, difficulties will arise.

INAPPROPRIATE POLICE BEHAVIORS

Most of the efforts to control police behavior are rooted in the law and departmental policies, rules, and regulations. These written directives stipulate inappropriate behavior and, in some cases, the behavior or actions that are expected in specific situations. As we noted previously, written directives cannot address every contingency and officers must often use their discretion. These discretionary decisions should be guided by ethics and values. When there is failure of ethics, the resulting behavior is generally considered to be illegal or inappropriate.

In many cases, however, no clear line separates acceptable from unacceptable behavior. The two are divided by an expansive "gray" area referred to as relative ethics, which we discussed earlier in this chapter. Some observers have referred to illegal police behavior as a "slippery slope," where officers tread on solid or legal grounds but at some point slip beyond the acceptable into illegal or unacceptable behavior. These slippery slopes will serve as a point of analysis for the behaviors addressed in this section, which contains information pertaining to a number of behavioral areas where officers frequently get into trouble: (1) lying and deception, (2) acceptance of gratuities and corruption, (3) improper use of force, and (4) improper sexual relationships.

Lying and Deception

At times, police officers must rely on deception as a tactic while performing their duties. In some cases their misrepresentations are accepted and considered as an integral part of a criminal investigation; in other cases they are not accepted and are viewed as violations of law. Barker and Carter (1994, 1990) examined police lying and perjury and developed a classification that centered on accepted lying and deviant lying. Accepted lying includes police activities to apprehend or entrap suspects. This type of lying is generally considered to be trickery. **Deviant**

lying refers to occasions when officers commit perjury to convict suspects or are deceptive about some activity that is illegal or unacceptable to the department or the general public.

Trickery

Trickery has long been a practice used by the police to apprehend violators and suspects. For many years it was the principal method used by detectives and police officers to secure confessions and convictions (Kuykendall, 1986). It is allowed by the law, and to a great extent, it is expected by the public. G. T. Marx identified three methods the police use to trick a suspect: (1) offering the illegal action as a part of a larger, socially acceptable, and legal goal; (2) disguising the illegal action so that the suspect does not know the action is illegal; and (3) weakening the suspect morally so that he or she voluntarily becomes involved (Marx, 1982:170).

The courts have long accepted deception as an investigative tool. In *Illinois v. Perkins* (1990), the U.S. Supreme Court ruled that police undercover agents are not required to administer the *Miranda* warning to incarcerated inmates when investigating crimes. The court essentially separated "trickery" from coercion. Coercion is strictly prohibited, but trickery by police officers is unquestionably acceptable. Lying, although acceptable by the courts and the public in certain circumstances, does result in an ethical dilemma. It is often a questionable means to accomplish a good end; the police use untruths to gain the truth relative to some event.

However, limits do exist for the use of deception to gain information. It would not be acceptable for police to use deception to engage an otherwise innocent person in an illegal act. For example, undercover officers sometimes lie to suspects about other offenses as a ruse to gain their confidence and information. The suspects, in an effort to prove their worthiness, may confess to fictional crimes or crimes they did not commit in order to gain acceptance by the undercover officer. The suspect's admissions could not be used as a basis for arrest absent corroborating evidence.

Entrapment. Another problem with deception is entrapment. **Entrapment** exists when the idea for a crime begins with the police rather than the suspect, and the police facilitate the commission of a criminal act. The courts examine the offender's predisposition to commit the crime. If there was no predisposition, then the police have engaged in entrapment. It would not be legal for police undercover officers simply to give drugs to suspects so that the suspects could be apprehended for possession. Neither could suspects be encouraged by undercover police officers to burglarize a business so that the suspects could be arrested? The question for the courts when reviewing allegations of entrapment is simple; was it the police or suspect who initiated the idea for commiting the crime.

Sting Operations. Police sting operations provide another strategy that has come under question. Langworthy (1989) and Marx (1982) maintained that police sting operations create crime. Police **sting operations,** are where the police buy stolen property from burglars and other property offenders, through a

184

*PART TWO
Supervising Human
Resources: Training,
Evaluation, and
Discipline*

phoney strorefront business. When these storefronts open, numerous offenders readily use their services. Langworthy's and Marx's research argues that a sting operation results in a significant increase in property crimes. It is their contention that storefronts entice otherwise inactive criminals into crime which results in a large number of offenses?

The types of deception accepted by the courts and the public can be extremely troublesome irrespective of their acceptance, especially when the deception results in harm to innocent persons. However, it is often difficult to discern who is innocent. The police objective in these cases is to secure a confession or other evidence for prosecution, not to determine guilt or innocence. Again, this situation indicates the need for police to use their discretional authority wisely and ethically.

Deviant Lying

In their taxonomy of police lying, Barker and Carter (1990) identified two types of deviant lying: lying that serves legitimate purposes and lying that conceals or promotes crimes or illegitimate ends.

Lying that serves legitimate goals occurs when officers lie to secure a conviction, obtain a search warrant, or conceal police omissions during an investigation. Barker (1994) studied police deviance in one city and found that officers believed that almost one-fourth of the police force would commit perjury to secure a conviction in court or to obtain a search warrant. Skolnick (1982) argued that the police culture justifies lying to achieve legitimate goals much in the same manner the courts have permitted police trickery during investigations. Lying becomes an effective, routine way to sidestep legal impediments. When left unabated by police supervisors and administrators, lying becomes organizationally accepted as an effective means to nullify legal entanglements and other obstacles which stand in the way of convictions. Examples include the use of nonexistent confidential informants to secure search warrants, the concealment of a coerced confession by an interrogator who went too far, or perjury by an officer to gain a conviction.

Some officers may argue that the police should be able to violate or bend the Constitution in order to apprehend felons, and they may justify a lie because they believe that the Constitution makes it too difficult for the police to do their job effectively. Without a doubt, such a position violates the Constitution and the ethical behaviors expected by Americans. Even more dangerous, however, is that officers might take this position one step further. In the most extreme cases officers have been convicted of planting drugs on individuals they believe to be involved in the narcotics trade. It goes without saying that if this behavior occurs, there will be instances when innocent persons are wrongfully arrested and prosecuted.

Lying to conceal or promote criminality is, without doubt, the most distressing form of police deception. Examples of this form of lying range from officers lying to conceal their use of excessive force when arresting a suspect to obscuring the commission of a criminal act. Barker and Carter (1990) and Skolnick (1982) reported that the practice is commonplace in some departments. They reasoned that the police culture approves and, in some cases, promotes it. Clearly, a police agency is in serious trouble when this type of behavior occurs.

From a supervisory standpoint, the issues surrounding lying and deception require their close attention. Supervisors cannot look the other way, even though it may be easier to ignore the behavior than to confront it. First, they must fully understand what is acceptable and what is unacceptable by the department, and they must draw a line. Second, this information must be communicated to officers on a regular basis. Third, supervisors must actively investigate the extent of deception and lying by individual officers. If they do so, officers are less likely to engage in unacceptable deception; when supervisors fail to inquire, in essence they are passively approving any wrongful activity. Finally, when problems are identified, supervisors must take immediate disciplinary action. If supervisors promote deception by failing to respond to it, they are only worsening the problem. Case Study 8–1 discusses systemic corruption problems in a police department.

Gratuities and Corruption

The acceptance of gratuities by police officers is an issue of longstanding debate and concern throughout the field. Restaurants frequently offer officers free or half-price meals and drinks; bars and liquor stores offer discounts for their alcoholic beverages; and businesses routinely give officers discounts for services or merchandise. Some departments prohibit such gifts and discounts but seldom

Case Study 8–1
Getting the Job Done

Smithville is a midwestern city with a high crime rate and poor relations between the police and the public. The new reform mayor and police chief campaigned on a platform of cleaning up crime in the streets and ineffectiveness in government. They launched a commission to investigate a "litany of problems" within the police department. The investigation found that officers routinely lied about the probable cause for their arrests and searches, falsified search warrant applications, and basically violated the rules of collecting and preserving evidence. They were also known to protect each other under a shroud of secrecy, and to commit perjury in front of grand juries and at trials.

These problems were found to be systemic to the agency. However, greed or corruption were not the motivating factors behind the giving of perjured testimony. Officers believed their false testimony and other similar activities were the only means by which they could put persons they believed guilty behind bars. Worse still, the study also

found that prosecutors routinely tolerated or at least tacitly approved such conduct.

The study also found that many police officers did not consider giving false testimony as a form of corruption, which they believe implies personal profit. Instead, they viewed "testifying" as simply another way to "get the job done."

1. Do the officers' means of lying about the basis for their arrests and searches justify the end result of making arrests?
2. What about the prosecutors' tolerance of the officers' unethical behavior? By what ethical standards should the prosecutor's office be held?
3. As a supervisor, when these kinds of behaviors come to light, what punishment, if any, do you think is warranted for the persons involved?
4. What actions, if any, could a supervisor take to oversee officers' activities to prevent and detect such behaviors?

186

PART TWO
Supervising Human
Resources: Training,
Evaluation, and
Discipline

enforce any relevant policy or regulation against them. Other departments attempt to ensure that officers do not accept free or discounted services or merchandise and routinely enforce policies or regulations against such behavior.

Arguments against Gratuities

There are two basic arguments against police acceptance of gratuities. The first is the slippery slope argument, discussed earlier, which proposes that gratuities are the first step in police corruption. Once gratuities are received, the ethics of police officers are subverted. The officers are then open to additional breaches of their integrity. Also, officers who accept minor gifts or gratuities are then obligated to provide the donors with some special service or accommodation.

Second, some argue that receiving a gratuity is wrong because officers are receiving rewards for services that they are obligated to provide as a term of employment. That is, officers have no legitimate right to accept compensation in the form of a gratuity.

As noted above, Kania (1988) attempted to categorically justify the acceptance of gratuities by police officers. He argued that shopkeepers and restaurant owners often feel an indebtedness toward the police, and gratuities provide an avenue of repayment. Gratuities, Kania argued, result in social cohesion between the police and business owners. He also maintained that the acceptance of gratuities does not necessarily lead to the solicitation of additional gratuities and gifts or corruption. Plainly, officers are able to differentiate between what is appropriate and what is not, and to develop their own ethical standards and adhere to them.

Kania may be correct in asserting that gratuities are harmless and even beneficial in some cases, but the evidence suggests that this occurs only in very few instances. Indeed, studies have shown the dysfunctional and corrupting influence gratuities can have on law enforcement. Perhaps the most notorious and disgraceful example can be found in the *Knapp Commission Report on Police Corruption* in New York City (1972). The commission found that not only were a large number of officers accepting gratuities, but that the active solicitation of gratuities and gifts had become institutionalized within the department. The commission found that officers actively and routinely solicited free meals from restaurants and hotels, free drinks from bars and clubs, Christmas payments, free merchandise and other gifts, and tips for various services rendered. If the gifts and gratuities were not forthcoming, police officers often issued summons or otherwise harassed the shopkeeper or owner.

The Knapp Commission characterized a majority of the officers as "grass-eaters" and described others as "meat-eaters." Grass-eaters are officers who freely accept gratuities and sometimes solicit minor payments and gifts. Meat-eaters, on the other hand, spent a significant portion of the workday aggressively seeking out situations that could be exploited for financial gain. These officers were corrupt and were involved in thefts, drugs, gambling, prostitution, and other criminal activities.

In some cases, at least, it seems that gratuities may be a first step toward corruption. Especially those officers who fail to understand when and where to draw the line. As a preventive measure, police departments should develop a clear policy regarding gratuities and ensure that all officers are familiar with it. In turn, supervisors should be fully informed of the policy and emphatically enforce it.

The Supervisor's Role

Supervisors, as a consequence of direct oversight of their subordinates, should keep appraised of their activities and continually stress the department's policies. Second, supervisors should periodically check with business owners, restaurant managers, and liquor establishments to gauge police practices toward those establishments. Supervisors should communicate the department's policies to business owners and ask their cooperation in dealing with individual officers. They should also ask that business owners contact them when officers solicit gifts or gratuities. Finally, supervisors should aggressively investigate any evidence or indications that officers may be violating departmental policies.

It is difficult to recognize a specific time when an officer has become corrupt. Part of the problem lies in defining corruption. Goldstein (1977:188) defined **corruption** as "acts involving the misuse of authority by a police officer in a manner designed to produce personal gain for himself or for others." The primary components are misuse of authority and personal gain. Using this definition, it appears that the solicitation of gratuities and gifts by police officers would be considered corruption. Such acts involve both the misuse of authority and personal gain.

Sherman (1974) developed a typology to describe police corruption: (1) rotten apples and rotten pockets, (2) pervasive unorganized corruption, and (3) pervasive organized corruption. Rotten apples and rotten pockets refer to situations where a few officers are involved in corrupt activities, some of whom cooperate with each other to further their corrupt ventures. An officer may steal money during a drug raid or several officers may shake down a business owner who consistently violates an ordinance. Pervasive unorganized corruption is corruption on the part of a majority of a department's officers, but with little organization or collaboration. For example, a number of different officers may be shaking down bar owners and merchants, but they do it independently without coordinating their activities with a higher authority. Finally, pervasive organized corruption is the working together of a large number of officers on a variety of corrupt activities. Pervasive organized corruption entails a structure where some officers are reporting and taking commands from higher-ranking officers who are masterminding the activities. Police commanders and supervisors generally are involved when pervasive organized corruption exists.

Supervisors are a department's first line of defense against corruption. For pervasive organized corruption to exist, rotten apples and rotten pockets had to first exist. If supervisors can prevent, or at least control, the corruption associated with rotten apples and rotten pockets, it is unlikely that more severe forms of corruption will emerge. Supervisors should review their subordinates' daily activities, inform business establishments and bars in their district of the department's policy regarding gratuities, and monitor any potential illegal activities of cliques that form in the work group. In essence, supervisors must proactively investigate and break-up potential corruptive activities.

Improper Use of Authority and Force

As noted above, citizens bestow a substantial amount of authority on police officers. A central problem in police supervision occurs when officers use this authority improperly. Improper use of authority can range from being disrespectful to the inappropriate use of deadly force. To this end, Carter (1994) has provided a typology of abuse of authority by police officers. His categories include (1) physical abuse/excessive force, (2) verbal/psychological abuse, and (3) legal abuse/violations of civil rights.

Physical Abuse and Excessive Force

Physical abuse and excessive force generally refer to occasions when the police use force, deadly or nondeadly. The use of physical force often results in substantial public scrutiny. Indeed, national attention has sometimes focused on instances where the police have improperly used their authority and employed excessive force. Perhaps the most notorious incident of excessive force was the Rodney King case in 1991, involving the Los Angeles Police Department. This incident had profound national affects on policing and how citizens view law enforcement. Local incidents may not receive national media coverage, but they often have the same dramatic and chilling effects on a community. All police officers are judged by the actions of one or a few officers.

Regardless of the type of force used, police officers must use it in a legally accepted manner. Police officers are allowed to use only that amount of force needed to effect an arrest. Thus, the amount of force that a police officer uses depends on the amount of resistance demonstrated by the person being arrested. This concept is taught to police officers in training academies through a **use of force continuum,** which includes actions ranging from verbal commands to deadly force. Figure 8–2 shows the use of force continuum.

The use of force continuum illustrates how officers respond to the actions of suspects. For example, if a suspect tries to physically assault an officer using his fists, the officer may be justified in using a police baton, pepper spray, or some other nonlethal means to ward off the attack and subdue the suspect. On the other hand, if the suspect is brandishing a knife, the officer may be justified in using a firearm. In addition to using that amount of force necessary to bring about the arrest of a suspect, the officer must also consider any alternatives to the use of force. In this instance, it may be reasonable and prudent for an officer to retreat and seek assistance from other officers or to contain the situation and wait for the suspect to surrender.

Nondeadly Use of Force

Police officers use a complicated decision-making process to respond to situations or calls (Bayley and Garofalo, 1989). Indeed, officers generally follow a continuum of escalating force as the citizens they encounter escalate and de-escalate their aggressiveness or potential for violence. Furthermore, the potential for violence between police officers and suspects exists in a very low percentage of police calls. Black and Reiss (1967) reported that the police used nondeadly force in only 5 percent of the observed police-citizen encounters in a study of high-crime areas in Boston, Chicago, and Washington. Similarly, Bayley and

Levels of Resistance	Levels of Control or Force
Suspect's Actions	*Officer's Response*

Psychological Intimidation
  Nonverbal clues which indicate a
  subject's attitude, appearance, physical
  readiness
	Officer Presence
	  Verbal direction

Verbal Noncompliance
  Verbal responses indicating an attitude
  of unwillingness
	Officer Presence
	  Verbal direction
	  Telling suspect what you want him or
	  her to do

Passive Resistance
  Physical actions that do not prevent
  officer's attempt to control, dead
  weight, active passiveness
	Officer Presence
	  Verbal direction
	  Soft, empty hand techniques
	  Wrist locks, pressure point control

Defensive Resistance
  Physical actions that prevent officer's
  control without attempting to harm the
  officer
	Officer Presence
	  Verbal direction
	  Soft, empty hand techniques
	
	  Strikes with hands, feet, knee, elbow in
	  response to defensive resistance; this
	  level of control should only be used
	  after lesser force has proved ineffective
	  in controlling the suspect and applied
	  only to nonvital areas.

Active Aggression
  Physical assault on the officer
	Officer Presence
	  Verbal direction
	  Soft, empty hand techniques
	  Hard, empty hand techniques
	  Soft and hard intermediate weapons.
	  Soft shall include radial arm locks, arm
	  bars, etc. Hard shall include strikes
	  with baton to nonvital areas.

Aggravated Active Aggression	Any of the above and deadly force
Deadly Force Encounters	Firearms, strikes to the head and other vital areas with impact weapons.

FIGURE 8-2. Use of Force Continuum for Law Enforcement Officers

Garofalo (1989) found that police used force in approximately 8 percent of potentially violent encounters.

Even though physical force is used in only a small percentage of encounters with citizens, it appears to be concentrated among a few officers. The Christopher Commission (1991), examining the Rodney King incident and the Los Angeles Police Department, found the use of force to be widespread and generally accepted by the department. More alarming was the discovery that only 5 percent of officers accounted for more than 20 percent of excessive force complaints.

190

PART TWO
*Supervising Human
Resources: Training,
Evaluation, and
Discipline*

Deadly Force

Deadly force is the highest level of force that may be used by an officer, and many of the same considerations and recommendations for controlling non-deadly force apply to its use. Deadly force, however, is more problematic because of the personal toll taken on officers and agencies as a result of scrutiny by the public and authorities. Justified or unjustified, deadly force often creates a number of legal concerns as well as public relations problems for policing.

Accurate statistics are unavailable on the frequency of police use of deadly force because reporting of such incidents by many departments is nonexistent. Fyfe (1988), extrapolating from available data, estimated that there were 1,000 such deaths each year. Geller (1986) estimated that the police fire shots at approximately 3,600 suspects a year, hitting about 50 percent of their targets; approximately 20 percent of the civilians shot by the police are fatally shot (Geller, 1992).

No Alternative. It is difficult to detail the police decision-making process in the use of deadly force. However, two issues appear to be used fairly consistently as justifications for its use. First, as the Christopher Commission (1991) found in Los Angeles while investigating the Rodney King incident, police officers often believe that there are no effective midrange force alternatives or tactics. In other words, officers felt that once a suspect exhibits significant resistance and danger, their only alternative was to use deadly force. This situation can be corrected by training and ensuring that officers adhere to the use of force continuum (shown Figure 8–2).

Split-Second Syndrome. The split-second syndrome implies that officers must make deadly force decisions in a precious few seconds. Fyfe (1986) noted that the syndrome makes three assumptions.

1. No two shootings are alike; therefore, it is virtually impossible to establish principles that can be used to diagnose potential shooting situations.
2. Police officers can be expected to make errors. The circumstances, stress, and time limitations should justify police actions, and any criticism of police officers is unwarranted, especially by nonpolice personnel who do not understand police procedures or appreciate the problems encountered by officers.
3. Finally, evaluation of police decision making should be based on the perceived exigencies. If a citizen has or is perceived to have committed an act justifying deadly force, any subsequent shooting by the police should be deemed necessary or permissible.

Fyfe makes the assertion that split-second syndrome leads to unnecessary violence. In some shooting instances, Fyfe believes police officers have the time to analyze the situation and employ alternatives to deadly force. Indeed, officers are frequently confronted with potentially violent situations and must respond accordingly. The deliberate actions by police in these situations may reduce the liklihood of its escalation. For example, when potentially deadly situations arise, such as fight calls or calls involving weapons, officers must quickly deploy tactics to control its potential escalation to a deadly force situation.

The role of the supervisor in controlling potentially deadly situations is also vital. Supervisors should counsel officers when they become lax and make sure they use proper tactics when approaching a suspect or answering a call. This level of preparedness is essential for officers and will help them when confronted with split-second decisions.

Verbal and Psychological Abuse

As will be discussed in Chapter 9, profanity is one of the most common complaints by citizens regarding officers behavior. While officers may believe profanity is necessary in some instances to control the situation, research shows the opposite often results. Research indicates that profanity is used for a variety of reasons: as a source of power to control others (Selnow, 1985), as a weapon to degrade or insult others (Paletz and Harris, 1975), as a method of alienating others (Selnow, 1985), as a method of labeling others (Warshay and Warshay, 1978), and as a way of defying authority (Paletz and Harris, 1975).

Unfortunately, profanity has become a part of the police culture and many officers' everyday speech. When profanity is used liberally in the work setting, it increases the likelihood that it will be used inappropriately.

Profane language tends to polarize a situation (Rothwell, 1971). A citizen will either passively submit or respond aggressively—in either case, it causes the citizen to distrust and dislike the police. When police officers use profanity, especially in an aggressive manner, the focus may quickly shift from the problem to the officer's language, and where it is used aggressively, profanity can easily create greater physical risks to the officer. Furthermore, even if the officer intended to resolve the situation, it may no longer be possible because of the harm caused by the language. Profanity can incite a situation and increase the potential for liability and citizens' complaints; therefore, heightening the possibility of the officer facing administrative action.

For all of these reasons, profanity by the police toward citizens is neither justified, wise, nor advised. Supervisors should discourage its use and review every instance where an officer used it with a citizen.

Violations of Civil Rights

Civil rights violations consist of police actions in which a citizen's constitutional or statutory rights are violated. These violations may involve false arrest, false imprisonment, and harassment. For example, a police officer who knowingly makes an unlawful search and charges the suspect with a crime, would violate the person's civil rights.

Supervisors play a key role in preventing violations of citizens' civil rights. Supervisors frequently back up officers when responding to calls and observe situations that lead to an arrest. They should ensure that officers' decisions to arrest are based on probable cause, not some lesser standard. They also should review arrest reports and question officers when arrests are not observed to ensure that the arrests meet the probable cause standard.

This is also critical because of the common complaint by citizens that officers base their decisions to arrest on factors other than a suspect's demeanor:

192

PART TWO
Supervising Human
Resources: Training,
Evaluation, and
Discipline

The homeless often claim to be victims of police abuse and harassment.

socioeconomic status, race, age, relationship between the suspect and victim, and the preference of the complainant. If police officers allow these factors to influence their decisions, they are abusing their authority. Officers are legally required to provide the same level of services to all citizens, and they should use consistent decision-making criteria when deciding to make an arrest.

Improper Sexual Relations

Although no accurate data exist, research indicates that a number of officers engage in improper sexual relationships. In a study of deviance in a southern city, Barker (1994) found that the officers believed that about one-third of the department engaged in improper sexual relationships while on duty. This in itself is problematic, because officers who participate in this activity are not only showing poor judgment but also may be compromising their ability to enforce the law objectively. Although many of the liaisons could be deemed romantic encounters, some of these activities may very well be associated with illicit activities.

Sapp (1994) noted that police officers, because of their authority, have a number of opportunities to engage in sexual misconduct. They have the authority to stop and talk with citizens and, in many cases, they can limit their freedom. They also perform most work activities while unsupervised and in relative isolation. Although the majority of police officers may never engage in sexual misconduct, some do.

The following are a few of the many examples where police officers' sexual activities have become public and created an embarrassment for the department.

- Two Spokane, Washington, police officers pleaded guilty to charges that they employed underage female prostitutes.
- The Spartanburg, South Carolina, police department investigated allegations that as many as 20 police officers engaged in sexual activities with prostitutes. Two officers resigned as a result of the investigation.
- A Tennessee sheriff was charged with attempted rape and sexual battery after the sheriff visited a female job applicant at her home.
- A Connecticut police department had to remove cellular telephones from its vehicles because officers were using them to call numbers that provided sexually explicit conversations with females.

Activities of this nature undermine the effectiveness of a police department in two ways. First, they create a public relations nightmare. When sexual deviance cases involving the police become known, citizens lose respect for their police, tend to be less cooperative, and are less likely to support them politically. Second, it undermines the operational effectiveness of a department; when problems of this nature occur, officers tend to believe they are immune from disciplinary controls and they can go about their jobs as they please.

Supervisors must closely scrutinize the activities of subordinates to prevent or reduce the incidence of sexual misconduct. If supervisors fail to investigate or pursue allegations of sexual misconduct, in essence they are condoning it. This may only lead to additional and possibly more outrageous conduct on the part of some officers while departments may not be able to completely eliminate such behavior, they can minimize it through assertive supervision.

Sexual Harassment in the Workplace

Another form of sexual misconduct that requires discussion is sexual harassment in the workplace. This form of sexual deviance generally involves supervisors or it occurs with the supervisors' knowledge and acquiescence. **Sexual harassment** is a form of sexual discrimination. The Equal Employment Opportunity Commission has provided guidelines which describe it:

> Unwelcome sexual advances, requests for sexual favors, and other verbal or physical conduct of a sexual nature constitute sexual harassment when (1) submission to such conduct is made either explicitly or implicitly a term or condition of an individual's employment; (2) submission to or rejection of such conduct by an individual is used as the basis for employment decisions affecting such individual; or (3) such conduct has the purpose or effect of unreasonably interfering with an individual's work performance or creating an intimidating, hostile, or offensive working environment [29 CFR. 1604.11(a)].

There are two theories of sexual harassment, both of which are relevant to supervision (Higginbotham, 1988). The first is *quid pro quo,* which occurs when a

194

PART TWO
*Supervising Human
Resources: Training,
Evaluation, and
Discipline*

sexual act is a condition of employment. For example, a supervisor may offer a subordinate the high rating necessary for promotion if the subordinate in turn provides sexual favors. The second is the hostile environment where employees are harassed because of their gender.

Seven sexual harassment behaviors exhibited by police officers have been identified (Sapp, 1994).

1. *Sexually motivated nonsexual contacts.* Here an officer will stop another citizen without legal justification simply to obtain information or get a closer look at the citizen.
2. *Voyeuristic contacts.* Here police officers attempt to observe citizens partially clad or nude. They observe apartment buildings or college dormitories. In other cases they roust citizens parked on lovers' lanes.
3. *Contacts with crime victims.* Crime victims generally are emotionally distraught or upset and particularly vulnerable to sexual overtones from officers. In these instances officers may make several return visits and calls with the intention of seducing the victim.
4. *Contacts with offenders.* In these cases officers may conduct body searches, frisks, and patdown searches. Sometimes officers may demand sexual favors. Offenders' complaints of sexual harassment will not be investigated by a department without corroborating evidence, which seldom exists.
5. *Contacts with juvenile offenders.* In some cases officers have exhibited some of the same behaviors for juveniles that they have for adults, such as patdowns, frisks, and sexual favors. There also have been cases where officers assigned as juvenile or school liaison officers have taken the opportunity presented by their assignment to seduce juveniles.
6. *Sexual shakedowns.* Here police officers demand sexual services from prostitutes, homosexuals, and others engaged in criminal activity as a form of protection.
7. *Citizen-initiated sexual contacts.* Some citizens are attracted to police officers and attempt to seduce them. They may be attracted to the uniform, authority, or the prospect of a "safe" sexual encounter. In other cases the citizen may be lonely or want a "break" when caught violating the law.

When supervisors engage in or allow other officers to participate in sexually offensive activities in the workplace, they have affected an employee's psychological well-being. If officers or supervisors repeatedly tell sexually explicit stories or jokes, or make sexual or indecent advances toward an employee, a hostile environment is created.

Women who attempt to cope with sexual harassment often find little organizational support and their complaints are not taken seriously (Kissman, 1990; Summers, 1991). Supervisors must be quick to correct such behavior and, when appropriate, take disciplinary action to prevent it from occurring in the future.

Departmental Guidelines

In light of the problems discussed above, it is imperative that agencies develop clear, written guidelines (rules, regulations, procedures, and policies). Indeed, it might well be argued that the *primary* function of a police supervisor is to control employees' behavior. Written guidelines are vital to preventing inappropriate police behavior from occurring. Simply, guidelines articulate how certain tasks can be best performed. Regardless of the rationale, written guidelines represent instructions that all officers must follow, and a tool supervisors can use to ensure that they do so.

However, police officers often view written guidelines as impositions on their discretion. Officers generally do not like policies that restrict the way they apply force perfom their duties, such as in the case of hot pursuit. If supervisors allow officers to act entirely on their own, behavioral, organizational, and community problems are very likely to occur. Passive or reactionary supervision will only result in the problem becoming worse. Therefore, supervisors should be proactive and attempt to eliminate problems before they happen.

CIVIL LIABILITY AND POLICE SUPERVISION

Types of Supervisory Liability

Supervision is about behavior, for it is the direct responsibility of supervisors to monitor and regulate officers' behavior and, when necessary, take disciplinary action to ensure that negligent or illegal behavior does not recur in the future. This section explores some of the legal consequences of the failure of police supervisors to control their officers' behavior.

The number of lawsuits against police officers and police departments is constantly increasing. Silver (1991) noted that police departments face about 30,000 civil actions annually. Kappeler and Kappeler (1992) examined the Section 1983 civil actions—civil rights cases emanating from Title 42 of the U.S. Code—against police departments from 1982 through 1991 and found that sufficient evidence warranted a jury trial in approximately half of the cases. Civil liability represents a substantial monetary loss each year, and the legal fees associated with 30,000 or so cases is staggering. Kappeler and Kappeler found in their study of U.S. district court cases that the average loss including judgment and attorneys' fees was $134,690.

Supervisory liability can be imposed by state or federal courts. Most claims of supervisory liability are state tort cases or Section 1983 cases at the federal level. State tort cases are liability cases filed against the police in state court. On the other hand, **Section 1983 cases** are federal civil rights proceedings for which three conditions must be met: (1) the conduct complained of was committed by a person acting under color of state law; (2) this conduct deprived a person of rights, privileges, or immunities secured by the Constitution or laws of the United States; and (3) the violation reached a constitutional level. Thus, if a police officer acting in an official capacity violates a citizen's constitutional or other federally guaranteed rights, the citizen can seek redress under Section 1983.

Supervisors must be mindful that a certain level of liability is attached to the job when they fail to supervise correctly. They should also remember that plaintiffs generally attempt to include as many officers, supervisors, and administrators in the lawsuit as possible to enhance the probability that the award will be greater and the defendants will have the ability to pay it. This is commonly referred to as the "deep pockets" approach.

196

Direct and Indirect Liability

PART TWO
*Supervising Human
Resources: Training,
Evaluation, and
Discipline*

Supervisors incur two types of liability: liability for what subordinates do, and liability for what supervisors do to their subordinates (del Carmen, 1991). The first category is addressed here; the liability associated with supervisory treatment or interaction with their subordinates is addressed in Chapter 9.

In terms of supervising subordinates, supervisors have *direct* and *vicarious* liability. **Direct liability** refers to the liability incurred for the actions of supervisors themselves, while **vicarious** or **indirect liability** is the liability of supervisors for the actions of their subordinates. For direct liability to exist, supervisors must be direct participants in the act. They incur direct liability in a number of ways (del Carmen, 1989).

1. Supervisors authorize the act. They give officers permission to do something that ultimately results in liability.
2. They participate in the act. They engage in activities with other officers which ultimately results in liability.
3. They direct others to perform the act. They order officers to do something which ultimately results in liability.
4. They ratify the act. Once the act is completed, they fail to admonish or take corrective action when it comes to their attention.
5. They are present when an act for which liability results occurs. They stand by and watch an act occur which results in liability and fail to take corrective action.

Supervisory Negligence

One of the most commonly litigated areas of liability is supervisory negligence. **Simple negligence** takes place when a supervisor fails to provide the degree of care and vigilance required for a situation. **Gross negligence** is a deliberate indifference to life or property. Generally, the courts require gross negligence to hold a supervisor liable.

As a result of case law, there are currently seven areas where supervisors have been found liable as a result of negligence: (1) negligent failure to train, (2) negligent hiring, (3) negligent assignment, (4) negligent failure to supervise, (5) negligent failure to direct, (6) negligent entrustment, and (7) negligent failure to investigate or discipline (del Carmen, 1991: 227). The hiring and academy training of police officers is usually not the responsibility of a supervisor, but the remaining five areas of liability fall squarely with the supervisor and are discussed below.

Negligent Assignment. **Negligent assignment** occurs when the supervisor assigns a task to a subordinate without first determining that the subordinate is properly trained or capable of performing the required work. Negligent assignment also occurs when a supervisor determines that an employee is unfit or unqualified for a position but fails to relieve the employee of that assignment.

An example of negligent assignment is the case of a supervisor who allows a subordinate to assume the duties of a police officer without receiving firearms training. If the officer subsequently negligently shot a citizen, both the supervisor and the officer would be liable. A second example might concern an officer against whom several complaints of sexual harassment have been lodged, and a supervisor failed to reassign the officer to a position within the department where there would be no opportunities for sexual harassment. Even if disciplinary action was taken, a supervisor must eliminate any opportunities for the act to recur. Supervisors must pay particular attention to their subordinates' behavior and make assignments to ensure that problems do not occur.

Negligent Failure to Supervise. Negligent failure to supervise is the failure of a supervisor to properly oversee subordinates' activities. In *Lenard* v. *Argento* (1983) the court held that at a minimum a plaintiff must demonstrate that the supervisory official authorized (implicitly or explicitly), approved, or knowingly acquiesced in the illegal conduct. For example, if a supervisor knows that an officer on a number of occasions has used unnecessary force to effect an arrest and fails to take corrective action, the supervisor can be held liable for failure to supervise in a subsequent action. Thus, anytime a supervisor becomes aware of a problem, action must be taken to rectify the problem. The courts have also examined individual cases. In *Grandstaff* v. *City of Borger* (1985) police officials were held liable for failing to take supervisory action after officers mistakenly opened fire and shot an innocent bystander who was attempting to offer assistance to the officers. The court reasoned that the department's failure to reprimand, discipline, or fire officers constituted a failure to supervise. A supervisor's failure to act is an abdication of authority, and the courts consider this negligent supervision.

Negligent Failure to Direct. Negligent failure to direct occurs when supervisors fail to advise subordinates of the specific requirements and limits of the job. For example, if a police department fails to provide officers with the limits to the use of deadly force and officers subsequently use deadly force inappropriately, the responsible supervisors can be held liable. Negligent failure to direct has a specific application relative to departmental policies and procedures. If a department does not have a policy dealing with a sensitive area and officers subsequently act inappropriately, the department will be found negligent for failure to direct. Supervisors must be knowledgeable about the law, departmental policies, and be able to properly advise officers about their content.

Negligent Entrustment. Negligent entrustment occurs when supervisors entrust officers with equipment and facilities, fail to properly supervise the officers' care and use of the equipment, and subsequently the officers use the equipment to commit an act that leads to a violation of a citizen's federally protected rights. In these cases the government must show that the officer in question was incompetent and the supervisor knew about the incompetence. A supervisor's defense in negligent entrustment is that the employee was competent to use the equipment and was properly supervised.

Supervisors must investigate complaints and work activities and take proper disciplinary actions when required. Clearly, police departments must have adequate disciplinary procedures and they must function to protect the rights of citizens. If a supervisor or department covers up or is inattentive to

Case Study 8–2
Insensitivity Causes Escalation to Black and Blue

Officer Burns is known to have extreme difficulty in relating to persons of color and other people who are culturally different. Burns admits to his sergeant that he grew up in a very prejudiced home environment and that he has little sympathy or understanding for people "who cause all the damn trouble." The officer never received any sensitivity or diversity training at the academy or within the department. The supervisor fails to understand the weight of the problem and has very little patience with Burns. To correct the matter, the supervisor decides to assign Burns to a section of town where minorities live so he will improve his ability to relate to diverse groups. Within a week, Burns responds to a disturbance at a housing project where residents are partying noisily and a fight is in progress. Burns immediately becomes upset, yelling at the residents to quiet down; they fail to respond, so Burns draws his baton and begins poking residents and ordering them to comply with his directions. The crowd immediately turns against Burns, who is forced to call for backup assistance. After the other officers arrive, a fight ensues between residents and officers. Several officers and residents are injured and numerous arrests are made. The following day the neighborhood council meets with the mayor, demanding that Burns be fired and threatening a lawsuit.

1. Is any liability or negligence present in this situation?
2. If liability and negligence are present, what kinds are they?
3. Could the supervisor have dealt with Burns's lack of sensitivity in a better manner? If so, how?

complaints of police misconduct, the department and supervisor are liable. Too often supervisors attempt to stall, discourage, or disregard complainants when they protest the actions of police officers. Such actions can ultimately lead to the fifth area of liability, **negligent failure to investigate or discipline charges.**

Obviously, the best defense of a department and supervisor in such cases is to establish a record of strong disciplinary procedures within the agency. This is accomplished through consistent supervisory practices and documentation. Plaintiffs, on the other hand, will attempt to show that either no action or inadequate action took place.

SUMMARY

This chapter has examined police behavior from an ethical and legal standpoint. First, ethics were discussed. Ethics form the foundation for police officer behavior. It is important that officers understand ethics and the role ethics play in their profession. Departments must ensure officers perform their duties within the guidelines of acceptable ethical behavior.

In terms of officer behavior, we discussed lying and deception, gratuities and corruption, the use of force, verbal and legal abuse, and improper sexual relations. At times, police officers fail to properly perform duties and responsibilities; in the worst cases, they might become involved in corruption or other deviant activities. In a number of these situations, police supervisors must shoulder responsibility for failure to supervise their subordinates properly. Supervisors are the primary control mechanism in police departments, and as noted in this chapter, assume a tremendous responsibility and liability for officers' conduct.

Finally, as a result of their position, supervisors assume a degree of liability. Civil actions against supervisors are a way that society holds them accountable for failing to properly oversee their subordinates.

KEY TERMS

ethics (p. 172)
deontological
  ethics (p. 173)
absolute ethics (p. 173)
relative ethics (p. 173)
"principle of double
  effect" (p. 174)
Code of Ethics (p. 176)
Police Code of
  Conduct (p. 176)
deviant lying (p. 183)
entrapment (p. 183)

sting operations (p. 183)
use of force
  continuum (p. 188)
sexual
  harassment (p. 193)
Section 1983 cases
  (p. 195)
direct liability (p. 196)
vicarious (indirect)
  liability (p. 196)
simple negligence (p. 196)
gross negligence (p. 196)

negligent
  assignment (p. 197)
negligent failure to
  supervise (p. 197)
negligent failure to
  direct (p. 197)
negligent
  entrustment (p. 198)
negligent failure to
  investigate or discipline
  charges (p. 198)

ITEMS FOR REVIEW

1. Define "ethics," and explain the different types of ethics.
2. Explain the elements of a profession, and discuss whether or not policing meets those criteria.
3. Describe how value statements relate to the ethical behavior of individuals and the organization.
4. Briefly review the several behavioral areas where officers frequently get into trouble through inappropriate behavior.
5. Explain the two types of liability that police supervisors may incur, as well as the five areas of liability.
6. Describe the nature and use of Section 1983.

SOURCES

BARKER, T. (1994). "An empirical study of police deviance other than corruption." In T. Barker and D. Carter (eds.). *Police Deviance*. Cincinnati: Anderson.

BARKER, T., and CARTER, D. (1990). "Fluffing up the evidence and covering your ass: Some conceptual notes on police lying." *Deviant Behavior* 11:61–73.

BARKER, T., and CARTER, D. (1994). "Typology of police deviance." In T. Barker and D. Carter (eds.). *Police Deviance*. Cincinnati: Anderson.

BAYLEY, D. H., and GAROFALO, J. (1989). "The management of violence by police patrol officers." *Criminology* 27(1): 1–25.

BLACK, D. and REISS, A. (1970). "Police control of juveniles." *American Sociological Review* 35:63–77.

BROOKS, L. W. (1986). "Determinants of police orientations and their impact on police discretionary behavior." Unpublished Ph.D. Dissertation. Institute of Criminal Justice & Criminology, University of Maryland.

CALIFORNIA DEPARTMENT OF JUSTICE, ATTORNEY GENERAL'S OFFICE PREVENTION CENTER (1992). *COPPS: Community oriented policing and problem solving*. Sacramento, Calif.: California Department of Justice.

200

PART TWO
Supervising Human
Resources: Training,
Evaluation, and
Discipline

CARTER, D., (1994). "Theoretical dimensions in the abuse of authority." In T. Barker and D. Carter (eds.). *Police Deviance.* Cincinnati: Anderson.

CHRISTOPHER COMMISSION (1991). *Report of the independent commission on the Los Angeles police department.* Los Angeles: City of Los Angeles.

COVEY, S. R. (1991). *Principle-centered leadership.* New York: Summit Books.

DAVIS, M. (1991). "Do cops really need a code of ethics?" *Criminal Justice Ethics* 10(2):14–28.

DEL CARMEN, R. V. (1991). *Civil liabilities in American policing.* Englewood Cliffs, N.J.: Brady.

DEL CARMEN, R. V. (1989). "Civil liabilities of police supervisors." *American Journal of Police* 8(1):107–36.

DEL CARMEN, R. V. (1981). "An overview of civil and criminal liabilities of police officers and departments." *American Journal of Criminal Law* 9:33.

DONAHUE, M. E. (1992). "Crisis in police ethics: Is professionalization an answer?" *American Journal of Police* 11(4):47–70

FAIR, F. K., and PILCHER, W. D. (1991). "Morality on the line: The role of ethics in police decision-making." *American Journal of Police* 10(2):23–38.

FELKENES, G. T. (1984). "Attitudes of police officers toward their professional ethics." *Journal of Criminal Justice* 12:211–30.

FRIEDRICH, R. J. (1977). "The impact of organizational, individual, and situational factors on police behavior." Ph.D. Dissertation. Department of Political Science, University of Michigan.

FYFE, J. (1988). "Police use of deadly force: Research and reform." *Justice Quarterly* 5(2):165–205.

GELLER, W. A. (1986). *Crime file: Deadly force: A study guide.* Washington, D.C.: National Institute of Justice.

GELLER, W. A., and SCOTT, M. S. (1992). *Deadly force: What we know.* Washington, D.C.: Police Executive Research Forum.

GOLDSTEIN, H. (1977). *Policing a Free Society.* Cambridge, Mass.: Ballinger.

GRANDSTAFF V. CITY OF BORGER, 767 F2d 161 (5th Cir 1985).

GREENING, J. A. (1939). Report from Committee on Profession of Police Service. Yearbook of the International Association of Chief's of Police.

HIGGINBOTHAM, J. (1988). "Sexual harassment in the police station." *FBI Law Enforcement Bulletin* 9:22–29.

ILLINOIS V. PERKINS, 110 S.Ct. 2394 (1990).

KANIA, R. (1988). "Police acceptance of gratuities." *Criminal Justice Ethics* 7(2):37–49.

KAPPELER, S. F., and KAPPELER, V. E. (1992). "A research note on section 1983 claims against the police." *American Journal of Police* 11(1):65–74.

KISSMAN, K. (1990). "Women in blue-collar occupations: An exploration of constraints and facilitation." *Journal of Sociology and Social Welfare* 17:139–49.

KLEINIG, J. 1996. *The ethics of policing.* New York: Cambridge University Press.

KLOCKARS, C. B. (1980). "The dirty harry problem." *Annals of the American Academy of Political and Social Science* 452:33–47.

KUYKENDALL, J. (1986). "The municipal detective: An historical analysis." *Criminology* 24(3):175–201.

LANGWORTHY, R. (1989). "Do stings control crime? An evaluation of a police fencing operation." *Justice Quarterly* 6(1):27–46.

LENARD V. ARGENTO, 699 F2d 874 (7th Cir 1983).

MARX, G. T. (1982). "Who really gets stung? Some issues raised by the new police undercover work." *Crime & Delinquency* 8:165–93.

MILLER, G. I. (1987). "Observations on police undercover work." *Criminology* 25(1):27–46.

O'MALLEY, T. J. (1997). "Managing for ethics: A mandate for administrators." *FBI Law Enforcement Bulletin* (April):20–25.

PALETZ, D. L., AND HARRIS, W. (1975). "Four-letter threats to authority." *Journal of Politics* 37:955–79.

REIBSTEIN, L. (1997). "NYPD Black and Blue," *Newsweek* (May 26):64–68.

RHOADES, P. W. (1991). "Political obligation: Connecting police ethics and democratic values." *American Journal of Police* 10(2):1–22.

ROTHWELL, J. D. (1971). "Verbal obscenity: Time for second thoughts." *Journal of Western Speech* 35:231–242.

SAPP, A. D. (1994). "Sexual misconduct by police officers." In T. Barker and D. Carter (eds.). *Police Deviance*. Cincinnati: Anderson.

SELNOW, G. W. (1985). "Sex differences in uses and perceptions of profanity." *Sex Roles* 12:303–12.

SHERMAN, L. (1982). "Learning police ethics." *Criminal Justice Ethics* 1(1):10–19.

SILVER, I. (1991). *Police civil liability.* New York: Matthew Bender.

SKOLNICK, J. L. (1982). "Deception by police." *Criminal Justice Ethics,* 1(2):27–32.

SMITH, D. A., and VISHER, C. (1981). "Street-level justice: Situational determinants of police arrest decisions." *Social Problems* 29:167–78.

STACK, S. and KELLEY, T. (1994). "Police suicide: An analysis." *American Journal of Police* 13(4):73–90.

STEINMAN, M., and ESKRIDGE, C. W. (1985). "The rhetoric of police professionalism." *Police Chief* (February):26–29.

SUMMERS, R. J. (1991). "Determinants of judgment and responses to a complaint of sexual harassment." *Sex Roles* 25:379–93.

U.S. DEPARTMENT OF JUSTICE, NATIONAL INSTITUTE OF JUSTICE, OFFICE OF COMMUNITY ORIENTED POLICING SERVICES (1997). *Police Integrity: Public Service with Honor.* Washington, D.C.: U.S. Government Printing Office.

VON DER EMBSE, T. J. (1987). *Supervision: Managerial skills for a new era.* New York: Macmillan.

WARSHAY, D. W., and WARSHAY, L. H. (1978). "Obscenity and male hegemony." Paper presented at the annual meeting of International Sociological Association (nd), Detroit, Michigan.

WASSERMAN, R., and MOORE, M. H. (1988). "Values in policing." *Perspectives on Policing,* No. 8. (November), Washington, D.C.: National Institute of Justice.

9

Officers' Rights, Discipline, and Appeals

No man is fit to command another that cannot command himself.

—WILLIAM PENN

The price of greatness is responsibility.

—WINSTON CHURCHILL

Discipline must be maintained.

—CHARLES DICKENS

INTRODUCTION

We discussed ethics and police misbehavior in the last chapter; this chapter examines the other end of the spectrum—rights and discipline. These are especially delicate and important aspects of police supervision; if ignored or handled improperly, they can foster serious internal and external problems, increased liability, and a loss of public respect and trust.

More than most segments of government, the police are under the close scrutiny of the public. Therefore, it is extremely important that police agencies develop sound disciplinary policies and ensure that supervisors are properly trained to intervene early when problems emerge. Supervisors also must have a good working knowledge of departmental rules and regulations as well as the resources available for dealing with disciplinary issues.

We begin this chapter by laying the groundwork with an overview of police officers' rights and limitations under the Constitution and federal court decisions. We then look at the traditional problems surrounding the discipline of police officers and the need for a sound disciplinary system, followed by a look at both positive and negative forms of discipline. We next consider the filing and investigation of citizen complaints, the means by which officers can appeal disciplinary measures that have been taken against them, and how disciplinary problems may be averted by early warning systems. We conclude the chapter with a discussion of legal considerations.

OFFICERS' RIGHTS AND LIMITATIONS

Although police officers may be compelled to give up certain rights in connection with an investigation of on-duty misbehavior or illegal acts, they *generally* are afforded the same rights, privileges, and immunities the United States Constitution guarantees to all citizens. These rights are the basis for legislation such as the Peace Officers Bill of Rights (discussed below), labor agreements, and civil service and departmental rules and regulations that guide an agency's disciplinary process.

Next, we briefly discuss the limitations that might be placed on the actions of police employees by virtue of their unique occupation and the standards of behavior that exist because of it.

Free Speech

Although freedom of speech is one of the most fundamental of all rights of Americans, the Supreme Court indicated in *Pickering* v. *Board of Education* (1968:568) that "the State has interests as an employer in regulating the speech of its employees that differ significantly from those it possesses in connection with regulation of the speech of the citizenry in general." Thus, the state may impose restrictions on its employees that it would not be able to impose on the citizenry at large. However, these restrictions must be reasonable.

If overly broad, a police regulation may be found to be an unreasonable infringement on the free speech interests of officers. A Chicago Police Department rule prohibiting "any activity, conversation, deliberation, or discussion which is derogatory to the Department" is a good example because such a rule obviously prohibits all criticism of the agency by its officers, even in private conversation (*Muller* v. *Conlisk*, 1970:901).

A related area is political activity. As with free speech, government agencies may restrict the political behavior of their employees to prevent them from being pressured by their superiors to support certain political candidates or engage in political activities under threat of loss of employment or other adverse action. The federal government and many states have such statutes.

A police officer may also be protected because of his or her political affiliations. For example, a newly elected sheriff, a Democrat, in Cook County, Illinois, fired the chief deputy of the process division and a bailiff of the juvenile court because they were Republicans. The Supreme Court ruled that it was a violation of the employees' First Amendment rights to discharge them from nonpolicy-making positions solely on the basis of their political party affiliation (see *Connick* v. *Myers*, 1983; *Jones* v. *Dodson*, 1984).

The First Amendment's reach also includes appearance. For example, the Supreme Court upheld the constitutionality of a regulation of the Suffolk County,

204

PART TWO
Supervising Human
Resources: Training,
Evaluation, and
Discipline

New York, police department that established several grooming standards—hair, sideburn, and moustache length—for its male officers to make officers readily recognizable to the public and to maintain the esprit de corps within the department (*Kelley* v. *Johnston*, 1976).

Searches and Seizures

The Fourth Amendment to the U.S. Constitution protects the right of people to be secure in their persons, homes, papers, and effects against unreasonable searches and seizures. In an important case in 1967, the Supreme Court held that the amendment also protected individuals' reasonable expectations of privacy, not just property interests (*Katz* v. *United States*, 1967).

The Fourth Amendment usually applies to police officers at home or off duty in the same manner that it applies to all citizens. However, because of the nature of their work, police officers can be compelled to cooperate with investigations of their behavior when ordinary citizens would not. Examples include equipment and lockers provided by the department to the officers. There the officers have no expectation of privacy that affords or merits protection (see *People* v. *Tidwell*, 1971). However, lower courts have established limitations concerning searches of employees themselves. The rights of prison authorities to search their employees arose in a 1985 Iowa case, where employees were forced to sign a consent form as a condition of hire; the court disagreed with such a broad policy, ruling that the consent form did not constitute a blanket waiver of all Fourth Amendment rights (*McDonell* v. *Hunter*, 1985).

Police officers may also be forced to appear in a lineup, a clear "seizure" of his or her person. Normally requiring probable cause, a federal appeals court upheld a police commissioner's order for 62 officers to appear in a lineup during an investigation of police brutality. The court held that "the governmental interest in the particular intrusion [should be weighed] against the offense to personal dignity and integrity." Again, the court cited the nature of the work, noting that police officers do "not have the full privacy and liberty from police officials that [they] would otherwise enjoy" (*Biehunik* v. *Felicetta*, 1971:230).

Self-Incrimination

The Supreme Court also has addressed questions concerning the Fifth Amendment as it applies to police officers who are under investigation. In *Garrity* v. *New Jersey* a police officer was ordered by the attorney general to answer questions or be discharged. The officer testified that the information obtained as a result of his answers was later used to convict him of criminal charges. The Supreme Court held that the information obtained from the officer could not be used against him at his criminal trial because the Fifth Amendment forbids the use of coerced confessions.

The firing of a police officer who refuses to answer questions that are directly related to the performance of his or her duties has been upheld by the courts. Delted "provided that the officer has been informed that any answers may not be used later in a criminal proceeding." Although there is some diversity of opinion among lower courts whether an officer may be compelled to submit to a polygraph examination, the majority of courts that have considered the question have held that an officer can be required to take the examination under certain conditions (*Gabrilowitz* v. *Newman*, 1978). These conditions are outlined in the States Peace Officers Bill of Rights (discussed later in this chapter).

Religious Practices

Police work often requires that personnel be subject to availablility 24 hours a day, seven days a week. Although it is not always convenient or pleasant, shift coverage requires that police employees work weekends, nights, and holidays. It is generally assumed that one who takes such a job in policing agrees to work irregular hours. Usually, the personnel with the least seniority must work the most undesirable shifts. However, there are occasions when one's religious beliefs are in direct conflict with the requirements of the job. For example, conflicts may arise between one's work assignments and attendance at religious services or periods of religious observance. In these situations the employee might be forced to choose between his or her job and religion.

Title VII of the Civil Rights Act of 1964 prohibits religious discrimination in employment. Thus, public employees can expect reasonable accommodation of religious beliefs but not to the extent that they have complete freedom of religious expression (*United States* v. *City of Albuquerque*, 1976; see also *Trans World Airlines* v. *Hardison*, 1977).

Sexual Misconduct

Although we discussed sexual misconduct in Chapter 8, it deserves further mention here. To be blunt, police employees have ample opportunity to become engaged in affairs or other clearly sexual behavior. This is complicated by the number of police "groupies" who are attracted to officers in uniform.

Instances of sexual impropriety in police work can range from casual flirting on the job to romantic involvement with other employees or citizens. Policing has experienced all manner of unusual incidents, including the discipline of female police officers posing nude in magazines.

Clearly, sexual misconduct is a delicate area, one in which discipline can be and has been meted out as police supervisors and managers attempt to maintain high standards of officer conduct. It also has resulted in litigation on the part of some officers who feel that their right to privacy has been intruded upon.

Residency Requirements

Many government agencies specify that all or certain members in their employ must live within the geographical limits of their jurisdiction. In other words, employees must reside within the county or city of employment. Such residency requirements have been justified by employing agencies on the grounds that employees should become familiar with and be visible in the jurisdiction of their employment or that they should reside where taxpayers pay them. Perhaps the

206

PART TWO
Supervising Human
Resources: Training,
Evaluation, and
Discipline

strongest rationale given by employing agencies is that employees must live within a certain proximity of their work in order to respond quickly in the event of an emergency. However, residency requirements are less common today than in the past. This is largely due to issues related to family matters including affordable housing, schools, and recreational facilities.

Moonlighting

The courts have traditionally supported police agencies in the placing of limitations on the amount and kinds of outside work their employees can perform (see *Cox* v. *McNamara,* 1972; *Brenckle* v. *Township of Shaler,* 1972; *Hopwood* v. *City of Paducah,* 1968; *Flood* v. *Kennedy,* 1963). For example, police restrictions on moonlighting range from a complete ban on outside employment to permission to engage in certain forms of work, such as investments, private security, teaching police science courses, and so on. The rationale for agency limitations is that "outside employment seriously interferes with keeping the [police and fire] departments fit and ready for action at all times" (Williams, 1975:4).

Misuse of Firearms

Police agencies regulate the use of firearms through written policies and frequent range training. Still, a broad range of potential and actual problems remain with respect to the use and possible misuse of firearms, as the following will show.

Police agencies generally have policies regulating officer use of handguns and other firearms both on and off duty. The courts have held that such regulations need only be reasonable and that the burden rests with the disciplined police officer to show that the regulation was arbitrary and unreasonable (see *Lally* v. *Department of Police,* 1974).

Police firearms regulations tend to address three basic issues: (1) requirements for the safeguarding of the weapon; (2) guidelines for carrying the weapon while off duty; and (3) limitations on when the weapon may be fired (Swanson et al., 1993).

Courts and juries are becoming increasingly harsh in dealing with police officers who misuse their firearms. The current tendency is to "look behind" police shootings to determine if the officer acted negligently or the employing agency negligently trained and supervised the officer.

In a number of case, the courts have awarded damages against police officers and/or their employers for other acts involving the misuse of firearms: an officer shot a person while intoxicated and off duty in a bar (*Marusa* v. *District of Columbia,* 1973); an officer accidentally killed an arrestee with a shotgun while handcuffing him (*Sager* v. *City of Woodlawn Park,* 1982); an officer shot his wife five times and then committed suicide with an off-duty weapon the department required him to carry (*Bonsignore* v. *City of New York,* 1981); and an officer accidentally shot and killed an innocent bystander while pursuing another man at nighttime (the officer had no instruction on shooting at a moving target, night shooting, or shooting in residential areas) (*Popow* v. *City of Margate,* 1979).

Lab testing can determine a weapon's functionality and whether a bullet originated from it.
Courtesy New York Police Department Photo Unit.

Alcohol and Drugs in the Workplace

Alcoholism and drug abuse are issues of great concern to administrators in contemporary policing; employees must be increasingly wary of the risks of succumbing to these problems. The supervisor must be capable of recognizing these problems and assist the employee in seeking counseling and treatment for their problems.

Indeed, in the aftermath of the November 1992 beating death of Malice Green by a group of Detroit police officers, it was reported that the Detroit Police Department had "high alcoholism rates and pervasive psychological problems connected with the stress of policing a city mired in poverty, drugs, and crime"; a psychologist asserted that "there are many, many potential time bombs in that department" (Salholz and Washington, 1992:45).

Peace Officers Bill of Rights

In the past decade, police officers have insisted on greater procedural safeguards to protect them against what they perceive as arbitrary infringement on their rights. These demands have been reflected in statutes enacted in many

208

PART TWO
Supervising Human
Resources: Training,
Evaluation, and
Discipline

states, generally known as the "**Peace Officers Bill of Rights**." These statutes confer upon an employee a property interest in his or her position, and mandate due process rights for peace officers who are the subject of internal investigations that could lead to disciplinary action. These statutes identify the type of information that must be provided to the accused officer, the officer's responsibility to cooperate during the investigation, the officer's rights to representation during the process, and the rules and procedures concerning the collection of certain types of evidence. Briefly, some common provisions of state Peace Officers Bill of Rights legislation are:

Written Notice. The department must provide the officer with written notice of the nature of the investigation, a summary of alleged misconduct, and the name of the investigating officer.

Right to Representation. The officer may have an attorney or a representative of his or her choosing present during any phase of questioning or hearing.

Polygraph Examination. The officer may refuse to take a polygraph examination unless the complainant submits to an examination and is determined to be telling the truth. In this case, the officer may be ordered to take a polygraph examination or be subject to disciplinary action.

It is imperative that supervisors become thoroughly familiar with statutes, contract provisions, and existing rules between employer or employee so that procedural due process requirements can be met, particularly in disciplinary cases where an employee's property interest might be affected.

DISCIPLINARY POLICIES AND PRACTICES

A Tradition of Problems

Throughout its history policing has experienced allegations of misconduct and corruption. In the late 1800s, New York police sergeant Alexander "Clubber" Williams epitomized police brutality when he spoke openly of using his nightstick to knock a man unconscious, batter him to pieces, or even kill him. Williams supposedly coined the term "tenderloin," when he commented "I've had nothing but chuck steaks for a long time, and now I'm going to have me a little tenderloin" (Morris, 1951:112). Williams was referring to opportunities for graft in the area bounded by 14th and 42nd streets and Fifth and Seventh avenues in New York—the heart of vice and nightlife, often referred to as Satan's Circus. This was Williams's beat, where his reputation for brutality and corruption became legendary (Inciardi, 1996).

Although police corruption and brutality are no longer openly tolerated, a number of events throughout history have demonstrated that the problem still exists and requires the attention of police officials. Incidents such as the beating of Rodney King by officers in the presence of supervisors, the controversy surrounding the testimony of former Los Angeles police detective Mark Fuhrman during the O. J. Simpson trial, and major corruption scandals in the New York,

Philadelphia, and New Orleans police departments have led many people to believe that police misbehavior today is worse than during the "helter-skelter" 1960s (MacNamara, 1995). This perception about corruption is supported by the Mollen Commission's 1994 report on the New York City Police Department, which suggested a worsening pattern of corruption existed then and at higher levels in the organization than was the case 20 years ago (Gaffigan and Mcdonald, 1997). It seems apparent why the issue of police misconduct has assumed the forefront of the policing agenda.

Without question, police agencies need to pay close attention to any signs of police misconduct and to respond quickly. It is also important that agencies enact policies to guide supervisors on the handling of disciplinary issues. These policies must be based on standards of fairness, consistency, and equity so that the interests of the organization, the involved officer, and the public are protected.

The National Advisory Commission on Criminal Justice Standards and Goals (1973) recommended that every police agency formalize policies, procedures, and rules to investigate citizen complaints against the police. The following are important requisites of a disciplinary policy (Ianonni, 1994:159–60):

- *Certainty.* Certainty of punishment is perhaps the greatest deterrent to misconduct. However, the fear of losing peer respect may outweigh the fear of punishment, and the fear of punishment may be a helpful tool for supervisors to gain conformity from some employees.
- *Swiftness.* Punishment should be swift as well as certain. Any delays in investigations create unnecessary anxiety for the accused employee and a perception among officers of weakness and indecisiveness on the part of the supervisor.
- *Fairness and impartiality.* Employees object to the inequitable application of punishment more than the sanction itself. When considering punishment, supervisors should set all personal feelings and emotions aside. Another important disciplinary consideration for the supervisor is whether employee made a mistake "of the head" or "of the heart." For example, an officer who decides to go fishing and intentionally misses court should be punished more severely than an officer who inadvertently notes the wrong time on the calendar and misses a court appearance. Case Study 9–1 discusses a case in which officers appeal a supervisor's disciplinary actions all too often.
- *Consistency.* Similar misconduct should result in similar punishment. However, the aggravating or mitigating circumstances of each case coupled with an employee's past performance should also be considered by a supervisor reviewing discipline. Overly severe or lenient punishment may create the opposite reaction from employees than what the supervisor intended.

A study by the International Association of Chiefs of Police (IACP, 1996) concluded that police officers disagree with discipline primarily when they believe it is inconsistent. A system of discipline that considers the seriousness of the offense, aggravating and mitigating circumstances, and the officer's career record helps to ensure that consistency is met (Barker and Carter, 1994). Officers understand that when they violate departmental rules and regulations, sanctions will

210

PART TWO
Supervising Human
Resources: Training,
Evaluation, and
Discipline

follow. They only expect to be treated fairly, honestly, and respectfully during the course of the investigation. In turn, the public expects the agency to develop sound disciplinary policies and conduct thorough inquiries into allegations of misconduct. Thus, public trust begins with sound policies and procedures.

Establishing Sound Written Guidelines

Policies provide an overall plan that helps to translate agency philosophy into practice. Policies guide employee behavior and conduct by setting acceptable and realistic parameters of control. A sound disciplinary policy represents the best interests of the accused employee, the agency, and the community. Sencio (1992) noted that an effective policy ensures that:

- Citizens are afforded the opportunity to lodge complaints and obtain information about the progress of the investigation.
- An impartial and objective investigation is carried out to obtain facts and support to refute the allegation.
- Employees' rights are not violated and they are protected from false, unjust, or vindictive accusations.
- The agency is protected from unsuitable employees and unwarranted criticism, while morale and competence are maintained.
- The community enjoys confidence in the police force and receives quality police service.

The following administrative, supervisory, and leadership factors also have a significant impact on the effectiveness of an organization's disciplinary poli-

Case Study 9–1
Making Enemies Fast: The "Misunderstood" Disciplinarian

Sergeant Jerold Jones does not understand why his officers appeal all of his disciplinary recommendations. He takes matters of discipline very seriously; it commonly takes him three to four weeks to investigate minor matters—three to four times longer than other supervisors. Jones believes that by doing so, he shows great concern for his officers. In fact, he does not even question the officers about their behavior until the investigation is nearly complete and he has interviewed everyone involved in the matter.

Jones decides to speak to his officers about the matter. He is surprised when they tell him that they do not trust him. They fail to understand why he needs so much time to investigate minor incidents. They feel that he is being secretive and is always looking for ways to find fault with their per-

formance. Jones argues that his recommendations are consistent with those of the other sergeants, and he provides some examples of similar cases handled by various supervisors. Apparently not convincing the officers, Jones receives another appeal the next day of one of his disciplinary recommendations of an officer concerning a minor traffic accident.

1. Are the officers' allegations of Sgt. Jones's unfairness valid?
2. What requisites of sound disciplinary policy that may be leading to the officers' appeals does Jones not understand?
3. Under the circumstances, should Jones simply ignore the officers' complaints? Are their perceptions that important?

cies and practices (Ross, 1992:21–22):

Adequate training and retraining.

Publicized rules of ethics and conduct.

Consistent leadership and supervision.

Coaching and counseling.

Regular performance evaluations.

Prompt corrective action against inappropriate attitudes and conduct.

To ensure that fair and consistent treatment of employees occurs, the police departments should consider the following factors in its disciplinary process (Stephens, 1994:21–22):

Determining factors. Consider all the factors and give each equal weight unless the circumstances dictate otherwise. The factors are also interactive, so don't isolate one or give it greater importance than it deserves.

Employee motivation. Give more positive consideration to employees who act in the best interests of the broader public than to those who are motivated by personal interests.

Degree of harm. Harm can be measured in various ways, including monetary costs to the department and community as a result of vehicle repairs or personal injury or excessive force claims. Harm may also be assessed in terms of the impact on the public's confidence owing to employee involvement in criminal behavior.

Employee experience. A new employee may be treated with more leniency in errors of judgment than a more experienced employee who may warrant more serious sanctions.

Intentional/unintentional errors. Unintentional errors occur when an employee's decision turns out to be wrong, even though it was in compliance with departmental rules and regulations at the time. For example, a supervisor who allows officers to continue a vehicle pursuit based on the belief that the vehicle was involved in an earlier robbery, and subsequently learns that it was not, should be not be reprimanded or punished. On the other hand, intentional errors generally are treated more seriously and occur when the employee knew or should have known the act would violate law, policy, or procedures.

Employee's past record. Repeated errors should be dealt with in a progressive and more serous manner. The lack of any previous disciplinary action may also be a mitigating factor, especially for a first offense.

Automated Records Systems

During the 1990s there were many advances in the technological aspects of police discipline. In 1991, for example, the Fresno, California police department automated its disciplinary process in an effort to establish a better system for tracking and sanctioning personnel for various offenses (Guthrie, 1996). The principle objectives of this automated system were to help the chief to administer the department in a more equitable fashion and to improve the department's ability to defend its personnel actions. Within minutes the database provides supervisors with five years of history about standards of discipline for any category of violation. A variety of reports can be produced, showing patterns of incidents for the supervisor. The system has provided several additional positive results, including:

Savings in time and money. Data concerning an officer's disciplinary history or trends in violations is available within minutes. A cost savings of $25,000 in staff time was estimated during the first year of implementation.

Complaint patterns identified. Data can be sorted by date, time of day, type of complaint, race of participants, officer involved, responsible supervisor, and so on. Habitual offenders also can be identified. This information helps the department's command staff to evaluate the need for policy modifications, training, and changes in the levels of discipline for certain offenses.

Improved case management. The automated system eliminates the need for supervisors and commanders to review a large volume of handwritten logs. The information is immediately available, reducing the time it takes to complete cases; this has a positive impact on officers' anxiety while awaiting a decision and has eliminated the incidence of lost cases.

This information is also helpful as a preventive measure and may be integrated into an early warning system, discussed in more detail below.

Keys to Effective Discipline

The real purpose of discipline is to get employees to comply voluntarily with departmental rules and regulations, work together as a team, respect each other, and perform to the best of their ability. In this sense, self-discipline provides the foundation for successful management. Without self-discipline an organization is sure to face significant problems. Black (1986) provided the following checklist to assist supervisors in developing self-discipline within the workforce:

1. *Understand your disciplinary responsibilities.* The road to success as a supervisor entails much more than simply being liked by subordinates. Judgment, fairness, and knowledge of the job provide the foundation upon which a supervisor's respect is earned. These traits provide the best means of ensuring the self-discipline of employees.
2. *Make sure employees receive sound instruction.* The employee who is half-taught is half-disciplined. Discipline means knowledge. Employees expect that supervisors will provide them with the necessary information, guidance, and coaching to increase their opportunities for improvement and advancement.
3. *Insist on high standards of performance.* The employee who is allowed to perform at a mediocre level has little incentive to improve.
4. *Maintain effective communication.* Effective communication begins the first day a supervisor and subordinate work together. Start by making sure that

When Sergeants Need Discipline

Sometimes police supervisors themselves require the sharp hand of discipline and even prosecution. Two examples follow.

Former New York City Sergeant Kevin Nannery was sentenced to one to three years in prison in June 1997 for perjury. Nannery, the highest ranking officer in the scandal, led a group that became known as "Nannery's Raiders,"

for their practice of breaking into apartments, stealing drugs and cash, and taking payoffs.

Atlanta Police Sergeant Randy Meyers, 44, was suspended for 30 days without pay after being videotaped beating a man who drove through a police roadblock. Meyers and other officers surrounded a 27-year old man, pummeled him with a baton, and doused him with pepper spray.

the subordinate understands all departmental rules and regulations and the reasons behind them. Recognize accomplishments early and remember that two-way communication breeds respect and is the hallmark of constructive discipline.

5. *Enforce discipline fairly.* A capable supervisor sees that all rules apply equally to all people. Don't ignore any discipline, but at the same time don't show favoritism.

6. *Set the pace for discipline.* Discipline begins with the supervisor. You cannot expect discipline from others if you are not disciplined yourself. The disciplined supervisor plans ahead and is organized. There is no lost motion or indecision.

FORMS OF DISCIPLINE

Officer misconduct and violations of departmental policy are the two principle areas where discipline is involved (McLaughlin and Bing, 1989). Officer misconduct includes acts that harm the public, including corruption, harassment, brutality, and civil rights violations. Violations of policy may involve a broad range of issues, including substance abuse and insubordination or minor violations of dress and tardiness.

Determining the Level and Nature of Action

When an investigation against an employee is sustained, the sanctions and level of discipline must be decided. Management must be very careful when recommending and imposing discipline because of its impact on the overall morale of the agency's employees. If employees perceive the recommended discipline as too lenient, a supervisor may be sending the wrong message: The misconduct is insignificant. On the other hand, discipline that is viewed as too harsh may have a demoralizing effect on the officer(s) and other agency employees involved and result in allegations that the leadership is unfair. This alone can have significant impact on the esprit de corps or morale of the agency.

We have discussed the importance of having a disciplinary process that employees view as fair and consistent, meaning that similar violations receive

213

214

PART TWO
Supervising Human
Resources: Training,
Evaluation, and
Discipline

similar punishments. It is also important that discipline is progressive and more serious sanctions are invoked when repeated violations occur. For example, a third substantiated violation of rude behavior may result in a recommendation for a one-day suspension without pay, whereas a first offense may be resolved through documented oral counseling or a letter of reprimand. The disciplinary actions commonly used by agencies are discussed below in order of their severity.

Counseling

Counseling is usually a conversation between the supervisor and employee about a specific aspect of the employee's performance or conduct. It is warranted when an employee has committed a relatively minor infraction or the nature of the offense requires only oral counseling. For example, an officer who is usually punctual but arrives at briefing 10 minutes late two days in a row may require nothing more than a reminder and warning to correct the problem.

Documented Oral Counseling

Documented oral counseling is usually the first step in a progressive disciplinary process and is intended to address relatively minor infractions. It is provided in cases where there are no previous reprimands or more severe disciplinary action of the same or similar nature.

Letters of Reprimand

Letters of reprimand are formal written notices regarding significant misconduct, more serious performance violations, or repeated offenses. It is usually the second step in the disciplinary process and is intended to provide the employee and agency with a written record of the violation of behavior. A letter of reprimand identifies what specific corrective action must be taken to avoid subsequent, more serious disciplinary action.

Suspension

Suspension is a severe disciplinary action which results in an employee being relieved of duty, often without pay. It is usually administered in cases where an employee commits a serious violation of established rules or after written reprimands have been given and no change in behavior or performance has resulted.

Demotion

Demotion places an employee in a position of lower responsibility and pay. It is normally used when an otherwise good employee is unable to meet the standards required for the higher position, or where the employee has committed a serious act requiring removal from a position of management or supervision.

Termination

The final and most severe disciplinary action is **termination.** It usually occurs when previous serious discipline has been imposed and the employee's subsequent behavior or performance has been inadequate or shown no improvement. Termination also may occur when an employee commits an offense so serious that continued employment would be inappropriate.

Transfer

215

CHAPTER 9
Officers' Rights,
Discipline, and
Appeals

Some agencies use the disciplinary **transfer** of an officer to a different assignment as a method of dealing with the problem. In some departments however, labor agreements prohibit transfers for disciplinary reasons.

An employee's disciplinary record is not a permanent record. The time period for maintaining and purging disciplinary records is often specified by state administrative code. In some jurisdictions, the maintenance of Internal Affairs Unit (IAU) files is a matter of confidentiality, making any violation an unlawful act. Therefore, the maintenance and security of IAU files is often assigned to the IAU supervisor.

Positive and Negative Discipline

The primary purpose of discipline is to ensure that employees perform their duties and responsibilities within established policies and procedures. When policies and procedures are violated, positive or negative disciplinary measures may be imposed. Although different in their philosophy, both positive and negative discipline seek to accomplish the same purpose: to correct negative behavior and promote the employees' voluntary compliance with departmental policies and procedures. Both positive and negative discipline are important tools for the supervisor.

Positive discipline (also known as progressive discipline or positive counseling) attempts to change employee behavior without invoking punishment. Consider the following scenario for example; a supervisor might use positive discipline when John, an employee, continues to be unproductive and tardy, causes interpersonal problems with coworkers, or has other problems on the job. To this point, John has been in control of the situation—"on the offensive" one might say—while his supervisor Jane and coworkers have been on the defensive. John is jeopardizing the morale and productivity of the workplace, but the preferred approach is to salvage him because of the agency's investment in time, funds, and training.

Finally, Jane calls John into her office. She might begin with a casual conversation, and then proceeds to outline all of John's workplace shortcomings. This demonstrates to John that Jane is very aware and concerned about his various problems. Jane explains to him why it is important that he improve (for reasons related to productivity, morale, and so on), and what benefits he might realize from improvement (promotions, pay raises, bonuses, and so forth). She also outlines what can happen if he does *not* show adequate improvement (reprimand, days off, transfer, or termination). Having gained John's attention, Jane gives him a certain time period (maybe 30, 60, or 90 days) in which to improve; she emphasizes, however, that she will be constantly monitoring his progress. She might even ask John to sign a counseling statement form that sets forth all of the problems and solutions, indicating that John has received counseling and understands the situation.

Note that Jane is now on the offensive, thereby putting John on the defensive and responsible for his own destiny. If he fails to perform, Jane would probably give him a warning; if the situation continues, more serious discipline would be appropriate. If John sues or files a grievance, Jane has proof

216

*PART TWO
Supervising Human
Resources: Training,
Evaluation, and
Discipline*

that every effort was made to help him salvage his position. This is a very effective means of getting subordinates to have an incentive to improve their behavior; at the same time it makes the department less vulnerable to successful lawsuits.

Negative discipline is punishment. It is generally used when positive efforts fail or the violation is so serious that punishment is required. Negative discipline may vary in its severity and involve a simple documented oral counseling, letter of reprimand, demotion, days off without pay, or even termination.

THE INVESTIGATION OF COMPLAINTS

The Origin of Complaints

A **personnel complaint** is an allegation of misconduct or illegal behavior against an employee by anyone inside or outside the organization. There are two types of complaints: internal and external. **Internal complaints,** those made from persons within the organization, may involve supervisors observing officer misconduct, officers complaining about supervisors, supervisors complaining about supervisors, civilian personnel complaining about officers, and so on. **External complaints** originate from sources outside the organization and usually involve the public.

Supervisors may receive complaints from primary, secondary, and anonymous sources. A **primary source** is one that is received directly from the victim. A **secondary source** is one that is made by another party, such as an attorney, school counselor, parent of a juvenile, and so on, on behalf of the victim. An **anonymous source** derives from an unknown person or persons and may be delivered to the police station by means of a telephone call or unsigned letter.

Every complaint, regardless of the source, must be accepted and investigated in accordance with established policies and procedures. However, some complaints may be disposed of without the formality of an investigation. In some cases, the accused employee's actions may be clearly within departmental policy, so a simple communication about that to the citizen from a supervisor should resolve the matter. For example, a citizen might be offended that officers following policy would handcuff an elderly shoplifting suspect. Other complaints may be so trivial that further inquiry or investigation is unnecessary; a citizen's call to the watch commander with a general complaint that the city employs too many police officers is not an issue that would be handled within a disciplinary process.

Anonymous complaints are the most difficult to investigate because there is no opportunity to obtain further information or question the complainant about the allegation. In addition, anonymous complaints are troublesome for the supervisor because of their potentially negative impact on an employee's morale. Officers often view anonymous complaints as unjust and frivolous and question why the department gives them any attention whatsoever. Therefore, supervisors must help officers understand that complaints, regardless of their source, cannot be ignored or disregarded, and that disciplinary processes are designed to protect both officers and the organization, as well as to preserve the public's trust.

Supervisors also should be aware that the most bizarre accusations sometimes may prove true. In one western city, an anonymous complaint was received alleging that a marked city police vehicle was observed during the early morning hours in another city 120 miles away and across state lines. An investigation found that officers working in the rural outskirts of the city were making bets on how far they could travel and return during the course of a shift. Photos of officers in uniform standing next to their vehicle and the city limits sign of the distant city were discovered and used as evidence against the officers during their disciplinary hearing. Supervisors also should understand that the reason behind a complainant's anonymity may be the result of a close relationship with or fear of the accused officer.

Types and Causes of Complaints

Supervisors may handle complaints informally or formally. The seriousness of the allegation and preference of the complainant usually dictate whether a complaint will be investigated in a formal or informal manner. A **formal complaint** is a written and signed or tape-recorded statement of a complainant's allegation. In a formal complaint, the complainant is kept informed of the investigation's disposition. Figure 9–1 provides an example of a complaint form used to initiate a personnel investigation.

An **informal complaint** is an allegation of minor misconduct made for informational purposes that can usually be resolved without the need for more formal processes. In the case of a citizen who calls the watch commander to complain about the rude behavior of a dispatcher but does not wish to make a formal complaint, the supervisor may simply discuss the incident with the dispatcher and resolve it through informal counseling as long as more serious problems are not discovered and the dispatcher does not have a history of similar complaints.

These examples are typical of the majority of complaints handled by supervisors. Few complaints involve serious acts of physical violence, excessive force, or corruption. The majority of complaints against police officers fall under the general categories of verbal abuse, discourtesy, harassment, improper attitudes, and ethnic slurs (Wagner and Decker: 1997). These comprise the issues that supervisors contend with on a daily basis.

Dugan and Breda (1991) reviewed 691 citizen complaints taken from 165 police and sheriff agencies representing 3,515 officers in Washington state. They found that 42 percent of complaints involved the "verbal conduct" of officers (see the discussion on police use of profanity in Chapter 8). Verbal conduct also accounted for 47 percent of all sustained complaints as did the majority of repeated offenses. It is clear that the verbal demeanor of officers generates a significant number of complaints. Supervisors must be attentive to officers' interpersonal skills and use of language.

Receipt and Referral

The process for receiving a complaint should be clearly delineated by departmental policy and procedures. Generally, a complaint will be made at a police facility and referred to a command officer or supervisor to determine its

****

Control Number _____

Date & Time Reported	Location of Interview	Interview
_____	_____	_____Verbal _____Written _____Taped

Type of complaint: ____Force ____Procedural ____Conduct
____Other (Specify)

Source of complaint: _____In Person _____Mail _____Telephone
_____Other (Specify)

Complaint originally _____Supervisor _____On Duty Watch Commander _____Chief
Received by: _____IAU _____Other (Specify)

Notifications made: _____Division Commander _____Chief of Police
Received by: _____On-Call Command Personnel
_____Watch Commander _____Other (Specify)

Copy of formal personnel complaint report given to complainant? _____Yes ____No

****

Complainant's name: Address:
_____ _____Zip_____

Residence Phone: Business Phone:

DOB: Race: Sex: Occupation:

****

Location of Occurrence: Date & Time of Occurrence:

Member(s) Involved: Member(s) Involved:
(1) _____ (2) _____
(3) _____ (4) _____

Witness(es) Involved: Witness(es) Involved:
(1) _____ (2) _____
(3) _____ (4) _____

****

(1)_____ Complainant wishes to make a formal statement and has requested an investigation into the matter with a report back to him/her on the findings and actions.

(2)_____ Complainant wishes to advise the Police Department of a problem, understand that some type of action will be taken, but does not request a report back to him/her on the findings and actions.

****

CITIZEN ADVISEMENTS

(1) If you have not yet provided the department with a signed written statement or a tape-recorded statement, one may be required in in order to pursue the investigation of this matter.

(2) The complainant(s) and/or witness(es) may be required to take a polygraph examination in order to determine the credibility concerning the allegations made.

(3) Should the allegations prove to be false, the complainant(s) and /or witness(es) may be liable for criminal and/or civil prosecution.

_____ _____
Signature of Complainant Date & Time

_____
Signature of Member Receiving Complaint

FIGURE 9–1. Police Department Formal Personnel Complaint Report

218

seriousness and need for immediate intervention. A telephone complaint alleging that an on-duty officer is drinking in a local bar would require that a supervisor investigate immediately. However, in the case of a citizen complaint about the attitude of an officer during a traffic stop, time is not critical and the complainant would normally be referred to the officer's immediate supervisor, or an internal affairs officer will investigate the matter and contact them at a later time, depending upon the department's established procedures.

In most cases, the supervisor handling the investigation will determine the nature of the complaint and the employees involved; the matter will be referred to the employee's supervisor to conduct an initial investigation. The supervisor would complete the investigation, recommend any disciplinary action, and send the matter to the IAU and the agency head to complete the disciplinary process. This method of review ensures the application of consistent and fair standards of discipline.

Complaints are usually accepted from any person who feels injured or aggrieved in some way. Complaints may be made through a variety of means, including in person, mail, or telephone. Technology has increased the capacity of police agencies to provide citizens with easier access. As a result, some departments have begun to include complaint forms on their Web page of the Internet.

The Investigative Process

Perez (1992) indicated that all but a small percentage of the 17,000 police agencies in the United States have a process for investigating police misconduct. Generally, the employee's supervisor will conduct a preliminary inquiry of the complaint, commonly referred to as fact-finding. Once it is determined that further investigation is necessary, the supervisor may further question employees and witnesses, obtain written statements from those persons immediately involved in the incident, and gather any evidence that may be necessary for the case, including photographs. As discussed below, it is at this time that a supervisor must be careful that the rights of the investigated employee are upheld. The initial investigation would be sent to an appropriate division commander and forwarded to an IAU for review.

Most investigations, especially those determined to be minor in nature, will be handled completely by an employee's supervisor. Where the allegations involve employees from more than one division or an outside agency, or in cases where the incident is of a more serious nature, investigations may be handled by the IAU.

Making a Determination and Disposition

Once an investigation is completed, the supervisor or IAU officer must make a determination concerning the culpability of the accused employee. Each allegation should receive a separate adjudication. The following are the categories of dispositions in common use.

Unfounded. The alleged act(s) did not occur.

Exonerated. The act occurred, but it is lawful, proper, justified, and/or in accordance with departmental policies, procedures, and rules and regulations.

220

PART TWO
Supervising Human
Resources: Training,
Evaluation, and
Discipline

Not sustained. There is insufficient evidence to prove or disprove the allegations made.

Misconduct not based on the complaint. Sustainable misconduct was determined but is not a part of the original complaint. For example, a supervisor investigating an allegation of excessive force against an officer might find that the force used was within departmental policy, but that the officer made an unlawful arrest.

Closed. An investigation may be halted if the complainant fails to cooperate or the action is determined to fall outside the administrative jurisdiction of the police agency.

Sustained. The act did occur and it was a violation of departmental rules and procedures. Sustained allegations include misconduct that falls within the broad outlines of the original allegation(s).

Once a determination of culpability has been made, the complainant should be notified of the department's findings. Details of the investigation or recommended punishment will not be included in the correspondence. As shown in Figure 9–2, the complainant will normally receive only the final disposition of the complaint, including a short explanation of the finding along with an invitation to call the agency if further information is needed.

EMPLOYEE GRIEVANCES

Notwithstanding all of the limitations on their rights and freedoms, police officers still may complain and file grievances about contractual or other matters. We next provide an overview of the means by which officers may address the perceived unfair disciplinary measures taken against them.

The Formal Processing of Grievances

The purpose of grievance procedures is to establish a fair and expeditious process for handling employee disputes that are not disciplinary in nature. **Grievance procedures** usually involve collective bargaining issues, conditions of employment, or other terms and conditions of employment or employer-employee relations. More specifically, grievances may cover a broad range of issues, including salaries, overtime, leave, hours of work, allowances, retirement, opportunity for advancement, performance evaluations, workplace conditions, tenure, supervisory methods, and administrative practices. Grievance procedures are often established as a part of the collective bargaining process.

The preferred method for settling officer grievances is through informal discussion where the employee explains his or her grievance to the immediate supervisor. Allowing employees to vent their frustrations is an important aspect of supervision and greatly enhances the chances of a grievance being resolved informally and to the satisfaction of the employee. Those complaints that cannot be dealt with informally are usually handled through a more formal grievance process, which we describe on the following page. A formal griev-

Police Department
3300 Main Street
Downtown Plaza
Anywhere, USA. 99999
June 20, 1998

Mr. John Doe
2200 Main Avenue
Anywhere, U.S.A.

Re: Internal Affairs #000666-98
 Case Closure

Dear Mr. Doe:

Our investigation into your allegations against Officer Smith has been completed. It has been determined that your complaint is SUSTAINED and the appropriate disciplinary action has been taken.

Our department appreciates your bringing this matter to our attention. It is our position that when a problem is identified, it should be corrected as soon as possible. It is our goal to be responsive to the concerns expressed by citizens so as to provide more efficient and effective services.

Your information regarding this incident was helpful and of value in our efforts to attain that goal. Should you have any further questions about this matter, please contact Sergeant Jane Alexander, Internal Affairs, at 555-9999.

Sincerely,

I. M. Boss,
Lieutenant
Internal Affairs Unit

FIGURE 9–2. Citizens' Notification of Discipline Letter

ance begins with an employee submitting the grievance in writing to his or her immediate supervisor (see Figure 9–3).

Levels of Action

The process for formally handling grievances will vary between agencies and may involve as many as three to six different levels of action. A typical grievance may proceed as follows:

Level I. A grievance is submitted in writing to a supervisor. The supervisor has five days to respond to the employee's grievance. If the employee is dissatisfied, the grievance moves to the next level.

Level II. At this level, the grievance proceeds to the chief of police who will be given a specified time (usually five days) to render a decision.

222

PART TWO
Supervising Human
Resources: Training,
Evaluation, and
Discipline

Police Department
Formal Grievance Form

Grievance #_____

Employee Name: _____ Work Phone: _____
Department Assigned: _____
Date of Occurrence:_____
Location of Occurrence: _____

Name of: 1.   Department Head:_____

             2.   Division Head: _____

             3.   Immediate Supervisor: _____

Statement of Grievance: _____
_____
_____
_____

Witnesses: _____
_____
_____

What article(s) and or section(s) of the labor agreement of rules and regulations do you
believe have been violated? _____
_____
_____
_____

What remedy are you requesting? _____
_____
_____

_____   _____
Employee Signature   Signature of labor representative
FIGURE 9–3. Employee Grievance Form

Level III.   If the employee is dissatisfied with the chief's decision, the grievance may proceed to the city or county manager, whichever is appropriate. The manager will usually meet with the employee and possibly representatives from the bargaining association to resolve the matter. An additional 5 to 10 days is usually allowed for the manager to render a decision.

Level IV.   If the grievance is still not resolved, either party may request that the matter be submitted to arbitration. **Arbitration** involves a neutral, outside person, often selected from a list of arbitrators from the Federal Mediation and Conciliation Service. An arbitrator will conduct a hearing, listen to both parties, and usually come up with a decision within 20 to 30 days. The decision of the arbitrator can be final and binding. This does not prohibit the employee from appealing the decision to a state court.

Advice for Supervisors

The actions of a supervisor in dealing with grievances are vital to their successful resolution. Failure to act quickly on grievances may result in serious morale problems within an agency. Snow (1990) offered this helpful advice for supervisors when dealing with employee grievances.

- *Give employees your attention.* Grievances are important to officers and must be dealt with quickly so officers do not feel that their concerns are being ignored.
- *Let officers vent.* Do not interrupt officers while they are expressing their grievances. Let them fully explain their concerns and never let them feel that you have already made a decision.
- *Search for the facts.* Separate facts from rumors and half-truths. Search for the underlying causes of problems—those small issues that are often symptoms of a larger hidden problem.
- *Seek the advice of peers.* Talk with other supervisors or experienced officers who may have dealt with similar issues and find out what their solutions were.
- *Do not trivialize grievances.* Grievances are often very emotional and volatile issues to the employee, and supervisors should treat them with dignity and respect, regardless of their veracity.
- *Explain your decision.* Take the time to explain the logic and reasoning of your decision with the employee. Even if an officer does not agree with a decision, often he or she may accept it based on your explanation and reasoning.
- *End on a positive note.* Ofttimes, an officer only wants someone to talk to and listen to his or her complaint. Supervisors should attempt to conclude interviews on a positive note and with some resolution in mind.

APPEALING DISCIPLINARY ACTIONS

The process for employees to appeal recommended disciplinary measures is frequently outlined in civil service rules and regulations, labor agreements, and departmental policies and procedures. Appeals processes normally follow an officer's chain of command. For example, if an officer disagrees with a supervisor's recommendation for discipline, the first step of an appeal may involve a hearing before the division commander, usually of the rank of captain or deputy chief. The accused employee may be allowed labor representation or an attorney to assist in asking questions of the investigating supervisor, clarifying issues, and presenting new or mitigating evidence. The division commander would have a specified period of time (normally five days) to review the recommendation and respond in writing to the employee.

224

PART TWO
Supervising Human
Resources: Training,
Evaluation, and
Discipline

If the employee is still not satisfied, an appeal hearing before the chief of police would be granted. This is usually the final step in appeals within the agency. The chief would also communicate a decision to the employee in writing (normally within 5 to 10 days). Depending on labor agreements and civil service rules and regulations, some agencies extend their disciplinary appeals beyond the department. In this case, employees may be afforded the opportunity and choice of bringing their issue before the civil service commission or city or county manager for a final review. In the most extenuating circumstances, employees may also have the right to an independent arbitrator's review of the discipline. The arbitrator's decision is usually binding.

PREVENTION THROUGH EARLY INTERVENTION

The Early Warning System

The early identification and intervention of employee misconduct or performance problems is vital to preventing ongoing and repeated incidents. An **early warning system (EWS)** allows police agencies to identify and intervene in employee problems at an early stage and before they become a crisis; if ignored, these problems can eventually lead to more serious misconduct or violations of departmental rules and regulations.

EWS helps police agencies respond proactively to patterns of behavior that may lead to more serious problems. Prior to EWS, few departments would deal proactively with repeated minor or unsubstantiated complaints. EWS views these patterns as precursors to more serious problems and may require that the officer's supervisor intervene with early prevention methods such as counseling or training.

The importance of EWS is illustrated by an example in Kansas City, Missouri, where a task force investigated use-of-force complaints against police officers. It was discovered that 29 officers of approximately 1,100 in the department were involved in nearly 50 percent of the 756 complaints filed (KCPD, 1991). The study also identified some common traits among the offending officers. They included poor report writing, authoritarian and abusive language toward the public, and an obsessive focus on strength building, wearing mirrored sunglasses, and carrying extra enforcement equipment, such as two sets of handcuffs. Some officers had as many as nine complaints against them; the department may have avoided more serious complaints had they developed a system of early detection (Ross, 1992).

Types of Early Warning Systems

Berkow (1996) separated EWS into two types. The first and most frequently used type is based on external citizen complaints against officers. As described above, these types of systems seek to identify those officers who exceed the norm in acceptable behavior. The second type of system tracks officers' use of force. Agencies commonly document any use of force by officers. Force is broadly defined and may include defensive tactics, batons, oleo capsicum (pepper) spray, Tasers, and so on. To get a complete picture of the officers' behavior, some agencies also monitor use of sick leave, vehicle accidents, and on-duty injuries.

Some agencies require that any use of force by an officer is reported (see Figure 9.4) and reviewed by a supervisor. By reviewing and approving use-of-force reports, the supervisor must make a judgment concerning whether the officer is acting within departmental policies and regulations. The circumstances surrounding the officer's decision to use force may also indicate the need for remediation or additional training. In the worst case, EWS will identify those officers whose track record indicates a need to intervene quickly and maybe even remove them from the street. Figure 9–4 provides an example of a use-of-force form.

Administering EWS

Department internal affairs units (IAUs) are generally responsible for administering the EWS. The EWS also may identify a variety of behavior or performance concerns, including complaints of misconduct, unauthorized use of force, multiple vehicle accidents, and other violations of departmental policy and regulations. An EWS would also seek to identify trends or patterns of behavior which, if left unattended, may lead to more serious problems.

Once a potential problem has been identified, the IAU reports the information to the officer's immediate supervisor, to be addressed in accordance with some established procedures. In some cases repeated incidence of violence may require officers to attend anger management training or verbal judo to learn how to de-escalate confrontational situations. The officer's supervisor reviews the information and intervenes with some preventive measure or measures such as counseling, remedial training, or temporary change of assignment. As noted in Chapter 7, referral to an employee assistance program (EAP) to deal with more serious psychological or substance abuse problems may also be necessary. They offer a variety of confidential family and personal services to help employees through their difficulties, such as stress or marital problems or drug or alcohol abuse (stress and wellness were discussed at length in Chapter 7).

Rooting Out Corruption in New York

Recently New York City Mayor Rudolph W. Giuliani and former Police Commissioner William Bratton introduced a new process to root out police corruption. The department's revitalized IAU developed a PRIDE computer system that helped it to track serious officer misconduct and corruption. In addition, the department instituted a number of other measures to protect against corruption, including integrity tests aimed at specific officers under suspicion of corruption, mandatory response by the IAU to any incident that could implicate officers criminally, increasing entry-level education to 60 college credits or two years' military service, simplifying the department's disciplinary system so that cases were handled more expeditiously, and independent oversight by the Mayor's Commission to Combat Police Corruption. The department also increased its minimum amount of service time for promotion to sergeant from three years to five years, so that the force would gain more experienced candidates, and it developed supervisory training that focused on "field-tested tools" needed to maintain alert and effective control of police officers (IACP, 1996).

The data provided in the EWS should help the supervisor to determine the proper intervention strategy. Repeated violations of departmental policy may

Date:
Type of Incident:
Location of Occurrence:

Officer Involved: Badge Number:
Area/Div Assigned: State Compensation Claim Filed   Y/N_____
Injuries/Officer: ___ None   ___ Treat/rel   ___ Hospitalized   ___ Fatal
Other Officers Involved: ___ Yes   ___ No   Number ___

Subject #1
Name (Last, First, MI)
Sex, Race, DOB:
Level of Resistance: ___ None   ___ Physical   ___ Firearm   ___ Other Weapon
Injuries to Subject: ___ Y/N
If Yes: ___ Treated/Released   ___ Hospitalized   ___ Fatal
Type of Force Used: ___ Physical   ___ Capstun   ___ K-9   ___ Firearm   ___ Carotid
___ Other (specify):
Charges:

Subject #2
Name (Last, First, Middle):
Sex, Race, DOB:
Level of Resistance: ___ None   ___ Physical   ___ Firearm   ___ Other Weapon
Injuries to Subject: ___ Y/N
If Yes: ___ Treated/Released   ___ Hospitalized   ___ Fatal
Type of Force Used: ___ Physical   ___ Capstun   ___ K-9   ___ Firearm   ___ Carotid
___ Other (specify):
Charges:

Witnesses

#1   Name (Last, First, Middle):
Address & Phone:

#2   Name (Last, First, Middle):
Address & Phone:

#3   Name (Last, First, Middle):
Address & Phone:

Supervisor:
Further Investigation Required   ___ No Further Investigation Required
Date: Signature:

Shift Lieutenant:
Further Investigation Required   ___ No Further Investigation Required
Date: Signature:

Division Commander:
Further Investigation Required   ___ No Further Investigation Required
Date: Signature:

FIGURE 9–4 Supervisor's Use of Force Form

require more serious discipline or even demotion or termination. In the most serious cases, a detailed analysis of the EWS data will ensure that the supervisor has the information necessary so that the process is fair.

Methods of Supervisory Monitoring

It is the supervisor's responsibility to intervene in any situation that may result in a violation of departmental policy or law. As discussed in previous chapters, however, much of what an officer does during a shift may not be known by the supervisor; it is impossible for a supervisor to have firsthand knowledge of every call and activity of each officer during a shift. Therefore, supervisors must rely on a variety of other means to monitor officer performance and conduct, including review of reports, periodic field observation of calls, citizen commendations and complaints, conversations with the officers, and listening to what other officers and supervisors are saying about the officer. The EWS provides the supervisor with those personnel that require attention.

Once the supervisor is informed of a problem, a plan must be developed to address it. In some cases, the problem may be as obvious as the officer's involvement in three traffic accidents within a three-month period of time. In this case, potential actions may include the recommendation of a driver's school or even having the officer's eyes checked. But what should be done with the officer who has no previous disciplinary record, yet has received four unsustained citizen complaints of rudeness? How might a supervisor deal with this situation? Initial counseling may reveal that this officer has a family or personal substance abuse problem that is affecting his or her conduct. Is this a disciplinary issue or something the supervisor should refer to professional counseling? This scenario illustrates the potential benefits of an EWS by pointing out the complexity of issues that may come to the attention of a supervisor.

Benefits and Potential Drawbacks

No disciplinary system is perfect, but developing a system to identify potential problems early offers many obvious benefits. However, an EWS also has potential drawbacks. The overall success of any system depends on how it is perceived by employees. Reiter (1993) identified the following benefits of an EWS:

Benefits

1. An employee's career may be salvaged before the problem becomes too serious.
2. It forces supervisors, particularly in field operations, to become actively involved in employee development.
3. It may provide the necessary progressive disciplinary steps to support termination of an employee who fails to respond to remediation and other supervisory techniques.
4. The agency can gain valuable information that can be used to develop positive changes in training, equipment, tactics, and policy.

228

PART TWO
*Supervising Human
Resources: Training,
Evaluation, and
Discipline*

5. Properly documented action in this system may defend the agency against a "custom and practice" allegation in a civil suit (that is, certain inappropriate behaviors of officers were routine, customary, and practiced often).

6. A workable and articulated system may encourage greater community confidence in the agency's ability to control and manage itself.

However, there may be several drawbacks to the use of an EWS, that require some discussion:

Drawbacks

1. The use of an EWS could have an adverse impact on an individual employee's career, particularly if supervisors or managers use it inappropriately.

2. The system could restrict some employees' field performance if they developed an attitude that "no action is safe action."

3. Some supervisors may simply go through the motions of their role and not truly become involved and supportive of the system.

4. If the police agency does create and implement an EWS and then fails to use it, it could be harmed by failure to identify an employee.

5. Plaintiff attorneys could use the EWS to accumulate resource information that might be helpful in a subsequent civil lawsuit.

Case Study 9–2
Downtown Sonny Brown

Officer Sonny Brown works the transport wagon downtown, an assignment that he has worked for several years on the day shift. Because of his length of service in this assignment, he has earned the nickname "Downtown" Brown. Brown loves "hooking and booking" drunks and takes great pride in keeping the streets safe and clean. Local business owners appreciate his efforts; even honoring him once as the Chamber of Commerce "Officer of the Year."

Sgt. Carol Jackson is recently promoted and receives her first patrol assignment in the downtown district. Because it has been awhile since she worked patrol, she decides to ride with Brown for a few days to learn about the district and its problems. Jackson is pleased at the warm reception Brown receives from business merchants but quickly becomes concerned about some of his heavy-handed methods of dealing with drunks. When questioned about his tactics, Brown replies, "This ain't administration, Sarge, it's the streets, and our job is to sweep 'em clean."

Jackson speaks with Brown's former supervisor, who said he had received several verbal citizen complaints against Brown, but none could be substantiated. Apparently no one was interested in the word of a drunk against a popular officer. Two days later, Sgt. Jackson is called to the county jail to meet with Hamstead, a booking officer who wants to talk with Jackson about a drunk that Brown had booked a few hours earlier. Another prisoner confided to Hamstead that the drunk had complained that Brown had injured him by kicking him off a park bench and pushing him down a hill to the transport wagon. Complaining of pain in his side, the drunk was then taken to the hospital and treated for three broken ribs. When asked later about the incident, the drunk refused to cooperate and simply told Hamstead, "I fell down."

1. How should Sgt. Jackson handle this matter?
2. What are her options? Her responsibilities?
3. What types of disciplinary policy changes should the department consider to prevent these situations from occurring?

All things considered, the benefits of an EWS appear to outweigh the potential drawbacks. The early warning system provides supervisors with information that is vital to the early identification and intervention of employee problems. This proactive approach to helping employees deal with their problems may also protect the agency against potential litigation. Case Study 9–2 illustrates how an EWS might have prevented police officer misconduct.

Developing a Preventive Policy

A carefully constructed disciplinary policy provides a framework for supervisors to intervene early in employee behavior problems. The Police Executive Research Forum (PERF) developed a model policy on how to handle officer misconduct. The purpose of establishing a disciplinary policy is threefold: It engenders the trust and confidence of the public, it helps supervisors to identify problems and areas where increased direction or training may be necessary, and it helps to protect the rights and due process of citizens and officers alike. Following are the essential components of PERF's (1981:2) model policy:

> *Prevention of misconduct.* Agencies should make every effort to eliminate any organizational conditions that may foster, permit, or encourage improper behavior by its employees. Preventing misconduct should be an agency's primary means of reducing and controlling it.

> *Recruitment and selection.* Testing that includes written psychological exams and interviews may ensure that the highest quality individuals are hired

The internal affairs office is the locus of investigations for allegations of police misconduct. Here, an internal affairs supervisor interviews an officer.
Lt. Phil Galeoto, Reno Police Department

230

PART TWO
Supervising Human
Resources: Training,
Evaluation, and
Discipline

and protect against the selection of those who may be unsuited for the difficult tasks of police work.

Training. Ethics training should be a major component of recruit training and revisited periodically for in-service classes. Departments should develop systems to ensure that rules, procedures, and outcomes of disciplinary processes are communicated to officers.

Written directives manual. Every officer should receive a complete manual of departmental general orders, procedures, and training bulletins. Particular attention should be paid to sections dealing with misconduct and officers' responsibility and accountability for protecting the civil rights of all citizens.

Supervisory responsibility. Training supervisors properly is critical to ensuring that officers' performance conforms with departmental policies and procedures. Emphasis should be placed on methods of identifying problems early, counseling and intervention strategies, training needs, and providing professional referral for more serious problems.

Community outreach. Meetings with community members and advisory councils are an excellent mechanism for establishing trust and collaborative approaches to general community problems and identifying potential crisis situations.

Data Collection and analysis. It is mandatory that records are kept of all internal affairs actions. General information about IAU actions should be communicated throughout the agency for training purposes.

As denoted above, an EWS will assist agencies in early intervention and prevention of problems.

LEGAL CONSIDERATIONS

The failure to discipline poses serious liability for police organizations and supervisors. What are the consequences of an agency's failure to develop an adequate policy and to investigate and prosecute violations by officers? Is an agency required to develop a system for receiving and handling citizen complaints against an officer? Generally, case law has held that liability exists if the plaintiff is able to prove that the disciplinary process was sufficiently lacking so that officers felt there would be no consequences for their actions. The existence of this situation is based on a number of factors, including the number of citizen complaints, how discipline is handled, and the department's failure to take action in matters they should.

In *Parish* v. *Luckie* (1992), the plaintiff claimed that she was the victim of a false arrest and rape by a member of the police department. The court found that the department had a history of avoiding and covering up complaints of physical and sexual abuse by officers. The officer in question also had a history of violent conduct. The chief would only investigate complaints against officers that were in writing and improperly applied the standard of "beyond a reasonable doubt" to determining whether or not the case was sustained.

Gutierrez-Rodriguez v. *Cargegena* (1989) provides an example of a supervisor's failure to address problems. There, Puerto Rican drug agents came upon the plaintiff and girlfriend in a parked car. The agents approached the vehicle in civilian clothes and with weapons drawn. The plaintiff, seeing them approaching, started his car and attempted to drive away. Without warning or notice that they were police officers, the officers began firing at the car, striking the plaintiff in the back and permanently paralyzing him. The plaintiff sued the squad, the supervisor, and the police chief under Section 1983. The court found evidence of numerous complaints against the supervisor—who had had 13 separate citizen complaints filed against him in three years. The court awarded a $4.5 million judgment.

Liability may also be established in the department's past practices. In *Bordanaro* v. *McLeod* (1989), the court found that the agency had a widespread practice of unconstitutional, warrantless entries and that the chief had knowledge or should have known that the practice was occurring. The court observed that when a large number of officers conduct themselves in a like manner, that alone is evidence of an established practice by the department.

In *Ramos* v. *City of Chicago* (1989), however, the court did not find the city liable for the plaintiff's allegations that he was beaten by police officers without provocation and that his beating was the result of an institutionalized practice by the Chicago Police Department. The court concluded that six unrelated incidents of police brutality over a 10-year period, in a police department of more than 10,000 officers, failed to prove that a policy or custom existed that condoned brutality. This case is important because the court considered the size of the department and locale in its decision.

SUMMARY

This chapter has demonstrated how important it is for agencies to institute sound disciplinary policies and practices. Policies and training are needed for supervisors to identify and respond to employee misconduct or performance problems at an early stage. Policies also ensure that discipline is administered in a consistent and equitable manner throughout the organization. A process that is based on consistency will increase credibility and foster positive employee morale and relations. A prompt, complete, and full investigation of alleged misconduct coupled with the appropriate level of discipline may minimize or even eliminate potential civil liability.

The public's trust and respect are precious commodities and can be quickly lost through the improper handling of an allegation of misconduct. Serving communities professionally and with integrity should be the goal of every agency and its employees to ensure that trust and respect are maintained. The public expects that police agencies will make every effort to identify and correct problems and respond to citizens complaints in an equally judicious manner. When errors in judgment or performance occur, it is the police department's responsibility to act quickly and in a visible, consistent, fair, and equitable manner.

232

PART TWO
Supervising Human
Resources: Training,
Evaluation, and
Discipline

KEY TERMS

Peace Officers Bill of
   Rights   (p. 208)
counseling   (p. 214)
documented oral counsel-
   ing   (p. 214)
letters of reprimand
   (p. 214)
suspension   (p. 214)
demotion   (p. 214)
termination   (p. 214)
transfer   (p. 215)

positive
   discipline   (p. 215)
negative
   discipline   (p. 216)
personnel
   complaint   (p. 216)
internal
   complaints   (p. 216)
external
   complaints   (p. 216)
primary source   (p. 216)

secondary source   (p. 216)
anonymous
   source   (p. 216)
formal complaint   (p. 217)
informal
   complaint   (p. 217)
grievance
   procedures   (p. 217)
arbitration   (p. 222)
early warning system
   (EWS)   (p. 224)

ITEMS FOR REVIEW

1. Delineate the rights that police officers possess and do not possess under the First, Fourth, and Fifth Amendments to the Constitution.
2. Explain what rights police officers maintain or do not hold with respect to sexual misconduct, residency, and moonlighting.
3. Briefly review the history of problems that have occurred with regard to police disciplinary problems.
4. Describe some guidelines and methods that exist for coping with disciplinary problems.
5. What are the keys to effective discipline?
6. What are the various forms of discipline?
7. Outline the process for investigating citizen complaints.
8. Describe the benefits of having an early warning system (EWS) to detect problems with officer behavior.
9. What are the consequences of an agency's failure to develop an adequate policy and a system to investigate and prosecute violations by officers?

SOURCES

BARKER, T., and CARTER, D. L. (1994). *Police deviance.* Cincinnati: Anderson.

BERKOW, M. (1996). "Weeding out problem officers." *Police Chief* (4): 22–29.

BIEHUNIK V. FELICETTA, 441 F2d 228 (1971).

BLACK, J. M. (1986). *The real meaning of discipline.* Gaithersburg, Md.: International Association of Chiefs of Police.

BONSIGNORE V. CITY OF NEW YORK, 521 F.Supp. 394 (1981).

BORDANARO V. MCLEOD, 871 F2d 1151, 1989.

BRENCKLE V. TOWNSHIP OF SHALER, 281 A2d 920 (Pa. 1972).

CONNICK V. MYERS, 461 US 138 (1983).

COX V. MCNAMARA, 493 P2d 54 (Ore. 1972).

DUGAN, J. R., and BREDA, D. R. (1991). "Complaints about police officers: A comparison among types and agencies." *Journal of Criminal Justice* (19): 165–71.

ELLIS, E. R. (1966). *The epic of New York City.* New York: Coward-McCann.

FLOOD V. KENNEDY, 239 NY S2d 665 (1963).

GABRILOWITZ V. NEWMAN, 582 F2d 100 (1st Cir 1978).

GAFFIGAN, S. J., and MCDONALD, P. P. (1997). *Police integrity: Public service with honor.* Washington, D.C.: U.S. Department of Justice.

GUTHRIE, M. (1996). "Using automation to apply discipline fairly." *FBI Law Enforcement Bulletin* 5: 18–21.

GUTIERREZ-RODRIGUEZ V. CARGEGENA, 882 F2d 553 (1st Cir 1989).

HOPWOOD V. CITY OF PADUCAH, 424 SW2d 134 (Ky. 1968)

INCIARDI, J. A. (1996) *Criminal justice.* 5th ed. Orlando, Fla.: Harcourt Brace.

INTERNATIONAL ASSOCIATION OF CHIEFS OF POLICE (1996). "Rooting out corruption and building organizational integrity: The New York experience." Workshop delivered at the 102nd Annual IACP Conference in Miami, Florida. Author: *Police Chief,* 10, pp. 33–34.

JONES V. DODSON, 727 F2d 1329 (4th Cir 1984).

KANSAS CITY (MISSOURI) POLICE DEPARTMENT (1991). "Recommendation of the task force on the use of force." (January).

KATZ V. UNITED STATES, 389 US 347 (1967).

KELLEY V. JOHNSTON, 425 US 238 (1976).

KENNY, D. J., ED. *Police and policing:* Contemporary Issues (1989). New York: Praeger.

LALLY V. DEPARTMENT OF POLICE, 306 So2d 65 (La. 1974).

MACNAMARA, J. (1995). Panel discussion on ethics and integrity, California Peace Officers' Association Meeting, Napa, Calif. (November).

McDONELL V. HUNTER, 611 F.Supp. 1122 (SD Iowa, 1985), affd. as mod., 809 F2d 1302 (8th Cir 1987).

McLAUGHLIN, V., and BING R. (1987). Law enforcement personnel selection. *Journal of Police Science and Administration* 15, pp. 271–276.

MARUSA V. DISTRICT OF COLUMBIA, 484 F2d 828 (1973).

MORRIS, L. (1951). *Incredible New York.* New York: Bonanza.

MULLER V. CONLISK, 429 F2d 901 (7th Cir 1970).

NATIONAL ADVISORY COMMISSION ON CRIMINAL JUSTICE STANDARDS AND GOALS (1973). *The Police.* Washington, D.C.: U.S. Government Printing Office.

PARISH V. LUCKIE, 963 F2d 201 (1992).

PEOPLE V. TIDWELL, 266 NE2d 787 (Ill. 1971).

PEREZ, D. W. (1992). *Police review systems.* Management information service.

PICKERING V. BOARD OF EDUCATION, 391 US 563 (1968).

POLICE EXECUTIVE RESEARCH FORUM. (1981). *Police handling of officer misconduct: A model policy statement.* Washington, D.C.: Police Executive Research Forum.

POPOW V. CITY OF MARGATE, 476 F.Supp. 1237 (1979).

RAMOS V. CITY OF CHICAGO, 707 F.Supp. 345 (1989).

REISS, A. J. (1970). "Police brutality—answers to key questions." In M. Lipsy (ed.). *Law and order police encounters.* New Brunswick, N.J.: Aldine.

REITER, L. (1993). *Law enforcement administrative investigations: A manual guide.* Tallahassee, Fla.: Lou Reiter and Associates.

ROSS, R. A. (1992). "Citizen complaint policy." *FBI Law Enforcement Bulletin* (May) 10: 21–22.

SAGER V. CITY OF WOODLAWN PARK, 543 F.Supp. 282 (D Colo. 1982).

SALHOLZ, E., and WASHINGTON, F. (1992). "Detroit's brutal lessons." *Newsweek* (November 30): 45.

SENCIO, W. J. (1992). "Complaint processing: Policy considerations." *Police Chief* 7:45–48.

SNOW, R. L. (1990). "A right to complain: Grievance procedures for small departments." *Law and Order* (5): 39–41.

STEPHENS, D. W. (1994). "Discipline philosophy." *FBI Law Enforcement Bulletin* 3: 20–22.

SWANSON, C. R., TERRITO, L., and TAYLOR, R. W. (1993). *Police administration.* 3d ed. New York: Macmillan.

TRANS WORLD AIRLINES V. HARDISON, 97 S Ct 2264 (1977).

United States v. *City of Albuquerque,* 12 EPD 11, 244 (10th Cir).

WAGNER, A. E., and DECKER, S. H. (1997). "Evaluating citizen complaints against the police." In R. G. Dunham and G. P. Alpert (eds.). *Critical issues in policing: Contemporary readings.* Prospect Heights, Ill.: Waveland.

WILLIAMS, R. N. (1975). *Legal aspects of discipline by police administrators.* Traffic Institute Publication 2705. Evanston, Ill.: Northwestern University Press.

PART THREE

Supervising Police Work: Deployment and Daily Operations

10

Deploying and Scheduling Personnel

There can't be a crisis next week. My schedule is already full.

—Henry Kissinger

We need a sense of value of time—that is, of the best way to divide one's time into one's activities.

—Arnold Bennet

When schemes are laid in advance, it is surprising how often the circumstances will fit with them.

—Sir William Osler

INTRODUCTION

The scheduling and deployment of patrol officers is a primary concern for police administrators, middle managers, and supervisors alike, all of whom struggle on a daily basis with balancing the needs of officers with those of the department and the community. For these practitioners, ensuring 24-hour, seven-day shift coverage each week is a complex task. This chapter examines the issues surrounding the scheduling and deploying of police officers to satisfy departmental service delivery objectives.

Note that we take a somewhat unique view in the presentation of this chapter's personnel deployment and scheduling material. First, we approach these matters from primarily a *qualitative* point of view, rather than one that is highly quantitative. This chapter does provide some basic quantitative information, such as formulas and calculations for determining adequate numbers of personnel for every day, around the clock. However, we believe that the complex aspects of deployment and scheduling can be accomplished or are greatly aided

237

by computer software (discussed in the section on patrol planning. Furthermore, once a police agency's executives adopt and implement a particular staffing schedule, that pattern will not be likely to change often. The daily challenge for supervisors is to ensure there are adequate personnel for a schedule, considering time off (vacations, sick time off, and training) and changes in workload demands (crime trends, special events, and crisis).

But what does change is the *philosophical,* or qualitative aspect of personnel deployment and scheduling. As we will see below, the adoption of the community policing and problem solving (COPPS) strategy by an increasing number of police departments across the country has fostered the need for greater examination, flexibility, and modification of personnel deployment. Once the COPPS philosophy is adopted, it is the supervisor's task to see that the personnel are deployed in keeping with the needs of that strategy and are given the necessary time to engage in COPPS activities.

This chapter begins with a look at the need for patrol planning, and then examines methods of determining resource allocation needs, including calculating the size of the patrol force. We then review some methods that may be used for performing a workload analysis and consider several alternative patrol responses. Next, we look at some of the basic types and elements of compressed shift schedules, such as the 4–10 plan, and compare permanent and rotating shifts. This section also includes a review of relevant federal legislation. Then we discuss deployment strategies, including the deployment demands of the COPPS initiative. We conclude the chapter with a brief discussion of the influence of unions on the scheduling and deployment of officers.

PATROL PLANNING

The largest, most costly, and most visible function in a police agency is patrol, yet patrol is that area of policing that receives the least amount of planning or analysis. As an example, patrol beats are all too often created by convenient streets, railroad tracks, rivers, and so forth, rather than by thoughtful planning and analysis of officer workload according to geographical areas. Few police agencies pay regular attention to evaluating and adjusting patrol plans to meet service demands. Instead, patrol is often the first division where a police administration seeks to reduce personnel in order to enhance specialized units or to create new programs. This practice often leaves the patrol division in need of personnel and frequently results in morale problems and unnecessary delays in responding to calls for service (CFS). The unfortunate consequence of this situation is that supervisors are left to manage the demands of patrol by reacting to crises rather than through thoughtful planning.

Planning is an important, powerful tool for helping police managers cope with the backlash of shrinking budgets and accompanying personnel cutbacks that have plagued police agencies since the 1970s. Patrol planning enables managers to properly assess service demands so that resources may be appropriately allocated across shifts and in proportion to workload. Computer software can be used to design various combinations of shift patterns, print staffing reports for up to a year's time, and provide quick access to all employee information, such as seniority date and shift preferences; employee phone numbers; and the ability to see an entire month's shifts at a glance, and quickly edit assignments. Several private corporations now produce and advertise such software in professional trade magazines, such as the *Police Chief*, published by the International Association of Chiefs of Police (IACP), *Law and Order* magazine, and so forth. Administrators and supervisors who want to maximize their resources would do well to invest in such software.

The lack of proper patrol planning may be attributed to several factors. First, few police agencies have planning units, so planning (aside from the budget) is usually nonexistent. The lack of data also presents a problem. Few police agencies have sufficient data for analyzing their CFS, time spent on calls by officers, time that officers are available for CFS and other work, the numbers of units assigned, and so on. Even when these data exist, few agencies have the trained staff to conduct in-depth analyses. The natural resistance to new ideas by many people may also create barriers to change. Many agencies are tradition bound and resist any new approaches to change patrol practices.

The primary purpose of patrol planning is to keep supervisors and managers apprised of how resources are utilized. This enables them to make informed decisions about departmental operations and to develop future plans. A patrol plan should be based on an analysis of data concerning the tasks that officers perform during their shifts of duty. These plans also should be flexible and reviewed constantly to meet the changing needs and goals of an organization.

The NYPD utilizes the COMPSTAT (computer statistics) process, meeting monthly to review crime trends, plan tactics, and allocate resources.
Courtesy New York Police Department Photo Unit.

RESOURCE ALLOCATION

Another important part of police leadership lies in how best to allocate resources, especially in a time when new resources are more difficult to obtain and the police are asked to do more with less. Next, we examine the early research concerning how the patrol function should be allocated, and then we look at some methods for determining how many officers are required to do the job.

Early Research

One of the earliest studies of patrol allocation was conducted in Trenton, New Jersey. In 1959 the Trenton Police Department contracted with the IACP to conduct a study to determine how many uniformed officers were needed to patrol the city's streets and neighborhoods. CFS were evaluated by location, time of day, and day of week. Incidents were also weighted to account for the longer time necessary to process more serious offenses. The study resulted in a plan that deployed personnel proportionally according to workload variations.

This study marked the beginning of allocation studies and replaced the traditional equal distribution of personnel that was often used in the past. Under a **flat system of deployment,** an equal number of officers would be distributed across shifts, days of week, and location. Flat systems fail to take into consideration variations in workload, and are prone to creating disproportionate demands on officers.

By 1975 various mathematical models were used for determining the appropriate allocation of personnel to patrol functions. Then, by the late 1970s, a number of computer-based allocation schemes were developed to improve the efficiency and effectiveness of patrol allocation plans (Gay et al., 1977). From these studies, more comprehensive workload factors were developed (Levine and McEwen, 1985:21) for consideration in determining allocation needs, which can be determined from dispatch information. They included the following:

- Total numbers of calls for service.
- Officer-initiated activities.
- Administrative activities.
- Number of CFS by hour, shift, beat, and reporting area.
- Average dispatch delay (in minutes).
- Average travel time (in minutes).
- Average on-scene time (in minutes).
- Average service time (in minutes).
- Average number of backup patrol units per call.
- Probability that all units are busy.
- Average number of free units.

Determining Patrol Force Size

The collection and analysis of data are the foundation of proper patrol deployment. Unfortunately, as we have mentioned, most police agencies do not adhere to such rational and scientific approaches. Three crude methods are commonly used by police departments to determine resource needs (Roberg and Kuykendal, 1995:284):

Intuitive. This is basically educated guesswork based on the experience and judgment of police managers. It is probably the most commonly used method for small agencies where the numbers of incidents and officers available are so few that more analytical analysis may be unnecessary for determining when and where officers should be deployed.

Workload. This requires comprehensive information, including standards of expected performance, community expectations, and the prioritization of police activities. Although rarely used by an entire police agency, it is most often used for determining resource needs for patrol or specific programs such as crime prevention.

Comparative. Often the most common method used by police agencies, the comparative method is frequently based on a comparison of agencies by the number of officers per 1,000 residents. Data are available in the *Uniform Crime Reports* (UCR), published annually by the Federal Bureau of Investigation. The UCR (1996:278) data reveal a national average of 2.3 full-time, sworn police officers per 1,000 residents in the United States; the range is 1.8 officers in communities with populations of 25,000 to 99,999 residents, to 3.1 officers in cities with 250,000 or more residents; agencies in rural counties averaged 2.8 officers per 1,000 residents.

Another method for determining allocation needs is to set an objective related to the amount of time an agency wants officers to be committed to CFS and available for other functions. There is no established guideline, but agencies often set an objective that would restrict the amount of time that officers are committed to CFS at 30–40 percent of the total time available per shift. Gay, Schell, and Schack (1977) found that officers spend approximately 23 percent of their patrol time on administrative matters, 23 percent on CFS, 40 percent on preventive patrol, and 14 percent on directed patrol. Levine and McEwen (1985:35) provided the following guide for agencies to determine allocation needs based on this formula:

Step 1. Set an objective for patrol performance (e.g., 30–40 percent committed to CFS).
Step 2. Select a time period to be analyzed.
Step 3. Determine CFS workload for this time period.
Step 4. Calculate the number of units needed based on the workload and the selected objective.
Step 5. Calculate the number of on-duty officers needed for each shift.
Step 6. Multiply by the **relief factor** (a variable that accounts for officers' days off, sick or training leave, vacation, or other reasons) to obtain the total number of officers needed.

Using these steps, Table 10–1 shows the basic data needed in calculating the number of patrol officers needed in a city's patrol force. Assume that, after discussing how busy patrol units should be, the department determines the following objective: "There should be sufficient units on duty so that the average unit utilization on CFS will not exceed 30 percent." Assume further that a mix of 70 percent one-officer and 30 percent two-officer units will be established for each shift. The data were collected during a four-week (28-day) period.

The first section of Table 10–1 shows the *total* number of CFS, assists, and traffic accidents by shift for the four weeks, along with the average times for these activities for each shift. With these activities and average times, the total amount of work for the patrol force amounts to about 745 hours for the midnight to 8 A.M. shift; 969 hours for the 8 A.M. to 4 P.M. shift; and 1,421 hours for the 4 P.M. to midnight shift. Over a 28-day period, the average work *per shift* amount to 26.6 hours, 34.6 hours, and 50.8 hours, respectively. (For example, for midnights, 1,027 calls for service × 32 minutes to handle each = 32,864; 225 assists × 22 minutes = 4,950; 109 traffic accidents × 63 minutes = 6,867, for a grand total of 44,681 minutes, or 745 hours, of work; 745 hours of work divided by 28 shifts = 26.6 hours of average work for the midnight shift tour of duty.)

To calculate the number of patrol units needed to meet the desired objective—average unit utilization on CFS will not exceed 30 percent—we use the following formula:

$$\frac{\text{Average hours of work per shift}}{(\text{Shift length})(\text{Unit utilization})} = \text{Number of units needed}$$

Again, using the midnight shift as an example, the calculation would be as follows:

$$\frac{26.6 \text{ hours}}{(8 \text{ hours})(30\%)} = 11.08 \text{ units}$$

The answer must be rounded to 11 units because no fractions of units are possible. Similar calculations for the day and evening shifts yield 14 units and 21 units, respectively. Table 10–1 shows the officers needed for these

TABLE 10.1. An Example of Data for Determining Patrol Force Size

	Midnights	Days	Evenings
1. Workload Data			
Calls for service	1,027	1,614	2,059
Average time (minutes)	32 min.	28	33
Assists	225	273	463
Average time (minutes)	22 min.	20	18
Traffic accidents	109	129	150
Average time (minutes)	63 min.	58	60
2. Hours of work for entire 4-week period	745	969	1,421
Average hours of work per shift	26.6	34.6	50.8
3. Units needed for 30%	11	14	21
4. Number of 1-officer units	8	10	15
Number of 2-officer units	4	4	6
5. Number of officers needed per shift	14	18	27
6. Total number of officers needed (relief factor = 2.2)	31	40	59

Source: U.S. Department of Justice, National Institute of Justice, *Patrol Deployment* (Washington, D.C.: U.S. Government Printing Office, 1985), p. 34.

shifts under the decision of a 70 percent/30 percent split between one- and two-officer units.

The final line in Table 10–1 multiplies the number of officers needed by the department's relief factor of 2.2 (to cover officers' absences from days off, sick leave, vacations, training, and so on) to give a total of 31 officers for the midnight shift, 40 officers for the day shift, and 59 officers for the evening shift. A total of 130 officers would be required to meet the objective of an average unit utilization of 30 percent. If an objective other than unit utilization had been selected, the same steps would have been followed to determine the number of units needed, but the calculations would have been different.

The selection of a unit utilization objective of 30 percent is subject to criticism; remember, there is no universal rule to guide the choice of a percentage. A department should consider the "big picture" of patrol resource allocation; certainly, however, the existence of a COPPS philosophy should be weighed into this decision.

Finally, the use of a relief factor of 2.2 in the above example and in Table 10–1 is also subject to debate. Another commonly accepted relief factor is 1.66, used in determining the number of police officers that are needed to staff a shift annually. Indeed, a very common calculation—one that uses the 1.66 relief factor—is that five officers are required to staff a position for an entire year:

$$3 \text{ (shifts)} \times 1.66 \text{ (officers)} = 4.97, \text{ or 5 officers}$$

Case Study 10–1 is an exercise in determining the number of officers needed for each shift.

Other Allocation Issues

Traditional approaches to determining patrol allocation needs are vested in the belief that, whenever possible, patrol resources should be distributed in proportion to the workload by day of the week, time of day, and location. These

---

Case Study 10–1
Letting the Count Determine the Amount

It is budget preparation time at the Deer County Sheriff's Office. Sgt. Fitzpatrick is assigned as the administrative supervisor to the patrol captain. The captain needs to prepare a justification statement for a budget staff meeting in two weeks, and at which he must defend to the chief the need for more positions. The captain asks Fitzpatrick to provide information on the total numbers of officers needed per shift.

Sgt. Fitzpatrick gathers the following data about the number of calls from the computer-aided dispatch system.

	Midnights	Days	Evenings
Workload Data:			
Calls for service	6,432	6,608	8,901
Assists	1,522	1,766	2,111
Traffic accidents	615	713	991

Using the above figures and the same procedure and general information presented in Table 10–1 and in Chapter 10, *as well as the same numbers of average times required to handle these calls per shift*, and assuming that data were collected over a 28-day period, how many total officers will Sgt. Fitzpatrick need? Using a relief factor of 1.66?

workload analysis factors are discussed in more detail below. The rationale for this approach rests with the concern that nonproportional staffing may result in varying levels of service. It may also create morale problems with those officers who must handle a disproportionate share of the workload.

More recent patrol deployment formulations take into account a broader range of workload analysis data and other factors. These include the average time required to travel to incidents due to geographic barriers (e.g., thoroughfares, freeways, bridges, mountains). Geographic barriers may have a significant impact on response times and should be considered when designing beats and car plans, which we discuss later in this chapter.

WORKLOAD ANALYSIS

Basic Approaches

A **workload analysis** produces essential data about patrol operations. Its primary objective is to provide supervisors with information about the pattern of service demands with the purpose of determining allocation needs, developing efficient and effective shift schedules, and deployment schemes.

A workload analysis provides information to assist with the temporal (short-lived) and geographic allocation of personnel. Temporal allocation can be attained by calculating the daily percentage of the total workload occurring during each shift and then assigning a comparable percentage of available officers to shifts. The same process can be used for distributing personnel in each area. Table 10–2 shows two plans for the allocation of patrol resources.

Option 1 in Table 10–2 is the traditional approach to deployment that many agencies use, with equal staffing on all three shifts. Under option 2 (assuming that 20 officers are sufficient for the evening shift), the department reduces the total number of officers required by matching allocations to CFS demands. The savings are obvious. As a bonus, the surplus of officers can either be transferred to

TABLE 10.2. Two Plans for Allocating Patrol Resources

| | | Deployment Options | |
| | Percentage of Total Calls for Service | Option One | Option Two |
Shift	by Shift	Equal Staffing	Efficiency[a]
Midnight	20%	20	9
Day	35%	20	16
Evening	45%	20	20
Total personnel deployed[b]		60	45

[a]The efficiency option assumes that the 20 officers assigned to the Evening Shift are sufficient to respond to all calls for service and provide adequate preventive patrol during the peak demand period.
[b]This total reflects only the number of officers deployed and not the total complement actually needed, because the relief factor was not considered.
Source: Adapted from U.S. Department of Justice, National Institute of Law Enforcement and Criminal Justice, *Improving Patrol Productivity,* Volume I: *Routine Patrol* by Gay et al. (Washington D.C.: U.S. Government Printing Office, July 1977) pp. 26–29.

an understaffed section of the department or redeployed as a special operations unit for enhancing crime prevention and directed patrol activities (Levine, 1982).

Deployment by Time and Location

Two of the most important factors in allocating personnel are location and time. The location of problems helps police in dividing the community into geographic beats or divisions of approximately equal workload. By analyzing the time incidents took place, appropriate shifts may be determined. Mobility and geographic barriers are also important factors in the consideration of allocation needs. Table 10–3 shows how the personnel workload can be determined by CFS per shift by calculating for every day the percentage of the total workload occurring during each shift and then assigning a comparable percentage of the available officers to those shifts. A similar process can be used in distributing personnel geographically; that is, the first step is to determine the workload in

TABLE 10.3. Sample Distribution of Personnel by Hourly Workload

Hours by Shift	Calls for Service	Percent of Total Hourly Workload	Percent of Manpower Assigned
0700–0759	58	2.11	Day Shift
0800–0859	77	2.80	
0900–0959	90	3.28	29.27
1000–1059	100	3.64	
1100–1159	107	3.90	
1200–1259	117	4.26	
1300–1359	123	4.48	
1400–1459	132	4.80	
1500–1559	158	5.75	Evening Shift
1600–1659	153	5.57	
1700–1759	165	6.01	47.03
1800–1859	172	6.26	
1900–1959	161	5.86	
2000–2059	164	5.97	
2100–2159	164	5.97	
2200–2259	155	5.64	
2300–2359	159	5.79	Midnight Shift
2400–0059	118	4.30	
0100–0159	101	3.68	23.68
0200–0259	90	3.28	
0300–0359	60	2.18	
0400–0459	45	1.64	
0500–0559	37	1.35	
0600–0659	40	1.46	
Total	2,746	99.98*	99.98*

*Total does not equal 100% because of rounding.
Source: U.S. Department of Justice, National Institute of Justice, *Patrol Deployment* (Washington, D.C.: U.S. Government Printing Office, 1985), p. 29.

each patrol district, then calculate the portion of the shift's workload handled in each area, and finally assign personnel accordingly.

Figure 10–1 provides an example of CFS demands for each hour of the day. Figure 10–2 is a sample of CFS workload demands according to day of the week, with each week broken down into 168 hours.

FIGURE 10–1. Sample 24-Hour Graph of Workload Distribution
Source: U.S. Department of Justice, National Institute of Justice, *Patrol Deployment* (Washington, D.C.: U.S. Government Printing Office, 1985), p. 27.

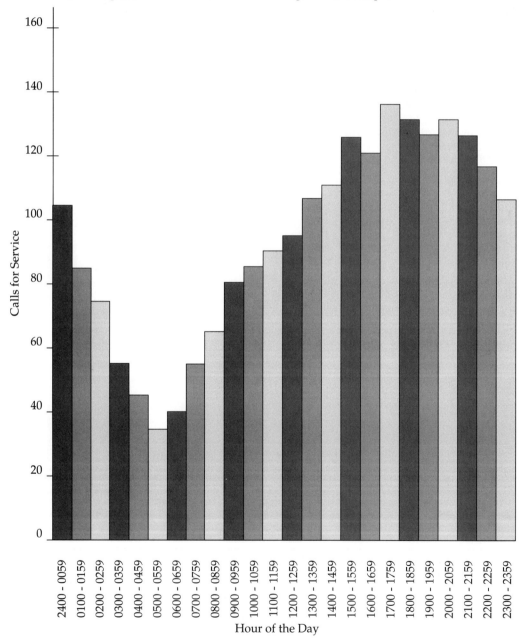

Car Plans

After patrol personnel have been assigned according to time and location needs, the supervisor can deploy them to beats or patrol car districts. Separate car plans should be established for each shift to equalize workloads for all officers. The boundaries for the beats in a six-car plan on the day shift might be very different from the boundaries in a six-car plan on the night shift because of various crime problems and public service demands. For example, a congested industrial area might present quite different problems on the day shift than on the night shift when plants are closed (Iannone, 1994). And, as we have seen earlier, the number of patrol vehicles in use will also vary by time of day and day of week.

Normally, the car plan in use will be dictated by the number of officers on duty and available for field patrol. If two-officer units are used, adjustments will

FIGURE 10–2. Sample Workload by Day of Week
Source: U.S. Department of Justice, National Institute of Justice, *Patrol Deployment* (Washington, D.C.: U.S. Government Printing Office, 1985), p. 28.

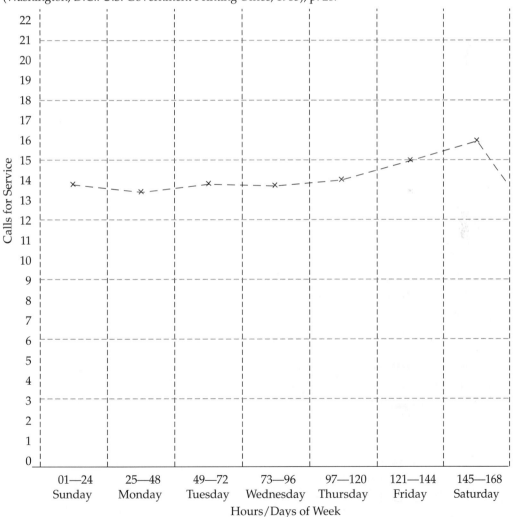

of course be necessary. Using one-officer units, a nine-car plan will be required to cover nine beats unless two of the beats use two-officer patrol units, in which case 11 officers would be required.

Ideally, patrol districts should be divided into beats that contain as nearly as practicable an equal distribution of workload. Each beat in a 10-car plan would theoretically contain 10 percent of the work; each beat in a 5-car plan would ideally contain 20 percent of the work; and so on. By experimenting with beat arrangements according to the ideal percentage of workload and the most desirable boundaries, a supervisor will eventually develop a variety of reasonably effective car plans from which the most workable can be selected. Beats will not be equal in size because area, as represented by street miles, is only one factor used in determining the relative need for patrol (Iannone, 1994).

Computer Models

Computer-based analysis and allocation models were developed as early as the 1960s. These models assisted administrators who often struggle with shift-related issues such as fixed versus rotating schedules, one- versus two-officer cars, and compressed schedules. Some of the first programs developed were the RAND Corporation's Patrol Car Allocation Model (PCAM), Public Systems Evaluation's Hypercube Queueing Model, and the Institute of Public Program Analysis's Patrol Plan/Beat Plan. These automated systems were capable of performing a number of staff distribution functions and could simplify the process of determining allocation needs and designing beats (Levine and McEwen, 1985).

The Statistical Package for Social Sciences (SPSS) also can be used to analyze workload and to develop schedules. This comprehensive statistical package is personal computer based, inexpensive, and simple to run with some training. It may also be merged with mapping programs that are commonly used by police.

Clearly, a comprehensive workload analysis provides the foundation for determining allocation needs and deployment schemes. It provides the basic information for determining the number of patrol officers that are required to staff shifts each day of the week. Once an analysis is completed, managers can select the most appropriate deployment schemes to attain departmental objectives.

ALTERNATIVE PATROL RESPONSES

Why Respond to Every Call? Seeking Alternatives

Our discussion thus far assumes that every call for service requires the response of a uniformed patrol officer. However, increasing workloads, shrinking budgets, and increased public demands for service are key factors forcing police administrators to consider alternative methods for handling nonemergency CFS. Research (Scott, 1981) has shown that as much as 30 to 40 percent of CFS do not require dispatching a patrol unit to the scene and could be handled by alternative methods of taking calls. These alternative response methods are commonly referred to as **differential police response (DPR).** These methods reduce patrol officers' workloads, allowing them to spend more time with directed patrol activities, initial investigations, case follow-up, and neighborhood problem-solving activities.

Differential response provides a tremendous opportunity for supervisors to gain some control over limited resources. The potential savings in officers' hours can have a significant impact on allocation and deployment.

Beginning in the mid-1970s, police departments began to question whether a patrol officer's response to every CFS, especially nonemergency situations, was needed to produce effective outcomes. Several studies concerning the patrol function were conducted during the 1970s and 1980s and greatly affected managerial assumptions about traditional strategies for responding to citizen CFS. Following are descriptions of some of those key studies that led police administrators to consider alternative patrol responses.

Kansas City Preventive Patrol Experiment. This evaluation of the effectiveness of random preventive patrol challenged several traditional assumptions held by police. Normal, proactive (saturation), and reactive (emergencies only) patrol were conducted in 15 of 24 beats in the city's south patrol division. The normal strategy involved conventional single patrol car response to CFS. The proactive strategy was to increase preventive patrol and police visibility by tripling the number of cars on patrol in another area. The reactive strategy was characterized by the virtual elimination of patrol cars. No significant differences in crime reduction were found in any of the experimental beat areas, regardless of the level of patrol. This experiment suggested that random police patrol was not a factor in deterring crime (Kelling, 1974).

Kansas City Response Time Study. This research evaluated whether rapid response to calls increased the likelihood of arresting offenders. It was discovered that the most important factor in arresting offenders was not the speed at which the police responded, but the delay in calling the police. Put simply, the fastest response could not compensate for delays in reporting the incident (Bieck and Kessler, 1977).

RAND Study of Managing Investigations. This study cast a first critical eye on detective work. Findings suggested that the way detectives were organized had little effect on the results of investigations. Factors such as case screening, which focuses on those cases with the highest possibility of arrest and weeds out those with few solvability factors, were more important. The RAND study also determined that the quality of the patrol officers' initial investigation was a significant factor in making an arrest (Greenwood, 1975).

Team Policing Experiment. Team policing was a popular reform effort that sought to improve crime prevention and reduction efforts by assigning teams of officers to a particular neighborhood and giving them responsibility for all services in that area. An evaluation of its implementation in seven cities in the United States suggested that the experiment was largely a failure. Findings revealed that poor planning and implementation by chief administrators, confusion by officers about their duties, and resistance by middle managers who resented sharing their authority with sergeants and officers, contributed to its failure (Sherman, 1973).

One- versus Two-Officer Patrol Cars. In a study of the effectiveness of one- versus two-officer patrol cars, Hale (1981) suggested that officer productivity and operational efficiency were increased in one-officer patrol units. Officer safety concerns may be addressed by establishing policy that requires the dispatching of two patrol cars to high-risk CFS. Wrobleski and Hess (1993) added that one-officer patrol vehicles can patrol twice the area, and that solo officers are generally more cautious and more attentive to their patrol duties because they do not have a partner to engage in conversation.

Newark and Flint Foot Patrol Studies. Evidence on the effects of foot patrol is somewhat mixed. In Newark, New Jersey, findings suggested that citizen fear of crime was reduced while citizen satisfaction with the police increased. However, foot patrols had no significant impact on reported crime or victimization (Police Foundation, 1981). In Flint, Michigan, findings suggested that the neighborhood foot patrol program appeared to decrease crime, increase citizen satisfaction with the police, and reduce public fear (Trojanowicz, 1986). The lack of sound experimental designs contributed to this inconsistent evidence regarding the effects of foot patrol (Green and Taylor, 1991). As a result, these findings should be interpreted with caution until more information is made available.

Newark and Houston Fear-Reduction Studies. These jurisdictions tested seven fear-reduction strategies, including citizen newsletters, police recontact with victims, neighborhood storefronts, increased citizen contact during patrol, community organizing, and coordinated community policing efforts. These studies were implemented to evaluate the impact of these strategies on the public's fear of crime. Findings indicated that these programs were least effective in reducing the public's concerns about property crime and most effective at reducing perceived civil disorder (Pate et al., 1986).

Newport News Problem-Oriented Policing. This study examined whether police officers could employ more rigorous analysis of the underlying causes of crime and reduce the prevalence of multiple incidents. Officers were trained and provided a problem-solving model called SARA (scanning, analysis, response, and assessment). The study showed that properly trained officers could employ problem solving as a daily practice. This study reported significant reductions in burglary and prostitution (Eck and Spelman, 1987).

Later we will discuss other methods for addressing nonemergency CFS.

Call Management: Prioritizing Calls for Service

Call management is a process for screening and prioritizing CFS. Today most police agencies have computer-aided dispatch (CAD) systems that may be programmed to prioritize calls by their importance. Obviously, more dangerous and in-progress calls such as robberies and assaults would receive the highest priority and an immediate response from patrol units, while a report of a theft that occurred two days prior may bring a delayed response. Police departments generally have clearly established dispatch protocols that determine the priority of call responses, such as the following:

Priority 1. Danger to life and/or property is imminent, or a crime of a serious nature is in progress. Examples include an armed robbery in progress, a shooting with the suspect on scene, or a major injury accident.

Priority 2. A threat to a person or property is possible or a breach of the peace is occurring. Examples include a loud argument or verbal disturbance, an unruly shoplifter in the custody of store security, and loud music or a party.

Priority 3. No threat to life or property exists, and a delay in response would not cause undue inconvenience to the citizen. Examples include theft of property which occurred days ago, a request for a house watch, or a dead animal in the road.

At times the volume of CFS will exceed the number of personnel who are available to respond. In this case police agencies are forced to hold the calls and delay their response. Generally, policies will guide the amount of time that a call may be delayed. For example, Priority 1 calls may require an immediate response in all cases, Priority 2 calls may be held for 15 minutes, and Priority 3 may be held for 30 minutes. When a pending call cannot be assigned to an officer within the established time limit, it is usually the responsibility of the dispatcher to notify a field supervisor or watch commander. The supervisor may need to direct communications to relieve an officer from a nonessential activity, such as lunch or another less serious call, or to hold the call for the next available officer.

Alternative Responses

A number of alternatives are available to reduce officer workload and increase productivity. Nearly all of these alternatives to traditional mobile response contain some mechanism to produce more time for officers to perform other

Computer-aided dispatch (CAD) systems may be programmed to prioritize calls based on their seriousness, and send the appropriate beat officers to handle the call for service. *Courtesy New York Police Department Photo Unit.*

important patrol activities. These alternative responses to CFS include telephone report units, delayed mobile response (stacking calls, setting appointments), referral to other sections (inside or outside the department), walk-in reports, and use of nonsworn personnel in lieu of patrol officers (e.g., civilian evidence technicians, animal control officers, community service specialists). Each is discussed briefly below.

Another reason for developing alternative response strategies is to ensure that adequate personnel are available to handle those calls requiring an immediate response. Experience suggests that citizens will accept, and often prefer the flexibility and convenience that alternative responses provide.

Telephone Reporting

One of the most effective call alternative strategies for relieving officer workload is the **Telephone Report Unit (TRU),** in which reports are handled over the telephone rather than by a patrol officer dispatched to the scene. TRUs provide several advantages for police agencies and the public. For example, a Priority 3 call (discussed above) may take 45 to 60 minutes for an officer to respond while a telephone report may be handled in 10 to 15 minutes and at the convenience of the caller. A telephone reporting unit may handle as much as 25 to 50 percent of an agency's noninvestigative reports. This accounts for a considerable amount of the workload and frees officers in the field to engage more in community problem solving.

To be effective, a call classification system and prioritization scheme are needed so that call takers can properly classify incoming calls. A training program is also required by call takers, dispatchers, and officers who must be familiar with the new procedures. Evaluations of this approach have consistently shown it to be more efficient than sending an officer to the scene and without a significant loss in citizen satisfaction. In addition to the volume of work that can be handled by TRUs, experience has shown that they provide major savings in the amount of time taken to complete a report and save money on vehicle maintenance costs. They also afford sworn officers more time for self-initiated activities and arrests (Levine and McEwen, 1985).

Delayed Response

A **delayed response** means that the presence of a police officer is required at the scene, but the incident is of sufficiently minor nature so that an immediate dispatch is unnecessary (e.g., "cold" larcenies and burglaries, unoccupied suspicious vehicle calls, and vandalism calls). Today the trend is to develop formal delayed response strategies that specify which types of calls can be delayed, and for how long. Factors to be considered are the seriousness of the call, the presence or absence of injuries, and the amount of damages. Most departmental policies state a maximum delay time, such as 30 or 45 minutes, after which the closest available unit must be assigned to handle the call (Levine and McEwen, 1985).

While the delayed response does not directly reduce officer workload, it does help make the existing workload more manageable. It increases the likelihood that officers will receive calls in their area of assignment, which results in fewer cross-beat dispatches and prevents the interruption of officers while on another assignment (e.g., COPPS activities).

The call taker must inform the citizen than an officer will not respond immediately; studies have found that once the call taker informs the citizen about the expected delay of police response, citizen satisfaction is not adversely affected by the delay (Levine and McEwen, 1985).

Walk-in/Mail-in Reporting

Many police agencies have also instituted programs that encourage citizens to come to the nearest police facility at their convenience to file a report, or the police may send a report package to citizens to be completed and returned by mail. The recent trend by police agencies to decentralize patrol operations through various COPPS initiatives has resulted in an increase in neighborhood police **ministations.** These provide a convenient place for citizens to complete walk-in reports or to pick up mail in reporting packages.

Use of Nonsworn Personnel

The use of volunteer and nonsworn personnel to handle nonemergency CFS has gained considerable popularity over the years. Many agencies utilize citizen volunteers who have been trained in citizen police academies, reserve police academies, and senior volunteer programs to handle a bulk of the workload traditionally handled by uniformed officers.

Another concept used by many police agencies to reduce patrol officer workload is the **Community Service Officer (CSO)** program. This program uses nonsworn personnel in the field and to respond to CFS, thus eliminating the requirement for an officer's presence. A CSO may engage in traffic accident investigations, take vandalism reports, perform parking enforcement, conduct basic crime scene investigations and collect evidence, dust for fingerprints, and perform other related duties. In some agencies, CSOs also staff ministations to handle telephone and mail-in reporting requests, again eliminating the need for an officer to respond.

Agencies also should explore the **civilianization** of police agencies. It makes little sense to assign a fully trained and qualified police officer to some administrative or support duties when they may be better handled by nonsworn personnel. Some of the areas being civilianized in police agencies include dispatching, research and planning, crime analysis, finance, parking enforcement, custody, technical/computer support, and animal control.

SHIFT SCHEDULING

General Recommendations

The question of whether to work around-the-clock shifts is not an option for the police. Police organizations are bound by their 24-hour responsibility to deploy officers to beats in shifts. When developing shifts, it is also important to consider the safety of officers. Primary concerns are the physical and emotional health and productivity of officers. O'Neill and Cushing (1991: 71–73) provided the following advice for administrators when creating shifts:

1. Create a system of steady shifts with selection based, at least in part, on fair and equitable criteria such as seniority grade. Shift selection could provide for 75 percent of the positions to be filled by seniority and 25 percent of the positions filled at management's discretion.
2. Establish a steady midnight shift in which the workweek is limited to four consecutive days. An officer's court dates would be scheduled for the day preceding the first night of work, and this would be considered a "workday."
3. Redeploy personnel so that only the required minimum number of officers and supervisors are on duty from 2 A.M. to 6 P.M. This would more accurately reflect the demand for service by assigning a greater number of officers to shifts where they are needed most.
4. In general, do not permit a change of shifts within a time period without making allowances for proper rest. In those rare instances when a change must be made, several days of advance notice must be given. There should be no changing of shifts for purely disciplinary reasons. Officers should be permitted to bid for another shift at least twice during a year, and vacancies should be announced.

Administrative decisions concerning shift scheduling may have significant impacts on officer performance and the quality of police service the community receives. The challenge for the supervisor is to employ a schedule that meets both the needs of the organization and the officers. An optimal shift schedule can minimize shortages by determining the correct starting times and days for the right number of officers so that, on an hourly basis, the number of officers on duty matches the patrol needs as closely as possible.

Traditionally, police have utilized a three eight-hour shift plan for patrol. For example, day shift officers would be assigned to work from 8 A.M. to 4 P.M., evening ("swing") shift officers work from 4 P.M. to 12 A.M., and night ("graveyard") shift officers are deployed from 12 A.M. to 8 A.M. However, in recent years alternative 9-, 10-, and 12-hour shifts have become popular (these are discussed below). Regardless of the shift schedule employed, police administrators should ensure that it provides adequate staffing levels and proper supervision and improves patrol effectiveness.

Permanent versus Rotating Shift Assignments: Advantages and Debilitating Effects

The issue of permanent versus to rotating shifts has been argued at length in police management literature. There are advantages and disadvantages to both shifts. The primary advantage of having personnel work a permanent or fixed shift is its simplicity and ease of assigning officers according to workload. Other advantages of fixed shifts include fewer physiological problems for personnel, fringe benefits for senior officers (e.g., better choices of days off), easier court scheduling, and the preference of most officers to work fixed shifts, which studies have long indicated (see Brunner, 1976). The disadvantages of fixed shifts include the time-honored tradition of placing rookie officers on the graveyard shift, thus leaving that shift with the greatest number of least experienced personnel; the stress placed on younger officers who may be assigned to higher workload shifts; and officers who lack the experience of working various shifts. Officers also may argue that permanent shifts result in officers losing touch with administration and other units that typically work dayshift.

Rotating shifts also offer some advantages and disadvantages. Advantages include the opportunity for rotating officers to experience the different kinds of work from one shift to another, and to have different times of the day off for their personal or family needs. But the disadvantages weigh heavily on officers. The frequency of rotating shifts—with some agencies rotating their officers as often as monthly or quarterly—creates fatigue and disruptions in officers' home life and their pursuit of higher education. The physical adjustment to rotating shifts may be the equivalent of "jet lag."

Because rotating shift work is debilitating and even dangerous, O'Neill and Cushing (1991) reported that police departments today are moving away from them, and that most major departments are moving or have moved out of what some psychologists have termed the "dark ages" and into a fixed-shift schedule or a more scientifically designed rotation. They argue that rotating shifts are to blame for poor performance, bad attitudes, absenteeism, and accidents.

Another reason for giving strong consideration to permanent shift assignments concerns the number of police agencies that are implementing COPPS. Under this philosophy, shift rotation can greatly frustrate the officers' attempts to solve neighborhood problems on their beats. Indeed, frequent shift rotation can be a death knell for the effectiveness of COPPS. Herman Goldstein (1990:160), the founder of the problem-oriented policing concept, argued that:

> The ultimate form of decentralization [is where] officers are assigned permanently, *for a minimum of several years* [emphasis added], to a specific area. Such an arrangement enables an officer to get to know the problems of a community, the strengths and weaknesses of existing systems of control, and the various resources that are useful in solving problems. Changes in the time during which a police officer works seriously detract from the potential to cement relationships between a police officer and [citizens]. If maintaining permanent assignments to both an area and a time of day is not possible, considerable effort must be invested in communications among officers serving the same area to ensure continuity and consistency in dealing with problems.

The research on shift work strongly suggests that administrators should carefully consider the benefits and hazards of various shift schemes. Human beings are naturally diurnal (day oriented) in their activity patterns. Shift work disrupts the body's complex biological clock, known as the circadian rhythm, and can result in stress-related illnesses, fatigue-induced accidents, family crises, and lower life expectancy. Furthermore, supervisors need to be aware of the higher probability of accidents and errors during shifts where they may be fatigued. Moore-Ede and Richardson (1985) noted that the *Exxon Valdez* incident (where 11 million gallons of crude oil was dumped into Alaska's Prince William Sound in 1989) and nuclear accidents at Three Mile Island, Pennsylvania (March 1979) and Chernobyl in the Ukraine (April 1986, killing 45 people and causing thousands more to suffer from the aftereffects), and the industrial chemical disaster in Bhopal, India (killing 6,000 people in 1984) all occurred during the early hours of the morning when the risk of employee fatigue was at its highest. A review of each of these accidents—and scores more involving automobiles, air-planes, trains, and ferries—have all cited shift-related fatigue as a factor.

Assigning Officers to Shifts

There are two principle forms of shift scheduling. The first is a flat system of scheduling, which we introduced at the beginning of the chapter, where an equal number of officers are assigned to each shift. The obvious problems with the flat system is that it does not consider the varying demands across shifts. Most jurisdictions may find the weekend late evening and early morning hours to be the busiest, thus presenting the most danger to officers because of the types of calls that they must respond to during those time periods. The day shift may also be busy, but calls involving noninvestigative theft and burglary reports or traffic- and accident-related incidents normally present little threat to officers. Also, a high percentage of typical day shift calls can be assigned to differential responses. A Department of Justice study showed that the typical distribution of calls by shift varied. In what they termed a "typical city," approximately 22 percent of the CFS occurred between 12 A.M. and 8 A.M. while 33 percent of the CFS are received from 8 A.M. and 4 P.M. and 45 percent between 4 P.M. and 12 A.M.

Compressed Work Schedules

Compressed work schedules have gained considerable momentum recently, with the strong support of police employees and representative labor organizations. This support is prompted by a changing mood in the workplace that is vastly different from that in the past because of numerous economic, legislative, and cultural changes (Williams and Eide, 1995). In both corporate America and government, employers are being forced to be more flexible in their work arrangements. In a study of 521 of the largest corporations in America, 94 percent offered a compressed work schedule (Williams and Eide, 1995). The trend for law enforcement began in the 1970s, with many agencies—including the Huntington Beach, California, police department and Sacramento County sheriff's department—moving toward 4–10 (officers working four days a week, 10 hours a day) plans.

However, there has been considerable debate among police practitioners about the benefits and problems associated with these 9-, 10-, and 12-hour compressed work schedules. While advocates claim improvements in the quality and quantity of work, reduced sick time, and lower attrition rates, managers remain skeptical and have voiced concerns to the contrary.

With each compressed schedule, certain benefits and concerns appear. Of utmost concern for the supervisor is that the compressed schedule adequately addresses workload demands. Following are some of the types of compressed work schedules that have been implemented and tested by agencies across the United States:

5-Day, 8-Hour Schedule [5–8]. The 5–8 work schedule remains the most commonly used by police agencies. In some jurisdictions an overlapping 7 P.M. to 3 A.M. shift is added to assist evening (swing) and night (graveyard) officers during what is traditionally the busiest time of their shifts—when bars and taverns empty, fights and domestic disturbances begin to occur, and buildings and residences are more often burglarized under cover of darkness.

4-Day, 10-Hour Schedule [4–10]. Under the 4–10 shift plan, officers work four 10-hour days a week, with three days off. This shift configuration also has a built-in overlap during shifts (see Table 10–4). When scheduled properly, the overlaps can be utilized to ensure that more employees are available during late afternoon and evening hours, which are typically peak workload times for agencies. Many police agencies have studied 4–10 plans extensively. They found that officers generally favor the shorter workweek because it offers them additional time for leisure, education, moonlighting, and so on. However, many police executives have decided against implementing the 4–10 plan for a host of reasons, including the fatigue factor, the greater need to control moonlighting, the need for more equipment to accommodate extra personnel during overlapping periods of duty, and the potential need for greater salary budgets to pay employees at overtime rates for exceeding eight hours a day (Iannone, 1995). In addition, this schedule makes training for 10-hour blocks problematic.

Table 10–5 presents a more detailed comparison of the 5–8 and the 4–10 duty shifts, using average types and amounts of days off that are taken by officers in a typical year. Several important aspects of the two shifts may be noted. First, 5–8 personnel are on duty 1,760 hours a year and can be scheduled to work for 220 shifts; 4–10 personnel are on duty for 1,680 hours a year and work 168 shifts. What is *not* shown in the table is that, while both 5–8 and 4–10 personnel will earn about the same hourly wage (because they work about the same number of hours per year), 4–3 (10) personnel will earn much more compensation for each shift and overtime hour worked.

3-Day, 12-Hour Schedule [3–12]. The 3–12 plan originated in the private sector nearly 40 years ago, but only within the past decade has it gained the attention of the police. Unlike 9- and 10-hour plans, it fits neatly into a 24-hour day for scheduling. Normally, officers are assigned to work three days a week, with four days off for three weeks, and four days a week with three days off for the fourth week of a 28-day cycle. Again, proponents claim the benefits of increased productivity and employee morale as justification for 3–12 shifts (Schissler,

TABLE 10.4. A Basic 8- and 10-Hour Duty Shift Configuration

Type of Shift	Day	Evening (Swing)	Night (Graveyard)
Three	8 A.M.–4 P.M.	4 P.M.–12 P.M.	12 P.M.–8 a.m.
8-hour	or	or	or
shifts*	7 A.M.–3 P.M.	3 P.M.–11 P.M.	11 P.M.–7 A.M.
4–10 hr.-shift[†]	7 A.M.–5 P.M.	3 P.M.–1 A.M.	9 P.M.–7 A.M.

*Swing or relief officers may work all three shifts to cover as needed.
[†]This shift has built-in overlapping of personnel.
Source: M. J. Levine and J. T. McEwen, *Patrol Deployment* (Washington, D.C.: U.S. Department of Justice, 1985).

TABLE 10.5. Comparisons of Scheduling Availability for the 8- and 10-Hour Duty Shifts

5–2 (8) Shift Scheduling Availability

BASE = 8 HRS./DAY × 365 DAYS PER YEAR = 2,920 HOURS

From the base, we subtract the following time off (averages are used; actual amount of time off taken per year will vary from agency to agency, officer to officer):

Days		Hours
Days off	2 days/week × 8 hrs./day × 52 wks./yr. =	832 hrs.
Vacation	16 days/week × 8 hrs. =	128
Holidays	3 days/year =	24
Sick/Injury	7 days/year =	56
Training	5 days/year =	40
Compensatory	8 days/year =	64
Compassionate	1 day/year =	8
Other (military, discipline)	1 day/year =	8
		Total: 1,160 hrs.

Hours and shifts for which personnel may be expected to be on duty are as follows: 2,920 hrs. (base) − 1,160 hrs. off duty = 1,760 hrs. (or 220 eight-hour shifts).

Note that an officer is available for duty only *60 percent* of the time.

4–3 (10) Shift Scheduling Availability

BASE = 10 HRS./DAY × 365 DAYS PER YEAR = 3,650 HOURS

From the base, we subtract the following time off (averages are used; actual amount of time off taken per year will of course vary from agency to agency, officer to officer):

Days		Hours
Days off	3 days/week × 10 hrs./day × 52 wks./yr. =	1,560 hrs.
Vacation	16 days/week × 10 hrs./day =	160
Holidays	3 days/year =	30
Sick/Injury	7 days/year =	70
Training	5 days/year =	50
Compensatory	8 days/year =	80
Compassionate	1 day/year =	10
Other (military, discipline)	1 day/year =	10
		Total: 1,970 hrs.

Hours and shifts for which personnel may be expected to be on-duty are as follows: 3,650 hrs. (base) − 1,970 hrs. off duty = 1,680 hrs. (or 168 ten-hour shifts).

Note that an officer is available for duty only *46 percent* of the time.

1996). Management voices concerns regarding increased fatigue and potential increased costs associated with the Fair Labor Standards Act (FLSA), discussed below, as primary issues. Nonetheless, the 12-hour plan is enjoying increased support among agencies (see, for example, Talley, 1995). Again, advocates cite higher officer morale, increased productivity, and reduced sick leave as the benefits.

5-Day, 9-Hour Schedule [5–2 (9)]. The 9-hour work schedule requires five working days followed by two days off, five workdays followed by three days off, and a final workday with another three days off. The 5–9 schedule is becoming popular with nonuniformed assignments, such as detectives and administration.

There is no single shift scheduling configuration that fits all needs, nor would we recommend one shift pattern over the others. Administrators should decide on the shift that accomplishes a balance between organizational objectives and employee needs. They should carefully evaluate the maintenance of staffing levels, productivity, fatigue, equipment, and overtime costs before deciding on a compressed schedule.

Split and Overlapping Shifts

We also need to mention that so-called split shifts—in which officers work a few hours, are relieved for a period, and then return to complete their tours of duty—should usually be avoided because of their adverse effects on officers. There are times, however, when such arrangements are desirable, such as those officers wishing to further their education or attend to other personal needs during the middle of their shift. Indeed, split shifts may be sought after by such personnel (Iannone, 1995).

On occasion, because of inordinately high workloads at certain peak periods, it may be desirable to institute overlapping shifts to meet these needs. For example, if certain problems arise at about 8 P.M. each evening, a 6 P.M. to 2 A.M. shift might be implemented. Like split shifts, overlapping shifts should be avoided because of possible adverse effects on morale and effectiveness, unless workload demands require additional officers during peak workload periods. In this case, such overlapping shifts should be eight consecutive hours in length—to avoid officers being assigned to work split shifts (Iannone, 1995).

Labor Considerations

For some police administrators, the **Fair Labor Standards Act (FLSA)** of 1938 has become a budgetary and operational nightmare (Randels, 1992). The act provides minimum pay and overtime provisions covering employees in both public and private sectors, and contains special provisions for firefighters and police officers. Although there is some discussion in Congress concerning the repeal or modification of the act, at the present time it remains a legislative force that administrators, middle managers, and supervisors must reckon with. Indeed, one observer referred to the FLSA as the criminal justice administrator's "worst nightmare come true" (Lund, 1991:4).

The act was passed to protect the rights and working conditions of employees in the private sector. During that time, long hours, poor wages, and substandard work conditions plagued most businesses. The FLSA placed a number of restrictions on employers to improve these conditions. Then, in 1985 the United States Supreme Court brought local police employees under the coverage of the FLSA. In this major (and very costly) decision, *Garcia* v. *San Antonio Transit Authority,* the Court held, five to four, that Congress imposed the requirements of the FLSA on state and local governments.

As indicated, police agencies operate 24 hours a day, seven days a week—often requiring overtime due to such activities as court appearances and training sessions. The FLSA comes into play when overtime salaries must be paid. It provides that an employer must generally pay employees time and a half for all hours over 40 worked in a week. Overtime must also be paid to personnel for all work in excess of 43 hours in a 7-day cycle or 171 hours in a 28-day period. Public safety employees may accrue a maximum of 480 hours of compensatory ("comp") time which, if not utilized as leave, must be paid off on separation from employment at the employee's final rate of pay or at the average pay over the last three years, whichever is greater (Swanson et al., 1993). Furthermore, employers usually cannot require employees to take comp time in lieu of cash. The primary issue with FLSA is the rigidity of application to what is compensable work. The act prohibits an agency from taking "volunteered time" from employees.

Today, an officer who works the night shift must receive pay for attending training or testifying in court during the day. Further, officers who are ordered to remain at home in anticipation of emergency actions must be compensated. Notably, however, the FLSA's overtime provisions do not apply to persons employed in a bona fide executive, administrative, or professional capacity. In policing, the act has generally been held to apply to all ranks below the most senior positions.

The *Garcia* decision prompted an onslaught of litigation by police and fire employees of state and local governments. The issues are broad but may include paying overtime compensation to K-9 and equestrian officers who care for department animals while "off duty," overtime pay for officers who access their work computer and conduct business from home, pay for academy recruits who are given mandatory homework assignments, and standby and on-call pay for supervisors and officers who are assigned to units that require their unsched-

---

Case Study 10–2
Who's on First?—Or, Who Should Work When?

Industry City is rapidly growing. In the past five years the police department has doubled its number of officers. As a result, it is not uncommon to find that the officers assigned to the evening and night shifts have less than three years of experience. There is also a shortage of qualified field training officers for the evening shifts because the majority of veteran officers work the day shift or are on special assignment. All sworn officers work a straight five-day, eight-hour week, with no shift rotation; all assignments are based on seniority.

Lately the union has expressed a great deal of unhappiness concerning the lack of opportunities for the younger officers to work other shifts and special assignments. Younger officers have also expressed some interest in the four-day, 10-hour shift

scheme. There also have been increased use of sick time and citizen complaints against graveyard shift officers. The union has sent a letter to the chief requesting a discussion of these matters. The training supervisor, Sgt. O'Neal, has been directed to provide the chief with an evaluation of the benefits, costs, and concerns of various compressed shift configurations.

1. What suggestions might Sgt. O'Neal provide regarding shift rotation?
2. Would a compressed shift plan have any advantages over the current five-day, eight-hour plan? Disadvantages?
3. What labor considerations might be posed by a shift rotation or compressed plan?

uled return to work. These are just a few of the many FLSA issues that are being litigated in courts across the nation.

The fiscal and operational repercussions of the FLSA could be staggering for some agencies, depending on past practices. For example, in one West Coast police department, the city was required to pay each of its six K-9 officers up to $35,000 in back pay for FLSA claims associated with the care, feeding, and training of the department's dogs. This example alone should be warning to police administrators to review their department policies and practices to ensure that they comport with FLSA requirements.

A companion issue with respect to criminal justice pay and benefits is that of equal pay for equal work. Disparate treatment in pay and benefits can be litigated under Title VII of the Civil Rights Act or statutes such as the Equal Pay Act or the equal protection clause. An Ohio case involved matron/dispatchers who performed essentially the same job as jailers but were paid less. In *Jurich* v. *Mahoning County* (1983), the court found this to be in violation of the Equal Pay Act and, since discriminatory intent was found, in violation of Title VII.

DEPLOYMENT STRATEGIES

Over the years several methods for deploying officers to patrol duties have been explored. The most common deployment schemes involve basic officer, split force, and special unit plans. We briefly discuss each method as well as directed patrol. We conclude this section with an in-depth look at the unique deployment requirements of a COPPS initiative.

Basic Officer Plan

Under the **basic officer plan,** officers are assigned to a geographic area that has been designed with neighborhoods in mind. This is a typical beat plan configuration that we described earlier. Most computer-aided dispatch systems adjust beat plans according to the number of officers available during any given shift. The basic officer plan assigns officers to fixed shifts.

Split Force

The **split force plan** divides patrol into two groups. One group consists of three-fourths of the patrol officers, who handle CFS in a normal fashion, while the second group performs specialized functions in high-crime areas, often in plainclothes. The split force concept is used by many agencies to free officers to engage in COPPS activities. All officers respond to emergency calls under this plan. An evaluation conducted by the Wilmington, Delaware, police department found that police productivity increased by 20 percent, whereas crime decreased 18 percent during the first year of implementation of the split force plan.

Special Units

Many agencies also have developed special teams to handle certain community concerns. These teams may be dedicated solely to COPPS, gang activities, adult repeat offenders, or traffic matters and may utilize a variety of patrol tactics, including bicycle patrol, foot beats, horse patrol, or other means of transportation. The key to the effectiveness of any specialized unit is that community problems drive the tactics. Departments must be sure that the various patrol tactics benefit the agency's responses to community problems. Few agencies can afford to implement these approaches solely to improve police-community relations.

Directed Patrol

Directed patrol efforts were implemented to increase patrol productivity. Supervisors use directed patrol to direct officers to put their available time to work in a more planned and rational manner than traditional random patrol. Directed patrol utilizes crime analysis and shift designs as a tool to accomplish its objectives. With these data a patrol supervisor can deploy officers to attend to specific beat problems.

Community-Oriented Policing and Problem Solving

Community policing and problem solving (COPPS) is an overarching management philosophy that affects how an entire organization addresses crime detection and prevention (COPPS will be discussed in detail in Chapter 13).

A COPPS strategy involves significant changes in how patrol officers are deployed, including an emphasis on flexible work schedules. Officers must be given the requisite time for neighborhood interaction and problem solving. Decisions must be made concerning matters such as duties and job descriptions of officers, functions to be performed, staffing levels, and neighborhood boundaries.

Police departments might need to redesign district and beat boundaries that match the major neighborhoods of the city, ensuring that the areas generating the greatest number of CFS are in the middle of districts and posts, thus providing for strong accountability for policing those areas. Frequently, some police officers have very little uncommitted time during a tour of duty while others have large blocks of uncommitted time. As noted earlier, no more than 30–40 percent of an officer's time should be devoted to handling CFS.

The time between calls is the key element in determining whether officers have time for problem solving. It is not uncommon to find that officers have ample time available between calls for other activities. However, the available time is normally spread throughout the shift, varying from 10 minutes between calls to 45 minutes. If we assume an average problem-solving activity takes 45 minutes, then the officer may have few blocks of uninterrupted time for an assignment. Time between calls varies considerably, depending on the number of calls for a particular shift, the types of calls, and how much time they require. One or two fewer calls can make a big difference in whether stretches of uninterrupted time will be available.

Obviously, citizen calls are important and cannot be ignored. Supervisors play an important role in helping officers find the time to engage in COPPS activities between CFS. In addition to the alternative reporting methods discussed above, there are three methods for overcoming the matter of finding time for problem solving while still handling calls effectively (Peak and Glensor, 1996:157–58):

1. Allow units to perform problem-solving assignments as self-initiated activities. Under this approach, a unit would contact the dispatcher and go out of service for a problem-solving assignment. The unit would be interrupted only for an emergency call in its area of responsibility.
2. Schedule one or two units to devote a predetermined part of their shift to problem solving. For example, a supervisor could designate one or two units each day to devote the first half of their shift or even just one hour to problem solving. Their calls would be handled by other units so that they have an uninterrupted block of time for problems.
3. Review the department policy on "assist" units. In some departments, several units show up at the scene of a call even though they are not needed. A department should undergo a detailed study on the types of calls for which assist units are actually appearing, with the aim of reducing the number of assists.

In many agencies, supervisors maintain the authority to reprioritize calls and delay officers' response. Again, it is important that a dispatcher advises the caller of any delayed response. As we discussed previously, slower police responses to nonemergency calls have been found satisfactory to citizens if dispatchers tell citizens that an officer might not arrive right away (Eck and Spelman, 1989).

In summary, the overall aim should be to provide officers with uninterrupted amounts of time for problem-solving assignments. There are many ways to accomplish this aim, but they require a concerted planning effort by the department.

THE INFLUENCE OF UNIONS

Police unions consider officer deployment and scheduling to be issues that should be negotiated with management, as a condition of work. The number of persons assigned to a patrol car or section of the community, how seniority and education will be used in assignments, and the hours worked and shift selection by seniority are issues that traditionally were considered management prerogatives but are now negotiable. Critics argue that this kind of union activity is detrimental to the effective management of the department and the provision of services to the community (Bouza, 1985). Others, however, blame the poor management and treatment of employees as fostering such union activity (see Kliesmet, 1985).

SUMMARY

The determination of the proper allocation of patrol personnel is of vital interest and concern to the police supervisor. This is due to the fact that the patrol function is the backbone of police work and requires the greatest numbers of personnel. In this chapter we examined the need for patrol planning, methods of determining resource allocation needs and performing a workload analysis, alternative patrol responses, types of compressed shift schedules, and deployment strategies, and demonstrated that ensuring 24-hour, seven-day-a-week shift coverage is not an easy task.

As service demands continue to increase and new strategies to control and prevent crime evolve, so will the deployment and scheduling of personnel. Today's police supervisors must therefore be more flexible and willing to modify their personnel deployment schemes that best fit the needs of the department, its personnel, and the public they serve.

KEY TERMS

flat system of
   deployment (p. 240)
relief factor (p. 241)
workload
   analysis (p. 244)
differential police response
   (DPR) (p. 248)

Telephone Report Unit
   (TRU) (p. 252)
delayed mobile
   response (p. 252)
ministations (p. 253)
community service officer
   (CSO) (p. 253)

civilianization (p. 253)
Fair Labor Standards Act
   (FLSA) (p. 259)
basic officer plan (p. 261)
split force plan (p. 261)
directed patrol (p. 262)

ITEMS FOR REVIEW

1. Describe the purposes of patrol planning and some of the factors that contribute to the overall lack of proper patrol planning in police agencies.
2. Discuss the three methods that police departments use most frequently to determine resource needs.
3. Explain the two plans for allocating patrol resources as shown in Table 10–2.
4. Describe some of the factors a police supervisor should consider in the proper deployment of officers by time and location.
5. Discuss some alternative patrol responses that the police can use in handling citizen calls for service, thus reducing officer workload.
6. Compare permanent and rotating shift assignments, including the advantages and debilitating effects of each.
7. Explain the benefits and drawbacks of the 5–8 and the 4–10 work shifts.
8. Describe how the Fair Labor Standards Act has affected shift scheduling.
9. Examine the primary methods for deploying officers—including the basic officer, split force, and special unit plans—and directed patrol plans.
10. Explain why the police must be deployed differently with the community policing and problem-solving strategy.

SOURCES

ASCHOFF, J. (1965). "Circadian rhythms in man." *Science* 148:1427–32.
BIECK, W., and KESSLER, D. (1977). *Response time analysis.* Kansas City, Mo.: Board of Police Commissioners.
BOUZA, A. V. (1985). "Police unions: Paper tigers or roaring lions?" In W. A. Geller (ed.). *Police Leadership in America: Crisis and Opportunity.* New York: Praeger.
BRUNNER, G. D. (1976). "Law enforcement officers' work schedules: Reactions." *Police Chief* (January): 30–31.

ECK, J., and SPELMAN, W. (1987). *Problem-solving: Problem-oriented policing in Newport News.* Washington, D.C.: Police Executive Research Forum.

ECK J., and SPELMAN, W. (1989). "A problem-oriented approach to police service delivery." In Dennis Jay Kenney (ed.). *Police and Policing: Contemporary Issues.* New York: Praeger.

GARCIA V. SAN ANTONIO METROPOLITAN TRANSIT AUTHORITY, 469 US 528 (1985).

GAY, W. G., SCHELL, T. H., and SCHACK, S. (1977). *Improving patrol productivity: Routing patrol, prescriptive package,* Vol. 1. Washington D.C.: U.S. Department of Justice.

GOLDSTEIN, HERMAN (1990). *Problem-oriented policing.* New York: McGraw-Hill.

GREEN, J. R., and TAYLOR, R. B. (1991). "Community-based policing and foot patrol: Issues of theory and evaluation." In Jack R. Greene and Stephen D. Mastrofski (eds.). *Community Policing: Rhetoric or Reality?* New York: Preager.

GREENWOOD, P. (1975). *The criminal investigation process.* Santa Monica, Calif.: RAND.

HALE, C. D. (1981). *Police operations and management.* New York: John Wiley.

IANNONE, N. F. (1994). *Supervision of police personnel.* 5th ed. Englewood Cliffs, N.J.: Prentice Hall.

JURICH V. MAHONING COUNTY (31 Fair Emp Prac 1275 (BNA) (ND Ohio 1983).

KELLING, G. L. (1974). *The Kansas City preventive patrol experiment: A summary report.* Washington D.C.: Police Foundation.

KLEISMET, R. B. (1985). "The chief and the union: May the force be with you." In W. A. Geller (ed.). *Police Leadership in America: Crisis and Opportunity.* New York: Praeger.

LEVINE, C. H. (1982). *Cutback management in the criminal justice system: A manual of readings.* Washington, D.C.: University Research Corporation.

LEVINE, M. J., and MCEWEN J. T. (1985). *Patrol deployment.* Washington, D.C.: U.S. Department of Justice.

LUND, L. (1991). "The 'ten commandments' of risk management for jail administrators." *Detention Reporter* 4 (June): 4.

MCEWEN, J. T., CONNERS, E., and COHEN, M. (1986). *Evaluation of the differential police response field test.* Washington, D.C.: National Institute of Justice.

MOORE-EDE, M. C., and RICHARDSON, G. S. (1985). "Medical implications of shift work." *Annual Review of Medicine,* p. 608.

O'NEILL, J. L., and CUSHING, M. A. (1991). *The impact of shift work on police officers.* Washington D.C.: Police Executive Research Forum.

POLICE FOUNDATION (1981). *The Newark foot patrol experiment.* Washington, D.C.: Police Foundation.

PATE, A. M., WYCOFF, M. A., SKOGAN, W. G., and SHERMAN, L. W. (1986). *Reducing fear of crime in Houston and Newark: A summary report.* Washington D.C.: Police Foundation and National Institute of Justice.

PEAK, K. J. and GLENSOR, R. W. (1996). *Community policing and problem solving: Strategies and practices.* Upper Saddle River, N.J.: Prentice Hall.

RANDELS, E. L. (1992). "The fair labor standards act: An administrative nightmare." *Police Chief* (5): 28–32.

ROBERG, R. R., and KUYKENDALL, J. (1990). *Police organization and management: Behavior, theory, and processes.* Pacific Grove, Calif.: Brooks/Cole.

SCOTT, E. J. (1981). *Calls for service: Citizen demand and initial police response.* Washington, D.C.: U.S. Government Printing Office.

SHERMAN, L. (1973). *Team policing: Seven case studies.* Washington D.C.: Police Foundation.

SCHISSLER, T. M. (1996). "Shift work and police scheduling." *Law and Order* (May): 61–64.

SWANSON, C. R., TERRITO, L, and TAYLOR, R. W. (1993). *Police administration.* 3d ed. New York: Macmillan.

TALLEY, G. B. (1995). "12-Hour Shifts: Comments from the field." *Police Chief* (December): 29.

TROJANOWICZ, R. C. (1986). "Evaluating a neighborhood foot patrol program: The Flint, Michigan project." In Dennis P. Rosenbaum (ed.). *Community Crime Prevention: Does it Work?* Beverly Hills, Calif.: Sage.

UNITED STATES DEPARTMENT OF JUSTICE, FEDERAL BUREAU OF INVESTIGATION (1996). *Crime in the United States, 1995.* Washington D.C.: U.S. Government Printing Office.

WILLIAMS, W. L. and EIDE, R. W. (1995). "LAPD conducts one year test." *The Police Chief* (December): 18–27.

WROBLESKI, H. M., and HESS, K. M. (1993). *Introduction to law enforcement and criminal justice.* St. Paul, Minn.: West.

11

Patrol and Special Operations

Big jobs usually go to the men who prove their ability to outgrow small ones.
—RALPH WALDO EMERSON

For one man that can stand prosperity, there are a hundred that will stand adversity.
—THOMAS CARLYLE

The best executive is the one who has sense enough to pick good men to do what he wants done, and the self-restraint to keep from meddling with them while they do it.
—THEODORE ROOSEVELT

INTRODUCTION

There are innumerable situations and problems confronting police supervisors as they direct daily patrol operations and ensure that officers' work activities are being conducted according to departmental expectations. During any tour of duty, police officers may encounter situations that are extraordinary and unique compared with the majority of general calls for service (CFS), thus requiring the special attention of supervisors.

This chapter addresses the following five complex, serious, and dangerous patrol situations that confront supervisors: domestic violence, crimes in progress, street drug enforcement, youth gang enforcement, and police pursuits. The chapter includes a discussion of tactics for handling problems as well as supervisors' responsibilities.

Note that several of the types of incidents discussed in this chapter—crimes in progress, police pursuits, and domestic violence—are often addressed at length in agency policy and procedure manuals which spell out how officers are to deal with them. Even some municipal ordinances and state statutes cover some of these problems, such as arrest policies for domestic violence cases, mandatory victim notification laws when offenders are released, and how police agencies deal with gang members. It is incumbent upon supervisors to ensure that officers adhere to pertinent laws, ordinances, and policies.

THE SCOPE OF PATROL OPERATIONS

To understand the scope of patrol operations, we must consider the myriad of possible CFS handled by police officers. They range from simple requests for information or assistance to emergency situations.

One of the primary responsibilities of supervisors is to manage and control the scene of dangerous calls and to assist officers' handling of such incidents. Also, a number of calls can be classified as tactical or critical incidents (discussed in Chapter 12), which have the potential to become life threatening; supervisors must manage those calls as well. Any of these situations can take a turn for the worse and result in personal injury to citizens or officers. For this reason the direct involvement of supervisors in these situations is most important.

Police officers also have a number of resources at their disposal when responding to CFS, ranging from providing information or assistance to the use of deadly force. Both officers and supervisors must ensure that these responses meet the needs of the situation and that only a minimum amount of force is used to establish control.

It should be noted that when officers engage in various situations, they attempt to achieve some goal or objective. Possible goals include (1) protecting an endangered citizen, (2) protecting the officer or other officers at the scene of a crime, (3) preventing a crime, (4) defusing a potentially violent situation, (5) solving a crime, (6) serving court papers, (7) ensuring the orderly flow of traffic and pedestrians, (8) helping or serving citizens, and (9) collecting information. The goal that officers select for a given situation is contingent upon the situation. Officers must be able to analyze the situation and exercise discretion when selecting the proper outcome. A supervisor's primary responsibility is to ensure that officers do so.

The following sections explore several types of CFS from operational and supervisory perspectives. These are commonly the kinds of CFS that require a supervisor's immediate attention and involvement.

DOMESTIC VIOLENCE SITUATIONS

A Unique Problem

Perhaps one of the most potentially problematic situations for police officers is domestic violence calls. **Domestic or family violence** refers to a number of situations, including spousal abuse, elder abuse, and child abuse. There is disagreement about what constitutes domestic violence, but most agree that abuse must occur. Abuse involved in such situations can refer to overt acts of aggression against another (Feld and Straus, 1989) or the injuries incurred as a result of the assault (Berk et al., 1983).

Historically, domestic violence, especially spousal abuse, was viewed as different and less serious than other forms of assault because the act was a private family matter; indeed, domestic violence has been perceived so differently from other forms of assault and criminality that some observers postulate that it is accepted as normal family behavior in some circles (Gelles and Straus, 1988). "A man's home is his castle" was traditionally the prevailing notion, and the sanctity of the home was not to be violated by the police unless "significant" criminal acts occurred there (Belknap, 1990; Fyfe and Flavin, 1991). There are no concrete data relative to the number of abuse cases that occur each year, but we know that spousal abuse and other forms of domestic violence remain a substantial problem for America's police.

Domestic violence calls are difficult for police for two reasons. First, handling domestic violence calls is fairly dangerous. A significant number of police officers are killed or injured each year while handling these calls. Second, domestic violence represents a weighty area for police liability. Each year a significant number of civil suits that originated from a domestic violence call are filed against the police. We will briefly discuss each area of difficulty.

An Element of Danger

Traditionally, police officers have perceived domestic violence calls as extremely dangerous, although there is some disagreement about how dangerous such calls are relative to other calls and incidents the police handle. For example, Konstantin (1984) maintained that the perceptions that family violence calls are dangerous has been perpetuated through police "folklore," and that domestic violence calls are fairly safe relative to other types of calls. However, studies indicate that domestic violence calls are fairly dangerous in some locations (see, for example, Uchida, Brooks, and Kopers, 1987). Today it would appear that both sides are partly correct; from 1985 to 1994, 65 of 704 (9.2 percent) of all police officers killed in the line of duty were addressing family-quarrel situations; 4 of 76 (5.3 percent) officers killed in a recent one-year period were engaged in such situations (U.S. Department of Justice, Federal Bureau of Investigation, 1996:33). In sum, while it appears that officers are becoming more careful in the handling of domestic situations, they still have good reason to be cautious when responding to such calls, regardless of where they work.

The Specter of Liability

As we mentioned above, a number of civil suits have been filed against police officers and agencies, alleging mishandling of domestic violence cases. These suits commonly allege excessive force, false arrest, or that police officers failed to take into custody a suspect who later returned to the scene of the disturbance and assaulted or killed his or her spouse or other relatives.

Domestic violence situations are often confrontational and the police become personally involved as a result of responding to such calls. Officers are more likely to arrest citizens in confrontational situations, and less likely to discriminate when effecting these arrests, especially when the conflicts become heated. Such actions frequently lead to citizens' complaints or allegations of false arrest.

Similarly, police officers are often accused of using excessive force in domestic violence situations. These types of calls sometimes escalate to the point of physical violence. When police officers intervene, the citizens involved in the fight often turn on the police officer, especially when they see their spouse being arrested, when they perceive that the officer is not taking the actions they desire. Also, because many domestic calls are physical confrontations, police officers generally resort to some form of physical force to subdue arrestees or to break up fighting parties. Thus, by their very nature domestic violence calls are conducive to physical violence and accusations that officers used excessive force. For this reason, many departments require that supervisors review and approve all domestic violence reports and in some agencies, a supervisor is required to respond to all calls.

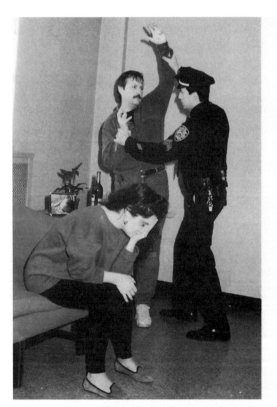 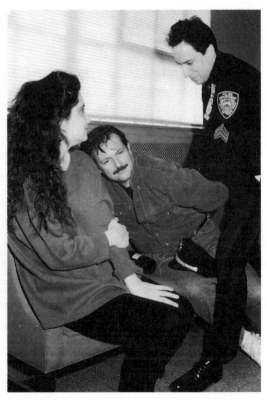

Role-playing is one of the best methods for teaching officers how to handle difficult situations. Here a supervisor participates in domestic violence training.
Courtesy New York Police Department Photo Unit.

Perhaps the most difficult problem confronting police officers in domestic violence calls is deciding how to respond to them. A major study of domestic violence in Minneapolis indicated that arresting abusers, as opposed to separating the combatants or mediating the disputes, resulted in a marked decrease in the number of future domestic altercations (Sherman and Berk, 1984). A number of states have enacted mandatory arrest statutes or have given police officers special powers in domestic disputes. For example, many states now require officers to make a misdemeanor arrest at the scene when there is evidence that one of the parties was physically assaulted. Police officers, in essence, have been given the authority to make misdemeanor arrests for misdemeanors which did not occur in their presence.

To test the findings in the Minneapolis study, it was replicated in several other cities. However, the results of the studies in Omaha, Charlotte, and Milwaukee indicated that arrest is no more effective in deterring future domestic assaults than other intervention methods.

Research obviously fails to provide the police with any concrete answers on how best to handle domestic violence cases. Supervisors should ensure that their officers follow the law and provide victims with maximum protection; that is, if the jurisdiction has a mandatory arrest policy, it should be followed. If a mandatory arrest law or policy does not exist, officers should inform victims of the process for obtaining arrest warrants or restraining orders. Finally, officers should ensure that they analyze domestic conflicts accurately and take only appropriate legal action. They also should refrain from using excessive force when making such arrests. These actions will protect the police department as well as the victim of domestic violence. Supervisors can best ensure that these actions occur by overseeing officers' actions at domestic violence calls. Case Study 11–1 discusses police response to a domestic violence call.

Case Study 11–1
Just Another Night at the Knox House

Officers Ben Collins and Earl James respond to another domestic violence call at the Knox household. The officers are very familiar with the Knoxes: Every Friday night, it seems, the husband and wife get drunk and eventually beat up on one another. Although the state has enacted a mandatory arrest law for domestic violence, it requires the arrest of the primary aggressor. Who exactly is the "primary aggressor" can never be determined at the Knox house; both husband and wife are uncooperative with the police. In the 38 previous responses to their home, only three arrests have been made—for assaults on the police officers, not domestic violence.

Tonight is not any different. Officers Collins and James arrive at the Knox home to face an onslaught of vulgarities by both of them, who are quite drunk and display the usual matching bruises. Sgt. Caplan also responds and observes his officers' vain attempts to resolve the situation. After witnessing the vulgarities, Caplan orders the two officers to leave the home and return back to their patrol duties. Three hours later, a neighbor calls police dispatch to report the sound of gunshots from the Knox residence. The police respond and find that Mrs. Knox has shot and killed her husband with a shotgun.

1. Could this situation have been prevented?
2. Is the supervisor liable in any manner?
3. Were any laws violated by the manner in which the police addressed the problem?

RESPONDING TO CRIMES IN PROGRESS

Lethal Potential

Crimes in progress comprise some of the most dangerous types of CFS to which police officers must respond. Many police officers are killed answering crimes in progress calls each year. For example, between 1985 and 1994, 269 of 708 (38 percent) of all police officers killed were responding to crimes in progress and other arrest situations (U.S. Department of Justice, Federal Bureau of Investigation, 1996:378). The danger comes from the fact that in most cases perpetrators know the police are coming and have time to seek a defensive advantage. Also, upon arrival the officers are ofttimes extremely vulnerable as they exit their patrol vehicle, approach the location, attempt to obtain information, and search out any suspects (see Table 11–1).

Another danger in responding to crimes in progress calls is automobile accidents. Between 1980 and 1993, 543 of 1,074 (50.6 percent) of all officers who were accidentally killed, died in automobile and motorcycle accidents (U.S. Department of Justice, Federal Bureau of Investigation, 1996:380). Many of these deaths occurred as officers responded to crimes in progress or hot pursuits. In addition to deaths and injuries, accidents also result in a large number of civil suits brought against police departments by citizens who are struck by police vehicles.

Police officers frequently do not use their emergency equipment (lights and siren) in an effort to "run silent" and keep perpetrators from being alerted to their response. This creates a dangerous situation, especially if officers are responding at a high rate of speed. Automobile accidents often occur, and police officers are held at fault. Therefore, police departments must ensure that when officers are not using their emergency equipment, they do not violate traffic laws and have their vehicles constantly under control. It is critical that supervisors ensure that officers follow state statutes and departmental policies in this regard.

Tactical Considerations

Once a crime has been reported, it is critical that dispatchers obtain as much information as possible. It is especially important that the exact location of the incident, descriptions of suspects and vehicles and their whereabouts, possible weapons involved, and witness and victim information are obtained. If a suspect is on the scene, the dispatcher should maintain contact with the caller and provide updated information to all responding officers.

Sufficient police units should be dispatched to the scene of a crime in progress. Supervisors should ensure that responding units converge on the scene from different directions so that police officers can observe as many getaway routes as possible. Indeed, supervisors should coordinate and direct officers' responses to ensure that the maximum number of avenues of escape are covered. Even when a description of the perpetrators or their vehicle is not available, officers should look for suspicious vehicles and conduct field interviews of suspicious persons. These field interviews often result in the capture of the suspects or the identification of eyewitnesses.

TABLE 11.1 Summary of Law Enforcement Officers Killed on Duty

(By circumstances at scene of incident, United States, 1978–95)

Circumstances at scene of incident	Total	1978	1979	1980	1981	1982	1983	1984	1985	1986	1987	1988	1989	1990	1991	1992	1993	1994	1995
Total	1,420	93	106	104	91	92	80	72	78	66	74	78	66	66	71	63	70	76	74
Disturbance calls	226	10	17	12	19	18	15	8	13	7	23	7	13	10	17	11	10	8	8
Bar fights, man with gun, etc.	122	5	13	6	14	11	10	7	6	5	10	4	5	5	8	2	5	4	2
Family quarrels	104	5	4	6	5	7	5	1	7	2	13	3	8	5	9	9	5	4	6
Arrest situations	563	39	47	49	38	36	31	33	29	26	27	33	24	30	14	26	29	31	21
Burglaries in progress/ pursuing buglary suspects	64	3	7	8	6	3	4	2	4	1	6	3	0	1	3	5	1	3	4
Robberies in progress/ pursuing robbery suspects	207	15	19	22	17	14	11	9	12	9	4	7	8	13	4	10	10	16	7
Drug-related matters	95	6	6	9	2	5	6	4	6	7	4	12	7	5	3	3	3	3	4
Attempting other arrests	197	15	15	10	13	14	10	18	7	9	13	11	9	11	4	8	15	9	6
Civil disorders (mass disobedience, riot, etc.)	1	0	0	0	0	1	0	0	0	0	0	0	0	0	0	0	0	0	0
Handling, transporting, custody of prisoners	60	7	3	1	1	3	3	3	4	5	6	2	6	2	6	2	1	1	4
Investigating suspicious persons/circumstances	207	8	9	16	10	11	10	12	9	11	5	23	10	9	10	7	15	15	17
Ambush situations	140	12	11	7	9	9	9	8	7	4	4	6	4	8	11	7	4	6	14
Entrapment/premeditation	77	11	8	2	5	7	6	4	5	2	3	2	2	2	5	5	2	0	6
Unprovoked attack	63	1	3	5	4	2	3	4	2	2	1	4	2	6	6	2	2	6	8
Mentally deranged	28	3	4	2	2	2	1	0	0	3	1	1	2	1	0	0	1	4	1
Traffic pursuits/stops	195	14	15	17	12	12	11	8	16	10	8	6	7	6	13	10	10	11	9

Note: These data include Federal, State, and local law enforcement officers feloniously killed in the United States, Puerto Rico, American Samoa, Guam, the Northern Mariana Islands, the Virginia Islands, and abroad.

Source: U.S. Department of Justice, Federal Bureau of Investigation, *Law Enforcement Officers Killed and Assaulted, 1987,* p. 31; *1990,* p. 17; *1994,* p. 17; *1995,* p. 31; FBI Uniform Crime Reports (Washington, DC: USGPO).

It is critical that the dispatcher, responding officers, and supervisor work as a team when responding to a crime in progress. Field supervisors must ensure that responding officers follow police procedures and are provided with the best possible information. This is important because initial tactical decisions made by officers is guided by information obtained by the dispatcher.

STREET DRUG ENFORCEMENT OPERATIONS

Relatively speaking, drugs in the United States is a rather recent phenomenon. In 1960 less than 5 percent of the nation's population and perhaps less than 25 percent of the criminal population had tried illegal drugs (Johnson et al., 1990). However, the substantial increase in marijuana after 1965, the heroin epidemic of 1965 through 1973, the cocaine epidemic of 1975 through 1984, and the recent crack epidemic resulted in substantial numbers of citizens and criminals using illegal drugs. This increase has led to a complete rethinking of police operations; almost everything police departments do today is directly or indirectly related to or affected by the drug problem.

Perhaps the best way to understand street drug enforcement is to consider the criminal activities associated with drugs, and then progress to enforcement tactics. The police can better assemble effective tactics if they first understand the problem. Also, it must be understood that there is no simple solution to drug-related criminality. Since there are a variety of types of drug dealers, drug users, and criminals involved in drug-related crime, the police must devise and adopt tactics that target each type. In short, there is no panacea for addressing the problem.

Drug-Related Criminality

Many people in the law enforcement community have long operated under the assumption that drugs and crime are directly and undisputedly related; that is, drugs cause crime. People who use drugs ultimately become involved in criminal activities. This view has been supported by the fact that many criminals are drug abusers, and drug abusers are disproportionately represented in the prison population. More than one-third (36 percent) of all male state prison inmates used illegal drugs daily in the month before their offense, and 31 percent were under the influence of drugs at the time of their current offense (Maguire et al., 1993).

Several types of drug dealers merit the special attention of police. The first class is street drug dealers. Research shows that many drug dealers are not dangerous and drift in and out of selling; they tend to use drug selling as supplemental income or to obtain drugs (Johnson et al., 1985). However, those drug dealers who sell drugs openly in the streets tend to commit high rates of predatory crimes and are much more dangerous to society.

A second type of drug offender includes juvenile drug users. When drug abuse begins at an early age, the abuse tends to extend into adulthood and abusers tend to graduate to more addictive drugs, such as methamphetamines, cocaine, and heroin. A large percentage of the individuals who commit significant numbers of predatory crimes also are drug abusers. Drug abuse does not necessarily lead to criminality, but the two problems seem to coexist. Regardless, early intervention may reduce criminality and more serious drug abuse.

Finally, a third type of offender that deserves special police attention is the hard core addict, who tends to commit large numbers of crimes in an effort to produce the income needed to maintain the drug habit. Although the vast majority of these crimes are property crimes, some addicts become involved in crimes against persons, such as robbery.

Enforcement Tactics

The selection and implementation of drug enforcement tactics depends largely on the nature and setting of the problem. For example, where the problem is dispersed across jurisdictional boundaries, law enforcement agencies often employ multijurisdictional task forces (Schlegal and McGarrel, 1991; Chaiken, Chaiken, and Karchmer, 1990). In jurisdictions where the problem is more concentrated in urban centers or neighborhoods, police tend to deploy a variety of additional tactics to counter drug activities.

Traditionally, the police have targeted the substance abuser and dealer by employing such tactics as undercover surveillance, **street sweeps,** and criminal prosecution (Hayslip, 1989). Today, the police have greatly expanded their approaches to drug problems by employing such strategies as improving the physical environment, removing offenders, reduced demand, improved intelligence, empowering residents, and community policing and problem solving. The police supervisor is actively involved in these approaches as they deploy their subordinates—plainclothes and uniformed patrol officers.

In terms of improving the physical environment, a number of agencies have trained officers in crime prevention through environmental design (CPTED) techniques. CPTED helps the officer identify environmental factors that may be linked to crimes—including drug dealing. By removing these environmental factors, the officer may be more successful in reducing or eliminating the particular drug problem. For example, police officers in Tampa, Florida, recognized that drug dealing in a public housing complex was often conducted in areas with poor exterior lighting, so the officers conducted a lighting survey. With the assistance of the local utility company and the city, the officers had the lighting upgraded and broken lights repaired, resulting in a reduction of drug activity in the area (Weisel, 1990). Other environmental design tactics such as neighborhood cleanups in Atlanta, erecting fences in North Charleston, South Carolina, and improved security and access control in Chicago, have resulted in similar successes at reducing drug traffic (Weisel, 1990).

Eradicating neighborhoods of dealers has long been a top priority of police. The police utilize a number of strategies focusing on dealers. In some cases, agencies simply saturate an area where dealers are concentrated and make mass arrests. This is often done by uniformed officers, in hopes of simply dispersing the dealers to other areas. **Buy-bust programs** are also a popular strategy. Here, undercover officers make street buys of drugs and the dealer is immediately arrested by another team of officers. Buy-bust programs often yield a high number of arrests.

Increased prosecution through career criminal programs are another method of removing dealers. Under career criminal laws, police can target the repeat offender and seek higher penalties of incarceration, thus removing the offender from the street for longer periods of time. Laws providing for the seizure of criminal assets from drug dealers are also commonly used by the police. Police agencies throughout the United States have seized boats, cars, planes, and cash from drug dealers under federal and state seizure laws (Weisel, 1990).

Reducing demand is another drug enforcement strategy that may be employed. Here, police focus more attention on the chronic user. The Drug Recognition and Enforcement (DRE) program is a popular strategy. Officers who are trained in drug recognition techniques (such as gaze nystagmus, which focuses on the condition and movement of the user's eyes) are able to identify the user. Programs like DRE provide the supervisor with a powerful tool for dealing with beat drug problems.

Improved intelligence also serves to assist police in addressing drug problems. For example, a landlord/tenant training program conducted by Nashville, Tennessee, police resulted in a collaborative effort in a public housing complex to rid the area of drug dealers. In other jurisdictions police have surveyed residents about drug problems and offenders in the area and instituted confidential "narcotic tip lines" to gather information about local drug problems (Weisel, 1990).

The emergence of community policing and problem solving has also resulted in numerous efforts between the police and residents to rid neighborhoods of drug problems. For example, in Philadelphia, police worked with a group of citizens—Concerned Black Men—to bring black role models to the community in hopes of reducing drug problems in poor neighborhoods. In Tulsa officers initiated a program known as Young Ladies Self-Awareness Organization to help youths with employment in hopes of diverting them from drugs (Weisel, 1990). Many police agencies now train their patrol supervisors and officers to employ problem-solving strategies to drug problems. This approach is discussed in more detail in Chapter 13.

America's drug problems are no longer the exclusive domain of large cities. Volumes of drugs are being sold and consumed in the smallest of cities and placing a tremendous load on police resources and personnel. The newer and innovative strategies for addressing this problem engage the police supervisor and officer in ways never before experienced.

POLICING YOUTH GANGS

Definition and Causation

Understanding the gang problem can come only after we have developed a concrete definition of gangs. For example, all neighborhood or street-corner groups are not "gangs," especially when many such groups are law abiding and seldom cause problems. In essence, there are near-groups, wanna-bes, and other groups that sometimes give the appearance of gangs. What behaviors must occur for a gang to exist? Klein and Maxson (1990) identified three criteria that distinguish **gangs:** (1) community recognition that the group is a gang; (2) recognition by the group itself that it is a gang; and (3) enough illegal activities to result in a consistent response from law enforcement and neighborhood residents. Sanders (1994:20) has defined a gang as

> any transpersonal group of youths that shows a willingness to use deadly vio-
> lence to claim and defend territory, and attack rival gangs, extort or rob money,
> or engage in other criminal behavior as an activity associated with its group,
> and is recognized by itself and its immediate community as a distinct danger-
> ous entity. The basic structure of gangs is one of age and gender differentiation,
> and leadership is informal and multiple.

The critical point in identifying a gang is that its members are willing to use violence to defend their territory. This violence is what separates gangs from other
groups of juveniles. Such a definition requires that the police associate specific
activities and social relationships to individuals.

Although gangs seem to be a recent problem, they have existed for many
years. They were present in many U.S. cities in the 19th century (Hyman,
1984); it has been estimated that in 1855 New York City alone had more than
30,000 gang members (Asbury, 1971). It has also been estimated that some of
the Hispanic gangs in Los Angeles have fourth-generation members (Donovan, 1988), and that the names of some Los Angeles gangs date back 60 years
(Pitchess, 1979).

Gangs and their membership are often a product of socioeconomic conditions and tend to develop and expand during periods of rapid social change and
instability. Further, deterioration of the family and other institutions of social
control tend to cause an increase in gang activity. When social conditions dete-
riorate, the gang tends to serve as an extended family for many juveniles.

However, it should not be assumed that juveniles join gangs only because
of poverty or for the pursuit of wealth. A 1995 study of the two largest youth
gangs in Los Angeles, the Crips and the Bloods, determined that most young
men who join gangs "grow up in dangerous family environments" and that
members may affiliate with gangs "to escape the violence of home, or drift away
because they are abandoned or neglected by their parents." There have also
been a number of studies which indicate that large numbers of gang members
come from the middle- and lower-middle classes (Spergel, 1990). Furthermore,
Cartwright, Tomson, and Schwartz (1975) speculated that much of the crime
committed by gang members is more for the social recognition from peers than
for the monetary benefits. Thus, gangs are social structures serving sociological
ends and not solely vehicles for economic independence.

Extent and Organization

Today, gangs are a substantial problem in most U.S. cities. A recent survey spon-
sored by the National Institute of Justice (see Curry et al., 1994) found 4,881
youth gangs flourishing in the nation's 79 largest cities. Nearly half of all gang

members (47.8 percent) were African-American youth. Hispanics accounted for 42.7 percent and Asians totaled 5.2 percent. It has been estimated that Los Angeles—considered to be the "gang capital of the United States—has upwards of 1,142 different gangs and more than 143,000 known juvenile participants (Schmalleger, 1997).

Although gangs represent a significant criminal population, they are not as pervasive as depicted by some law enforcement officials and the news media; these groups often tend to attribute any crime involving juveniles to gangs or any group of juveniles to be a gang, especially in areas where gangs exist. While much violence, drug dealing, and criminal activity is gang related, a substantial amount of such activities are not so related. When media and law enforcement officials overestimate the gang problem, the public's fear of crime and social disintegration tends to increase. Communities can very easily fall into the trap of a self-fulfilling prophecy of escalating social disintegration and crime.

Horizontal Structure

Organizationally, gangs develop horizontal and vertical characteristics. The horizontal structure of gangs refers to a gang's creation of chapters or sets and coalitions with other gangs. As gangs have concentrated on the drug trade, especially crack cocaine, "supergangs" have spread across the country. Now, intercity youth gangs such as the Bloods and Crips have begun to expand into multiple gangs or units within communities and into multiple communities. Horizontal expansion has resulted in the greatest concern for law enforcement and public officials. It means that no city, regardless of size, is immune from the gang problem. Any city that has a drug market is a potential target for gangs. This also has resulted in the incorrect identification of juveniles and groups of juveniles as gangs or gang members, which adds to community fear.

Vertical Structure

The vertical structure of gangs refers to the development of a command hierarchy consisting of several types of members. Each gang has a small group of members forming the gang's core—a clique of individuals who are considered the primary gang leaders. The gang's core is generally the most prone to use violence. Each gang usually has a following of younger wanna-bes, usually 8 to 14 years of age, who desire to emulate and ultimately join the gang. There are also scavengers—nonmembers who hang around gangs attempting to reap benefits such as drugs or employment for petty activities. Associates are peripheral members who have become associated with core gang members through business or social activities. Associates occasionally work with or provide services to gang members, depending on need. Thus, membership can be very extensive, with the largest numbers consisting of noncore members.

Police Responses and Implications for Supervisors

Gangs create police problems as a result of their violence and criminality, particularly in drug trafficking. Gang violence is constantly being headlined in the nation's news media. Both innocent citizens and gang members are the frequent victims of gang violence. Basically, gangs participate in three types of violence: random, intergang, and intragang violence. **Random violence** occurs when gang members attack innocent citizens as a part of a criminal act or to impress their superiors with their savagery (Klein and Maxson, 1990). Intergang violence refers to the violence between different gangs as they (1) retaliate for past aggression or acts, (2) protect or compete for territory, or (3) recruit new members, especially in another gang's territory. Any time different gangs confront each other, there is the possibility of violence.

Today about two-thirds of all large cities (cities of more than 200,000 population) in the United States have a specialized gang unit, while about half of all smaller cities (less than 200,000) have a gang unit (Weisel and Painter, 1997).

A five-year study of gangs in five cities—San Diego, Chicago, Kansas City, Austin, and metropolitan Dade County (Miami), Florida—was illuminating in terms of recent police responses to gangs. First, it is important to note that in these cities, as in many communities across the nation, there was strong political or community pressure in the late 1980s or early 1990s to develop responses to gangs, often because of major crimes or confrontations that had occurred. Police departments typically responded by forming some type of special unit—often suppression oriented—as an initial response to major episodes of gang violence. Over time, these units evolved into a broadened response to gangs, integrating investigations, intelligence gathering, and prevention and enforcement activities.

All of the five agencies in this study, like many others across the country, engaged in some limited form of community outreach, such as making presentations to community groups concerned with how to recognize whether a youth had joined a gang, and so forth. Often, a sergeant served this training function, speaking about gangs and disseminating information about them.

Graffiti provides gang officers with important intelligence information.
Courtesy Reno, Nevada Police Deparmtent

A review of these agencies' responses determined that the police reactions to the local dynamics of gang problems generally "fit" the agency's orientation to handling crime and disorder. Rather than implement a "one size fits all" approach to gang problems, police agencies refined their approaches over time. One noteworthy trend discovered in this study was that, from 1991 to 1996, most of the agencies shifted from an emphasis on suppression to a variety of strategies that focused on education and a much stronger reliance on the involvement of line personnel instead of relying solely on a gang unit.

From these efforts, two major trends have been identified in police responses to gangs: better data collection, management, and dissemination; and enhanced collaboration with agencies external to the police agency (schools, local code enforcement agencies, probation agencies, community groups, and so on).

The important role of patrol officers in the control and prevention of gang-related violence suggests that increased efforts must be made to bring these personnel into the information loop. And as the patrol officers' role is enhanced, there will no doubt be an increased need for patrol sergeants to develop or maintain gang expertise, and a move toward competent supervision of line officers who often must be able to recognize gang graffiti or signs and determine whether or not an incident was gang related.

The second gang-related problem, drug trafficking, poses additional problems for law enforcement. Part of the problem is determining the extent to which gangs are involved in drugs. While drug use and sales are common gang activities, the media and police to some extent have given the impression that the majority of cities' drug problems are attributable to gangs. This may not be totally accurate and should be carefully analyzed by individual jurisdictions before control and prevention strategies are implemented.

Tactical Considerations

Gangs have become thoroughly entrenched in some cities while they are only beginning to appear in others. Regardless of the extent of development and entrenchment, it must be recognized that gangs represent one of the most significant problems facing the police. As such, no effort or resource should be spared in combating their presence.

If law enforcement efforts are to be effective, the police must use multiple community-based strategies, including community building, social intervention, juvenile development programs, and law enforcement suppression.

Community Building

The degree of police success in dealing with gangs is, to a large extent, limited by the level of commitment within the community or affected neighborhood. Empowerment basically means working with neighborhoods and community groups to develop cooperative relationships with the police. The police can help institute community mobilization where none exists. This means organizing groups, getting people involved, and helping them become involved in working toward community objectives. This is accomplished by identifying current neighborhood organizations such as churches, community centers, clubs, and other social organizations. Police officers can meet with these groups and assist them in their development and encourage them to become involved. Once organizations are identified, they may be networked with other organizations and government entities to increase the resources available to them. Although slow at first, this process has the potential to affect significant changes in neighborhoods.

Social Intervention

As noted above, one of the primary reasons that juveniles join gangs is to fill a void left by a deficient family structure. The police should work with other social agencies to fulfill these social needs through youth outreach and street counseling programs. The types of services provided by these programs include crisis intervention, counseling, temporary shelters, drug prevention and treatment, police athletic leagues, gang mediation, role modeling, and miscellaneous social services. The police can be instrumental by going into a neighborhood, assessing its needs, and ensuring that the right blend of programs are implemented to deal with social disintegration and crime problems. This mix generally entails a number of programs that are coordinated and networked to ensure that as many youths as possible are the beneficiary.

Juvenile Development

Juvenile development programs are designed to enhance the life skills of juveniles. Programs in this category include after-school educational tutoring, job preparation, leadership skills training, job placement, and gang education. The purpose of these programs is to provide juveniles with the skills necessary to cope with their current environment and to succeed in life. Many inner-city youths need help in obtaining jobs and preparing for their futures, and early intervention is an important way to prevent them from entering criminal careers later. In many instances the school systems have failed and social agencies typically neglect juveniles. Therefore, it falls on the police to provide these badly needed services.

Law Enforcement Suppression

The enforcement of gang activities entails a substantial effort of intelligence and suppression strategies. Once a gang problem begins, it will only spread and become more severe unless the police effectively control it. This control is effected through intelligence operations that identify key gang members and gang activities on the one hand, and police enforcement or suppression of gang activities on the other.

The first step in containing a gang problem is the assembling of gang-related intelligence. Most major police departments now have **Gang Intelligence Units (GIUs)** which perform this function. The critical task for the GIU is to identify the core members of the gang and target them for enforcement. As noted above, there are a number of wanna-bes, associates, and other individuals who interact and otherwise come into contact with gang members on a regular basis. If the police are to be maximally successful, they must target the core gang members who are the most prone to violence. This entails a substan tial intelligence effort.

Intelligence is collected by questioning suspected gang members who are arrested, talking with rival gang members, and talking with residents in gang neighborhoods. Police may learn quite a lot of information about gang leadership by observing members activities at "hangouts" and parties. This will also help police discern the core members from other members.

There are many ways that officers can collect information on gang activities. Officers should be attentive to gang graffiti, which generally mark gang boundaries. When graffiti for different gangs appear in the same location, it generally means that rival gangs are fighting over territory. The police should collect information on assaults and homicides of gang members by rival gangs. Such acts of violence are almost always followed by retaliation. Most gangs live by the credo "an eye for an eye." Finally, the police should pay particular attention to disputes involving drug sales. This usually indicates a potentially larger, violent problem.

In terms of enforcement, Sanders (1994) noted that gang members are sometimes reluctant to commit violence because of retaliation from rival gangs and the attention and resulting enforcement actions by the police. He cited several instances in San Diego where gang members would report suspects to the police in an effort to avoid police scrutiny. These examples demonstrate the effectiveness of police enforcement and suppression activities.

Clearly, some of the most effective suppression techniques include street sweeping or neighborhood crackdowns. A primary example of this technique is the Chicago Police Department's "Flying Squad" (Dart, 1992). In 1991, the department added 100 officers to its gang crime section. This squad, formed after additional personnel were added to the unit, consisted of 40 uniformed officers and three supervisors. The squad used unmarked patrol cars and worked from 5:30 P.M. to 2:00 A.M. Each night two geographical areas of approximately five city blocks were targeted. The targets were identified as a result of reported gang activity, GIU intelligence, and citizen complaints. Once on location, the unit strictly enforced all laws, including nuisance ordinances, to ensure minimal gang activity. This is a primary example of how departments can use street sweeps or neighborhood crackdowns to contend with gang activity.

However, these police activities are best implemented in conjunction with community building, social intervention, and youth programs. Law enforcement suppression treats the symptoms for a short time; other strategies such as those discussed above are required to have any long-term success.

If the above strategies are to be effective, supervisors will need to work closely with officers and assist them in obtaining the resources necessary to develop diverse responses to the complex problem of youth gangs.

VEHICULAR PURSUITS

A High-Stakes Operation

When considering the numbers of officers killed in traffic accidents, few patrol operational issues are of greater concern to police administrators and the general public than hot pursuits. Civil litigation arising out of collisions involving police pursuits reveal it as a high-stakes undertaking with serious and sometimes tragic results. The significance and loss of life associated with **police**

pursuits are graphically represented in statistics maintained by the National Highway Traffic Safety Administration (NHTSA) (1995). For example, 247 people died in the United States in 1995 as a result of police pursuits; 116 were occupants of other vehicles, 10 were police officers, and 10 were uninvolved citizens. Injuries and deaths that involve innocent third parties or that stem from minor traffic violations are extremely difficult to justify and create the greatest public concern.

The following case studies demonstrate the dangerous nature of hot pursuits:

- In Omaha, Nebraska, a 70 mile-per-hour pursuit of a motorcyclist through a residential neighborhood for expired license plates ended when the motorcyclist ran a stop sign, crashing into another vehicle and killing the female passenger on the motorcycle.
- A sheriff's deputy in Florida intentionally rammed a vehicle during a pursuit for an outstanding misdemeanor warrant, causing a collision and killing a backseat passenger.
- A police officer pursuing a shoplifter in Mobile, Alabama, crashed into a mall security vehicle, seriously injuring the guard.

Many injuries have resulted from police roadblocks, legal interventions (ramming suspects' vehicles) and shooting at fleeing felons and misdemeanants over the years. These and many other tragic stories are all too common. The injuries

The danger of high-speed police pursuits is all too evident in the number that result in accidents, with injuries or death.
Courtesy Sparks, Nevada Police Department

and losses of life are even more tragic when evaluating the circumstances preceding the decision to engage in high-speed chases. Case Study 11–2 examines a hot pursuit gone awry.

A Look at the Research

Data concerning police pursuits prior to 1982 are noticeably absent from the literature. Two early reports—by the New Jersey Physicians for Automobile Safety (1968) and the NHTSA (1970)—provide the most insight about what occurred with police pursuits.

The New Jersey physicians' report, which described the findings of a 10-year study of newspaper articles of police pursuits, concluded that 20 percent of pursuits ended in a death, 50 percent involved some injury, and 70 percent resulted in an accident. The NHTSA study revealed similar findings and estimated that between 50,000 and 500,000 police pursuits occur each year in the United States, resulting in 6,000 to 8,000 crashes. Of those crashes, 300 to 400 persons are killed and 2,500 to 5,000 are injured. In 90 percent of the cases, police initiated the pursuit as a result of a traffic violation.

Case Study 11–2
Can "the Long Arm of the Law" Reach Too Far?

Saturday night downtown is usually very hectic, with the teenage cruisers, drunks, and "fender-bender" accidents. Motorcycle officers have little time to relax on those nights. During the beginning of a shift, Officer Thompson observes a blue 1996 Camaro go through a stop sign at Second and Main Avenues. When he attempts to stop the vehicle, a high-speed pursuit ensues. Thompson radios the license plate of the vehicle as it accelerates to more than 70 miles per hour, and drives away from the downtown into a residential neighborhood. Thompson continues to pursue the vehicle at speeds exceeding 50 miles per hour when the dispatcher advises him that there are no warrants on the vehicle or its owner. At that point his supervisor, Sgt. Bevins, in accordance with departmental policy, orders Thompson to terminate the pursuit, which Thompson does. While on an unrelated traffic stop about an hour later, Thompson observes a blue 1996 Camaro pass by. He runs to his motorcycle and gets close to the Camaro as it enters an industrial park. Thompson, now determined not to lose the vehicle, and knowing there are no exits from the park, decides to wait at the park's en-

trance for the vehicle to exit. He turns off the motorcycle's lights.

Suddenly, the Camaro speeds toward Thompson at a high rate of speed. Thompson immediately turns his headlights on and activates his siren and red lights. The driver of the Camaro, startled by the lights and siren, swerves to miss Thompson's motorcycle and crashes into a ditch, seriously injuring all four juvenile passengers. The ensuing investigation revealed that the Camaro was *not* the same vehicle that Thompson had pursued earlier in the evening; the driver had taken his father's car and gone to the industrial park, which was a popular place to race.

1. What, if any, errors in judgment did Thompson commit?
2. Evaluate the supervisor's decision in this matter.
3. On what basis might claims of negligence and liability be filed against Thompson? The supervisor? The city (for any lack of training and control over its officers)? Will such claims be successful?

Aside from these early statistics, several more recent studies of police pursuits stand out for their comprehensiveness and scope and help us to understand the causal factors and outcomes of police pursuits. In 1983 the California Highway Patrol (CHP) conducted a detailed analysis of 683 pursuits initiated by 5,800 CHP officers and 4,150 officers of 10 allied California law enforcement agencies (CHP, 1983). In 1985 Erik Beckman, a professor at Michigan State University (MSU) and pioneer in police pursuit studies, released an evaluation of 424 pursuits involving 40 police departments and 35 sheriff's departments in nine western and southern states. Beckman (1987) made the following recommendations:

1. There should be a written pursuit policy reinforced through training and supervision.
2. Policy must be based on the balance between known offenders and the need for apprehension against the degree of hazard created by the pursuit.
3. Restrictions should be placed on pursuits.
4. There should be practical and classroom training for all officers.
5. Records should be kept on all pursuits and those periodically analyzed.
6. Special attention should be given to ramming and roadblocks.
7. There should be further data collection and exchange, research, and technology development.

Similar concerns and findings were also revealed in studies of the Metro-Dade, Florida (Alpert and Dunham, 1984) and Baltimore County, Maryland, police departments (1985), and the State of Illinois (Auten, 1991). These provide additional and comprehensive information about police pursuit practices and risks.

Following 1992 legislation in California that required police agencies to report pursuit data to the CHP, the National Highway Safety Administration developed a voluntary system for capturing pursuit-related traffic data nationwide. Reporting data for 1992 revealed that 7,323 occurred statewide. Of these pursuits, 1,698 (23.2 percent) involved traffic accidents; 1,210 (16.5 percent) resulted in injuries; 28 (0.4 percent) involved fatalities; 5,642 arrests were made; and 3,687 of those persons arrested were charged with felonies while 1,669 were charged with misdemeanors.

It would appear from these data that the pursuits involved a much higher percentage of serious incidents than has been reported in previous research. However, a much different picture is presented when reviewing the initial incidents that precipitated the pursuits. Of the 7,323 pursuits, 2,155 (29.4 percent) were initiated for felony offenses, 1,117 (15.3 percent) for misdemeanors, and 3,987 (54.4 percent) for a minor traffic infraction (CHP Report, 1992). These data are consistent with previous research findings.

Enacting Defensible Policies

In 1996 the debate over whether the police endanger the public's safety with high-speed chases was further fueled as the nation observed video footage of deputies stopping and beating illegal immigrants along a freeway in Riverside, California. In another incident shortly afterward, a van transporting 25 undocumented aliens collided with a Border Patrol vehicle near San Diego, killing two aliens and injuring 19 others (Walchak, 1996).

The concern about "hot pursuit" is not new. In 1971 the International Association of Chiefs of Police (IACP) recognized the increased concern among police administrators concerning hot pursuits and responded with a model policy, urging the adoption of written policies by local agencies. At the IACP's annual conference in 1996, its membership adopted a resolution and the model pursuit policy to serve as a guideline for police executives. The resolution and policy, based on recommendations from the National Commission on Law Enforcement Driving Safety, was provided to the IACP's Highway Safety Committee. The resolution and policy as shown in Table 11–2 is purposely generic in nature so that agencies can adapt it to their specific needs.

Pursuit policies provide general guidelines for the officer and supervisor. Alpert (1983) identified the following issues that should be considered in a pursuit policy.

1. When to continue (initiate a pursuit).
2. Police units authorized to participate and their roles.
3. Supervisory roles and responsibilities.
4. Multijurisdictional pursuit issues.
5. Driving tactics.
6. Permissible and impermissible exceptional tactics.
7. Air support.
8. Termination.
9. Capture of suspect.
10. Reporting and postpursuit analysis.

The courts will evaluate these policy issues when considering whether an agency or its officers and supervisors should be held culpable for damages or injuries resulting from pursuits.

Pursuit Liability

The liabilities associated with pursuits should be a primary concern of every police administrator. The courts have awarded numerous six- and seven-figure settlements to plaintiffs seeking redress for injuries, damages, or deaths resulting from police pursuits (Zevitz, 1987). The development of pursuit policies and officer and supervisor training can help to protect agencies against liability suits.

It is the responsibility of command personnel and supervisors to ensure that officers thoroughly understand and comply with pursuit policies. In addition to the issues identified above, the courts have considered other factors in evaluating pursuit liability (Falcone et al., 1994:60).

The reason for the pursuit. Does it justify the actions taken by the officer?

Driving conditions. Any factor that could hinder an officer's ability to safely conduct a pursuit should be considered sufficient reason to terminate it.

The use of police warning devices. Typically, state statutes require lights and siren.

Excessive speed. This often depends on environmental conditions. For example, a 30 mile-per-hour pursuit in a school zone may be considered excessive and dangerous.

TABLE 11.2. IACP Model Vehicular Pursuit Policy

Following are selected portions of the Sample Vehicular Pursuit Policy that was approved at the 103rd Annual Conference of the International Association of Chiefs of Police in Phoenix, Arizona, on September 30, 1996. Note the responsibilities of the supervisor as they pertain to communications, coordination, participation, and possible termination as they relate to the pursuit:

I. *Purpose*
   The purpose of this policy is to establish guidelines for making decisions with regard to pursuits.

II. *Policy*
   Vehicular pursuit of fleeing suspects can present a danger to the lives of the public, officers, and suspects involved in the pursuit. It is the responsibility of the agency to assist officers in the safe performance of their duties. To fulfill these obligations, it shall be the policy of this law enforcement agency to regulate the manner in which vehicular pursuits are undertaken and performed.

III. *Procedures*
   A. Initiation of Pursuit
      1. The decision to initiate pursuit must be based on the pursuing officer's conclusion that the immediate danger to the officer and the public created by the pursuit is less than the immediate or potential danger to the public should the suspect remain at large.
      2. Any law enforcement officer in an authorized emergency vehicle may initiate a vehicular pursuit when the suspect exhibits the intention to avoid apprehension by refusing to stop when properly directed to do so. Pursuit may also be justified if the officer reasonably believes that the suspect, if allowed to flee, would present a danger to human life or cause serious injury.
      3. In deciding whether to initiate pursuit, the officer shall take into consideration:
         a. Road, weather, and environmental conditions.
         b. Population density and vehicular and pedestrian traffic.
         c. The relative performance capabilities of the pursuit vehicle and the vehicle being pursued.
         d. The seriousness of the offense.
         e. The presence of other persons in the police vehicle.
         Upon engaging in a pursuit, the officer shall notify communications of the location, direction, and speed of the pursuit, the description of the pursued vehicle, and the initial purpose of the stop. When engaged in pursuit, officers shall not drive with reckless disregard for the safety of other road users.
   C. Supervisory Responsibilities
      1. When made aware of a vehicular pursuit, the appropriate supervisor shall monitor incoming information, coordinate and direct activities as needed to ensure that proper procedures are used, and have the discretion to terminate the pursuit.
      2. Where possible a supervisory officer shall respond to the location where a vehicle has been stopped following a pursuit.

Source: International Association of Chiefs of Police, Sample Vehicle Pursuit Policy, *Police Chief* (January 1997), p. 20.

Demonstrations of due regard in officers' actions. Officers who choose the course of safety will create the least danger to all parties affected and maintain the highest degree of protection from liability.

The use of deadly force. There are few instances in which officers can justify driving tactics that result in the death of a fleeing driver. Situations that could result in the death of a fleeing party, such as roadblocks, boxing in, and ramming, should be viewed in light of the Supreme Court's decision in *Tennessee* v. *Garner* (1985). There, the court held that the use of deadly force, where the suspect poses no threat to the officer or to others, is not justified.

Departmental policies and state law. These must be obeyed; to do otherwise greatly increases the potential liability of both the officer and department.

Appropriate supervision and training. In the absence of such measures, the department will be subject to a finding of negligence, and liability will attach.

Clearly, officers have a duty to apprehend people who violate the law, and citizens have a duty to obey police officers. The challenge for police officers lies in striking a balance between the need to apprehend fleeing motorists and the dangers inherent in pursuit. And the role and responsibilities of supervisors are deeply ingrained in the liability chain of every pursuit. By exercising proper control over their officers, supervisors can protect them and the public from potential injury or death and the department from unnecessary litigation.

SUMMARY

This chapter has addressed five types of calls for service commonly handled by police that pose substantial danger in terms of life and property: domestic violence situations, crimes in progress, drug and gang enforcement, and vehicle pursuits. If police are to effectively address these situations, supervisors must apply the proper control and guidance to ensure that officers follow departmental procedures and the law.

As we noted at the chapter's beginning, the supervisor is at the heart of the police response to patrol operations. Supervisors are responsible for ensuring that commanders are notified of situations and that adequate resources are provided. They must also take charge at the scene until other support units arrive. The supervisor, in essence, often must make critical operational and tactical decisions while using appropriate resources.

KEY TERMS

domestic or family
   violence   (p. 268)
street sweeps   (p. 275)
buy-bust
   programs   (p. 275)

gangs   (p. 277)
random violence   (p. 278)
juvenile development
   programs   (p. 281)

Gang Intelligence Units
   (GIUs)   (p. 281)
police pursuits   (p. 283)

ITEMS FOR REVIEW

1. Describe the problems and potential for liability that might occur when the police deal with domestic violence situations.
2. Explain the supervisor's role in situations where the police respond to crimes in progress.
3. Compare the different enforcement tactics that the police use for dealing with the drug problem.
4. Define a gang, and explain why people become members of gangs.
5. Describe the two major trends that have been identified in police responses to gangs. What are some specific activities that the police have used to control gang activities?
6. Explain the supervisor's role in vehicular pursuits. Describe the factors the courts consider in evaluating pursuit liability.

SOURCES

ALPERT, G. P. (1997). "The management of police pursuit driving: Assessing the risks." In R. G. Dunham and G. P. Alpert (eds.). *Contemporary Issues in Policing: Contemporary Readings.* Prospect Heights, Ill.: Waveland.

ASBURY, H. (1971). *Gangs of New York: An informal history of the underworld.* New York: Putnam. (Originally published in 1927)

AUTEN, B. (1991). *Police pursuit driving in Illinois, 1990.* Chicago: University of Illinois Police Training Institute.

BECKMAN, E. (1985). *A report on law enforcement and factors in police pursuits.* (10):I. Michigan State University, School of Criminal Justice.

BECKMAN, E. (1987). "Identifying issues in police pursuits: The first research findings." *Police Chief* (7): 61–63.

BELKNAP, J. (1990). "Police training in domestic violence: Perceptions of training and knowledge of the law." *American Justice Society* 14(2): 248–67.

BERK, R. A., BERK, S. F., LOSEKE, D. R., and RAUME, D. (1983). "Mutual combat and other family violence myths." In D. Finkelhor, R. Gelles, G. Hotaling, and M. Straus (eds.). *The Dark Side of Families: Current Family Violence Research.* Beverly Hills: Sage.

CALIFORNIA HIGHWAY PATROL (1983). *California highway patrol pursuit study.* Sacramento, Calif.: California Highway Patrol.

CALIFORNIA HIGHWAY PATROL REPORT. (nd). *Police pursuit data: Report to the legislature.* Management Services Division, Sacramento, Calif.: California Highway Patrol.

CARTWRIGHT, D. S., TOMSON, B., and SCHWARTZ, H. (1975). *Gang delinquency.* Monterey, Calif.: Brooks/Cole.

CHAIKEN, J. M., CHAIKEN, M. R., and KARCHMER, C. (1990). *Multijurisdictional drug law enforcement strategies: Reducing supply and demand.* Washington, D.C.: U.S. Department of Justice.

CURRY, G. D., BALL, R. A., and FOX, R. J. (1994). *"Gang crime and law enforcement recordkeeping."* Washington, D.C.: National Institute of Justice.

DART, R. W. (1992). "Chicago's flying squad tackles street gangs." *Police Chief,* December: 96–104.

DONOVAN, J. (1988). "An introduction to street gangs." A paper prepared for Senator J. Garamendi's Office, Sacramento, Calif.

FALCONE, D. N., CHARLES, M. T., and WELLS, E. (1994). "A study of pursuits in Illinois." *Police Chief* (7):59–64.

FELD, S. L., and STRAUS, M. A. (1989). "Escalation and desistance of wife assault in marriage." *Criminology* 27:141–61.

FYFE, J., and FLAVIN, J. (1991). "Differential police processing of domestic assault complaints." Paper presented at the annual meeting of the Academy of Criminal Justice Sciences, Nashville, Tenn.

GELLES, R. J., and STRAUS, M. A. (1988). *Intimate violence.* New York: Simon and Schuster.

HAYSLIP, D. (1989). *Local-level drug enforcement: New strategies.* NIJ Reports/No. 213, April–May. Washington, D.C.: National Institute of Justice.

HYMAN, I. A. (1984). *Testimony before the subcommittee on elementary, secondary, and vocational education of the committee on education and labor.* U.S. House of Representatives.

JOHNSON, B. D., WILLIAMS, T., DEI, K. A., and SANABRIA, H. (1990). "Drug abuse in the inner city: Impact on hard-drug users and the community." In M. Tonry and J. Q. Wilson (eds.). *Drugs and Crime.* Chicago: University of Chicago Press.

JOHNSON, B. D., GOLDSTEIN, P., PREBLE, E., SCHMEIDLER, J., LIPTON, D. S., SPUNT, B., and MILLER, T. (1985). *Taking care of business: The economics of crime by heroin abusers.* Lexington, Mass.: Lexington Books.

KLEIMAN, M. (1988). "Crackdowns: The effects of intensive enforcement on retail heroin dealing." In M. Chaiken (ed.). *Street-level drug enforcement: Examining the Issues.* Washington, D.C.: National Institute of Justice.

KLEIN, M. W., and MAXSON, C. L. (1989). "Street gang violence." In N. Weiner and M. Wolfgang (eds.). *Violent Crime, Violent Criminals.* Newbury Park, Calif.: Sage.

KONSTANTIN, D. N. (1984). "Homicides of American law enforcement officers." *Justice Quarterly* 1: 29–45.

MAGUIRE, K., PASTORE, A. L., and FLANAGAN, T. J. (eds.) (1993). *Sourcebook of criminal justice statistics, 1992.* U.S. Department of Justice, Bureau of Justice Statistics. Washington, D.C.: U.S. Government Printing Office.

MAXSON, C. L., and KLEIN, M. W. (1990). "Street gang violence: Twice as great, or half as great?" In R. Huff (ed.). *Gangs in America.* Newbury Park, Calif.: Sage.

NATIONAL HIGHWAY TRAFFIC SAFETY ADMINISTRATION (1995). *National Highway Traffic Safety Administration Statistics.* Washington, D.C.: NHTSA.

PITCHESS, P. J. (1979). *Street gangs.* Los Angeles: Human Services Bureau, Los Angeles Sheriff's Office.

SANDERS, W. B. (1994). *Gangbangs and drivebys: Grounded culture and juvenile gang violence.* New York: Aldine De Gruyter.

SCHLEGEL, K., and MCGARRELL, E. F. (1991). "An examination of arrest practices in regions served by multijurisdictional drug task forces." *Crime and Delinquency* 37(3): 408–26.

SCHMALLEGER, F. (1997). *Criminal justice today.* 4th ed. Upper Saddle River, N.J.: Prentice Hall.

SHERMAN, L., and BERK, R. A. (1984). *The Minneapolis domestic violence experiment.* Washington, D.C.: Police Foundation.

SHERMAN, L. (1990). *Police crackdowns.* NIJ Reports (March–April). Washington, D.C.: National Institute of Justice.

SPERGEL, I. A. (1990). "Youth gangs: Continuity and change." In M. Tonry and N. Morris (eds.). *Crime and Justice: A Review of Research.* Vol. 12. Chicago: University of Chicago Press.

UCHIDA, C., BROOKS, L. W., and KOPERS, C. S. (1987). "Danger to police during domestic encounters: Assaults on Baltimore County police, 1984-1986." *Criminal Justice Policy Review* 2:357–71.

U.S. DEPARTMENT OF JUSTICE (1984). *Attorney general's task force on family violence among friends and relatives.* Washington, D.C.: U.S. Government Printing Office.

U.S. DEPARTMENT OF JUSTICE, FEDERAL BUREAU OF INVESTIGATION (1991). *Crime in the United States: 1985-1990.* Washington, D.C.: U.S. Government Printing Office.

U.S. DEPARTMENT OF JUSTICE, FEDERAL BUREAU OF INVESTIGATION (1996).*Law enforcement officers killed and assaulted, 1994.* Washington, D.C.: U.S. Government Printing Office.

WALCHAK, D. G. (1996). "Vehicle pursuits—What are the issues?" *Police Chief* (7):7.

WEISEL, D. L. (1990). *Tackling drug problems in public housing: A guide for Police.* Washington, D.C.: Police Executive Research Forum.

WEISEL, D. L., and PAINTER, E. (1997). *The police response to gangs: Case studies of five cities.* Washington, D.C.: Police Executive Research Forum.

ZEVITZ, R. G. (1987). "Police civil liability and the law of high speed pursuits." *Marquette Law Review* 70(2): 237–84.

ZIMMER, L. (1990). "Proactive policing against street-level drug trafficking." *American Journal of Police* 9(1): 43–74.

12

Tactical Operations and Critical Incidents

You gain strength, courage, and confidence by every experience in which you really stop to look fear in the face. You are able to say to yourself, "I lived through this horror. I can take the next thing that comes along". . . You must do the thing you think you cannot do.

—ELEANOR ROOSEVELT

I am more afraid of an army of 100 sheep led by a lion that an army of 100 lions led by a sheep.

—TALLEYRAND

INTRODUCTION

No matter where they are located in this country, police agencies face the potential each day for being confronted with a variety of tactical situations and critical incidents. Tactical operations and critical incidents may arise as a result of criminal conduct (a bombing or hostage incident), an accident (a train or plane crash), or environmental hazards (chemical spills) that pose serious threats to the police and citizens alike. Many police supervisors and veteran officers can recall occasions when they were required to deal with nature—on a tornado watch or cleaning up in its aftermath, at floods, in the wake of a major earthquake or fire, or an explosion.

A supervisor's direction and control during the first few critical minutes of these situations will often determine their ultimate outcome and the safety of those involved (Kaiser, 1990). Many agencies provide officers and supervisors basic operating procedures for handling these situations as well as the procurement of necessary personnel and equipment to prevent the further escalation of a crisis.

This chapter explores several types of tactical operations and critical incidents from the perspective of responses and supervision. We begin with a discussion of tactical responses to dangerous, confrontational situations, including barricaded persons, hostage situations, and civil disorder and riots. Then we examine other extremely dangerous types of calls for service: bombing incidents, major fires, airplane crashes, and the containment of hazardous materials. We conclude the chapter with an examination of police responses to natural disasters.

Background information and case studies are provided to illustrate the true complexities of supervising and managing for safe outcomes. An underlying theme running throughout this chapter is that supervisors must be well informed about the resources that are available to them from federal, state, and local agencies, as well as the protocol for working within established interagency cooperation, as set forth in mutual aid agreements.

PREPLANNING AND MANAGING MAJOR OPERATIONS

Key Elements and Critical Times

A key element of a supervisor's success in handling major operations is the development of comprehensive policies and procedures for tactical operations and disaster responses. The Federal Bureau of Investigation (FBI) has adopted a four-phase framework—preconfrontation/preparation, immediate response, deliberate/specific planning, and resolution—for deploying personnel and equipment with tactical situations; this process will be discussed later in this chapter.

The most critical period of time for controlling a crisis is during those initial moments when officers and supervisors arrive at the scene. They must quickly contain the situation, analyze the extent of the crisis, request additional resources and special teams if needed, and communicate available information and intelligence to headquarters. Their initial actions as first responders provide a vital link to the total police response and will often determine its ultimate outcome.

An example of how a tactical situation can have disastrous results is the response of the Bureau of Alcohol, Tobacco, and Firearms (ATF) to the 1993 incident involving a religious cult, the Branch Davidians, in Waco, Texas. Essentially, the ATF was investigating David Koresh and his followers for firearms violations. On the morning of February 28, ATF agents stormed the group's fortified compound; Koresh and his well-armed followers had become aware of the impending attack and consequently prepared themselves for the ATF's arrival. Subsequently, a 90-minute gun battle transpired and four ATF agents were killed. The ensuing investigation of the raid revealed a number of flaws in the operational plan, and that ATF raid coordinators were aware they had lost the element of surprise that was essential to the success of the raid (Department of the Treasury, 1993). The FBI was ultimately called in to take charge of the situation; after a standoff of more than 50 days, FBI agents assaulted the compound and approximately 70 people died (most succumbing to a fire set by Koresh and his followers). Much of the ensuing investigation focused on tactics used and the supervision and management of the incident.

Initial Duties and Responsibilities

The following checklist of questions provides the supervisor with necessary information to make a quick assessment of the personnel, equipment, and other resources needed during the initial stages of any critical incident.

1. What is the exact nature and size of the incident (e.g., flood, barricaded suspect holding 2 hostages, a civil disorder involving 500 persons)?
2. What is the exact location and description of its surroundings?
3. Are dangers to persons and property present, such as armed suspects, fire, or hazardous materials?
4. Are there any unusual circumstances present, such as snipers, explosives, or broken utilities?
5. Is there a need to evacuate, and are antilooting measures required?
6. Is traffic control needed?
7. Is an inner perimeter needed to control the immediate scene?
8. Are additional personnel needed for inner and outer perimeters, evacuation, rescue, and special weapons and tactics (SWAT)? Are negotiators or other specialists needed?
9. Will a **command post** (CP) and staging area for additional personnel and emergency support be needed?
10. What emergency equipment and personnel is needed, and what safe routes are available for their response to the staging area?
11. What other equipment, supplies, and facilities will be needed?
12. Are there any injured persons who require medical assistance or transport to the hospital?
13. What other needs are there? For example, food and drink for long-term incidents, tactical units, rescue operations, bomb squad, K-9, and tow trucks? (Ianonni, 1996).

It is often difficult to predict the length of time needed to bring a crisis under control. Some hostage situations may be concluded within minutes while others, like the Waco incident, can last for days or weeks. Natural disasters present another problem. While tornadoes and earthquakes may occur in only minutes, the cleanup and restoration of damaged bridges, freeways, and buildings can take months or even years. DeJong (1994) recommended that supervisors adhere to the principles of containment, communication, coordination, and control when responding to critical incidents.

Containment. **Containment** ensures that a crisis does not escalate beyond a supervisor's control or resources. Containment also protects innocent people from entering areas of danger, and allows police to isolate a suspect for apprehension in a tactical situation.

Communication. Communicating the status of a crisis to dispatch for higher headquarters and other responding personnel is a first priority for the on-scene supervisor. **Communication** may be accomplished by answering the questions above. For more prolonged operations, an emergency operations center (EOC) and/or CP should be established as a single point for command and control and centralized communications during critical incidents.

Coordination. Once effective communications have been established, the **coordination** of ongoing logistical needs becomes a priority for the on-scene commander. This would involve requests for additional personnel, equipment, and specialized units such as SWAT, hostage negotiators, hazardous materials team, and so on.

Control. At this stage, personnel and equipment are deployed to the incident. The three previous elements should be implemented before any response is attempted. Case Study 12–1 is an exercise in police response to a hostage situation.

Tactical Responses

Tactical problems present many unique concerns and dangers for the supervisor's consideration. The FBI's training for managing confrontational situations adopts DeJong's principles into a four-phase framework for organizing and deploying personnel and resources to tactical incidents:

Preconfrontation/Preparation Phase. Preparation and planning are the keys to successful outcomes of situations that may be confrontational and require a tactical response. Training should address individual officers' tactical skills, team skills (such as hostage negotiators, SWAT, and command post staff)

Case Study 12–1
"When the Going Gets Tough . . ."

An estranged husband, Donald Blair, goes to his ex-wife's school, where she is a fifth-grade teacher. A residential area borders the school on the north side; on the south side is a large shopping center with a restaurant and several other small stores; a four-lane thoroughfare borders the school on the west side; and a day care center and a retirement home are on the east. Blair enters the cafeteria, where the majority of the school's children, teachers, and principal are having lunch. He pulls out an AR-15 automatic weapon, screams to his ex-wife that she's made his life miserable, and threatens to kill her. He also states that no one is to leave the room or he will kill them. The school nurse, passing by in the hallway, overhears the commotion and

immediately contacts the police. Sgt. Hawthorne is in charge of this district and responds quickly by going to the scene. The first officers to arrive see several teachers and school children running away from the school building. One teacher points out Blair's pickup truck parked in front of the school; inside are several survival guides, empty ammunition boxes, and pipe-bomb materials.

1. As supervisor on the scene, use the 13-point checklist provided on page 294 to identify what Sgt. Hawthorne would need to do during the initial stages to gain control of this situation.
2. What additional personnel, equipment, and other resources might be needed?

and systems skills (the agency's capabilities to manage a command post). Multiagency exercises provide one method for training and testing an agency's preparation and capabilities.

Contingency Planning. Contingency planning focuses on identifying any potential problems, logistical requirements, strategies and tactics, communication needs, and command and control requirements for any tactical situation. Contingency planning provides a basis for developing standard operating procedures.

Immediate Response Phase. Control of the scene and isolating the threat is paramount in any response to a tactical situation. An initial assessment of the situation may be provided by answering the questions provided in the checklist on page 294.

Establishing an inner and outer perimeter will help to isolate the suspect and keep all nonessential personnel at a safe distance from danger. As a situation progresses in severity or time, officers must also pay attention to a variety of concerns, including ongoing intelligence about suspects and hostages, if applicable; establishing a command post to handle logistics, tactics, and negotiations separately; and documenting all actions taken.

Deliberate/Specific Planning Phase. During this phase, officers develop strategies for responding to the incident. These may include maintaining negotiations, emergency or deliberate assault, or surrender. Before initiating tactical response plans, all tactical personnel must be carefully briefed and the plans coordinated with all other responses.

Resolution Phase. Resolution entails maintaining control, negotiations, and intelligence during an incident. The goal is to end the incident without injury to anyone. Surrender is preferred, but assault may be necessary, depending on the circumstances. Supervisors should consider all available intelligence information before employing assault tactics. A direct assault should be the last resort. An after-action report should be completed following every tactical incident, identifying which tactics were successful and which were not, so that appropriate changes can be made for future operations.

Again, these matters will guide supervisors during the first few minutes of their arrival at scenes requiring tactical operations; the type of situation will dictate further measures that a supervisor and his or her subordinates must take.

The remainder of this chapter examines a number of types of critical incidents that police confront, with particular attention given to the role of the first-line supervisor.

BARRICADED PERSONS AND HOSTAGE SITUATIONS

Armed suspects who take hostages or barricade themselves into a building represent one of the most dangerous situations that the police confront. By virtue of their motives, hostage takers are extremely dangerous to police officers and citizens.

Categories

The four categories of hostage takers are: (1) traditional (a criminal trapped at the scene of a crime or escaping from a crime scene, (2) terrorists, (3) prisoners who take a hostage or hostages while escaping, and (4) the mentally disturbed.

The traditional or criminal type of hostage takers often seize captives to gain leverage to bargain for their own freedom. The second type, terrorists, are probably the most dangerous of the four types (Beall, 1976). When terrorists take hostages, the operation is usually well planned and executed; furthermore, terrorists are often prepared to die for their cause, will quickly kill hostages (Mickolaus, 1976), may be sophisticated fighters, and have probably studied antiterrorist strategies used by police. Fortunately, the United States has had few terrorist acts. However, the World Trade Center bombing in New York City in March 1993 and the bombing of the federal building in Oklahoma City in April 1995 (both of which are discussed below) clearly demonstrated that this nation has become more vulnerable to such catastrophes.

The third type of hostage situation involves prisoners in jails or prisons who take hostages, usually correctional personnel, to get publicity for perceived inhumane conditions and other grievances. The final type of hostage taker, the mentally disturbed person, is the most prevalent and perhaps least dangerous if properly trained police personnel are dealing with them. These hostage takers are either paranoid schizophrenic, have a bipolar disorder, have antisocial personalities, or suffer from hallucinations, feelings of persecution, or depression. While these psychological conditions seem unmanageable, properly trained hostage negotiators can ususally resolve these incidents without violence.

Motives

Remsberg (1986) has identified four reasons why people take hostages:

1. *Persons seeking attention.* This motive for hostage taking is prevalent among gang members, criminals, or persons with mental disorders. For example, the four gunmen who took the 30 hostages in a 1991 Sacramento hostage incident (discussed below) were attempting to obtain recognition and respect—**attention**—for their gang.
2. *Power.* **Power** is a motive behind situations where the hostage taker has a psychological need to control or dominate. For example, an employee may take hostages in the workplace to prevent being dismissed.
3. *Revenge.* This is the motive when the hostage taker is attempting to right some wrong. Many hostage situations involving families are the result of **revenge.**
4. *Despair.* **Despair** is often the motive for a perpetrator who sees no hope in his or her job, financial situation, or family life. Hostage takers with the despair motive commonly commit suicide or force the issue so that the police will kill them. This was the case in each of the following situations:

   - *Mastic, New York.* On July 18, 1989, Jimmy Hyams shot and killed his 18-year old daughter during an argument about her boyfriend. After a seven-hour barricade incident, Hyams turned his gun on himself, committing suicide. A Suffolk County police officer was also wounded during the incident.

- *Fort Worth, Texas.* On August 1, 1989, Manny Cabano walked into the Tarrant County courthouse and shot and killed his girlfriend, Juanita Hermosillo, with a .357 magnum handgun. Cabano ended the incident by killing himself after a seven-hour standoff with police.
- *Stockton, California.* On August 16, 1989, Dang Cha Xiuong violated a restraining order for the third time and took his wife and eight children hostage for 34 hours. In the end, Dang killed his wife, then shot himself (Fuselier et al., 1991).

Many hostage takers are experiencing multiple stressors, ranging from family to financial problems. They frequently lack family support systems and therefore have no emotional outlets, and they often feel isolated, alienated, and desperate (Fuselier et al., 1991).

Magnitude

These are high-profile incidents for the media; consequently, every detail of the event is usually reported in the news. For all of these reasons, the police must be careful to follow proper procedures in barricade and hostage situations.

An incident illustrating how dangerous and deadly hostage situations can become occurred in Sacramento, California, in April 1991 (Paddock and Ingram, 1991). Four gunmen took about 30 hostages in an electronics store. The gunmen released several hostages throughout the day. Later in the evening, they demanded four bulletproof vests. After several hours, the sheriff's deputies provided the gunmen with two vests. Upon receiving the second vest, a SWAT team sniper shot at but missed one of the gunmen, and deputies immediately stormed the electronics store. The other gunmen began shooting at the deputies and hostages, with the deputies returning fire. In the end, three hostages and three gunmen were killed and 11 other hostages were wounded. One hostage, who was two months pregnant, suffered a miscarriage.

In the aftermath of the siege, several of the hostages criticized the police for antagonizing the gunmen during the eight hours of negotiations. Law enforcement officials outside the department also criticized the Sacramento Sheriff's department's tactics (Paddock and Frammolino, 1991). The department was further criticized for the SWAT team's missing the gunmen—the incident that initiated the gun battle.

This incident demonstrates the inherent dangers of confronting barricaded persons or hostage situations. It also confirms the need for police officials to proceed deliberately but cautiously, and demonstrates the speed at which injuries and death can occur once an assault is initiated.

Supervisory Tasks

Although there are no hard-and-fast rules that apply to such cases, the supervisor in charge at the scene must decide whether to accede to the hostage taker's demands or refuse to do so. Generally, no "deals" will be made. But the supervisor must judge each case on its own merits, and recognize that the successful negotiation of a hostage's release will take considerable time and patience.

The motivation of hostage takers is an important factor to consider when responding to situations. For example, if the hostage taker's motive is *attention*, negotiators should respond in a firm, caring manner. Getting tough only exacerbates the situation. The *power*-motivated hostage taker requires a different approach. Here the negotiator displays power and force but must be willing to give and take. Homicide is even more likely when *revenge* is involved. Negotiators should express compassion but should be prepared to move at the slightest opportunity. Finally, the *despair*-motivated hostage taker is the most difficult. The negotiator must provide encouragement and support realistically, not false hope which can backfire and result in violence.

As part of a tactical plan for neutralizing and arresting the hostage taker, the supervisor must attend to the following tasks or delegate them appropriately (adapted from Iannone, 1994:272):

1. *Secure the premises.* Officers should be posted at the front and rear of the premises and in other locations to prevent an escape.
2. *Command post.* Locate the command post in a safe, strategic area upwind from the scene to avoid contamination if gas is used.
3. *Injured persons.* Give aid, interview, and remove.
4. *Communications.* Notify headquarters of the situation.
5. *Personnel support.* Acquire necessary personnel to cordon off the area and for operations at the scene.
6. *Special equipment.* Request gas grenades, masks, body armor, marksmen and rifles, portable communications equipment, loudspeakers for communicating with the suspect, portable lights and generators, helicopter patrol, and ambulance and fire vehicles as needed.
7. *Staging area.* Locate a staging area where officers and equipment are to report upwind from the scene of the incident.
8. *Identify officers as they report.* Assign officers to positions where they can secure escape routes without exposing themselves to crossfire.
9. *Evacuation.* Persons in the area who may be endangered by gunfire or other police operations should be removed to a safe location.
10. **Field intelligence.** Collate intelligence from police and civilians about the suspect, his or her victim, and their location. Determine the type of crimes the suspect has committed, the purpose in barricading him- or herself or seizing a hostage, the suspect's physical and mental condition, attitudes toward the police and society, and a physical description. Disseminate the latter information to personnel, so they will not mistake the hostage for the suspect.

Negotiations, for the most part, are extremely effective in bringing hostage situations to a successful end. However, the police must be prepared to respond quickly with a tactical plan if negotiations fail and the lives of hostages are endangered.

Excellent training programs are conducted by the FBI and other entities for professional hostage negotiators. Obviously, this is a delicate and difficult subject that requires much more discussion and in-depth analysis than we are able to provide here.

CIVIL DISORDERS AND RIOT CONTROL

Tendencies toward Disorder

Civil disorder is a natural part of our society and has been present ever since there were governments. Our country was born out of civil disorder: The Boston Tea Party, which helped to initiate the American Revolution, was an act of civil disobedience resulting from the perception that the tax on imported tea was unfair. The British thought it a *good* tax to stop *smuggling.* In 1863 the Draft Riots in New York City—where the poor regarded conscription as inequitable—left approximately 2,000 people dead. More contemporaneously, the riots during the civil rights movement and the Vietnam War had a profound effect on most American citizens. Several U.S. cities experienced devastating riots, and many of our best-known universities had major demonstrations where students were pitted against university administrators and the police.

Civil disorders are far more common today than most people realize. Furthermore, they can erupt from a wide range of causes, making planning and reacting more difficult. For example, in 1992 Chicago police arrested more than 1,000 people and had 95 officers injured after the Chicago Bulls won the National Basketball Association championship. As we have mentioned, the 1992 riots in the wake of the Rodney King verdicts in Los Angeles were among the worst the country has witnessed since the 1970s; New York City had a similar riot in its Crown Heights area the year before. Riots in the late 1980s in New York City (with 277 Operation Rescue demonstrators arrested at an abortion clinic) and in Miami (1 looter lost his life and 22 people were wounded after a police officer shot and killed an African American in a traffic incident) demonstrate that, although such disorders are not commonplace, there is a strong potential for several riots each year in the United States. Furthermore, they are not limited to large cities; many riots and disorders occur in medium-sized cities and towns.

Tactical Considerations

Adams (1994) noted that crowds develop into unruly mobs through a series of three stages. During the first stage, the crowd consists of a conglomeration of individuals who are attracted by the excitement or a feeling of some impending event. They tend to be individualistic, but they have the potential to rapidly band together, especially if some event causes them to focus their attention. In the second stage, leaders or agitators are able to gain the attention of individuals and get them to focus on some objective or perceived threat. Primary leaders attempt to provide a focus while secondary leaders move through the crowd inciting them to action. Crowd leaders generally develop informally based on opportunity. In the third stage, the mob reaches critical mass and focuses on some objective. At this point the crowd is likely to get out of control, which can result in the destruction of property and injury to citizens.

When a crowd situation occurs, the police have four primary objectives: containment, dispersal, reentry prevention, and the arrest of violators (Adams, 1994). Anytime there is a disorder, the police should first attempt to contain it or prevent the problem from growing larger. Containment is achieved by establishing blockades and barriers to prevent others from entering the area. This should be accomplished only when the police have adequate personnel on the scene; to attempt containment without adequate resources may only worsen the situation and risk the safety of officers and citizens.

Once adequate resources are available, the police should quickly contain the situation and begin to disperse members of the crowd. This is accomplished by forcing the passive participants on the edges to leave the area. Some will resist and move back into the core of the crowd while others will leave peaceably. Reducing the size of the crowd will effectively lessen the courage of the remaining participants. As the crowd becomes smaller, it will be easier for the police to deal with the core or more troublesome members.

Finally, the police should attempt to arrest those persons who are responsible for inciting the riot and the individuals who cause personal injury or property damage. However, the decision to make an on-scene arrest must be weighed against the potential that the arrest might further incite the rioters and cause more harm. Also, a physical arrest should not be attempted unless the police have the resources to ensure that the arrest can be effected. Another effective police tactic involves taking video and still photographs of the crowd. Photographs serve to discourage rioters from criminal behavior and to frighten the more timid into leaving the area. They also serve as evidence and can be used in court to document individuals' behavior. Finally, photographs can be used for arrest purposes at a later period to identify those who violated laws.

BOMB INCIDENTS

A Contemporary Problem

Bombs have traditionally been the weapons of choice for urban terrorist groups because of the damage they inflict on life and property. The 1990s witnessed a number of major bombing incidents:

> *World Trade Center Bombing.* In February 1993 a car bomb exploded in the 110-story World Trade Center building in New York City, killing six and injuring 1,000 people. An FBI task force joined with the New York City police to bring 22 Islamic fundamentalists to trial, four of whom were convicted.

> *Unabomber.* In April 1996 federal agents arrested Theodore Kaczynski and charged him with the crimes committed by the so-called Unabomber. The Unabomber targeted university and airline employees, among others, and had evaded authorities for more than 18 years, during which time 3 people were killed and 23 others injured in mail package bombing incidents. Kaczynski pleaded guilty to all charges in an effort to escape the death penalty.

Oklahoma City Bombing. The bombing of the Alfred P. Murrah Federal Building in Oklahoma City in April 1995 killed 168 people and injured more than 500 others. Timothy McVeigh was arrested for the bombing by federal authorities and sentenced to death in 1997. His accomplice, Terry Nichols, was convicted of conspiracy and eight counts of manslaughter on December 23, 1997.

Olympic Bombing. During the Summer Olympic Games in Atlanta in July 1996, a pipe bomb exploded at Centennial Olympic Park, killing two people and injuring more than 100. The FBI reported the device as a homemade pipe bomb. While leads continue to be actively investigated, no one has been charged with this crime.

The initial response and responsibility for lives and property at these incidents often rested with a field supervisor and officers assigned to the beat where the incident occurred. The ability of the supervisor to control and protect the scene and direct necessary resources to the area is often critical to the outcome of the investigation.

These horrific incidents provide graphic examples of the devastation and loss of life that a bombing can cause. In such incidents, a supervisor must be capable of handling them with routine precision.

The bombing of the Alfred P. Murrah Federal Building in Oklahoma City in April 1995 caused 168 deaths.
Courtesy Capt. Jim Nadeau, Washoe County, Nevada, Sheriff's Office.

Conducting a Search

Explosive devices may be easily concealed. A supervisor should organize a search that is systematic and thorough so that it can be completed in the least possible amount of time. Some agencies have trained dogs available to search for explosives. The dogs' speed is particularly useful for such a situation. Another method of search is to match a police officer with an employee or an inhabitant of the building. This person is more likely to be familiar with the premises and be able to identify suspicious packages or out-of-place items. For example, a lunchbox or package on a desk may not look out of place to a police officer but may be obviously suspicious to an employee. Police should caution employees assisting in the search not to touch any suspected device and to summon an officer.

If a device is not found, the supervisor should so advise the person who is responsible for the premises. Supervisors must avoid telling anyone the building is safe or suggesting that employees or inhabitants may return. This is the duty of the property owner or representative on scene. For a supervisor to announce that the building is safe for employees or inhabitants to return may incur a tremendous liability for the police if a bomb were to explode and injure anyone.

When a Device Is Found

If a suspected bomb is found, the responding supervisor should ensure that trained bomb specialists are summoned to the scene. There should be no attempt by on-scene officers to remove or disarm the device while waiting for expert assistance. The supervisor should direct officers to establish a perimeter a safe distance around the device in the event of an explosion so that no one suffers injuries if the bomb explodes.

Evacuation Concerns

The dangers inherent in any bomb incident, or other crisis described below, may require that a police officer or supervisor make a decision concerning the evacuation of persons from a business or residence. Under many circumstances the police do not have the legal authority to force people to leave their personal property or business. Exceptions may be persons who are mentally incompetent, crippled, aged, young, or sick; in these instances the police may assume responsibility for their safe removal from danger.

Every police agency should request an opinion from a legal advisor concerning their authority and responsibility for evacuating citizens, and develop clear departmental policies and procedures for supervisors to follow during such incidents. On one hand, a supervisor's failure to take action that might ensure a person's safety may result in criticism and liability; on the other, a supervisor's decision to force the evacuation of persons from their residence or business assumes the responsibility for the protection of their property from theft or damage.

MAJOR FIRES

The magnitude and scope of a major fire present immediate dangers to the public as well as police and fire personnel responding to such incidents. During any major fire, the field supervisor should meet with the incident commander of the fire department to determine what police control measures may be required. The supervisor should direct any resources necessary to support the fire department in their immediate rescue and evacuation efforts. Additionally, personnel should be assigned to the perimeter to control traffic and crowds of onlookers and protect fire apparatus and hoses. A vehicle driving over a fire hose can rupture it and risk the lives of firefighters who may be inside a structure using the water for protection and suppression of the fire.

When a fire is extinguished, the police supervisor should coordinate with fire department investigators to protect the scene for investigation. The police are also responsible for the protection of the property from looters. In some cases, police may have to establish a perimeter around an entire neighborhood affected by a fire and check the identification of persons asking to enter the property to retrieve personal belongings.

The Oakland Hills, California, fire on October 20, 1991, provides a good example of the complexities and dangers involved in major fires. On that day, hot, dry, gusts of winds swept the Monterey pine- and eucalyptus-covered upscale neighborhoods in the Oakland-Berkeley hills. Twenty-five firefighters were on-scene overhauling hot spots from a fire the previous day when embers blew into dry areas and quickly ignited a fire that was soon out of control. Police and fire officials initiated immediate evacuation efforts and requested mutual aid. In the end, twenty-five people died, 150 were injured, and more than 3,000 living units were destroyed in a 5.25-mile area. Damages totaled more than $1.5 billion. An after-action report pointed to the need for enhanced mutual aid, availability of water, stricter fire codes and ordinances, improved communications, and vegetation management (Parker, 1992).

AIRPLANE CRASHES

Recent Tragedies

On July 17, 1996, Paris-bound TWA Flight 800 departed New York's Kennedy Airport with 230 passengers on board. Within minutes of takeoff, a midair explosion sent the Boeing 747 crashing into the ocean off Long Island, killing everyone on board. This was the beginning of one of the most tragic incidents and longest investigations in airline history.

The aftermath of a large commercial airplane falling from the sky with hundreds of passengers is catastrophic. Police and fire personnel are usually the first to arrive at the scene of a major airline crash; they must assume the gruesome tasks of fire suppression, lifesaving, and containment and protection of the scene until the responsible airline officials and investigators arrive. The police supervisor must also be concerned with crowd and traffic control and the looting of the personal effects of passengers.

The wheels from downed TWA Flight 800, on July 17, 1996, off
Long Island, New York, are carefully brought to shore; 230
passengers died.
Courtesy New York Police Department Photo Unit.

The containment of a crash scene is often complicated by the large area or
type of terrain involved. The crashes of TWA 800 and ValuJet Flight 592 (which
killed 109 passengers when the DC-9 plunged into the Florida Everglades) presented the uncommon problem of debris being strewn over a large area above
and below water. Such complicated investigations require the collaborative efforts of local police and Federal agencies (FBI, Federal Aviation Administration,
and so forth).

Military Aircraft

Military aircraft are particularly problematic and present many potential dangers for the on-scene supervisor and officers. Depending on the type of military
aircraft involved, the existence of conventional and nuclear weapons, explosives charges for ejection canopies, and the presence of classified or top secret
materials make the handling of a military aircraft accident more difficult to supervise than civilian aircraft crashes. As a result, many agencies located near
military bases conduct joint crash response exercises and have developed mutual aid agreements for handling these occurrences.

A supervisor's primary tasks in these cases are similar to those for any aircraft accident and include coordinating immediate lifesaving and rescue operations, and containing and protecting the scene until responsible authorities
arrive. In most cases, and in accordance with National Transportation Safety

Board (NTSB) regulations, Federal Aviation Administration (FAA) investigators will respond and assume responsibility for the investigation and coordinate their efforts with the assistance of local authorities.

HAZARDOUS MATERIALS

The U.S. Department of Transportation estimates that a half-million interstate shipments of **hazardous materials** are transported daily across the United States (Donahue, 1993). This creates a tremendous potential for accidents to occur in any small town or large metropolitan area. The following news articles illustrate the potential dangers involved in hazardous materials accidents:

- Three pipefitters at the Newport News, Virginia, Navy shipyard were found dead after lethal gas and raw sewage flooded a pumproom in the aircraft carrier USS*Harry S. Truman*. About 1,800 sailors had to be evacuated (*New York Times*, July 14, 1997).
- Two warehouse workers in Port Fourchon, Louisiana, were hospitalized for exposure to toxic fumes after hundreds of barrels of drilling fluids and other chemicals caught fire (*USA Today*, June 4, 1997).
- A fire and explosion at a farm chemical distribution plant in West Helena, Arkansas, killed 3 firefighters and injured 16 others. Nearby residents had to be evacuated because of the threat of danger caused by burning toxic chemicals (*Washington Post*, May 9, 1997).
- A toxic gas explosion at the Accra Pac Aerosol Packaging plant in Elkhart, Indiana, killed 1 worker and sent 34 others to the hospital (*USA Today*, June 25, 1997).

Police Preparedness

The above incidents reinforce the need for police education and training concerning hazardous materials. Police are often among the first responders to hazardous materials accidents and may quickly become victims themselves if the proper precautions are not taken. However, only recently has the need for such training been recognized.

A 1986 report by the Office of Technology Assessment stated that only 25 percent of police, fire, and emergency medical service personnel received any hazardous materials training. This finding prompted the Occupational Safety and Health Administration (OSHA) to establish minimum training levels for emergency response personnel, including police. As a result, states now include hazardous materials training (HAZMAT) into their mandatated Peace Officers Standards and Training (POST) curriculums.

In most cases the responsibility of police is limited to containment of the scene and notification to the proper authorities. Many local fire departments now have a special HAZMAT team trained to deal with these conditions. Larger situations may require the response of state or federal agencies for assistance.

When on the scene of a suspected hazardous materials situation, the supervisor should quickly evaluate the threat, notify the proper authorities, and establish a perimeter large enough to protect the public and officers from the affects of the hazard or spill. When containing the scene, supervisors should take into consideration how large a perimeter is needed as winds, water, and other environmental conditions may aggravate a problem. Supervisors must also be aware that hazardous materials are susceptible to fire or explosion.

Multiagency Response Plans

A hazardous materials accident of any size will require the response of several agencies, including police, fire, specialized HAZMAT response teams, and ambulance services for those injured. OSHA recommends that agencies develop response plans that account for the many different types of emergencies that might occur in any jurisdiction. These plans should include the following issues:

1. Preemergency planning and coordinating with outside parties.
2. Personnel roles, lines of authority, training, and communication.
3. Emergency prevention.
4. Determining safe distances.
5. Site security and control.
6. Evacuation routes and procedures.
7. Decontamination procedures.
8. Emergency medical treatment and first aid.
9. Critiques of response and follow-up.
10. Proper use of personnel and equipment (Donahue, 1993:5).

A hazardous materials accident in Casa Grande, Arizona, in April 1983, exemplifies how a lack of preplanning, misunderstandings about command and control, and communications problems can lead to ambiguity of authority and coordination between responding agencies. Police and fire units responded to reports of smoke coming from a railcar parked near the city's downtown. Railroad officials failed to inform responding personnel that the car contained chemical white phosphorous. Decisions to evacuate were delayed for 40 minutes, and no formal system was established for the evacuation of households in imminent danger. Officials never established a command post and failed to transmit information about the dangers to additional responding units. Subsequently, five police officers succumbed to toxic smoke because they lacked self-contained breathing apparatuses. Despite the availability of six HAZMAT teams in the state, none were called for assistance. Mutual agreements were not activated until late into the incident. Crowd problems developed because police failed to announce the dangers through the media. This occurrence serves as a case study in how not to respond to a critical incident involving hazardous materials.

NATURAL DISASTERS

When Nature Rages . . .

Every year, millions of people throughout the United States are victims of natural disasters. The aftermath of an earthquake, flood, fire, or earthquake presents many challenges for the police. A few examples follow:

Hurricane Andrew. The devastation caused by Hurricane Andrew as it ripped into South Florida, Dade County, and Louisiana on August 24, 1992, made it one of the worst natural disasters to occur in the United States in terms of damage and losses. When the winds finally subsided, 15 people were killed, 250,000 people were left homeless, and 2 million people were left without phones or adequate food and water. In total, the hurricane inflicted an estimated $18 billion dollars in damage (Getz, 1996).

Ohio Floods. In March 1997 rains caused the Ohio River to flood, creating a state of emergency for 10 Indiana counties and requiring the governor to call out the National Guard to assist law enforcement and emergency services personnel with the evacuations of hundreds of families (*Indianapolis Star/ News*, 1997).

Mount St. Helens. On May 18, 1980, Mount St. Helens in Washington erupted with the power of 500 atomic bombs, spewing tons of fiery ash into the air. Within minutes, 61 people were killed and over two million fish, animals, and birds were destroyed. The eruption caused major damage to the states of Washington, Idaho, and Montana (Tilling et al., 1990).

Andover, Kansas, Tornado. On April 26, 1991, a tornado with winds of up to 250 miles per hour struck the small town of Andover, Kansas. Police drove frantically through the streets with lights and sirens in an attempt to warn residents. In the end, 13 people died and more than 350 homes were destroyed, displacing 20 percent of the city's population (Robrahn, 1991).

Nature challenges the police in many ways. Floods can quickly destroy bridges and roads, making it difficult for police to respond to citizens' needs.
Courtesy Washoe County, Nevada, Sheriff's Office Photo Unit.

Northridge, California, Earthquake. On January 17, 1994 an earthquake with a magnitude of 6.7 on the Richter Scale struck the densely populated San Fernando Valley in northern Los Angeles, resulting in a death toll of 57, 1,500 injured, and the displacement of thousands of residents. Over 12,000 buildings suffered moderate or serious damage, freeway bridges and structures collapsed, and 11 major roads into downtown Los Angeles had to be closed. One of the first recorded deaths was that of a Los Angeles motorcycle officer who accidently drove off a collapsed portion of a freeway while responding to the emergency (EQE Summary Report, 1994).

The above examples demonstrate that natural disasters do not discriminate by jurisdiction. The largest and smallest of communities may be victim to the catastrophic effects of a natural disaster. Within minutes of each of these events, large numbers of people were endangered and police and emergency services personnel were faced with a variety of complex problems. These events also required significant coordination to control and reduce the aftereffects. Figure 12–1 shows the life cycle of disasters and describes the process through which emergency managers prepare for and respond to them.

The effective management of disaster situations requires that police supervisors know what to do and to respond quickly. Life saving measures, rescues, and evacuation of persons from danger will occupy much of a supervisor's

FIGURE 12–1 Disaster Life Cycle

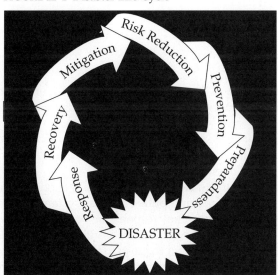

The disaster life cycle describes the process through which emergency managers *prepare* for emergencies and disasters, *respond* to them when they occur, help people and institutions *recover* from them, *mitigate* their effects, *reduce the risk* of loss, and *prevent* disasters such as fires from occurring.
Source: Federal Emergency Management Agency (FEMA) http://www.fema.gov/about/what. October 20, 1997

decision making during the initial stages of a disaster. Coordinating the responses of other emergency and fire personnel and support agencies will also be a concern of field supervisors.

Mutual Aid Agreements

The existence of interagency **mutual aid agreements** are essential for responding to disasters. Mutual aid agreements provide a coalition of reinforcements from neighboring agencies for jurisdictions that have been struck by a natural disaster. In many jurisdictions, written mutual aid agreements are developed within the planning process for emergency responses. These joint powers agreements allow for the sharing of resources among participating agencies and the establishment of clear policies concerning command and control when a disaster occurs. Mutual aid agreements are also commonly used to share personnel and equipment in a major tactical situation. Few agencies have the capability of handling a major tactical incident and must rely on the assistance of larger neighboring metropolitan agencies, county sheriff's departments, or state and federal agencies for assistance.

The Incident Command System

The **incident command system (ICS)** was originally developed as a process to manage fires, but it has been adopted by many jurisdictions to handle major disasters and emergencies.

The purpose of the ICS is to eliminate many of the problems discussed above. The components of ICS work interactively to provide direction and control over incident responses:

1. *Common terminology.* It is essential that joint operations with diverse users adopt common terminologies to reduce confusion and communications problems.
2. *Modular organization.* ICS establishes a logical hierarchical command structure with an incident commander at the head to manage all major functional areas during an incident.
3. *Integrated communications.* A common communications system including radio networks, telephones, and public address systems are established.
4. *Unified command structure.* A key responsible person for each jurisdiction involved in a multijurisdictional situation would be responsible for providing assistance and resources, upon request, to the incident commander.
5. *Consolidated action plan.* An action plan is a guide for successful resolution of the emergency and should include all potential agencies and resources for any incident.
6. *Manageable span of control.* The numbers of people supervised within the ICS should be maintained at an optimum of three to seven. The kind of incident, nature of the task, and hazards may influence span of control considerations.
7. *Comprehensive resource management.* ICS requires the continuous monitoring and status (assigned, available, out-of-service) of all personnel and equipment resources (ICS, 1983).

Case Study 12–2
"Dealing with Spills That Kill"

Metro City is a medium-sized community located in the Midwest. Three smaller incorporated cities border its jurisdiction. Union Rails, Inc., has informed the police chief of Metro City that it plans to increase the number of trains going daily through the downtown area, and that several of those trains will be carrying hazardous industrial materials. Each railcar containing such materials will be appropriately marked, and bills of lading identifying the cargo and its hazard will be available. The railroad requests a meeting with local officials to discuss the area's HAZMAT response capabilities in the event of an accident. Metro City has no such plan. As a police supervisor for planning and development, Sgt. Young has been directed to provide the police chief with recommendations concerning the impact of transporting hazardous materials through the urban area; Young must also determine what the jurisdictions need to do to prepare for the increase in rail traffic.

1. Which governmental agencies in the quad-city area would need to be involved in developing this plan?
2. What types of personnel training would be required, and where could the police agencies acquire this training for their officers?
3. What other issues might Sgt. Young need to identify for the chief?

When the ICS is properly instituted, it provides an excellent management model for handling multiagency and complex disaster responses. The ICS offers many benefits to the police supervisor working in the field. While the supervisor is engrossed in quickly assessing the magnitude of the incident, coordinating the responses of needed resources, and communicating information to superiors, the ICS command structure establishes cross-agency communications, availability of resources, and accurate and timely information. As indicated, this is crucial for the field supervisor in making proper operational decisions and may very well help to reduce the loss of lives and destruction of property during a crisis situation. Case Study 12–2 discusses the importance of planning and interagency cooperation in a hazardous materials crisis.

SUMMARY

This chapter has examined the supervisor's role in tactical operations and critical incidents, including barricaded persons and hostage situations, civil disorders and riots, bombing incidents, major fires, airplane crashes, hazardous materials, and natural disasters.

It is evident that these kinds of incidents require carefully preplanned responses. It simply will not do for supervisors to await their occurrence before developing plans to cope with them. The cost in human lives and property is potentially too great for supervisors to learn how to respond to these situations "on the job." Thus, it behooves police supervisors to be well versed in their agency's policies and procedures, as well as other resources and mutual aid agreements, for addressing these situations. Anything less would risk serious injury to officers and the public.

KEY TERMS

command post (p. 294)
containment (p. 294)
communication (p. 295)
coordination (p. 295)
control (p. 295)
contingency planning
   (p. 296)
Deliberate/specific phase
   planning (p. 296)

immediate response
   planning (p. 296)
resolution phase (p. 296)
attention (p. 297)
power (p. 297)
revenge (p. 297)
despair (p. 297)
field intelligence (p. 299)
civil disorders (p. 300)

hazardous materials
   (HAZMAT) (p. 306)
mutual aid
   agreements (p. 310)
incident command system
   (ICS) (p. 310)

ITEMS FOR REVIEW

1. Describe some of the personnel, equipment, and other resources that are needed during the initial stages of any critical incident.
2. Supervisors must adhere to the principles of containment, communication, coordination, and control when responding to critical incidents. What is involved with each principle?
3. Explain the four-phase framework for organizing and deploying personnel and resources at tactical problems.
4. List the four types of hostage takers and some of the approaches the police could take in dealing with them.
5. Describe the primary objectives of the police in dealing with civil disorder.
6. Explain the supervisor's duties in a bomb search.
7. Discuss the kinds of natural disasters that can occur, and how supervisors can help to ensure that their agencies are prepared to deal with them.

SOURCES

ADAMS, T. F. (1994). *Police field operations.* Englewood, N.J.: Prentice Hall.

BEALL, M. D. (1976). "Hostage negotiations." *Military Police Law Enforcement Journal* 3(Fall): 20–27.

DE JONG, D. (1994). "Civil disorder: Preparing for the worst." *FBI Law Enforcement Bulletin* (3): 1–7.

DONAHUE, M. L. (1993). "Hazardous materials training: A necessity for today's law enforcement." *FBI Law Enforcement Bulletin* (11): 1–6.

EQE SUMMARY REPORT (March 1994). *The January 1994 Northridge earthquake.* San Francisco: EQE International.

FUSELIER, G. D., VAN ZANDT, C. R. and LANCELEY, F. J. (1991). "Hostage/barricade incidents: High-risk factors and actions criteria." *FBI Law Enforcement Bulletin* (1): 6–12.

GETZ, R. J. (1996). "Planning for disaster: Lessons learned from hurricane Andrew." *Law and Order* (5): 80–88.

IANONNI, N. F. (1994). *Supervision of police personnel.* Englewood Cliffs, N.J.: Prentice Hall.

INCIDENT COMMAND SYSTEM. (1983). *Fire Protection Publications.* Oklahoma State University, Stillwater.

INDIANAPOLIS STAR/NEWS (1997). "Floods still plague 10 Indiana counties." (March 7).

KAISER, N. (1990). "The tactical incident: A total police response." *FBI Law Enforcement Bulletin* (8):14–18.

MICKOLUS, E. F. (1976). "Negotiating for hostages: A policy dilemma." *Orbis* 19 (Winter): 1309–25.

NEW YORK TIMES. "3 shipworkers die in leak of methane gas." 14 July 1997: A7.

PADDOCK, R. C., and FRAMMOLINO, R. (1991). "Hostages recall terror of siege in Sacramento." *Los Angeles Times* (April 16): A1, A26.

PADDOCK, R. C., and INGRAM, C. (1991). "3 hostages, 3 gunmen die in Sacramento store siege." *Los Angeles Times* (April 5): A1, A3.

PARKER, D. R.(N.D.). "REPORT OF THE OAKLAND BERKELY HILLS FIRE." Oakland Office of Fire Services, Oakland, California.

Remsberg, C. (1986). *The tactical edge: Surviving high risk patrol.* Northbrook, Ill.: Calibre Press.

ROBRAHN, S. (1991). "A national reminder of tornado destruction" [On-line]. internet. "Tornado Terror . . . " (J.A. On-line ed.).

TILLING, R. I., TOPINKA, L., and SWANSON, D. A. (1990). *Eruptions of Mount St. Helens: Past, present and future.* United States Geological Service Special Interest Report.

USA TODAY.(1997). "Indiana blast kills 1, forces evacuation." (June 25): (1997). 3A.

USA TODAY.(1997). "Port Fourchon, Louisiana." (June 4): 8A.

U.S. DEPARTMENT OF THE TREASURY (1993). *Report of the department of the treasury on the bureau of alcohol, tobacco, and firearms investigation of Vernon Wayne Howell, also known as David Koresh.* Washington, D.C.: U.S. Government Printing Office.

WASHINGTON POST (1997)."Three die, 16 injured in Arkansas blast, fire." (May 9): A15.

13

Community-Oriented Policing and Problem Solving

We are continually faced with a series of opportunities, brilliantly disguised as insoluble problems.

—John Gardner

The difficulty lies, not in the new ideas, but in escaping from old ones, which ramify, for those brought up as most of us have been, into every corner of our minds.

—John Maynard Keynes

Any solution to a problem changes the problem.

—R. W. Johnson

INTRODUCTION

A recent survey found that 50 percent of police officials serving cities with populations of more than 50,000 people were following the community-oriented approach to policing; an additional 20 percent planned to inaugurate it within a year (Peak and Glensor, 1996). According to one source, community-oriented policing "has become a mantra for police chiefs and mayors in cities big and small across the country" (Witkin and McGraw, 1993:28).

What is this concept that is sweeping the nation? This chapter responds to that question, providing a closer look at what we have termed community-oriented policing and problem solving (COPPS), and examining the very important role of the supervisor.

First, we briefly discuss the evolution of policing, from its beginning in England to its present-day status in the United States. Within this discussion is an assessment of some of the shortcomings of the professional era of policing that prevailed during most of the past 50 years, with its strong reliance on quantitative measures of police performance (e.g., response times, citations, arrests, and clearance rates). We then briefly review how policing is learning from its past and improving its ability to identify and respond to crime, neighborhood disorder, and public fear.

Next, we examine the COPPS philosophy in detail, including its origin and the process that is employed by the police for problem solving. Finally, we discuss implementation: the keys to its success, and how to fail. The role of the supervisor is emphasized throughout this discussion.

POLICING IN THE UNITED STATES: AN OVERVIEW

English Roots

To understand the roots of present-day policing and how it got to its present status with the contemporary emphasis on COPPS, we must first look back in time to early 19th-century England and the efforts of **Sir Robert Peel.** Actually, two powerful trends in England and the United States contributed to the onset of policing in both countries: urbanization and industrialization. These developments generally increased the standard of living for both Americans and western Europeans. Suddenly factories needed dependable people who could be trusted with machines.

After the end of the Napoleonic Wars in 1815, England faced worker protest against new machines, food riots, and an increase in crime. In 1822 the prime minister appointed Peel to establish a police force to quell the country's problems. Peel, a wealthy member of Parliament, found that many people objected to the idea of a professional police force, thinking that it might restrain their liberties. For seven years Peel's efforts to gain support for full-time, paid police officers failed (Johnson, 1981).

Peel finally succeeded in 1829, when Parliament passed the Metropolitan Police Act of 1829. Peel proved to be farsighted and keenly aware of the needs of both a professional police force and the public that would be asked to maintain it. He wrote that the power of the police to fulfill its duties depended on public approval of their actions; as public cooperation increased, the need for physical force by the police decreased; officers needed to display absolutely impartial service to the law; and force should be employed by the police only when attempts at persuasion and warning had failed, and then only the least degree of force possible should be used (Radzinowicz, 1968).

Americans, meanwhile, were observing Peel's successful experiment with the "bobbies" (London officers nicknamed after Sir Robert Peel) on the patrol beat. By the 1840s, when industrialization began in earnest, people began to watch the police reform movement in England more closely.

Eras of U.S. Policing

Political Era: 1840s to 1930s

The movement to initiate policing in the United States began in New York City in 1844, when the legislature established a full-time, preventive police force.

This new body was placed under the control of the city government and city politicians (Johnson, 1981). Soon policing began to spread to New England cities, New Orleans, and Cincinnati, which adopted plans for a new police force in 1852; Boston and Philadelphia followed in 1854, Chicago in 1855, and Baltimore and Newark in 1857. By 1880 virtually every major U.S. city had a police force based on Peel's model.

These new police forces, however, were born of conflict and violence. An unprecedented wave of civil disorders swept the nation from the 1840s until the 1870s. These often made for hostile interaction between citizens and the police, who were essentially a reactive force. The use of the baton to quell riots, known as the "baton charge," was not uncommon. It was not until the late 19th century that large cities gradually became more orderly (Richardson, 1970).

Partly because of their closeness to politicians, police forces during this era provided a wide array of services to citizens (Monkkonen, 1981). Police organizations were typically decentralized, with cities divided into precincts and run like small-scale departments—hiring, firing, managing, and assigning personnel as necessary. Decentralization encouraged foot patrol, even after call boxes and automobiles became available (Eck, 1984).

The strengths of this so-called **political era of policing** centered on the integration of the police into neighborhoods. This strategy proved useful because it helped contain riots and the police assisted immigrants in establishing themselves in communities and finding jobs. But there were weaknesses as well: The intimacy with the community, closeness to politicians, and a decentralized organizational structure—and its inability to provide supervision of officers—also led to police corruption. Police often ruled their beats with the "end of their nightsticks" and practiced "curbside justice" (Kelling, 1987:203, 207).

In summary, the 19th-century police officer was essentially a political operative rather than a professional committed to public service. Because the police were primarily a political institution and were perceived as such by the public, they did not enjoy widespread public acceptance. And, as political appointees, officers enjoyed little job security. Salaries were determined by local political factors. Police behavior was very much influenced by the interaction between individual officers and citizens (Walker, 1977).

Professional Era: 1930s to 1980s

The idea of policing as a profession began to emerge slowly in the latter part of the 19th century. Reform ideas first appeared as a reaction to the corrupt and politicized state of the police; partisan politics was considered to be at the heart of the problem. Slowly, the idea of policing as a profession began to gain ground. Two ideas about the proper role of the police in society also appeared. One emphasized improvement in the role of police with respect to scientific techniques of crime detection, and the other was that police officers could play a greater role in social work (Walker, 1977).

Then, in the 1930s, the **professional era of policing** came into existence. The professional model demanded an impartial law enforcer who related to citizens in professionally neutral and distant terms—personified by television's Sergeant Joe Friday on "Dragnet": "Just the facts, ma'am." The emphasis on professionalization also shaped the role of citizens in crime control. Citizens now became relatively passive in crime control, mere recipients of professional crime control services. Police were the "thin blue line" between civility and lawlessness. Professionalism in law enforcement was often identified in terms of firearms expertise, and the popularity of firearms put the police firmly in the antigun-control camp (Walker, 1977).

Citizens were no longer encouraged to go to "their" neighborhood police officers. The principal policing strategies were random preventive patrol by automobile, rapid responses to calls for service and retrospective investigations. A police presence was maintained, but the "personal" approach ended and was replaced by the case approach. Officers were evaluated by the numbers of arrests they made, the calls for service they addressed, or the number of miles they drove during a shift. The crime rate became the primary indicator of police effectiveness. Generally speaking, officers were not supposed to leave their patrol vehicles to mingle with the public; that activity was considered malingering and interfered with their random preventive patrol functions.

Civil service systems were created to eliminate patronage and ward influences in hiring and firing police officers. In some cities, officers could not live in the same beat they patrolled in order to isolate them as completely as possible from political influences (Goldstein, 1977). Police organizations became *law enforcement* agencies, with the sole goal of controlling crime. Any noncrime activities they were required to do was considered "social work." The "professional model" of policing was in full bloom.

From this emphasis on production and unity of control flowed the notion that police officers were best managed by a hierarchical pyramid of control. Police leaders routinized and standardized police work; officers were to enforce laws and make arrests whenever possible. Discretion was limited to the extent possible. When special problems arose, special units (e.g., vice, juvenile, drugs, tactical) were created instead of assigning problems to patrol officers. This began the introduction of "scientific management" to policing, discussed in Chapter 3.

The 1900s also became the age of the crime commission, most notably the **Wickersham Commission** reports in 1931. A report on "Lawlessness in Law Enforcement" indicated that the use of "third-degree" interrogation methods on suspects by the police—including the infliction of physical or mental pain to extract confessions—was widespread in America. The commission's recommendations to eliminate the corrupting influence of politics included:

- The selection of chief executives on merit.
- The testing of patrol officers who also must meet minimum physical standards.
- The provision of decent salaries, working conditions, and benefits to patrol officers.
- Adequate training, for both preservice and in-service officers.
- The use of policewomen (in juvenile and female cases), crime-prevention units, and bureaus of criminal investigation.

The major development of the 1930s was a redefinition of the police role and the ascendancy of the crime-fighter image. Professionalism came to mean a combination of managerial efficiency, technological sophistication, and an emphasis on crime control. The social work aspects of policing—the idea of rehabilitative work, which had been central to the policewomen's movement—fell into almost total eclipse (Walker, 1977).

The role of citizens in crime control and prevention also changed under the professional model of policing. While officers were to remain in their "rolling fortresses," randomly patrolling from one call to the next, citizens were essentially removed from the fight against crime.

As noted, during the professional era of policing the emphases were on law, technology, crime fighting, and the principal police strategies were rapid response, random patrol, and retrospective investigations. They also employed performance measurements such as numbers of citations, arrests, and clearance rates. As Herman Goldstein (1987:2) observed, "More attention [was] being focused on how quickly officers responded to a call than on what they did when they got to their destination." Furthermore, this era relied on quantitative measurements of and evaluation methods for officers' performance. Many departments, after recruiting the best and brightest people into the police field, required that they "park their brain" by the stationhouse door upon reporting for a tour of duty, and function like robots for the next 8 or 10 hours—going where they were sent, doing what they were told to do, following policies and procedures to the letter, and accomplishing little in the way of long-term problem solving.

A primary weakness with the traditional model was a failure to provide the patrol officer with the necessary tools, training, and incentives. Under the traditional model, officers were bored and had little sense of challenge or accomplishment. Nor were street officers given the *time* to do much thoughtful crime control or prevention. Unfortunately, we undermined the ingenuity, resourcefulness, abilities, and energies of our most valuable front-line resource: the patrol officer.

Community and Problem-Solving Era: 1980s to Present

As a result of frustration with the dominant model of policing, Goldstein (1987) formulated the concept of problem-oriented policing while exploring new methods for improving policing. Goldstein observed that more attention was focused on how quickly officers responded to a call than on what they did when they got to their destination. As a result Goldstein (1990) argued for a radical change in the direction of efforts to improving policing—a new framework that could help move the police from their preoccupation with form and process to a much more direct, thoughtful concern with substantive problems.

We are now seeing in cities and counties across the country (and indeed around the globe) that when given the necessary resources for undertaking "street-level analysis," patrol officers can have a significant impact on crime and disorder (Goldstein, 1990:68-69). Experience demonstrates that when police officers use COPPS techniques and are given the information, training, communication, and equipment to be analysts at the street level—and *if* the community is willing to become involved in this problem-solving effort—positive results will ensue.

Figure 13–1 illustrates the three eras of policing in relation to officers' authority, function, organizational design, relationship with the community, tac-

FIGURE 13-1. The Three Eras of Policing

	Political Era 1840s to 1930s	Reform Era 1930s to 1980s	Community Era 1980s to present
Authorization	politics and law	law and professionalism	community support (political), law and professionalism
Function	broad social services	crime control	broad provision of services
Organizational Design	decentralized	centralized, classical	decentralized, task forces, matrices
Relationship to Community	intimate	professional, remote	intimate
Tactics and Technology	foot patrol	preventive patrol and rapid response to calls	foot patrol, problem solving, public relations
Outcome	citizen, political satisfaction	crime control	quality of life and citizen satisfaction

Source: Summarized from George L. Kelling and Mark H. Moore, "From Political to Reform to Community: The Evolving Strategy of Police." In *Community Policing: Rhetoric or Reality.* Edited by Jack R. Greene and Stephen D. Mastrofski 6, 14–15, 22–23. New York: Praeger Publishers, 1991.

tics and technology, and desired outcomes. Next, we discuss community policing and problem solving in more detail.

NEW DIRECTIONS WITH COMMUNITY-ORIENTED POLICING AND PROBLEM SOLVING (COPPS)

Since the 1980s COPPS has emerged as the dominant direction for thinking about policing. It is an approach to crime detection and prevention that provides police officers and supervisors with new tools for addressing the recurring problems that plague communities and consume the majority of a department's time and resources. The California Department of Justice (1995) provided the following definition:

> Community-oriented Policing and Problem Solving is a philosophy, management style, and organizational strategy that promotes pro-active problem solving and police-community partnerships to address the causes of crime and fear as well as other community issues.

Two principle and interrelated components emerge from this definition: community engagement (partnerships) and problem solving. Although separate and distinct, they are not mutually exclusive. As noted by Darrel Stephens (1995), former chief of police and current city manager of St. Petersburg, Florida:

Engaging the community without problem solving provides no meaningful service to the public. Problem solving without [partnerships] risks overlooking the most pressing community concerns. Thus the partnership between police departments and the communities they serve is essential for implementing a successful program in community policing.

COPPS, with its focus on collaborative problem solving, seeks to improve the quality of policing. However, this is no simple task and several steps must be taken to accomplish this goal:

1. The police must be equipped to define more clearly and to understand more fully the problems that they are expected to handle.
2. The police must develop a commitment to analyzing problems.
3. The police must be encouraged to conduct an uninhibited search for the most effective response to each problem (Goldstein, 1987:5-6).

The SARA process discussed below provides the police with the tools necessary to accomplish these steps.

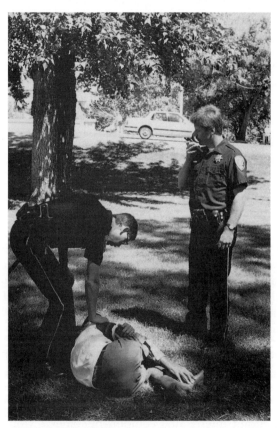

COPPS broadens officers' understanding of problems. Here, Homeless Evaluation and Liaison Program (HELP) officers assist a homeless person.
Lt Phil Galeoto, Reno Police Department

The first comprehensive experimentation with COPPS was conducted in Newport News, Virginia, in the mid-1980s. In that study, researchers, police officers, and community members developed a four-step **SARA (scanning, analysis, response, assessment)** problem-solving process to address repeated burglaries, prostitution-related robberies, and thefts from vehicles. The evaluation sought to answer two questions: Can police officers utilize a problem-solving process to address various crime concerns? And, second, can police officers apply COPPS to their routine daily activities?

The results were impressive. Burglaries in a targeted apartment complex were reduced by 34 percent, prostitution-related robberies were down 39 percent, and thefts from vehicles decreased more than 50 percent (Eck and Spelman, 1987). This study, along with others conducted in Baltimore County, Maryland; Madison, Wisconsin; and by agencies across the nation, convinced many police executives of the enormous potential of COPPS.

COPPS broadens officers' understanding of problems. It moves them from viewing incidents separately and individually toward recognizing that incidents are often related and symptoms of deeper problems. As we examine crime data, we have learned that crime is often concentrated. COPPS also teaches officers why and how crimes occur repeatedly, and what strategies they may employ toward crime-reduction strategies. Moreover, this requires officers to take a more in-depth interest in incidents by acquainting themselves with the conditions and factors that cause them. Once the causes are identified, police are better prepared to address those underlying conditions. As Fyfe (1993) observed, "Can anyone imagine the surgeon general urging doctors to attack AIDS without giving thought to its causes?"

THE SARA PROCESS

SARA (see Figure 13–2) provides officers with a logical step-by-step framework to identify, analyze, respond to, and evaluate crime, the fear of crime, and neighborhood disorder. This approach, with its emphasis on in-depth analysis and collaboration, replaces officers' short-term, reactive responses with a process vested in longer-term outcomes. Next, we discuss each component of the SARA process in detail.

Scanning: Problem Identification

Scanning means problem identification. It initiates the problem-solving process by conducting a preliminary inquiry to determine if a problem really exists and whether further analysis is needed. A problem differs from an isolated incident, which is something police are called to or happen upon that is unrelated to any other incidents in the community. A problem may be defined as "a cluster of two or more similar or related incidents that are of substantive concern to the community and to the police."

If the incidents to which the police respond do not fall within the definition of a problem, then the problem-solving process is not applicable and the officers should handle the incident according to normal procedure (crime report,

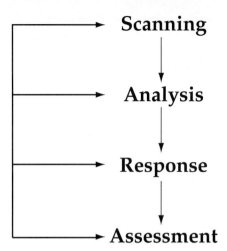

FIGURE 13-2. The SARA Problem-
Solving Process
Source: John E. Eck and William Spelman,
*Problem Solving: Problem-Oriented Policing
in Newport News* (Washington, D.C.: U.S.
Department of Justice, National Institute
of Justice, 1987), p. 43.

advisement, referral, and so on). The problems derived from repeated incidents
may vary and include:

- A series of burglaries at an apartment complex.
- Drug activity at a city park.
- Thefts of a particular type of car from several lots.
- Graffiti at a particular location or throughout a jurisdiction.
- Parking and traffic problems.
- A series of gang-related drive-by shootings.
- Robberies of convenience stores.
- Juvenile loitering-related crime at a mall.
- Aggressive panhandling at a downtown center.
- Repeat alarms to commercial businesses.

Numerous resources are available to the police for identifying problems, including calls for service data—especially repeat calls, crime analysis information, police reports, and the officers' own experiences. Other sources of information include other government agencies, public and private agencies, business,
media reports, and information obtained from the public. Scanning helps the officer to determine whether a problem really exists before moving on to an in-
depth analysis.

When considering how problems may be similar, officers should consider
the following:

Behaviors. This may include behaviors related to specific crimes such as bank
robberies, auto thefts, and burglaries, or numerous crimes resulting from
specific behaviors such as juvenile loitering, gang activity, and cruising.

Location. Research indicates that a relatively few "hot spots" (5 percent) account for nearly 49 percent of all calls for service (Sherman, 1993). Hot spots may include concentrations of crime at a public housing project owing to gang violence, a street corner where there are open market drug sales, or downtown juvenile cruising that contributes to fights, vandalism, thefts, and so on.

Persons. Both victims and offenders account for a disproportionate percent of crime. Research shows that 20 percent of repeat or "career" offenders account for 80 percent of all crimes (Spelman, 1990). Victimization research reveals that a mere 4 percent of victims account for 44 percent of total crime (Farrell and Pease, 1993).

Time. In Chapter 10 we discussed how crime and calls for service may vary greatly according to the time of day and day of the week. We also know that seasonal changes may impact crime, especially in communities where winter sports or summer vacations bring large numbers of people to the jurisdiction.

Events. Special events such as the Super Bowl, Mardi Gras, and air shows may bring hundreds of thousands of people together for a weekend and create tremendous demands on policing. Agencies must plan for these events and the types of crimes commonly associated with them.

As indicated, crime is often concentrated. By identifying those incidents that are similar in nature with one or more of the above characteristics, officers may then explore the extent of the problem using more comprehensive analysis.

Analysis: Determining the Extent of the Problem

Analysis is the heart of the problem-solving process. It is the most *difficult* and *most important* step in the SARA process. A common criticism of incident-driven policing is that officers often skip analysis in their haste to find solutions. Without analysis, long-term solutions are limited and the problem is likely to persist.

In the analysis phase of SARA, officers gather as much information as possible from a variety of sources. A complete and thorough analysis consists of the identification of the seriousness of the problem, all persons affected, and the underlying causes. Officers also should assess the effectiveness of current responses.

Many tools are available to assist with analysis. Crime analysis may be useful in collecting, collating, analyzing, and disseminating data relating to crime, incidents not requiring a report, criminal offenders, victims, and locations. Mapping and the **Geographic Information System (GIS)** can identify patterns of crime and hot spots. Police offense reports also can be analyzed for suspect characteristics, mode of operation (MO), victim characteristics, and information about high-crime areas and addresses. **Computer-aided dispatch (CAD)** is also a reliable source of information because it collects data on all incidents and specific locations from which an unusual number of incidents require a police response.

One explanation of crime may be found in the routine activity theory (Cohen and Felson, 1979). The **routine activity theory** postulates that a crime will occur when three elements are present: (1) a suitable victim; (2) a motivated offender, and (3) a location. The **problem analysis triangle** (see Figure 13–3) helps

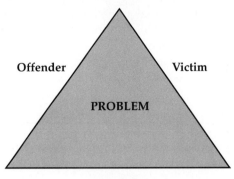

Location

FIGURE 13-3. Problem Analysis Triangle
Source: Bureau of Justice Assistance, U.S.
Department of Justice, *Comprehensive Gang
Initiative: Operations Manual for Implementing
Local Gang Prevention and Control Programs,*
draft (October 1993), pp. 3–10.

officers to visualize the complexities of crime and the relationship between its three elements. Figure 13–4 applies the problem analysis triangle to problem drug sales at a city park.

The concept of "guardians" is another important factor in our understanding crime and developing preventive strategies. **Guardians** are defined as those people or things that can exercise control over each side of the triangle and make it more resistant to crime. Consider the example of drug sales at Lexington Park (see Figure 13–4). The offenders are described as drug dealers and drug buyers. Potential guardians may include parents of buyers and sellers, parole and probation officers, police, park personnel, adopting a park curfew, increased lighting at night, stricter laws, enhanced sentencing, and so on. Analysis helps identify potential guardians. Next, the officer would identify potential guardians for the victim and location sides of the triangle to gain a complete understanding of the problem. Guardians are important to crime prevention, and greatly improves the officers' ability to affect one or more sides of the triangle.

Response: Formulating Tailor-Made Strategies

Once a problem has been clearly defined, officers may seek the most effective responses. A **response** should be developed in relation to each side of the problem analysis triangle. For example, focusing solely on the offender leaves room for new offenders because the location or victims have not changed.

We have stressed the importance of long-term solutions; however, officers cannot ignore the fact that more serious situations may require immediate action. For example, in the case of an open-air drug market involving violence between rival gangs, police may initially increase the number of patrols in the area to arrest offenders, gain control of public space, and secure the safety of residents and officers. Once this is accomplished, longer-term responses, which include the collaborative efforts of officers, residents, and other agencies, may be considered.

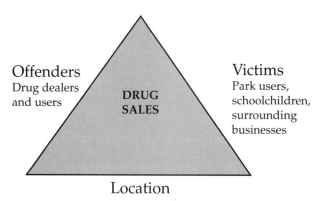

FIGURE 13-4. Drug Sales Problem Triangle
Source: Bureau of Justice Assistance, U.S. Department of
Justice, *Comprehensive Gang Initiative: Operations Manual
for Implementing Local Gang Prevention and Control
Programs,* draft (October 1993), pp. 3–10.

Responses to substantive problems rarely involve a single agency or tactic or quick fixes. For example, officers often see arrest as the only response to a problem even though alone it is rarely sufficient to provide a more permanent resolution. More appropriate responses frequently involve the police and public and other appropriate agencies, including those from business, social services and government.

Officers have many options in responding to problems. However, officers should not expect to eradicate every problem they take on. The elimination of some social problems, such as gangs and homelessness, is impractical and improbable. For example, it is more practical to attack the smaller and more manageable harms associated with these problems; such as grafetti, drug sales, and intimidation in the case of gangs.

The prevention of crime should be as important to the officer as the apprehension of offenders. Ronald Clark (1992) provided police officers with guidance on situational crime prevention (see Table 13–1).

Another important prevention tool for COPPS is **crime prevention through environmental design (CPTED).** CPTED teaches officers how building space, architectural design, lighting, and other features of the environment contribute to criminal opportunities. Both situational crime prevention and CPTED provide officers with tools necessary to employ comprehensive prevention strategies.

Assessment: Evaluating Overall Effectiveness

The final stage of SARA is **assessment.** Here, officers evaluate the effectiveness of their responses and may use the results to revise their responses, collect more data, or even redefine the problem. For some problems, assessment is very simple: observing a location to see whether a problem resurfaces. For example, in one East Coast city, when asked how he determined whether his COPPS efforts in a local park were successful, an officer simply mentioned that more families were using the park. Case Study 13–1 examines recurring problems in another city park.

TABLE 13.1. Problem Solving: Situational Crime Prevention Techniques

INCREASING THE EFFORT

1. *Target Hardening*—Obstructing the vandal or thief by physical barriers such as locks and safes.
2. *Access Control*—Denying access to offenders through such methods as gates and reception desks.
3. *Deflecting Offenders*—Channeling offensive behavior in more acceptable directions, such as through the provision of litter bins or relocation of bus stops.
4. *Controlling Facilitators*—Controlling such crime facilitators as spray-paint cans and digital (push-button) public telephones.

INCREASING THE RISKS

5. *Entry/Exit Screening*—Increasing the risk of detection for those not in conformity with entry or exit requirements (e.g., border searches and merchandise tags).
6. *Formal Surveillance*—Deterrence through official in-person (e.g., police) and technological (e.g., camera) surveillance.
7. *Surveillance by Employees*—Using employees to increase deterrence (e.g., hotel doormen and groundskeepers).
8. *Natural Surveillance*—Capitalizing on natural surveillance provided by people going about their everyday business (e.g., pruning hedges or neighborhood watch groups).

REDUCING THE REWARDS

9. *Target Removal*—Removing the targets of crime by means such as cash-reduction measures to reduce robbery and the provision of hotel safes for guest valuables.
10. *Identifying Property*—Marking property to improve chances of recovery, such as automobile VINs and Operation Identification.
11. *Removing Inducements*—Removing inducements to crime, through the publishing of gender-neutral phone lists and immediate cleaning of graffiti.
12. *Rule Setting*—Regulating employee and customer/clientele behavior through rule setting that removes any ambiguity between acceptable and unacceptable conduct and that encourages conformity with rules.

Source: Adapted from Ronald V. Clarke (ed.), "Introduction." In *Situational Crime Prevention: Successful Case Studies.* New York: Harrow and Heston, 1992, pp. 12–21. Used with permission.

In most cases, however, assessments should be comprehensive and may include such measures as before-and-after comparisons of crime and call for service data, environmental crime prevention surveys, and neighborhood fear-reduction surveys. The nature of the problem will often dictate the methods of assessment.

A COPPS-ORIENTED SUPERVISOR

What Constitutes a Good COPPS Supervisor?

The Police Executive Research Forum (1990) provided a list of characteristics of a good COPPS supervisor. This supervisor:

1. Allows officers the freedom to experiment with new approaches.
2. Insists on good, accurate analyses of problems.

Case Study 13–1
Problems Plague the Park

Paxton Park holds tremendous significance for the predominately older African-American and Hispanic residents of the city's Hillsborough district. Referred to as "instant park," it was literally constructed within a day by residents during the late 1960s. Since then, it has deteriorated and become a haven for drug dealers and gang members. Today, few residents dare use the park day or night.

Residents frequently report to the police all manner of suspicious activities in the park, including sightings of persons under the influence harassing children and the use of houses bordering the park as crash pads for drug users. In most instances the police response is to send a police unit by the park to disperse the drug dealers. Few arrests are ever made.

On occasion, the countywide consolidated narcotics unit and the department's special weapons and tactics unit initiates a program to make massive arrests. This approach usually brings about a large number of arrests, but it also generates complaints of excessive force and racism by offenders and residents alike. Six months ago the department initiated a narcotics tip line for residents, but very few calls have been made since it was installed.

Sergeant Brewer was recently assigned to the Hillsborough district. He has recently attended a COPPS training seminar and believes that the drug and other problems at the park could be handled in a different manner than in the past. He calls a team meeting to discuss how they might approach the problem.

1. Use the problem analysis triangle to thoroughly identify the problem and potential guardians.
2. What responses might be considered by the team (be sure to include all organizations that may help)?
3. How could Sgt. Brewer evaluate the team's successes?

3. Grants flexibility in work schedules when requests are proper.
4. Allows officers to make most contacts directly and paves the way when they are having trouble getting cooperation.
5. Protects officers from pressures within the department to revert to traditional methods.
6. Runs interference for officers to secure resources, protects them from criticism, and so on.
7. Knows what problems officers are working on and whether the problems are real.
8. Knows officers' beats and important citizens in it, and expects subordinates to know it even better.
9. Coaches officers through the process (SARA), giving advice and help in managing their time.
10. Monitors officers' progress and, as necessary, prods them along or slows them down.
11. Supports officers, even if their strategies fail, as long as something useful is learned in the process and the process itself is thought through well.
12. Manages problem-solving efforts over a long period of time; does not allow efforts to end just because officers get sidetracked by competing demands for time and attention.
13. Gives credit to officers and lets others know about their good work.
14. Allows officers to talk with visitors or at conferences about their work.

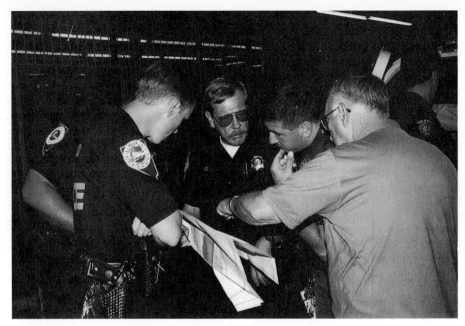

Interagency cooperation is essential for solving community problems.
Courtesy Washoe County, Nevada, Sheriff's Office Photo Unit.

15. Identifies new resources and contacts officers.
16. Stresses cooperation, coordination, and communication within and outside the unit.
17. Coordinates efforts across shifts, beats, and with outside units and agencies.
18. Realizes that this style of policing cannot simply be ordered; officers and detectives must come to believe in it.

Change Begins with the Supervisor

Robinette (1993) asserted that the traditional police supervisor, shift commander, or midlevel executive is largely unprepared for the requirements of the COPPS strategy. The problem is that most officers do not see their supervisors as sources of guidance and direction, but as authority figures to be satisfied by numbers of arrests and citations, the manner in which reports are completed, the officer's ability to avoid citizen complaints, and so on. This view of supervisors varies considerably from the characteristics of a good COPPS supervisor listed above.

Organizational change begins or ends with an agency's supervisors. The link between street officers and the organization is through their sergeant. Indeed, the quality of an officer's daily life often depends on the supervisor. However, there is some cause for supervisors' reluctance to change as Goldstein (1990:29) noted:

> Changing the operating philosophy of rank-and-file officers is easier than altering a first-line supervisor's perspective of his or her job, because the work of a sergeant is greatly simplified by the traditional form of policing. The more

routinized the work, the easier it is for the sergeant to check. The more emphasis placed on rank and the symbols of position, the easier it is for the sergeant to rely on authority—rather than intellect and personal skills—to carry out their duties. [S]ergeants are usually appalled by descriptions of the freedom and independence suggested in problem oriented policing for rank-and-file officers. The concept can be very threatening to them. This . . . can create an enormous block to implementation.

Goldstein maintained that the most effective means of altering the current attitudes of supervisors is to convince them that adopting a different style of supervision makes good sense in today's environment.

A difficult hurdle that supervisors must overcome is the idea that giving line officers the opportunity to be creative and take risks does not diminish their own role or authority. Risk taking and innovation require mutual trust between supervisors and line officers. It means changing from being a "controller," primarily concerned with rules, to that of "facilitator" and "coach" for officers engaged in COPPS work. As noted, supervisors must learn to encourage innovation and risk taking among their officers. They must also be well skilled in problem solving, especially in the analysis of problems and evaluation of efforts. Conducting workload analysis and finding the time for officers to solve problems and engage the community are important aspects of supervision. A supervisor must also be prepared to intercede and remove any roadblocks to the problem-solving efforts of their officers.

Furthermore, supervisors should understand that not all patrol officers or detectives will enjoy COPPS work or be good at it. A supervisor should assist officers with managing their beats and time utilized for COPPS activities. Some agencies accomplish this by assigning a specialized team to COPPS. We believe this risks creating the illusion that COPPS is no more than a specialty function or program. Also, supervisors should not contribute to the COPPS initiative becoming a mere public relations campaign; the emphasis is always on results (Police Executive Research Forum, 1990).

Gaining Time for Officers

One of the debates often heard with respect to COPPS is whether officers have enough time to engage in problem-solving activities. On the one hand, officers complain that they are going from call to call and have little time for anything else. On the other hand, administrators say there is plenty of time for problem solving because calls account for only 50 to 60 percent of an officer's time. The supervisor would seem to be caught in the middle of this debate, and is certainly in a key position to determine whether or not adequate time is indeed available to the patrol officers and, if not, that it be made so.

Obviously, citizens' calls for service are important and cannot be ignored; neverthless, supervisors must find a means of more effectively managing these calls in order to make more time available for officers to engage in COPPS activities.

Finding Time for Problem Solving

There are four methods for overcoming the problem of finding time for problem solving while still handling calls effectively.

1. *Allow units to perform problem-solving assignments as self-initiated activities.* Under this approach, a unit would contact the dispatcher and go out of service for a problem-solving assignment. The unit would be interrupted only for an emergency call in its area of responsibility. Otherwise, the dispatcher would hold nonemergency calls until the unit becomes available or send a unit from an adjacent area after holding the call for a predetermined amount of time.

2. *Schedule one or two units to devote a predetermined part of their shift to problem solving.* A supervisor could designate one or two units each day to devote the first half of their shift or perhaps only one hour to problem solving. Their calls would be handled by other units so that they have an uninterrupted block of time for problems. Of course, this approach means that the other units will be busier. The trade-off is that problem solving holds the greatest promise for reducing CFS.

3. *Take more reports over the telephone.* The information in nonemergency incidents is recorded on a department report form and entered in the department's information system as an incident or crime. The average telephone report taker can process four times as many report calls an hour as a field unit.

4. *Review the department policy on "assist" units.* In some departments several units may show up at the scene of an incident even though they are not needed. This problem is particularly acute with alarm calls. A department should undergo a detailed study on the types of calls for which assist units actually appear, with the aim of reducing the number of assists.

As a more general approach, a department should review its patrol plan to determine whether units are fielded in proportion to workload. Time between calls is a function not only of the number of incoming calls but also of the number of units in the field. More units result in more time between calls.

Delaying response time to calls for service can also provide more time for officers. Response time research has determined that rapid responses are not needed for most calls. Furthermore, dispatchers can set citizens' expectations of when an officer will arrive. As we described earlier, citizens find slower police responses to nonemergency calls satisfactory if dispatchers tell them an officer might not arrive at their home right away. Managers have also garnered more time for officers by having nonsworn employees handle noncrime incidents (Eck and Spelman, 1989).

Table 13–2 provides a 15-step exercise that may help supervisors capture more time for officers to engage in problem solving (Vaughn, n.d.).

Valuing the Line Officer

We believe the necessary shift to COPPS centers on those singular individuals who compose the backbone of policing—the patrol officer. We also maintain that the most powerful resource an organization possesses is a thinking, creative, and innovative police officer who—when supported by information, the community, training (in problem identification, analysis, and response), and internal support systems that reward and motivate the officer—is capable of providing long-term solutions to problems.

TABLE 13.2. A 15-Step Exercise for Recapturing Officers' Time

331

CHAPTER 13
Community-Oriented
Policing and Problem
Solving

1. Assemble a group of patrol officers and emergency communications center personnel representing each shift.
2. Have each of them write down three to five locations where the police respond repeatedly to deal with the same general problem and people.
3. Determine the average number of responses to those locations per month and approximately how long the problem has existed.
4. Determine the average number of officers who respond each time to those incidents.
5. Determine the average length of time involved in handling the incidents.
6. Using the information from points 3, 4, and 5, determine the total number of staff hours devoted to each of these problem locations. Do this for the week, month, and year.
7. Identify all the key players who either participate in or are affected by the problem—all direct and indirect participants and groups such as the complaining parties, victims, witnesses, property owners and managers, bystanders, and so forth.
8. Through a roundtable discussion, decide what it is about the particular location that allows, or encourages, the problem to exist and continue.
9. Develop a list of things that have been done in the past to deal with the problem, and a candid assessment of why each has not worked.
10. In a free-flowing brainstorming session, develop as many traditional and nontraditional solutions to the problem as possible. Include alternative sources such as other government and private agencies that could be involved in the solution. Encourage creative thinking and risk taking.
11. After you have completed the brainstorming session, consider which of those solutions are (a) illegal, (b) immoral, (c) impractical, (d) unrealistic, or (e) unaffordable.
12. Eliminate all those that fall in categories (a) and (b).
13. For those that fall in categories (c), (d), and (e), figure out if those reasons derive from thinking in conventional terms like "We've never done it this way," "It won't work," "It can't be done." If you are satisfied that those solutions truly are impractical, unrealistic, or unaffordable, then eliminate them, too. If there is a glimmer of hope that some may have merit with just a little different thinking or approach, then leave them.
14. For each remaining possible solution, list what would have to be done and who would have to be involved to make it happen. Which of those solutions and actions could be implemented relatively soon and with a minimum of difficulty?
15. If the solution were successful, consider the productive things officers could do with the time that would be recaptured from not having to deal with the problem anymore.

Source: Jerald R. Vaughn, *Community-Oriented Policing: You Can Make It Happen* (Clearwater, Fla.: National Law Enforcement Leadership Institute, n.d.), pp. 6–7. Used with permission.

A major departure of COPPS from the conventional style of policing lies with the view that the line officer has much more discretion and decision-making ability and is trusted with a much broader array of responsibilities. We believe the necessary shift to a COPPS perspective centers on supervisors, who should encourage officers to take the initiative in identifying and responding to beat problems. This recognizes the potential of highly trained and educated officers, "who have been smothered in the atmosphere of traditional policing" (Goldstein, 1987:17). It also gives officers a new sense of identity and self-respect; they are more challenged and have opportunities to follow through on individual cases—to analyze and solve problems—which will give them greater job satisfaction. Using patrol officers in this manner also allows the agency to provide sufficient challenges not only for the better-educated officers, but also a challenge for those officers who are not interested in being promoted. We ought to be recruiting as police officers people who can "serve as mediators, as dispensers of information, and as community organizers" (Goldstein, 1987:21).

COPPS appeals to the reasons why most officers chose policing as a profession. When asked why they originally wanted to join the police force, officers consistently say they did so in order to help people (Sparrow, 1988). By emphasizing work that addresses people's concerns, and giving officers the discretion to develop a solution, COPPS helps to make police work more rewarding.

IMPLEMENTING COPPS

Gaining the support of supervisors and officers is the first step in implementing COPPS. However, to make COPPS a part of the routine daily activities of officers requires an entire organizational transformation that cannot be accomplished overnight.

Keys to Successful Implementation

Four key components of implementation profoundly affect the way police agencies do business: leadership and management, organizational culture, field operations, and external relations (Glensor and Peak, 1996).

Leadership and Management

COPPS requires changing the philosophy of leadership and management throughout the entire organization. This begins with the development of a new *vision/values/mission statement*. All *policies and procedures* should be reviewed to ensure they are in accord with the department's COPPS objectives. *Leadership* should be promoted at all levels and a shift in *management* style from controller to facilitator is necessary. The organization should invest in *information systems* that will assist officers in identifying patterns of crime and support the problem-solving process. Progressive leaders will need to prepare for the millennium by developing long-term *strategic planning* and continuous *evaluation processes*, but at the same time be flexible and comfortable with change. *Finances and resources* will no longer be firmly established within boxes in the organizational chart. Rather, they will be commonly shared across the organization, with other city departments and the public engaged in neighborhood problem solving.

Organizational Culture

Human resources is the "heart and soul" of organizational culture. For employees, **human resources** answers the question, "What's in it for me?" Any major change in an organization requires a review of all human resources to be conducted. Community engagement and problem solving requires new skills, knowledge, and abilities for everyone in the organization. Therefore, such areas as *recruiting, selection, training, performance evaluations, promotions, honors and awards,* and *discipline* should be reviewed to ensure they promote and support the organization's transition to COPPS. Agencies must also work closely with the various *labor organizations,* which will be concerned with any proposed changes in shifts, beats, criteria for selection, promotion, discipline, and so on. It is wise to include labor representatives in the planning and implementation process from the beginning.

Field Operations

The primary concern with field operations is to structure the delivery of patrol services to assist officers in dealing with the root causes of persistent community problems. The first issue raised is whether a **specialist approach** or a **generalist approach** will be used. It is not uncommon, especially in larger police agencies, to begin COPPS implementation with an experimental district comprised of a team of specially trained officers. However, the experience of many agencies over the past 15 years suggests that departmentwide implementation should occur as quickly as possible. This will eliminate the common criticism that COPPS officers do not do "real police work" and receive special privileges. This attitude, if allowed to fester, can quickly impair any implementation efforts. The need for available time presents a supervisory challenge that begins with *managing calls for service.* This requires comprehensive workload analysis, call prioritization, alternative call handling, and differential response methods (see Chapter 10). A *decentralized approach* to field operations involves assigning officers for a minimum of one year to a beat and shift so that they can learn more about a neighborhood's problems.

External Relations

Collaborative responses to neighborhood crime and disorder are essential to the success of COPPS. This requires new relationships and the sharing of information and resources between the police and community, local government agencies, service providers, and business. This requires that agencies educate and inform their external partners about police resources and neighborhood problems, using surveys, newsletters, community meetings, and public service announcements. The *media* also provide an excellent opportunity for police to educate the community. Press releases about collaborative problem-solving efforts should be sent to the media and news conferences held to discuss major crime-reduction efforts. Case Study 13–2 considers a number of problems caused chiefly by large crowds of juveniles at a popular 24-hour eatery.

How to Fail

We conclude with a humorous yet insightful list of tips on how the "tradition-bound chief" can undermine the successful implementation of COPPS (Eck, 1992). *Warning: Following these suggestions will guarantee failure!*

The Burger Barn is the most popular fast-food restaurant in town and it is open 24 hours a day. It is located in the middle sector of town where two busy four-lane highways intersect; this is a commercial area that is adjacent to a low-income residential area consisting of mobile homes, apartment complexes, and small single-family homes.

Sergeant Maas has noticed a tremendous increase in calls for service (CFS) at the location. On checking computer-aided dispatch records, he discovers that CFS to the Burger Barn had indeed increased to nearly 90 a month. Further analysis reveals that the majority of CFS occur during the late night/early morning hours, peaking between 1:00 A.M. and 3:00 A.M. The CFS mostly involve large crowds of juveniles, fights, noise disturbances, shots fired, and traffic congestion and accidents. A few police officers have even been injured while attempting to break up fights.

The restaurant's manager has attempted to limit access to the building during the peak hours, allowing only five juveniles inside at any one time. Unfortunately, this approach has resulted in long lines forming outside and increased the number of disturbances and fights. Employees are frequently harassed by angry customers waiting for service in the building. Many of the juveniles are cruising and driving carelessly, paying little attention to the traffic signals and contributing significantly to congestion which creates a backup on the adjoining highway, generating a letter of complaint from the state highway patrol to the police chief.

1. Use the problem analysis triangle to thoroughly identify the problem and potential guardians.
2. What responses might be considered? Be sure to include all organizations that may help.
3. How would Sgt. Maas evaluate their successes?

1. *Oversell it.* COPPS should be sold as a panacea for every ill that plagues the city, the nation, and civilization. Some of the evils you may want to claim is that COPPS will eliminate crime, fear of crime, racism, police misuse of force, homelessness, drug abuse, gangs, and other social problems. By building up the hopes and expectations of the public, the press, and politicians, you can set the stage for later attacks on COPPS when it does not deliver.
2. *Don't be specific.* This suggestion is a corollary of the first item. Never define what you mean by the following terms: community, service, effectiveness, empowerment, neighborhood, communication, or problem solving. Use these and other terms indiscriminately, interchangeably, and whenever possible. At first, people will think the department is going to do something meaningful and won't ask for details. Once people catch on, you can blame the amorphous nature of COPPS and go back to what you were doing before.
3. *Create a special unit or group.* Less than 10 percent of the department should be engaged in this effort lest COPPS really catches on. Since the "grand design" is the return to conventional policing anyway (once everyone has attacked COPPS), there is no sense in involving more than a few officers. Furthermore, special units are popular with the press and politicians.
4. *Create a soft image.* The best image for COPPS will be a uniformed female hugging a small child. This caring and maternal image will warm the hearts

of community members suspicious of the police, play to traditional stereo-types of sexism with policing, and turn off most cops.

5. *Leave the impression that COPPS is only for minority neighborhoods.* This is a corollary of items 3 and 4. Since a small group of officers will be involved, only a few neighborhoods can receive their services. Place the token COPPS officers in areas with minority public housing. With any luck, racial antagonism will undercut the approach, and it will appear that poor, minority neighborhoods are not getting the "tough on crime" approach they need.

6. *Divorce COPPS officers from "regular" police work.* This is an expansion of the soft image concept. If COPPS officers do not handle calls or make arrests, and instead throw block parties, speak to community groups, walk around talking to kids, visit schools, and so on, they will not be perceived as "real" police officers by their colleagues. This will further undermine their credibility and ability to accomplish anything of significance.

7. *Obfuscate means and ends.* Whenever describing COPPS, never make the methods for accomplishing the objective subordinate to the objective. Instead, make the means more important than the ends, or at least put them on equal footing. For example, to reduce drug dealing in a neighborhood, make certain that the tactics necessary (e.g., arrests, community meetings) are as, or more, important than the objective. These tactics can occupy everyone's time and still leave the drug problem unresolved.

8. *Present community members with problems and plans.* Whenever meeting with community members, officers should listen carefully and politely and then elaborate on how the department will enforce the law. If the community members like the plan, go ahead. If they do not, continue to be polite and ask them to go on a ride-a-long or witness a drug raid. This avoids having to change the department's operations while simultaneously demonstrating how difficult police work is and why nothing can be accomplished. In the end, members of the community will not get their problems solved but will see how nice the police are.

9. *Never try to understand why problems occur.* Do not let officers gain knowledge about the underlying causes of problems; COPPS should not include any analysis of a problem and as little information as possible should be sought from the community. Keep officers away from computer terminals. Mandate that they get permission to talk to members of any other agency. Do not allow officers to go off their assigned areas to collect information. Prevent access to research conducted on similar problems. Suppress listening skills.

10. *Never publicize a success.* Some rogue officers will not get the message and will go out anyway to gather enough information to solve problems. Try to ignore these examples of effective policing and make sure that no one else hears about them. When you cannot ignore them, describe them in the least meaningful way (see item 2). Talk about the wonders of empowerment and community meetings. Describe the hours of foot patrol, the new mountain bikes, or shoulder patches. In every problem solved, there is usually some tactic or piece of equipment that can be highlighted at the expense of the accomplishment itself.

SUMMARY

This chapter began with a discussion of how policing has evolved and how traditional police methods, while not totally ineffectual, have not significantly reduced crime or citizens' fear of crime. It is clear that the police cannot hope to address today's crime problems alone. They cannot singlehandedly contain the burgeoning crime, drug, and gang problems that now beset our society and drain our federal, state, and local resources.

Police are discovering that COPPS—with its emphasis on community engagement and problem solving—is dramatically altering the traditional, reactive, incident-related methods of the past. If the police are to have any success in resolving substantive and recurring community problems, they must develop better methods of identifying and responding to the underlying causes that contribute to their occurrence. The SARA process provides a framework for officers and supervisors to identify problems, perform comprehensive analysis, develop tailor-made responses, and assess their efforts. Such in-depth inquiry and effort supplants conventional reactive, incident-driven responses and facilitates more effective responses to the increasing demands currently being placed on the police.

KEY TERMS

Sir Robert Peel   (p. 315)
political era of
   policing   (p. 316)
professional era of
   policing   (p. 316)
Wickersham
   Commission   (p. 317)
SARA   (p. 321)
scanning   (p. 321)
analysis   (p. 323)

Geographic Information
   System (GIS)   (p. 323)
computer-aided dispatch
   (CAD)   (p. 323)
routine activity
   theory   (p. 323)
problem analysis
   triangle   (p. 323)
guardians   (p. 324)
response   (p. 324)

assessment   (p. 325)
crime prevention through
   environmental design
   (CPTED)   (p. 325)
human resources   (p. 332)
specialist
   approach   (p. 333)
generalist
   approach   (p. 333)

ITEMS FOR REVIEW

1. Describe the three primary eras in policing: political, professional, and community policing and problem solving.
2. Define COPPS, focusing on its two primary components: community engagement and problem solving.
3. Explain the scanning and analysis phases of the SARA process, focusing on the various sources of information that are available to analyze the problem.
4. Describe what activities are involved in the response and assessment phases of the SARA process.
5. List at least a dozen characteristics of a good problem-solving supervisor.
6. Delineate some of the specific methods by which police officers may obtain time to engage in problem-solving activities.
7. Analyze some of the key elements and problems of implementing COPPS.
8. Explain some of the means by which the implementation of COPPS may fail.

SOURCES

337

CHAPTER 13
Community-Oriented
Policing and Problem
Solving

CALIFORNIA DEPARTMENT OF JUSTICE (1995). *COPPS: Community-oriented policing and problem solving.* Office of the Attorney General, Crime Violence Prevention Center, Sacramento, California.

CLARK, R. V. (1992). *Situational crime prevention: Successful case studies.* New York: Harrow and Hesoton.

COHEN, L. E., and FELSON, M. (1979). "Social change and crime rate trends: A routine activity approach." *American Sociological Review* 44 (August): 588–608.

ECK, J. E. (1992). "Helpful hints for the tradition-bound chief." *Fresh Perspectives.* Washington, D.C.: Police Executive Research Forum (6):1–7.

ECK, J. E. (1984). *The investigation of burglary and robbery.* Washington, D.C.: Police Executive Research Forum.

ECK, J., and SPELMAN, W. (1989). "A problem-oriented approach to police service delivery." In Dennis Jay Kenney (ed.). *Police and Policing: Contemporary Issues.* New York: Praeger.

ECK, J., and SPELMAN, W. (1987). *Problem-solving: Problem-oriented policing in Newport News.* Washington, D.C.: Police Executive Research Forum.

FARRELL, G., and PEASE, K. (1993). *Once bitten, twice bitten: Repeat victimisation and its implications for crime prevention.* Crime Prevention Unit Paper 46. London: Home Office.

FYFE, J. (1991). "Some hard facts about our wars on crime." *The Washington Post National Weekly Edition* (April 8–14), p. 25.

GLENSOR, R. W., and PEAK, K. J. (1996). "Implementing change: Community-oriented policing and problem solving." *FBI Law Enforcement Bulletin* (7):14–20.

GOLDSTEIN, H. (1977). *Policing a free society.* Cambridge, Mass.: Ballinger.

GOLDSTEIN, H. (1990). *Problem-oriented policing.* New York: McGraw-Hill.

GOLDSTEIN, H. (1987). "Problem-oriented policing." Paper presented at the Conference on Policing: State of the Art III, National Institute of Justice, Phoenix, Arizona, June 12.

JOHNSON, D. R. (1981). *American Law Enforcement History.* St. Louis: Forum Press.

KELLING, G. L. (1987). "Juveniles and police: The end of the nightstick." In Francis X. Hartmann (ed.). *From Children to Citizens, Vol. II: The Role of the Juvenile Court.* New York: Springer-Verlag.

MONKKONEN, E. H. (1981). *Police in urban America, 1860-1920.* Cambridge: Cambridge University Press.

PEAK, K., and GLENSOR, R. (1996). *Community policing and problem solving: Strategies and practices.* Upper Saddle River, N.J.: Prentice Hall.

POLICE EXECUTIVE RESEARCH FORUM, (1990). "Supervising problem-solving." Training outline. Washington, D.C.: Police Executive Research Forum.

RADZINOWICZ, L. (1968). *A history of english criminal law and its administration from 1750,* Vol. IV: *Grappling for Control.* London: Stevens & Son.

RICHARDSON, J. F. (1970). *Urban policing in the United States.* New York: Oxford University Press.

ROBINETTE, H. M. (1993). "Supervising tomorrow." *Virginia Police Chief* (Spring): 10.

SHERMAN, L. W. (1993). "Repeat calls for service: Policing the " 'hot spots.' " In Dennis Jay Kenney (ed.). *Police and Policing: Contemporary Issues.* New York: Praeger.

SPARROW, M. K. (1988). *Implementing community policing.* National Institute of Justice, Perspectives on Policing 9 (November): 6.

SPELMAN, W. (1990). *Repeat offender programs for law enforcement.* Washington, D.C.: Police Executive Research Forum.

STEPHENS, DARREL. (1995). "Community problem-oriented policing: Measuring impacts." In Larry T. Hoover (ed.). *Quantifying Quality in Policing.* Washington, D.C.: Police Executive Research Forum.

VAUGHN, J. R. (n.d.). *Community-oriented policing: You can make it happen.* Clearwater, Fla.: National Law Enforcement Leadership Institute.

WALKER, S. (1977). *A critical history of police reform: The emergence of professionalism.* Lexington, Mass.: Lexington Books.

WITKIN, G., and MCGRAW, D. (1993). "Beyond 'Just the facts, ma'am'." *U.S. News and World Report* (August 2): 28.

PART FOUR Epilogue

14

Future Trends and Challenges

The future is waiting, if we can just remember the access code.
—Wayne Hanson

The most reliable way to anticipate the future is by understanding the present.
—John Naisbitt

Some men see things as they are, and ask why?
I dream things that never were, and ask why not?

—Robert F. Kennedy

INTRODUCTION

What will the future bring? We have all asked this question at one time or another, and in one form or another. However, without the ability to employ a crystal ball, read palms, or run a planchette over a Ouija board with any accuracy, we look to other, more tangible and credible means of determining what the future holds. We would also do well to remember that the future is of utmost importance for supervisors, and it is largely affected and controlled by human actions, rather than by blind luck or fate.

This final chapter opens by examining the need for studying the future of policing in order to make the unknown more predictable. We then consider some widely used methods by which futurists attempt to forecast our future. Included in this section are some predictions that appear imminent with respect to demographics and crime in the United States. We then consider what the experts predict in terms of anticipated changes in policing in the 21st century, including management styles, organizational changes, the quality of life within police agencies, and community policing and problem solving. We conclude the chapter with a look at the impact of high technology on the future of policing.

WHY STUDY FUTURES IN SUPERVISION?

We all think about the future; it is a normal part of everyday living. We attend classes to better our future life, schedule meetings and appointments, consider our retirement programs, prepare notes for classes and speeches, and even pay our bills as a hedge against problems tomorrow. The trouble is that when the future finally arrives, we often find that it is embarrassingly different from our expectations: We simply did not plan effectively. The future is therefore a dynamic concept, always changing and making us unsure of what lies ahead. To use the driving experience as an analogy, we must constantly look at and be aware of several aspects of the road ahead—our speed and that of other drivers, traffic signals and signs, weather and road conditions—to reach our destination. And we *certainly* cannot afford to plummet into the next century with our eyes fixed firmly on the rearview mirror!

And so it is with police officers and supervisors. Historically, the role of the police has been to maintain the status quo. But reliance on the status quo will not prepare the police for the future. Previous chapters of this book, dealing with many kinds of personnel and operational issues, have made clear the need for possessing strategies for future problems. We have learned from riots, financial cutbacks, natural and man-made disasters, strikes, and other exigencies that the police simply must anticipate the future. They must plan for the unknown and expect the unforeseen.

Furthermore, the police, perhaps more than anyone, must plan with an eye toward community approval of their actions. Unless the public see the police as amicable, they will perceive them as adversaries. History has taught us that civil unrest—often following perceived police brutality or unjustified shootings—can be destructive and long lasting, and police leaders should be aware of this (Tafoya, 1990). The specter of liability also reminds us of the cost of failure.

In the past quarter century, policing has made important strides, but much work remains to be done. For 45,000 years humankind huddled in the darkness of caves, afraid to take that first step into the light of day. Police leaders are now "out in front," paving the way for others to follow. They do not wait for someone else to set the pace. Bold leadership is essential today, to prepare for the future of police reform (Tafoya, 1990). More than ever before, police supervisors must shoulder the responsibility for seeing that the best and brightest individuals are recruited and trained, and then become the best they possibly can be in their performance. And supervisors must have a vision of how those individuals—and the ever evolving high technology that they will be using (see the technology section, below)—can be directed in the most efficient and fair manner.

THE NEED FOR FUTURES RESEARCH

Despite the existence of a body of literature that one way or another reflects concern about social, technological, and economic change, the police have until recently traditionally remained largely uninterested in **futures research.** A recent survey by Conser and Diller (1994) determined that nearly one-half (44 percent) of 126 respondents felt that their police departments were resistant to change. According to Swanson, Territo, and Taylor (1993:675), three possible reasons exist for this disinterest: (1) a time horizon—for many police agencies, this is no longer than the next budget cycle; (2) a "hot stove" approach to managing, meaning that "we'll handle today's crisis now and worry about tomorrow when it gets here"; and (3) a lack of any need to consider what conditions might bc like in 10 to 20 years.

These reasons for the lack of attending to futures research would seem generally to be very true of policing. As one author (Tafoya, 1983:14) put it, "Most disciplines are almost totally absorbed with the problems of today and steeped in the tradition of yesterday." However, since the early 1980s there has been a growing interest among police executives in futures research, an interest fueled largely by the growing imperative to make sense out of a turbulent and sometimes chaotic environment, as well as the highly visible work of such police futures authors as William Tafoya, who developed the nation's first graduate-level police futures courses. Tafoya was also the founder of the Society of Police Futurists International, based in Baltimore, Maryland. Since 1982 the Management Science Unit of the FBI Academy has offered a three-credit graduate course on "Futuristics: Forecasting Techniques for Law Enforcement Managers."

Another outgrowth of this increased interest in the future is the creation by some police departments of a futures research unit standing alone or within their planning division; these units assess trends, countertrends, shifting values, and other indicators, and attempt to provide an understanding of what they mean, where a department is going, and what should be done.

Other police leaders, need to focus on the future. Futurists think in terms of time frames of five years and beyond. However, police leaders tend to focus on the *immediate* future—from the present to two years ahead—dealing with problems that need resolution, trying to "stay on top of things," and "putting out fires." Future outcomes *can* be influenced by decisions of today; this axiom is critical for police leaders to understand because the choices made today will definitely affect their agencies in the next century.

John Naisbitt (1984:xxiii), in his seminal book *Megatrends*, observed that "The most reliable way to anticipate the future is by understanding the present." Unfortunately, there is still a great deal to be learned about the present status of police supervision and management. Much of what we know or think we know is based on research conducted in the 1970s, 1980s, or even much earlier. Our society has changed in large measure since those studies were conducted. Most people who will read this text cannot imagine a time when computers did not exist; comic-strip detective Dick Tracy's two-way wristradio that dazzled people not many years ago is now a reality.

So more current research is needed. Who are the police officers of today? What are their beliefs? What is the police culture? What role do the police play in contemporary society? What organizational structures and philosophy predominates? Do police practices differ by region of the country? Is there a difference between recruits in a police agency and those persons who are already working there? What is the career path and opportunity for advancement in most police departments? What is the current attitude of citizens toward the police? We need new data if we are to understand the present and prepare police leaders for the future (Gaines et al., 1991).

PREDICTING THE FUTURE

Environmental Scanning, Drivers, Scenario Writing

In the past two decades there has been a surging interest in forecasting the future of policing. Tafoya (1983) called forecasting the "purest form of futuristics," likening the headlights of a car being driven in a snowstorm. The lights provide enough illumination to continue, but not enough so the driver can proceed without caution. What lies ahead is unknown. Next, we examine some of the methods that are employed by people engaged in futures research in their efforts to make the unknown more predictable.

Environmental Scanning

Contemporary futures research has two major aspects: environmental scanning and scenario writing. **Environmental scanning** is an effort to put a social problem under a microscope, with an eye toward the future. We may consult experts such as demographers, social scientists, technologists, and economists for their opinions. A Delphi process may also assist, gathering experts, looking at all possible factors, and getting an idea of what will happen in the future. Thus, environmental scanning permits us to identify, track, and assess changes in the environment (Peak, 1997).

Drivers

Through scanning, we can examine the factors that seem likely to "drive" the environment. "Drivers" are factors or variables—economic conditions, demographic shifts, governmental policies, social attitudes, technological advances— that will have a bearing on future conditions. Three categories of drivers will serve to identify possible trends and impacts on the U.S. criminal justice system beyond the year 2000: (1) social and economic conditions (e.g., size and age of the population, immigration patterns, nature of employment, and lifestyle characteristics); (2) shifts in the numbers and types of crimes, including the potential for new types of criminality and technological advances that might be used for illegal behavior; and (3) developments in the criminal justice system itself (e.g., changes in the way the police, courts, and corrections subsystems operate; important innovations) (Peak, 1997).

Three important drivers contribute to the changing nature of crime in the West: (1) the advent of **high technology** in our society, (2) the distribution and use of narcotics, and (3) a declining population in the 15 to 24 age bracket. The nature of crime is rapidly changing. With regard to technology, the new crimes of data manipulation, software piracy, bank card counterfeiting, and embezzlement by computer are here to stay. These new crimes will require supervisors to have the ability to direct people with specialized, highly technological backgrounds. The abuse of narcotics continues to spread in numbers and throughout various social classes, and it consumes an ever-increasing amount of police

The spoils of war—gangs, guns, and drug-related violence—will continue to challenge the police into the 21st century.
Courtesy New York Police Department Photo Unit.

time and resources. The decline in the size of the 15 to 24 cohort, the crime-prone youth of our society, significantly affected crime rates. With the exception of violent crime, we have witnessed a decline in several types of crime involving youth. However, this demographic benefit is about to change. As a consequence of the "baby boomerang" (the offspring of baby boomers), there are now 39 million children in this country who are under the age of 10, millions of them living in poverty and without parental supervision. Thus, we are likely to face a future wave of youth violence that will be even worse than in the past 10 years (Fox, 1996).

Scenario Writing

Scenario writing is simply the application of drivers to three primary situations or elements: public tolerance for crime, the amount of crime, and the capacity of the criminal justice system to deal with crime. An important consideration is whether each will occur in high or low degrees. For example, drivers may be analyzed in a scenario of *low* public tolerance for crime, a *high* amount of crime, and a *high* capacity of the criminal justice system to deal with crime. Conversely, a scenario might include a view of the future where there is a *high* tolerance for crime, a *low* amount of crime, and a *low* capacity for the system to cope with crime.

A CHANGING SOCIETY

Demographic Change

Future police recruiting efforts will be greatly affected by the shift in the nation's **demographics.** A change toward more older workers, fewer entry-level workers, and greater numbers of women, minorities, and immigrants in the population will force policing and private industry to become more flexible in competing for qualified applicants. Agencies must devise new strategies to attract 21- to 35-year-olds and offer better wage and benefits packages, such as day care, flexible hours, and paid maternity leave, in order to compete with private businesses (McCord and Wicker, 1990).

We are rapidly becoming a more diverse, senior, and divided society. By 2010 one in every four Americans will be 55 years or older, and this aging component of the population is more likely to suffer the harmful consequences of a victimization, such as sustaining injuries that require long-term medical care.

The minority population is also increasing rapidly; by 2000 an estimated 34 percent of U.S. children will be Hispanic, African American, or Asian American (Peak, 1996). The United States now accepts nearly one million newcomers each year. In less than 100 years we can expect the white majority in the United States to end, as the growing number of minorities together become the new majority. And when these minorities groups are forced to compete for increasingly scarce, low-paying service jobs, inter-group relations sour and can even become combative, as we have seen recently in several major cities. The gap between the haves and have-nots is widening. An **underclass** of people, those who are chronically poor is growing (Peak, 1996).

We also live in a violent country. There are about 43 million personal and property crime victimizations in the country each year; about 14 million serious (Part I) crimes are reported to the police (Maguire and Pastore, 1996).

Case Study 14–1
Loganville Looks Beyond the Horizon

The City of Loganville has a number of new department heads with varying levels of experience. Furthermore, recent crime, budget, and other crises have underscored the need for the city's departments to work more collaboratively and to address problems of the future. Accordingly, the city manager is convening a strategic planning workshop in one week to bring all department heads together, to orient them concerning the city council's long-term priorities and to discuss and address the above problems. Of course, the chief of police will attend and represent the police department. Sgt. Jennifer Smith, with nine years on the force and three years in the planning and research division, has been assigned by the chief to locate and prepare the requisite information that will be necessary for this workshop.

1. What types of information will the chief need? Where will Sgt. Smith obtain this information?
2. Using the data that are collected, what are the drivers that will most affect the future of *your* city in its changing environment?
3. What kinds of future challenges would those drivers pose for the police in your community?

The nature of crime is also changing rapidly in the United States, in great measure owing to the advent of high technology. Crimes will compel the development of new investigative techniques, specialized training for police investigators, and the employment of individuals with specialized, high-tech backgrounds.

Police Adaptation to Greater Diversity

As U.S. society becomes more diverse in the future, so must the supervisory ranks of policing. The proportion of women in state and local police agencies has risen to about 9.6 percent—4.8 percent of all state, 8.1 percent of municipal, and 15.4 percent of sheriff's employees (U.S. Department of Justice, Bureau of Justice Statistics, 1996). Women are a growing presence in the police field.

Minority police officers, like women, are slowly but steadily increasing their representation in state and local police agencies. From 1987 to 1990, for example, the percentage of African Americans in local police departments increased from 9.3 to 10.5 percent while the percentage of Hispanics went from 4.5 to 5.2 percent (U.S. Department of Justice, 1991:5, 11).

As contemporary policing increasingly adopts the community policing and problem solving philosophy (COPPS, discussed below), the growing presence of women may help improve the tarnished image of policing, improve community relations, and foster a more flexible, less violent, approach to keeping the peace. Increasing the number of women in supervisory levels could influence police policy and serve as role models for younger female officers.

African-American police officers face problems similar to those of women who attempt to enter and prosper in police work. Until more African-American officers are promoted and can affect police policy and serve as role models, they are likely to be treated unequally and have difficulty being promoted—a classic Catch-22 situation.

ANTICIPATED CHANGES IN POLICING

Among the most important changes likely to affect police supervisors and administrators in the future are participative management, for better educated officers who are unwilling to accept orders unquestioningly; flattening the organizational hierarchy; the quality of life within police agencies; and COPPS. These trends, discussed below, and the other trends discussed previously, will significantly affect how supervisors will go about their jobs in the years ahead (Bennett and Hess, 1996).

Participative Management
for More Highly Educated Officers

In the past the emphasis of police supervision was on submission to authority. However, a different set of values and expectations has been established for the future—**participative management.** The autocratic leader of the past will not work in the future. As Witham (1991:30) noted, "The watchwords of the new

Female and minority officers are more commonplace today. Their representation will increase as agencies strive to recruit officers who better reflect a community's diversity. *Courtesy Washoe County, Nevada, Sheriff's Office Photo Unit.*

leadership paradigm are coach, inspire, gain commitment, empower, affirm, flexibility, responsibility, self-management, shared power, autonomous teams, and entrepreneurial units."

Police officers of the future will not normally possess military experience and its inherent obedience to authority, but they will have higher levels of education and will tend to be more independent and less responsive to traditional authoritative approaches to their work. They also will be more receptive, participative, supportive, and humanistic approaches. These officers will want greater opportunities to provide input into their work and to address the challenges posed by neighborhood problem solving. In short, the new officers will not want to function like automatons during their tour of duty, blindly following general orders, policies and procedures, and rules and regulations.

These officers will be "bright, resourceful, and versatile, cross-trained in law enforcement, firefighting, and paramedical services. Administrators will care less about marksmanship and physical size and more about mental capacity and diplomas" (Metts, 1985:31).

Changes will not happen overnight, however, because many senior administrators who have come up through the ranks will oppose drastic changes in the "old style" of management. As one author observed, "The field of law enforcement management is full of dinosaurs, and they are becoming extinct" (Story, 1992:7).

Flattening the Organization

An area of concern among futurists is policing's organizational structure. Increasing numbers of police executives are beginning to question whether or not the traditional pyramid-shaped police bureaucracy will be effective in the future. Hillary Robinette (1989), retired special agent of the Management Science Unit of the Federal Bureau of Investigation, believes that the typical departmental organization chart of the future will no longer resemble a pyramid. Instead, he maintains that the top will be pushed down and the sides will expand at the very base of what used to look like a pyramid. Advancement will be across the organization and not up.

Indeed, many police executives are flattening their organizations. And, as we discussed in Chapter 4, communication within the pyramid structure is often made difficult by many barriers and frustrated by the numerous levels of bureaucracy. By changing the organization to a more horizontal design, the flow of information and ideas is better facillitated.

Quality of Life within Police Agencies

The quality of life within police agencies will present new supervisory challenges for the future. The median age of the U.S. workforce will be almost 40 early in the next century. The increase in older workers also will be reflected in the police workforce and will call for different motivational incentives and supervisory practices. Older officers will be less willing to change tasks or assignments.

Supervisors will mentor and coach their team members in their professional development. Some officers will need remedial writing; others assistance in learning a second language; all will need training in technology. Leadership training for newly promoted or promotable supervisors will be critical to the success of quality of life in the department.

Supervisors will have to demonstrate and teach the new methods of high-performance policing, as values, quality of life, and consensus will become more important than traditional order giving and statistical measurements of productivity.

Tomorrow's supervisor will be a team builder who will be guided by five principles; supervisors can examine their actions in light of these principles (Robinette, 1993:15–16):

1. *Free and equal access to police service.* A supervisor must test each decision against its equity effect and ask, "Is the action I am about to take, or the decision I am about to make, equitable and fair to those affected?"
2. *Fidelity to the public trust.* Here a supervisor asks, "Is it the right thing to do?"
3. *Balancing the needs of safety and security with the needs of enforcement.* A supervisor must determine whether his or her choice is lawful or involves unnecessary risks to life and property.
4. *Cooperation and coordination of activity with the community and other public agencies.* A supervisor must query whether the choice of action or decision is based on the best possible beneficial outcome for all the parties involved, and whether the action is defensible in the public forum.
5. *Objectivity.* The final supervisory test may be the most difficult. The objectivity test examines one's personal motives for choice and action. It forces the supervisor to ask why a particular action or decision is chosen over others, and whether his or her intentions are honorable.

Despite the increasing specialization that is likely to characterize policing in the 21st century, patrol officers will remain the backbone of the profession because of their sheer numbers and frequency of contact with the public. The importance of retaining competent patrol officers becomes increasingly apparent, as officers become less isolated from the public, and as cooperative efforts between the public and other citizens expand. Police officers who continue to serve, and be perceived, as soldiers of occupation in minority neighborhoods are unlikely to be effective in either crime control or the maintenance of order.

Community-Oriented Policing and Problem Solving (COPPS)

At various points throughout this book, primarily Chapter 13, we have discussed how supervisors and their subordinates must adapt to the new way of thinking and acting under the spreading COPPS philosophy of policing. Here we address this concept from a futures perspective.

As we noted in Chapter 13, the traditional police first-line supervisor has until recently been largely unprepared by training or experience for the implementation of COPPS. The command and control model of policing during the past 50 years measured the supervisor's success in the statistical accomplishments of his or her unit. Arrests, citations, calls for service, response time, and case closings were all counted in this quantitative approach. Good line officers followed orders and stayed out of trouble, filled out forms and reports correctly, and did not abuse citizens. Orders came down from the top. Sergeants checked the accuracy and compliance of paperwork going up and down the chain of command, doing more and more of the lieutenant's administrative work and spending less and less time on the street. As a result, sergeants observed their officers only once during the shift, during roll call (Robinette, 1993).

Our changing society requires a different leadership methodology. **Diversity**—cultural, gender, and ethnic—will characterize both the police work group and the community of the future, making it difficult for the supervisor to manage according to traditional standards. In those departments that implement the COPPS strategy, supervisors will have more freedom to intervene, innovate, and reallocate resources and task personnel. They will need to set clear, achievable goals and define outcomes, recognize and accommodate differences, and provide recognition, visibility, celebration, and rewards for team accomplishment. The new supervisor will be in the neighborhood talking to people, taking reports, and meeting with policing team members regularly (Robinette, 1993).

Will policing endure in the 21st century? More than any other single factor, as we noted above, the critical determinant of this endurance will be in the kind of people who enter policing in the next decade. The most significant question that police supervisors and administrators should ask is, "What are the predominant characteristics of tomorrow's police candidates?" If change is not implemented, the status quo will prevail, and those who enter policing in the next 10 years will be taught the same conventional policing methods as past generations of police officers. And, this would be a great disservice to their potential.

If past practices of selecting a police candidate—based on physical prowess and a propensity to be a "good soldier"—continue, policing is likely to regress to the norm: the legalistic style of policing. If, however, the majority of people selected to enter policing in the future are disposed to share decision making and are flexible, resilient, and well educated, these foundations will endure—and the United States will serve as a very positive model for emerging nations looking for guidance from the most democratic nation in the world (Tafoya, 1997).

HIGH TECHNOLOGY

It is not surprising that most of today's technological developments may be adopted by the police, given the nature of their work, tools, and crime problems. Indeed, as will be seen in this section, computer technology has already brought about several exciting developments in policing.

Supervisors are certainly implicated in these advances. Local area neworks (LANs) will so affect organizational communications that supervisors of the 21st century will need specific training and hands-on experience with the technology in the same way that firearms and defensive tactics training was important to an earlier generation of supervisors. Next, we discuss several of those technologies.

New Developments

A growing number of U.S. police departments, including small agencies, are using laptop computers with wireless connections to crime and motor vehicle databases. These systems are felt to pay for themselves in increased fines and officer safety. Officers can access court documents, in-house police department records, and a computer-aided dispatch (CAD) system, as well as enter license numbers into their laptop computers. Through a national network of motor vehicle and criminal history databases, they can locate drivers with outstanding warrants, expired or suspended licenses, and many other things. Furthermore, instead of using open radio communications, police officers use their computers to communicate with each other by means of E-mail (Ghaemian, 1996).

Geographic Information System

Some cities are also developing a Geographic Information System (GIS), that enables officers to plot criminal activity on an electronic map. Layers of information can then be added to the map to create a picture of crime trends. One unique way officers can use community policing strategies is to develop a database of problems and solutions. When an officer answers a call for service or encounters a problem, he or she can enter it into the database along with all information about the problem, the action taken, and a list of resources that were applied to the problem. The next time officers confront a similar problem, they can search the database and get a report on everything that was done with that problem in the past (Kavanaugh, 1996).

Electronics in Traffic Investigations and Enforcement

A multicar accident can turn a street or highway into a parking lot for many hours, sometimes days. Police need to collect evidence relating to the accident, including measurement and sketches of the scene and vehicle and body positions, skid marks, street or highway elevations, intersections, and curves. These tasks typically involve a measuring wheel, steel tape, pad, and pencil. The cost of traffic delays—especially for commercial truck operators—is substantial for every hour traffic is stalled.

Some police agencies have begun using a version of a surveyor's "total station," which electronically measures and records distances, angles, elevations, and the names and features of objects.

In addition, several companies now manufacture and provide traffic cameras to the police.

Imaged Fingerprints and Mugshots

Instead of transporting prisoners to a central booking facility in downtown Boston—a task that took 40,000 hours of officers' time each year—officers at the 11 district police stations can electronically scan a prisoner's fingerprints, take digital photographs, and then route the images to a central server for easy storage and access. This network gives investigators timely access to information and mugshot lineups and is saving the police department $1 million in labor and transportation costs while freeing officers from prisoner transportation duties (Newcombe, 1996).

Computerized Mapping for Crime Control

Computerized mapping is an effective tool to help police departments track criminal activity in neighborhoods—known in community policing as "hot spots." Combined with a technique known as **geocoding** (which verifies addresses and links other geographic information with them), computer mapping software can combine data sets to provide a multidimensional view of crime and its potential contributing factors (U.S. Department of Justice, National Institute of Justice Program Focus, 1996).

Three-Dimensional Crime Scene Drafting

Today, three-dimensional computer-aided drafting (3-D CAD) software can be purchased for a few hundred dollars. By working in 3-D, CAD users can create scenes that can be viewed from any angle. Suddenly, nontechnical people can now visualize and make sense of very technical evidence. Juries can "view" crime scenes and see the location of evidence; they can view just what the witness says he or she saw.

Gunshot Locator System

A primary obstacle for the police is to determine the location of gunshots. Technology is now being tested that is similar to that used to determine the strength and epicenter of earthquakes. Known as a Gunshot Locator System, it uses microphone-like sensors placed on rooftops and telephone poles to record and transmit the sound of gunshots by radio waves or telephone lines.

Firearms Training

A device known as "FATS," for Firearms Training System, is said to be "as close to real life as you can get" (Joyce, 1995).

Many agencies today use computerized latent fingerprint systems. Here detectives use the system to capture a serial attacker. *Courtesy New York Police Department Photo Unit.*

Recruits and in-service officers alike use the system, which ranges in cost from $32,000 to a military model selling at $5 million. The students are given a high-tech lesson in firearms and can be shown a wide variety of computer-generated scenarios on a movie screen. An instructor at a console can control the scene. Using laser-firing replicas of their actual weapons, students learn not only marksmanship but also judgment—when to shoot and not to shoot.

Other High-Tech Tools

A number of other tools can be instituted in police work provided the public will accept their use. **Artificial intelligence (AI)** is a system where computers are programmed to exhibit characteristics of human intelligence. **Expert systems** are AI programs that capture the knowledge of experts for use with new situations. **Virtual reality** combines computers and sensory apparatus to create simulated, controlled environments and experiences. **Robotics** employs computers to accomplish a useful action and **speech recognition** (where computers perform functions based on verbal input of the user).

POLICING METHODS OF THE FUTURE

The high-speed technological revolution in policing will introduce new weapons for criminals and the police alike. Some futurists believe that the old methods and equipment for doing police work will fall by the wayside in the future, replaced perhaps by electric and methane-fueled scooters and bubble-topped tricycles for densely populated areas; steamwagons and diesel superchargers for police in the rural and suburban areas; and methane-filled helium dirigibles, equipped with infrared night goggles and sophisticated communications and lighting devices, for patrol and assistance in planning barricades to trap high-speed drivers and search and rescue operations (Thibault, 1982). Others see the future of policing differently. The 21st-century cop may patrol by means of jet backpack flight equipment, and officers will be able to tie in to "language banks" of translators through their wrist radios (Cronkhite, 1984).

In terms of organization and operations, other noted speculators, such as former Madison, Wisconsin, police chief David Couper (1990), see the organization of policing in the 21st century as more demilitarized and decentralized in its organization. Officers will identify citizens as "customers" and work as "neighborhood police specialists"; these officers will be assigned to a specific neighborhood within their districts and provide a full range of police services. Couper also sees a training emphasis on community organization and conflict management (Couper, 1990).

Supervisors will be "area coordinators" who are interested in their subordinates' ability to foster teamwork in their neighborhoods; the supervisors will provide the coaching, support, and resources necessary for officers to perform quality work. The organizational hierarchy will be flatter, allowing for greater employee input and communication. Officers might wear blazers instead of military-style uniforms, and will not be troubled with their "social work" orientation as opposed to the crime-fighter bent of the past. Officers will see themselves as community workers and organizers, and have a variety of tools and resources, including arrest, at their disposal. They will serve as mediators, negotiating settlements in all kinds of community problems from pollution to marital property disputes (Couper, 1990).

Other predictions are less certain but just as plausible. A panel of police management experts, scholars, and executives participating in a 15-month study developed a long-term view of the future of policing. The events presented below are expected to occur by the year listed, assuming a continuation of the present economic, sociocultural, and political environment (Ward, 1991:3-4).

1999: Urban unrest and civil disorder of the 1960s and 1970s variety will take place throughout the United States.

2000: Computer-based instruction will become the standard for training in over 70 percent of police agencies. More than 70 percent of the "invasion of privacy" lawsuits will successfully demonstrate the inadequacies of and inaccuracies in police computerized files. Crimes using high technology will become so complex that the police will be unable to do more than take initial reports.

2005: Disparity between the haves and the have-nots will be identified as *the* major cause of traditional crime.

2025: Formal education will become the standard for entry and advancement in more than 70 percent of police agencies. More than 70 percent of police executives will adopt a nontraditional (proactive/goal-oriented) leadership style.

2035: Private security agencies will assume more than 50 percent of *all* law enforcement responsibilities.

2050: Law enforcement will achieve professional status. More than 50 percent of police agencies will have personnel competent to conduct rigorous

---

Case Study 14–2
"A Futures Forum"

Harrisburg is a medium-sized, industrial community with a progressive mayor and council. Together they have implemented a new program called Leadership Harrisburg, which is a one-year program to bring together professionals from the business and government sectors to discuss common issues, challenges, methods, and concerns. Sgt. Dale Williams is a patrol supervisor with 10 years' total experience, including four years as a supervisor. He has just graduated from the local university where he also just completed a supervision course (using this textbook). He has applied for and been accepted as a participant at Leadership Harrisburg. The project's director selected Williams to attend and represent the police department. He was advised that the first meeting will be in two weeks, when he is to make a 10-minute presentation on the profession, his position in it, and its future challenges.

1. Using some of the materials discussed throughout this text, how would *you* explain the role of a police supervisor to this diverse group?

2. If you were in Sgt. Williams's position, what would be some of the important *current* themes and issues, their complexities and challenges, that you would take to the forum concerning a supervisor's job?

3. Describe how the supervisor's role is changing? What are some of the *future* issues and challenges of this position?

empirical research. Medical (biochemical, genetic, nutritional, and brain) research will discover the means of identifying and treating proneness to violence.

SUMMARY

This chapter has examined the need for studying the future of policing and some methods for forecasting its future. It also reviewed some anticipated changes in policing and the impact of high technology on the field. The superiors of the future will need to be innovative, aware of the vast technological possibilities in their respective fields, and ensure that their personnel are trained and, where appropriate, certified in the proper use of these technologies.

The challenges posed in this chapter for the police supervisors of tomorrow may indeed appear to be daunting. Meeting the high standards of supervision is not easy and will only become more difficult as social, technological, and political changes occur. It is not expected that traditional police personnel problems will decline, either. Such matters as age discrimination, employment misconduct, sexism, new employee attitudes, and poor work performance will not be resolved in the near future.

Tomorrow's supervisors must know more than their predecessors and be both flexible and principled. They also must be careful listeners with high mental and physical energy, and have confidence in their decisions. It is these challenges that confront those selected few who wear the stripes of a police supervisor.

KEY TERMS

futures research (p. 343)	participative management	artificial intelligence (AI)
environmental scanning	(p. 349)	(p. 354)
(p. 344)	diversity (p. 351)	expert systems (p.3 54)
high technology (p. 344)	computerized mapping	virtual reality (p. 354)
demographics (p. 346)	(p. 353)	robotics (p. 354)
underclass (p. 346)	geocoding (p. 353)	speech recognition (p. 354)

ITEMS FOR REVIEW

1. Explain why it is important for the police to study the future and to engage in futures research.
2. Describe some of the methods used by futurists to predict the future.
3. Delineate some of the anticipated changes in policing, focusing on the most important changes that are likely to affect police supervision and management in the future.
4. List some of the high-technology developments that have occurred and how they will affect policing in the future.
5. Describe some of the projected police methods of the future.
6. Explain what is anticipated with respect to diversity in our society, and why it is important for the police to manifest a more diverse workforce as well.

SOURCES

BENNETT, W. W., and HESS, K. M. (1996). *Management and supervision in law enforcement.* 2d ed. Minneapolis/St. Paul, Minn.: West.

CONSER, J. A., and DILLER, J. J. (1994). "From theory to practice: The implementation of futuristics in selected policing agencies." Paper presented at the Annual Meeting of the Midwestern Criminal Justice Association, Chicago, Illinois, September 14–16.

COUPER, D. C. (1990). "Comparing two positions on the future of American policing." *American Journal of Police* 9(3):161–69.

CRONKHITE, C. L. (1984). "21st century cop." *National Centurion* (April).26–29, 47–48.

FOX, J. W. (1996). *Trends in Violence.* Washington D.C.: U.S. Department of Justice, Bureau of Justice Assistance, p. i.

GAINES, L. K., SOUTHERLAND, M. D., and ANGELL, J. E. (1991). *Police administration.* New York: McGraw-Hill.

GHAEMIAN, K. (1996). "Small-town cops wield big-city data." *Government Technology* 9 (September):38.

JOYCE, P. (1995). "Firearms training: As close to real as it gets." *Government Technology* 8 (July):14–15.

KAVANAUGH, J. (1996). "Community oriented policing and technology." *Government Technology* 9 (March):14.

MAGUIRE K. and PASTORE, A. L. (eds.) (1996). *Sourcebook of criminal justice statistics, 1995.* U.S. Department of Justice, Bureau of Justice Statistics. Washington D.C.: U.S. Government Printing Office.

McCORD, R., and WICKER, E. (1990). "Tomorrow's America: Law enforcement's coming challenge." *FBI Law Enforcement Bulletin* 59 (January):31–33.

METTS, J. R. (1985). "Super cops: The police force of tomorrow." *The Futurist* (October):31–36.

NAISBITT, J. (1984). *Megatrends: Ten new directions transforming our lives.* New York: Warner.

NEWCOMBE, T. (1996). "Imaged prints go online, cops return to streets." *Government Technology* 9 (April):1, 31.

PEAK, K. J. (1997). *Policing America: Methods, issues, challenges.* Upper Saddle River, N.J.: Prentice Hall.

ROBINETTE, H. (1989). "Operational streamlining." *FBI Law Enforcement Bulletin* (September):7–11.

ROBINETTE, H. (1993). "Supervising tomorrow." *Virginia Police Chief* (Spring):10–16.

STORY, D. (1992). "What happens after all the dinosaurs are gone? (The passing of the torch)." *Law and Order* (October):47–48.

SWANSON, C. R., TERRITO, L., and TAYLOR, R. W. (1993). *Police administration* (3d ed.). New York: Macmillan.

TAFOYA, W. L. (1983). "Futuristics: New tools for criminal justice executives." Part I. Paper presented at the 1983 Annual meeting of the Academy of Criminal Justice Sciences, March 22–26, San Antonio, Texas.

TAFOYA, W. L. (1990). "The changing nature of the police: Approaching the 21st century." *Vital Speeches of the Day* 56 (February):244–46.

TAFOYA, W. L. (1997). "The future of community policing." *Crime and Justice International* 13 (July):4–6.

THIBAULT, E. A. (1982). "Proactive police futures." In Gene Stephens (ed.). *The Future of Criminal Justice.* Cincinnati, Ohio: Anderson.

U.S. DEPARTMENT OF JUSTICE, BUREAU OF JUSTICE STATISTICS BULLETIN (1996). *Local Police Departments, 1993* (April):4.

U.S. DEPARTMENT OF JUSTICE, BUREAU OF JUSTICE STATISTICS BULLETIN (1991). *State and local police departments, 1990.* Washington, D.C.: U.S. Government Printing Office.

U.S. DEPARTMENT OF JUSTICE, NATIONAL INSTITUTE OF JUSTICE PROGRAM FOCUS (1996). "The Chicago police department's information collection for automated mapping (ICAM) program." (July):2.

WARD, R. H. (1991). "From future shock to power shifts: Police face a challenging new era." *Criminal Justice International,* (May–June):3–4.

WITHAM, D. C. (1991). "Environmental scanning pays off." *Police Chief* (March):26–31.

Name Index

359

Subject Index